EUROPEAN STAMP ISSUES
AND THE AFTERMATH OF THE SECOND WORLD WAR

1944-49

Published in 2023

Copyright © 2023 David Parker

All rights reserved. Apart from any fair dealing for the purpose of private study, research, criticism or review, as permitted under the Copyright, Designs and Patents Act, 1988, no part of this publication may be reproduced, stored in a retrieval system, or transmitted in any form or by any means, electronic, electrical, chemical, mechanical, optical, photocopying, recording or otherwise, without the prior written permission of the copyright owner. Enquiries should be addressed to the Publishers.

Every attempt has been made by the author and publisher to secure the appropriate permissions for materials reproduced in this book. If there has been any oversight we will be happy to rectify the situation in future editions.

A CIP catalogue record for this book is available from the British Library.

ISBN: 978 0 85704 358 0

Halsgrove
Halsgrove House,
Ryelands Business Park,
Bagley Road, Wellington,
Somerset TA21 9PZ
Tel: 01823 653777
Fax: 01823 216796
email: sales@halsgrove.com

Part of the Halsgrove group of companies
Information on all Halsgrove titles is available at: www.halsgrove.com

Printed and bound in India by Parksons Graphics

EUROPEAN STAMP ISSUES
AND THE AFTERMATH OF THE SECOND WORLD WAR

1944-49

DAVID PARKER

Halsgrove

A NOTE ON THE CAPTIONS DESCRIBING THE STAMPS ILLUSTRATED

Exact dates of issues are not always known and the captions give the best information available from Michel, Scott and Stanley Gibbons catalogues. Sometimes only the month and year are known, and occasionally only the year.

If an illustration is an issue comprising a single stamp it is noted as, for example, (1 June 1946).

If selected examples from a set are shown it is noted as (from set 10 February 1948).

If the issuing of a set ranged over a lengthy period it is noted as (from set 25 April 1947+).

If all the stamps in a set are shown it is noted as (set 12 September 1949) or (set 9 August 1946+).

If a set includes a variety of papers, and/or perforations and/or colour changes, as well as dates of issue, it is noted as (from series 21 November 1948+).

To Pamela - with love

CONTENTS

CHAPTER 1	Introduction	7
CHAPTER 2	United Kingdom	13
CHAPTER 3	Germany	15
CHAPTER 4	Soviet Union	43
CHAPTER 5	France	65
CHAPTER 6	Belgium	80
CHAPTER 7	Luxembourg	90
CHAPTER 8	The Netherlands	95
CHAPTER 9	Denmark	100
CHAPTER 10	Norway	103
CHAPTER 11	Finland	108
CHAPTER 12	Poland	115
CHAPTER 13	Czechoslovakia	133
CHAPTER 14	Austria	145
CHAPTER 15	Italy	157
CHAPTER 16	Yugoslavia	174
CHAPTER 17	Albania	186
CHAPTER 18	Hungary	192
CHAPTER 19	Romania	205
CHAPTER 20	Bulgaria	225
CHAPTER 21	Greece	237
BIBLIOGRAPHY		243
INDEX		244

Map of Europe between the wars. It shows (i) the separation of East Prussia from the rest of Germany by the 'Polish Corridor' and Danzig, (ii) Poland situated significantly eastwards from its post 1945 settlement, (iii) Carpathia-Ukraine as the most eastern region of Czechoslovakia, (iv) Bessarabia as part of north-eastern Romania, and (v) Italy stretching round the northern Adriatic Sea to embrace Trieste and the Istrian Peninsula.

CHAPTER 1

INTRODUCTION

The causes of the Second World War in 1939 lay in the outcome of the First World War. When the Armistice took effect on 11 November 1918 three great Empires lay torn apart. In 1917 Tsar Nicholas II of Russia had abdicated in the face of impending revolution and was murdered the following year after the Bolsheviks had seized power and a vicious civil war erupted across the empire. During these tumultuous years Estonia, Latvia and Lithuania along with Tsarist occupied parts of Poland wrestled themselves free from Russian control, although not without short sharp military conflicts with Bolshevik forces. In 1918 the centuries-old Imperial Hapsburg domain, incorporating the joint Austrian Empire and Kingdom of Hungary lay defeated with several hitherto subordinate states, notably Bohemia and Slovakia, and Slovenia, Croatia and Bosnia, and Polish Galicia, already striving militarily and diplomatically for independence. By the time of the Armistice, the German Empire had endured a naval mutiny, its people were facing starvation, and its armies on the Western Front were in retreat. A civilian government relieved the despairing military commanders of imperial authority, then pressurised Kaiser Wilhelm II into abdication, and finally accepted humiliating terms from the Allies as the price of an Armistice.

Europe was about to undergo a radical realignment of national borders in what turned out to be a generally well-intentioned but doomed attempt by the victorious Allies - primarily Great Britain, France and the USA - to satisfy the nationalist sentiments surging within the larger ethnic communities formerly subject to Tsarist, German and Austro-Hungarian authority. Everyone was eager for the spoils of war, but no-one was satisfied. Mutual suspicion, hostility and readiness to resort to arms abounded. The new small republic of Austria resented the Allied rejection of its plea for close links with Germany, and the once proud Kingdom of Hungary chafed at its reduction to a small impoverished state surrounded by hostile Romania, Czechoslovakia and Yugoslavia. Every one of them thought their new borders were unfairly circumscribed. Franco-German relations remained strained after the 1919 Treaty of Versailles transferred Alsace and Lorraine back to France after their loss to Germany in a war half a century earlier. And Germany resented the loss of Eupen and Malmedy to Belgium, and the German speaking Sudetenland to Czechoslovakia. Polish-German relations were particularly bitter when the Treaty separated East Prussia from the rest of Germany by awarding Poland an extensive corridor of land reaching up to the valuable port of Danzig. As Poland had been resurrected out of Russian, German and Hapsburg territory, not surprisingly it was forever wary of the ambitions of all its neighbours - not only Soviet Russia and a resurgent Germany but also Czechoslovakia with whom it contested mineral rich Silesia, and Lithuania with whom it fought a bitter border war in 1920.

In southern Europe Italy and the new Kingdom of the Serbs, Croats and Slovenes (soon to be renamed Yugoslavia) remained at odds over land around Trieste, and mutual jealousies between these two countries on opposite sides of the Adriatic Sea soured the inter-war years. The small historic states of Bosnia, Croatia, Serbia and Montenegro along with Slovenia had muted their deep-seated ethnic and religious divisions long enough for a superficially united kingdom to be created and receive international recognition. However, the fragile kingdom never shed the Balkan habit of political violence and assassinations, a factor Hitler and Mussolini took full advantage of during the Second World War - as they did of territorial jealousies everywhere across Europe. Although the post-1918 peace treaties sought to create countries largely peopled by those of similar ethnic backgrounds, their success was only partial as Europe was far too complex a mix for such understandable but simplistic solutions. The ethnic Germans who hated finding themselves in Poland and Czechoslovakia were prime examples.

In addition to its territorial losses, Germany had to acknowledge guilt for the war, pay a huge reparations bill, and virtually demilitarise. Social discontent soared, Communist and ultra Nationalist groups (the Frei Corps) fought on the streets and vied for power, and civilian politicians found it impossible to shake off the recurrent charge that they were responsible (and not the much-admired army) for Germany's humiliation in 1918. National Socialist Party membership grew steadily as Hitler and his associates battled the Communists with a campaign aimed at recovering lost territory, military power and national pride, and

EUROPEAN STAMP ISSUES AND THE AFTERMATH OF THE SECOND WORLD WAR: 1944–1949

establishing Aryan racial supremacy. Hitler became Chancellor of Germany in 1933 on the strength of these policies and set about fulfilling them. A largely willing Austria was absorbed into a Greater Germany in 1938. An internally divided and isolated Czechoslovakia was browbeaten into disintegration in 1938 and 1939. And in September 1939 Danzig was attacked as a prelude to Poland's shattering defeat and dismemberment by Germany, and its unlikely (but temporary) ally, the Soviet Union. The Second World War had begun.

In 1940 Denmark and Norway were conquered, and then Belgium, Luxembourg and the Netherlands as German forces rushed through the Low Countries to defeat a well-armed but politically paralysed and socially demoralised France. Finally in June 1941 Hitler reneged on his short-lived pact with Stalin, and invaded Russia. Only Great Britain held out, protected by its navy and air force and the English Channel.

Angered by a pro-Allied coup in Yugoslavia prior to his planned invasion of Russia, Hitler along with Mussolini swiftly crushed the fragile kingdom in April 1941. New Serbian, Croatian and Montenegrin puppet states were created allowing all the traditional ethnic and religious jealousies to mutate into vicious civil conflicts. Mussolini had long coveted Albania as part of Italy's recreation of a Roman Empire, and King Zog, once a grateful recipient of Italian aid, had been duly ejected in 1939. Eager for further conquests, in 1940 Mussolini had invaded Greece only to be doubly humiliated when Greek forces pushed the Italians back to Albania and Hitler had to intervene to reverse the situation.

Elsewhere in the Balkans Hungary, Bulgaria and Romania had been vulnerable to pre-war German and Russian machinations, and after varying degrees of vacillation each one decided that Nazi Germany was the power to back, not least because Communism was anathema to their ruling classes. Trade deals tied the countries to Germany which in due course pressed its political views and racial prejudices upon them. Hitler's dominance over the Balkans through alliances or invasion meant swathes of land changed hands as retribution or rewards. Hitler gave Hungary a part of Slovakia it coveted, and Bulgaria was ceded southern Dobrudja from Romania and parts of Macedonia and Thrace from Greece. In 1939 Romania had felt particularly aggrieved, yet utterly helpless, when the Soviet-German alliance obliged it to return its post-1918 acquisitions - Bessarabia and northern Buckovina - to Russia. Despite this, in 1941 Romania became Hitler's generally willing ally, which seemed to work well when Bessarabia and Buckovina were retaken after the invasion of Russia along with swathes of south-western Soviet territory. However, when seemingly against the odds after eighteen months of disaster the Soviet Union turned the tide of war against Germany, Hitler's Balkan allies of Bulgaria, Hungary and Romania were faced with an ominous future.

In May 1945 much of Europe and western Russia lay in ruins. Thousands of cities, towns and villages had been destroyed and much of the countryside laid waste. Many millions had died, millions were homeless and starving, and millions more were displaced refugees, forced labourers and prisoners of war. The horror of it all was as bewildering to the victors as it was to the defeated, with national and local administrations in disarray, transport systems wrecked, and widespread vengeance being wreaked upon oppressors and those who had collaborated with them. In the end it was the various occupying forces - primarily the Americans, British and Russians - who had to create some sort of military and civil administrations to bring a degree of order out of utter chaos and devastation. And as they did so, three factors contributed to a divided Europe - the mutually antagonistic East and West - that quickly took shape. The first was the wartime agreements between the 'Big Three' Allies (Russia, Great Britain and the USA) over European reconstruction. Most importantly this included the division of defeated Germany and Austria into occupied regions, and the spheres of political influence that Russia, Great Britain and the USA would retain over liberated countries. Although France was reluctantly accorded the status of an 'Ally', its humiliating defeat and sycophantic Vichy collaboration effectively ended its centuries-old right to be a Great Power - despite France's long denial of the fact. The second was *real politick* in the overwhelming presence of the Soviet armies who had battled their way into the Balkans, the Baltic States, Poland, Czechoslovakia, eastern Germany and Berlin. Indeed, across Europe each country's future primarily depended upon whose army reigned supreme there in 1945. The third was the deeply divided right and left wing political parties and associated organisations that existed in so many European countries battling vigorously for influence and power. Indeed throughout the war the assorted resistance movements in many countries from France in the west to the Balkans in the east had adopted strong right and left wing views which meant they usually viewed each other with suspicion, and often outright hostility, while still fighting the Germans and their collaborators. Nowhere was this as constant and brutal as in politically divided and poverty stricken Greece and the mutually hostile puppet states Hitler created out of the unstable Kingdom of Yugoslavia. At times resistance groups preferred to fight each other than the Germans. The Nazi creed of National Socialism was essentially a Teutonic and highly nationalistic

INTRODUCTION

ideology crowned with a concept of Aryan superiority whereas the Soviet Union's Bolshevik dictatorship was overlaid, and indeed masked, by the international appeal of the Communist creed centred upon the inevitable triumph of the proletariat over its avaricious oppressors. Small wonder it attracted many converts across war-torn Europe in the 1940s when people looked for a better world than that imposed upon them by pre-war monarchies and unstable democracies, and then the wartime Nazi and Fascist dictators.

Although national Communist Parties generally attracted a small percentage of the population compared with less radical Liberal and Socialist parties, they were skilful at creating and working within left-wing coalitions that accumulatively formed a majority capable of forming a government. They were equally skilful at securing key ministries for themselves, notably the Ministries of the Interior and Justice that controlled domestic affairs and the police, and the Ministry of Agriculture that could work towards attracting the peasant vote. And as Stalin recognised only to clearly, the post-war readiness of the Communists to work cooperatively alongside other parties in East Germany, Poland, Czechoslovakia, Hungary, Romania and Bulgaria - at least for a few years - cast a convenient diplomatic veil over his ultimate intentions. As we shall see, when backed by virtually unassailable Soviet political and military support it was just a matter of time, and timing, before the Communists purged the coalition of its more moderate members and seized complete control.

In several countries, though, it was the Communist parties whose ambitions were frustrated because Stalin decided not to support them or because other parties were too strong or USA interests were too great, or because all these factors were present. The Communists did, though, pose great threats to other parties of both left and right in the immediate post-war years, notably in Italy, Finland and Greece. However Stalin was largely satisfied with establishing a compliant ring of subservient and dependent countries from the Baltic to the Black Sea buffering the western monarchies and democracies, something Tsarist Russia had dreamed about for generations. In contrast in Western Europe nations kept their constitutional monarchs and republican presidents but largely with governments that made a marked turn to the left. Indeed every country needed to rebuild its houses, factories, transport system, trade and infrastructure, develop new international alliances, and seek to re-establish its culture, identity and pride after the trauma of war. It is all these stories, and many others, that this book covers using stamp issues as the illustration and evidence for the twists and turns of each nation's post-war fortunes.

All countries were proud of their postal services, and also of their membership of the Universal Postal Union (UPU). On 9 October 1874 twenty two nations had signed a convention in Berne agreeing the reciprocal exchange and unimpeded transit of mail and the uniformity of international tariff levels. The meeting instituted an organisation that became known as the UPU to maintain this agreement: it began its work on 1 July 1875. As its 75th anniversary in 1949 approached several countries suggested that every member should honour it with a stamp issue, and the UPU agreed. There was a variety of designs and dates. Some examples are given below while others appear in later chapters. (1.1 - 1.8)

1.1 Italy: 50l Globes and modern mail transport: 2 May 1949.

1.2 Czechoslovakia: 5k Mounted postman and mail van: from set 20 May 1949.

1.3 Romania: 30l Flag and ancient and modern communications: from set 30 June 1949.

1.4 The Netherlands: 10c Entwined posthorns: from set 1 October 1949.

1.5 Luxembourg: 80c Postmark across the world: from set 6 October 1949.

1.10 Hungary: Stamp Day: 30fi XVIth century mail cart: 21 December 1947. They were sold at philatelic exhibitions where a 50fi premium gained admission.

1.6 Finland: 15m Finland's lakes and forests: 8 October 1949.

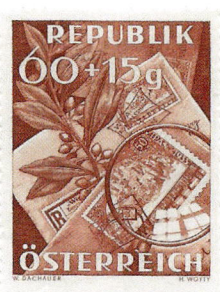

1.11 Austria: Stamp Day: 60g+15g Covers and magnifying glass: 3 December 1949.

1.7 Denmark: 40o UPU ribbon circling the world: 9 October 1949.

1.12 Poland: Torun Philatelic Congress/Exhibition: 15z Torun ramparts and mail coach: 4 September 1948.

1.8 Greece: 1,000d 'Youth of Marathon': 21 May 1950.

1.13 Finland: Helsinki 12m Philatelic Exhibition: early mail carrier's badge: 27 October 1948.

Annual Stamp Days were common, with issues highlighting aspects of each country's postal service past and present. The surtax usually supported national and international philatelic exhibitions which were golden opportunities to raise a regime's profile and profits.(1.9 - 1.13)

1.9 Bulgaria: Stamp Day and New York Philatelic Exhibition: 70l+30l Images of New York and poster: 31 May 1947.

Although France was not unusual in possessing historic state and private postal services it was unusual that a series of post-war Stamp Day issues lauded those responsible for them. Perhaps it helped restore a shattered national pride. In December 1944 it was the Arms of Jean-Jacques Renouard de Villayer (1607-91) who created post boxes in Paris in which pre-paid letters could be placed for delivery across the city. In October 1945 the stamp pictured King Louis XI (reigned 1461-83) who set up a web of postal relays across France, largely devoted to gaining intelligence about his enemies. In June 1946 it featured Guillaume Fouquet de la Varane (1560-1616) who opened up the royal postal services to private citizens. In March 1947

INTRODUCTION

1.14 France: Stamp Day: 2f+3f Louis XI: 3 October 1945; 3f+2f Guillaume Fouquet de la Varane: 29 June 1946; 4.50f+5.50f Marquis de Louvois: 15 March 1947; 6f+4f Etienne Arago: 6 March 1948; 15f+5f Duc de Choiseul: 26 March 1949.

it portrayed Francois-Michel le Tellier, Marquis de Louvois (1641-91) whose organisational skills as Secretary of State under Louis XIV included the superintendence of posts. In March 1948 the stamp featured Etienne Arago (1802-92) whose varied career included, briefly, director of the national Post Office in 1848 when the first adhesive stamp was introduced. In March 1949 the stamp portrayed Etienne Francois, Duc de Choiseul (1719-85), whose portfolio of state offices in the 1760s and 1770s included Superintendent of Posts.(1.14)

In May 1946 a particularly attractive French stamp that was a mirror image of Jean Baptiste Simeon Chardin's 1732 painting 'Lady sealing a letter' supported the National Postal Museum.(1.15)

1.15 France: 2f+3f Postal Museum Fund: 25 May 1946.

Stamp anniversaries were often commemorated, not least because they were signs of national stability and pride in a Europe torn by two World Wars.(1.16 - 1.19) Sometimes politics affected the dates. In the USSR it was just the 25th anniversary of the post-revolutionary postal service that was celebrated in 1946, not the far longer Tsarist one. Conversely in Czechoslovakia the Communists who seized power in 1948 were keen to highlight national continuity and therefore celebrated thirty years of independent stamp issues - from 1918. The shattering and occupation of the country by Germany was ignored. The 75th anniversary of Hungary's stamps in 1946 was dated from soon after Hungary gained internal autonomy within the Dual

1.16 Hungary: 75th anniversary of first Hungarian stamps: 1.5m.p.+1.5m.p. Lion freed from chains: from set 1 May 1946.

Monarchy of the Empire of Austria and Kingdom of Hungary in 1867 and marked the country's precarious survival of two World Wars.

An efficient postal service was considered a sign of a healthy national infrastructure, and a reasonably literate society. Carefully designed stamp issues were a key part of the identity of countries, not least as many emerged from pre-1914 Empires and then Second World War occupation. Advances in printing technology allowed countries to circulate colourful sets of stamps that contained carefully crafted images that purveyed a favourable view of the government and its policies. These small and seemingly innocuous pieces of paper reached every corner of the country and helped reinforce specific political priorities and historical interpretations by marking selected anniversaries, military victories and past ruling figures along with celebrations of the lives and achievements of national scientists, architects, artists, poets, playwrights and novelists. Among contemporary themes they were often used to honour current leaders, celebrate modern advances in selected areas of life, and instil a sense of purpose and trust in the prevailing regime. Often such commemorative issues contained a surtax raising funds for charities, notably for war widows and orphans or the fight against tuberculosis, and for rebuilding national institutions and financing war memorials. And as many stamps reached many foreign countries, the opportunities for propaganda via air mail sets were rarely missed.

As this book shows, each country's stamp issues highlighted the particular political, social and economic course it took after the fighting came to a close, and how post-war governments wanted others within, and beyond, their borders to perceive them. Ranging from the strikingly attractive to the starkly realistic, and from the subtly allegorical to the simple slogan, they were skilfully designed instruments of state policy and international Cold War confrontation.

1.18 Czechoslovakia: 30th anniversary of Czech stamps: miniature sheet 18 December 1948.

1.19 Belgium: Stamp centenary: 50f King Leopold I (reigned 1831-65) and modern mail transport: from set 1 July 1949.

1.17 USSR: 25th anniversary of the Soviet Postal Service: 15k Soviet stamps and map: from set 6 November 1946.

CHAPTER 2

THE UNITED KINGDOM

In 1945 Great Britain emerged militarily victorious but exhausted psychologically, economically and financially. The country had not been invaded but many cities and towns had been bombed, killing 67,000 civilians, and 383,000 servicemen from the United Kingdom and Crown Colonies had died. On 26 July Churchill resigned after the General Election, to many people's surprise, had returned a Labour government under Clement Atlee. This represented not so much a criticism of Churchill's wartime leadership but rather a justifiable conviction that Atlee was far more committed to the social reforms in education, health and housing so many families desired. Fortunately, despite Churchill's lukewarm interest, several major committee's had worked throughout the war to identity the principles and methods of creating a national health service, universal secondary education, and good quality council housing. Far less clear to most people was that many parts of the Empire were keen to shake off Imperial shackles, that Britain relied on huge American loans, that the age of rationing and austerity would last several more years, and that British society was about to undergo radical change.

Compared with other European countries Great Britain issued very few sets of stamps and certainly did not see them as instruments of propaganda. Indeed the General Post Office (GPO) constantly denigrated such attitudes. The only special wartime set comprised six stamps issued on 6 May 1940 featuring Queen Victoria and King George VI with the dates '1840' and '1940' to mark the centenary of the first adhesive postage stamp. (2.1) It had no inscription, and neither did the Victory Issue on 11 June 1946 which accompanied the official Victory celebrations over the Whitsun Bank Holiday that year.(2.2) Indeed the government had only issued the pair of stamps after huge pressure from philatelists, coupled with clear evidence that other countries were calling for Victory issues, and belated but welcome thoughts of heightened revenue earnings from sales. The 2½d featured the emblems of the four UK nations and images of reconstruction - a tractor, house, factory and ship. Although not triumphalist the shading did suggest a V for Victory behind the king's head. The 3d was less admired, and depicted a dove and olive branch of peace above what some critics thought were Masonic instruments rather than clear signs of rebuilding.

2.1 2d Centenary of the first pre-paid adhesive postage stamp: from set 6 May 1940.

2.2 2½d and 3d Victory: set 11 June 1946.

No further issues appeared until 1948. On 26 April two stamps, a simple 2½d and a more regal £1, marked the Silver Wedding of King George VI and Queen Elizabeth with the same portrait by the fashionable portrait photographer Dorothy Wilding.(2.3) The (GPO) had been widely criticised for only providing a special postmark for Princess Elizabeth's wedding in 1947, and hurriedly had set about avoiding a second round of abuse by royalists, philatelists, MPs, and Treasury officials scenting further revenue opportunities. The stylish £1 stamp proved particularly popular.

2.3 2½d and £1 Silver Wedding: 26 April 1948.

The set to mark the 1948 Olympic Games in London had been in preparation long before the hurried but popular Silver Wedding issue. London had been the intended venue for the 1944 Summer Games, and despite all the post-war difficulties the government and British Olympic Committee felt holding the Games in 1948 would help restore British morale and pride. Existing venues such as the Empire Stadium and Pools at Wembley and local football grounds were used, and competitors were housed in nearby London colleges and military camps. A record 59 nations sent athletes but Germany and Japan were not invited and the Soviet Union declined to participate. Great Britain came 12th, with 23 medals, including 3 golds. Issued on the opening day, 29 July 1948, the 2½d featured a globe and laurel wreath, the 3d an allegory of Speed, the 6d olive leaves and the Olympic rings, and the 1/-, perhaps a little ambiguously, depicted the figure of Winged Victory flying above a globe highlighting Europe.(2.4).

2.6 2½d and 3d UPU: from set 10 October 1949.

2.4 2½d and 1/- Olympic Games: from set 29 July 1948.

2.5 1d and 2½d Liberation of the Channel Islands: set 10 May 1948.

The Channel Islands were liberated from German occupation on 9 May 1945, and three years later two stamps (1d and 2½d) without any inscriptions were issued across the islands, and by the UK's main Post Offices, with two different pictures of men with horses and carts gathering vraic (seaweed) for use as fertiliser. (2.5) For some time the Channel Islands had wanted their own stamp issues but the government and GPO had demurred, worrying about possibly inappropriate designs and fearing Scotland, Wales, Northern Island and the Isle of Man would follow suit. However the Channel Island authorities themselves put forward the 'vraicing' idea as a scene all islanders would immediately recognise, and after lengthy discussions a short commemorative set for 9 May 1948 was agreed. In fact as 9 May was a Sunday 10 May was chosen. The islanders' response was muted, with critics lamenting any reference to the war and liberation, and pointing out that tractors now carried out 'vraicing'. Outside the Channel Islands the images were mystifying, and seen as rather depressing. The Channel Islands had to wait until 1959 for the British Post Office to issue regional stamps, and 1969 to achieve postal independence.

Conscious that Great Britain had led the way in the use of prepaid gummed stamps, on 10 October 1949 the GPO issued four inscribed UNIVERSAL POSTAL UNION 1874-1949.(2.6) Originally the date of issue was to be 9 October - the actual date of the Berne Convention - but in 1949 this was a Sunday. Each design featured the globe. Generally considered the most attractive stamp, the 2½d showed the inscription encircling two hemispheres. The 3d depicted the UPU monument in Berne, where the 1874 conference took place, the 6d depicted the Goddess Concordia clutching messages, and the 1/- a posthorn encircling the globe.

CHAPTER 3

GERMANY

At the fall of Nazi Germany the Soviet Union, Great Britain and the USA implemented the territorial agreement they had reached at their wartime conferences. All lands annexed by Germany before and during the war were returned to their pre-war owners - Austria became independent again, the Sudetenland returned to Czechoslovakia, Memel to Russia's Lithuanian Soviet Republic, Alsace-Lorraine to France, northern Slovenia to Yugoslavia, and Eupen and Malmedy to Belgium. In addition the Konigsberg region of East Prussia became part of the Soviet Union but most of East Prussia along with Germany east of the rivers Oder and Neisse (including much of Pommern, Brandenburg, Niederschlesien and Oberschlesien) became part of a redefined Poland. The rest of Germany was divided into four occupation zones with Berlin in the middle of the Soviet Zone also divided into four distinct zones.

The American Zone in southern Germany included much of Bavaria and Hesse, and parts of Wurttemberg and Baden. The British were responsible for northern Germany and created the new states of Lower Saxony and North Rhine-Westphalia along with a redefined Schleswig-Holstein. The British agreed to the Americans having open access to, and administering, the ports of Bremen and Bremerhaven. The French Zone in the west embraced the Rheinland Pfalz, south Baden and Wurttemberg-Hohenzollern. Originally no French zone was envisaged but partly to satisfy General de Gaulle's hurt pride, and partly to offload some occupation costs, the Allies agreed. A lengthy zone abutting France was carved out of the British and American zones. The French found many Germans particularly sour at the notion of France being numbered among the victors. For an initial period the French Zone included the key industrial region of the

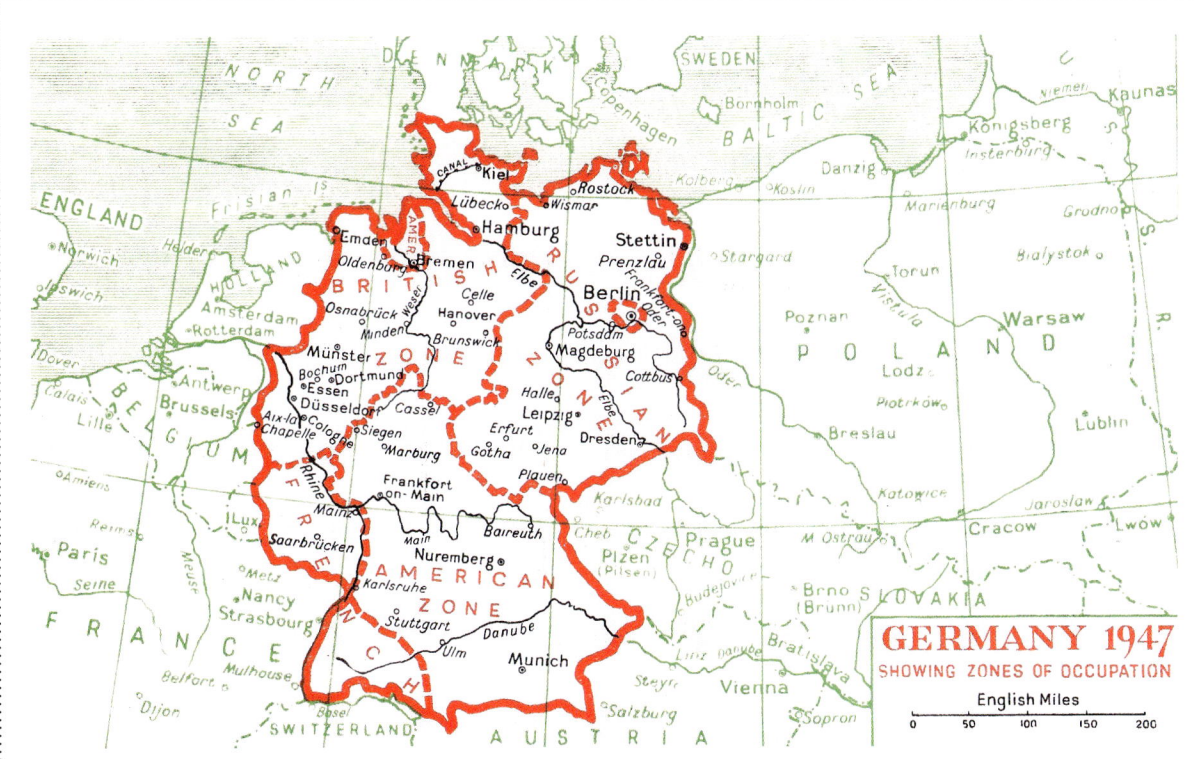

Map of post-war Germany showing the Allied Zones of Occupation. The small Bremen enclave in the north of the British Zone was created to give seaport facilities to the American occupation forces. Berlin was divided into its own four occupation zones.

Saar but in 1946 France created the Saar Protectorate which placed it outside the Allied Control Council jurisdiction. The eastern Soviet Zone included Thuringia, Saxony, Saxony-Anhalt, Brandenburg and Mecklenburg-Vorpommern.

After Germany's surrender the Allies had to administer a completely wrecked country. Food was desperately short, many starved, and the Black Market was rampant. Towns had been bombed to oblivion, local administration was paralysed, transport systems were shattered, power and fuel supplies non-existent, and millions of displaced persons and forced labourers from numerous countries were wandering the streets and countryside adding to the fears of robbery and violence. Vengeance was high on many people's agenda, notably in the Soviet army after the horrors of German brutality in the USSR.

The original plan was to govern Germany as a single unit through the Allied Control Council but this collapsed in 1946-47 because although the USA and UK favoured it France wanted Germany partitioned and kept weak, and the Soviet Union quickly introduced its alternative ideas on land redistribution and nationalisation into its zone. In addition whereas the UK, USA and USSR zones accepted ethnic Germans expelled from Poland, Czechoslovakia, Hungary and Yugoslavia, France controversially refused to accept any in its zone except Germans native to it. On 1 January 1947 the British and American zones merged, the French zone belatedly joined them on 1 August 1948, and the three zones formally became the German Federal Republic, or West Germany, on 23 May 1949. Henceforth until de facto independence in May 1955 the military governors were replaced by civilian high commissioners who exercised ultimate control, although with an increasingly light touch.

On 7 October 1949 the Soviet Zone became the German Democratic Republic, or East Germany, and the gradual granting of limited sovereignty was accompanied by the usual Stalinist control of policies and developments. Here the Social Democratic Party had been forced to merge with the Communist Party in 1946 to form the new Socialist Unity Party which henceforth dominated elections and the domestic government. Relations between the Soviet Union and the Western Allies had steadily deteriorated since 1945, with each 'side' fearing the latent aggression and underhand intentions of the other. Finally in 1948 Stalin reacted to the Allied plan to introduce the new Deutsche Mark into West Berlin by imposing a blockade to which the Western Allies reacted by flying in supplies until Stalin acknowledged defeat.

Initially the Allies agreed to reduce Germany's industrial output, even when reconstructed, to less than half its pre-war level. Indeed some saw Germany's future as primarily pastoral - thereby guaranteeing its inability to threaten its neighbours again. However, concerns that such a policy would inflict lasting hardship, engender mounting hostility, fail to absorb the millions of refugees, encourage Communism, and also mean long-term Allied financial support, later led to a policy of controlled encouragement of cross-border trade and a return to a free market economy. Indeed the imposition of a much reduced steel quota had led to the bankruptcy of many businesses relying on steel components, and the economy in the UK and American zones almost collapsed in 1948. In that year the USA's Marshall Plan offering vast sums of economic aid to European countries was extended to the western zones, and the timely introduction of the new Deutsche Mark stemmed inflation. Stalin ordered East Germany to refuse any Western aid, and continued to dismantle German factories and ship them to the USSR. Thousands of workers as well as vast amounts of produce were sent to the USSR to help rebuild its economy, and in East Germany living conditions for many remained squalid.

EARLY OCCUPATION ISSUES IN THE FOUR ZONES

One immediate result of Germany's defeat was for local postal administrations to accommodate to Allied occupation by partially or completely obliterating Hitler's image on definitive stamps and any signs of swastikas on commemorative and Official issues. Some overprints was approved by surviving district administrations and some were undertaken on the initiative of local postmasters. The overprints varied widely in their defacing of Hitler, and certainly not all of them obliterated the *Deutsches Reich* inscription as required by the Allies.

Among many examples, as early as 22 April 1945 Allied occupied Saulgau in Wurttemberg obediently issued a 12pf Hitler head definitive stamp overprinted with that date, the location *Wurrtemberg* and a V, (3.1), and a couple of weeks later when Germany surrendered Westerstede in the British zone also overprinted Hitler's head with a V and added that letter's Morse code sign. (3.2)

3.1 12pf Hitler definitive overprint Wurttemberg: 22 April 1944.

3.2 20pf Hitler definitive overprint Westerstede: from set May 1945.

3.3 25pf Allied Military Post: from series 19 March 1945+ (25pf first issued 1 July 1945).

For a short period the Allies halted the postal service, but soon local deliveries of censored post cards to designated centres were allowed, although international mail was barred for almost a year, except for foreign workers stranded in Germany. Couriers were organised for Official and business mail as ordinary van deliveries were crippled by the shortages of vehicles and fuel and much of the rail network needed rebuilding. Postal services within each zone were run by its military government, although routine administration was gradually handed over to German officials.

Allied Military Post stamps, inscribed *A M POST* with a Gothic M (Mark) monogram, were introduced in March 1945 in Aachen, which had been the first German city to surrender to the Americans in October 1944. They became the Allied Military Post's general issue throughout the American and British zones in June 1945, about a month after the overall German surrender. Stamps were printed initially in Washington (March to June 1945), then in London (August and September 1945) and in Brunswick (August 1945 to January 1946), and there were several sizes of perforations.(3.3)

3.4 42pf and 1m Numeral issue; from set February 1946+.

BRITISH, AMERICAN & SOVIET UNION ZONES: FEBRUARY 1946 to JUNE 1948

It was intended that general issues would apply to all four zones from February 1946 but the French decided to continue their own issues so from that date - until June 1948 when the Deutsche Mark row erupted - only the British, American and Soviet zones used common stamps. From February 1946 a bland definitive set inscribed Deutsche Post featured values within a geometric framework.(3.4)

This was superseded from 7 March 1947 by a lengthy set promoting Germany's physical and psychological recovery.(3.5) The lower values pictured a gardener, hand sower, factory worker, and a bricklayer alongside a female reaper. The higher values featured symbolic hands breaking free from chains releasing a dove of peace holding a sprig of olive.

On 15 May 1947 two identical stamps marked the fiftieth anniversary of the death of Dr Heinrich von Stephan (1831-97).(3.6) As Prussian and later Imperial Germany's Postmaster General and finally Minister of Postal Services he unified Germany's postal services and in calling the International Postal Conference in Berne in 1874 effectively created the Universal Postal Union which celebrated its 75th anniversary in 1949.

Other sets common to these three zones centred on Hanover and Leipzig Trade Fairs. Hanover Trade Fair was started in 1947 by the British Military Government as a means of boosting the economy. It proved successful, became annual, and soon replaced Leipzig Fair in East Germany as the major trade fair for West Germany. Despite its modern creation, on 22 May 1948 the pair of stamps promoting the 1948 event featured a medieval weighing balance.(3.7)

In contrast Leipzig Fair had been held since the Middle Ages and enjoyed Imperial protection. Held twice, sometimes three times a year, the fair attracted merchants from far afield right up to the Second World War. Revived in 1946, they soon became part of a Communist policy of promoting East Germany as a successful independent country rather than a permanently occupied zone. Issued in pairs each spring and autumn the stamps told a chronological story of Leipzig Fair. The first pair, issued on 5 March 1947, showed Leipzig receiving its charter in 1160 (24pf+26pf) and foreign merchants arriving under Imperial protection in 1268 (60pf+40pf).(3.8) On 2 September 1947 the second pair depicted officials collecting ground rents in 1365 (75pf) and the Emperor Maximilian I granting the Fair its charter in 1497 (12pf).(3.9) On 2 March 1948 the third pair featured merchants and officials at the customs barrier in 1388 (50pf) and merchandise arriving in 1433 (84pf).(3.10) East Germany issued later sets in the same format (see 3.102, 3.103).

EUROPEAN STAMP ISSUES AND THE AFTERMATH OF THE SECOND WORLD WAR: 1944–1949

3.5 6pf, 8pf, 16pf, 60pf and 2m Recovery: from set 7 March 1947+.

3.6 75pf Dr Heinrich von Stephan: from set 15 May 1947.

3.7 24pf Hanover Fair; from set 22 May 1948.

In 1948 a major currency reform across the western zones began to reinvigorate the stagnant economy by encouraging the American style market principle and ending the overhang of money that had been created by financing the war by printing fiat money. A new Deutsche Mark (DM) was introduced by Ludwig Erhard, the brilliant German Director of Economics in the American and British Zones. From 20 June families received 40 new Deutsche Marks (DM) per head and companies 60 DM per employee. Cash and savings were exchanged at a ratio of 100 old Reichmarks to 6.5 DM, debts at 100:10 and wages, prices and rent at 1:1. The Nazi price controls and wage freezes were soon relaxed, and in complete contrast to the Soviet zone, competition and the private ownership of businesses were encouraged. Savers, though, suffered badly but the changes wrenched the economy into a higher gear.

When, on 18 June 1948, the British, French and Americans introduced the reformed currency, the USSR reacted violently by attempting to freeze the western Allies out of Berlin which resulted in the famous Berlin airlift. The Soviet Zone also introduced its own currency reform and, from 24 June, its own postage stamps.

3.8 24pf+26pf Leipzig receives its charter 1160: from set 5 March 1947.

3.9 12pf Leipzig Fair granted its charter 1497: from set 2 September 1947.

3.10 50pf Merchants at the customs barrier 1388: from set 2 March 1948.

GERMANY

BRITISH & AMERICAN ZONES : JUNE 1948 to 21 SEPTEMBER 1949

Initially the British and American Zones used most of the 1946 numeral and 1947 'recovery' stamps overprinted with rows of post-horns either in a single central band or all over to signify the new currency. (3.11) For a time the Soviet Zone rejected any mail bearing them, making communications difficult as initially no other stamps were available in the western zones.

From 1 September 1948 the overprints were replaced by twenty-eight definitives featuring five famous buildings, four of them heavily damaged in the war but undergoing gradual restoration.(3.12) There were numerous variations in perforation sizes. The Romer, a grand medieval house in Frankfurt am Main that became the city hall, was a victim of a massive Allied air raid on 22 March 1944. The Romanesque Frauenkirche (Cathedral) in Munich was left roofless after bombing. The huge neoclassical Brandenburg Gate built between 1788 and 1791 at an entry point into Berlin by the Prussian King Frederick William II, and the scene of many Nazi parades, was left much damaged but still standing after ceaseless bombing. The imposing Holsten Gate with its massive round towers was a relic of the Hanseatic city of Lubeck's medieval fortifications. On 28 March 1942 much of the old city centre was destroyed in a British air raid, but the Gate stood firm.

3.11 The two post-horn overprints on 40pf and 84pf Recovery stamps: from set 21 June 1948.

3.13 Cologne Cathedral: 12pf+8pf Three Wise Men and 50pf+50pf West Front: from set 12 August 1948.

Cologne Cathedral - *Kolner Dom* - was the fifth image. It had been the subject of a slightly earlier surtaxed set on 12 August 1948 to celebrate its 700th anniversary and support its restoration.(3.13) Begun in 1248 to house the prestigious relics of the Biblical Three Kings, building continued erratically until it ceased completely about 1560. In 1842 work resumed on the original plans paid for partly by civic effort and partly by Prussia, and in due course it was avidly promoted as the symbol of German nationhood, and reconciliation between the country's hitherto warring Catholics and Protestants. Its completion in 1882 was a national event. During the Second World War it was hit by bombs at least a dozen times but remained standing but scarred in a devastated landscape. The 12 August set featured a crowned head (6f+4pf), possibly representing the Holy Roman Emperors who worshipped there, the Three Wise Men (12pf+8pf), the completed cathedral (24pf+16pf) and its vast western facade (50pf+50pf).

On 1 December 1948 a 2DM blue label inscribed *BERLIN NOTOPFER STEURMARKE (BERLIN EMERGENCY TAX STAMP)* introduced a new obligatory tax on all internal mail posted in the British and American, and later the French, Zones.(3.14) It

3.12 2pf Frankfurt Romer, 20pf Berlin Brandenburg Gate, 50pf Munich Frauenkirche, 60pf Cologne Cathedral, and 2DM Lubeck Holstentor: from set 1 September 1948+.

3.14 2DM Berlin Emergency Tax: 1 December 1948+.

3.16 30pf Hanover Fair: from set 22 April 1949.

3.1 10pf+5pf Help Berlin: from set 9 December 1948.

3.17 20pf+10f Across Germany Cycle Race; from set 15 May 1949.

raised funds to ensure flown aid reached the western areas of the city after the Soviet land blockade, although after the blockade ended it remained in use on certain items to help the city. On 9 December 1948 the Brandenburg Gate reappeared on two surtaxed stamps inscribed *HELFTBERLIN (HELP BERLIN)* and they, too, raised funds for the city and airlift.(3.15) This could well have been a deliberate provocation as the Gate was in the Soviet Zone by the border with the British Zone. Several Communist countries refused to recognise any stamps depicting the Gate, and as the Bizone (British and American Zones) had chosen it to adorn the well-used definitive values for regional letters (first 24pf, then 20pf) and for foreign letters (first 50pf, then 30pf) this, too, could be seen to be a deliberate provocation.

On 22 April 1949 the third Hanover Trade Fair - fast becoming the Western Zones answer to the Leipzig Fair - was marked by a carefully designed set of three stamps depicting a map of the world behind a magnificent sailing ship and richly clothed Hanseatic merchant.(3.16) Although the trade fair was a post-war innovation medieval Hanover had been connected to the Hanseatic League city of Bremen by the River Leine and was a gateway to the Ruhr, Rhine and Saar. Hans Holbein (c1497-15430) had painted portraits of several German merchants living in London in the 1530s, including members of the wealthy von Wedigh family - the one here is thought to be Hermann Hillebrandt von Wedigh, aged 39, in 1533.

Two other sets were issued in 1949, one on 15 May to support the *OUER DURCH DEUTSCHLAND (ACROSS GERMANY)* Cycle Race.(3.17) The race had been held intermittently since 1911, but had become popular in the later 1930s and was resurrected in 1947. The eastern European Communist countries had held a Peace Race

3.18 Portraits of Goethe: set 15 August 1949.

(Friedensfahrt) in 1948 between Warsaw and Prague. It attracted riders from across the world, and became an annual event, and perhaps this had led the Western Zones to support a rival race.

The second set, on 15 August 1949, comprised three different portraits of Johann Wolfgang von Goethe (1749-1832) to mark the bicentenary of the birth of this literary 'giant' whose works embraced philosophy, poetry, novels, plays, aesthetic criticism and scientific inquiry.(3.18) The 10pf+5pf shows him relaxing on a tour of Campagna from a painting by Johann Heinrich Tischbein in 1787. The 20pf+10pf is taken from a portrait by Josef Karl Steiler in 1828, and 30pf+15pf must show an earlier portrait as the artist Ferdinand Jagemann died in 1820.

Goethe stood partly in the tasteful and carefully crafted Age of Reason and partly in the emerging intuitive and individualistic era of Romanticism. Born in Frankfurt, for many decades he held several high offices under the Duke of Saxe-Weimer to whom he became friend, confidante and chief adviser. Alongside the Duke Goethe was involved in the unsuccessful invasion of Revolutionary France in 1792 and the more successful siege of Mainz in 1793. He was, though, an admirer of Napoleon Bonaparte whom he met in 1808 and thought would create an enlightened alternative society to the corrupt *ancien regime*. His novels such as the romantic tragedy *The Sorrows of Young Werthur* and the journey of self-realisation in *Wilhelm Meister's Apprenticeship* and the dramatic Part One of Faust, in which Mephistopheles brings Faust all he desires in return for his soul, brought him critical and popular acclaim. Faust was one of many of Goethe's works later set to music by, among others, Robert Schumann, Hector Berlioz and Charles Gounod. His *Metamorphosis of Plants* led him to ponder aspects of evolution and his *Theory of Colour* influenced many artists. His works interested and inspired many others including Georg Hegel, Friedrich Nietzsche, and Friedrich Schiller. His portraits appear in numerous Allied Occupation stamps and as an internationally renowned German figure he contrasted starkly with the culturally bankrupt Nazi regime.

On 21 September 1949 the French Zone joined with the British and American Zones to become the Federal German Republic, known as West Germany.

FRENCH ZONE : 1945 to 21 SEPTEMBER 1949

Initially the French invested little in relieving German poverty and distress: indeed they ensured the produce of forests, farmland and Saar mines primarily helped their own recovery. However by the end of 1945 the French accepted that no latent Nazi threat existed: all Nazi teachers and lecturers had been dismissed, and within a couple of years the French and Germans were working together to encourage new cultural initiatives - as represented in many of the Zone's stamps. The French, though, could rarely resist including a few portraits of personalities favourable to France.

3.19 3f Arms of the Rhineland: from set 17 December 1945+.

Stamp shortages after the war meant most mail in the French Zone bore hand written or rubber stamp inscriptions saying *Tax Percue* or *Gebuhr Bezahlt (Fee Paid)*. Eventually, from 17 December 1945 a clearly inscribed ZONE FRANCAISE BRIEF POST (FRENCH ZONE LETTER POST) set appeared depicting the heraldic shields of the historic German provinces within the Zone just before their realignment and amalgamation in 1946. The 1pf and 10pf featured the Palatinate, 3pf and 12pf the Rhineland, 5pf and 20pf Wurttemberg, 8pf and 30pf Baden, and 15pf and 24pf the Saar.(3.19)

3.20 2m Friedrich Schiller and 5m Heinrich Heine: from set 17 December 1945+.

Three higher values portrayed major German writers. The 1m featured Goethe. The 2m featured Friedrich Schiller (1759-1805), playwright, poet, philosopher and friend of Goethe.(3.20) His play, *The Robbers*, telling of an older brother leading a rebel gang in the forests while his younger brother schemed to inherit the noble estate, secured his reputation as a dramatist and critic of contemporary social mores. Later, living in Weimar near Goethe, the two celebrities fostered the theatre there, not least by the production of their own plays. Schiller's later plays - *Don Carlos, Mary Stuart, The Maid of Orleans* and the *Wallenstein* trilogy - stem from his historical studies on liberty and repression, and the human ability to sacrifice oneself for ideals. Schiller, too, is portrayed on several other Allied Occupation stamps.

The 5m featured Heinrich Heine (1797-1856) whose dissident writings upset the authorities but brought him fame across Germany especially when his satirical poems were set to music by Robert Schumann and Felix Mendelssohn.(3.20) Heine was devoted to his homeland but feared its narrow conservatism and censorship, and lived in Paris from 1831 onwards as he believed the 1830 French revolution which had brought the 'Citizen King', Louis Philippe, to the throne would pave the way for revolutions elsewhere. Small wonder he featured on the French set.

3.21 16pf Rastatt and 45pf Baden girl by lake: from Baden set 1 May 1947+.

3.22 84pf Hollental Gorge and 1m Freiburg Cathedral: from Baden set 1 May 1947+.

3.23 60pf Johann Hebel and 75pf Hans Grien; from Baden set 1 May 1947+.

Germans accused of crimes in the Second World War were still taking place.(3.21) Three (3pf, 15pf, 45pf) portrayed a young woman in provincial dress by yachts on one of Baden's many lakes.(3.21) The 84pf featured the deep Hollental Gorge (Hell's Valley) in the Black Forest through which Marie Antoinette passed on her way to marry the Dauphin, and the 1m Freiburg's Gothic Cathedral which somehow survived the intense 1944 bombing raids without any direct hits.(3.22)

Other values depicted uncontroversial cultural figures. Johann Hebel (1760-1826) (2pf, 12pf, 60pf) was a Lutheran teacher and poet who lived much of his adult life in Karlsruhe in Baden-Wurttemberg.(3.23) His early fame rested on his *Allemannische Gedichte*, a collection of poems of rural life written in Alemannic, a Germanic dialect common in many parts of Baden-Wurttemberg. It was much admired by Goethe. Later works, equally successful, were his humorous yet moral *Calendar Stories* and narrative *Bible Stories* for older children. The artist Hans Baldung Grien (c1484-1545) (10pf, 20pf, 75pf) trained under Albrecht Durer in Nuremberg but spent most of his life in Strasbourg working on commissions for churches (notably Freiburg's altar piece) and portraits (notably of Baden aristocracy) and his favourite subject - witchcraft.(3.23)

From 21 June 1948 the stamps were re-issued in new colours and the new currency values - some inscribed *pf* or *d.pf* for Deutschepfennig, and others DM. A new 30pf stamp depicted a girl in a festive Black Forest headdress, and an additional 50pf stamp featured Stephanie de Beauharnais, Grand Duchess of Baden (1789-1860). (3.24) Through Napoleon Bonaparte's marriage to her relative Josephine de Beauharnais, Stephanie became a member of the Imperial family, and in 1806 was married to the heir of the Grand Duchy of Baden, a state Napoleon was keen to make an ally. In 1811 she became Grand Duchess, and in 1818 a widow who became a noted patron of the arts until her death in 1860.

In April and May 1947 the first stamps appeared in a series that were titled either Baden or the Rheinland-Pfalz (Rhineland-Palatinate) or Wurttemberg. Their subjects were different but they had the same designer, the celebrated Lithuanian-born Vytautas Kazimieras Jonyas (1907-97). The title *Zone Francaise* was not used. Here, as in the other Allied Zones, the re-aligned provinces had been created with self-sufficiency in administration and economy uppermost in mind. Significantly the hitherto all-powerful militaristic state of Prussia was formally abolished and broken up in 1947.

By January 1948 the Baden set ran to 13 stamps. Two (16pf, 24pf) depicted the historic city of Rastatt on the border with France where Prussian troops had defeated the Baden revolutionaries in 1849 and where trials of

3.24 30pf Black Forest girl, 50pf Stephanie de Beauharnais and new colour 60d.pf Johann Hebel: from Baden set 21 June 1948+.

3.25 12pf Trier, 20pf Palatine house, 24pf Worms Cathedral, 50pf Mainz Cathedral and 84pf Gutenfels Castle: from Rheinland-Pfalz set April 1947+.

3.26 10pf Harvesting grapes and 16pf Asselstein: from Rheinland-Pfalz set April 1947+.

3.27 15pf Karl Marx, 30pf Johannes Gutenberg, 60pf Ludwig van Beethoven and 1m Charlemagne: from Rheinland-Pfalz set April 1947+.

From November 1948 ten values appeared with 'pf' omitted, five of which were new values and five existing values in new colours.

The corresponding initial set for the Rheinland-Pfalz had fifteen stamps. Several featured historic buildings. The 45pf and 50pf pictured the largely Romanesque Mainz Cathedral which had been badly damaged by Allied bombs in 1942, and the 24pf Worms Cathedral, also Romanesque in style, and also damaged in the war. (3.25) Both had been reduced to stables and barracks during the French Revolutionary Wars. The 12pf depicted Trier's huge Roman city gate, the Porta Nigra, that Napoleon Bonaparte ordered to be restored, the 20pf a traditional Palatinate house, and the 84pf the medieval Gutenfels Castle that guarded the River Rhine. (3.25) Perhaps the French forgot that here Marshal Blucher crossed the Rhine in pursuit of the French army on New Year's night 1813-14.

The 10pf depicted a young woman harvesting grapes in this famous wine-making region, and the 16pf the famous Asselstein (rock tower) near Annweiler.(3.26)

The 2pf and 60pf featured the death mask of the German composer Ludwig van Beethoven (1770-1827). (3.27) He had set several of Goethe's works, notably his play *Egmont* to music, composed *Eroica* to celebrate Napoleon as a revolutionary leader (although he changed the dedication in disgust at him becoming Emperor) and also the *Battle Symphony* to celebrate Wellington's victories over the French in 1813. The 15pf depicted Karl Marx (1818-83), born in Trier, whose studies of social tensions led to his *Communist Manifesto* and *Das Capital* and their calls for a proletarian revolution and the establishment of a classless Communist state.(3.27) The 30pf and 75pf portrayed Johannes Gutenberg (c1400-69) whose introduction of a mechanical movable-type printing press into Europe revolutionised the spread of ideas and learning.(3.27) He was born in Mainz and lived and worked mainly there and in Strasbourg. The 1m depicted Charlemagne (748-814), the King of the Franks whose ambition, military skills and aggressive diplomacy briefly united western and central Europe for the first time since the Roman Empire and led to a flowering of cultural activity.(3.27) The stamp portrays him after the pope had crowned him Emperor of the Romans in 800.

From 21 June 1948 the set was re-issued in new colours and new currency values, as at Baden. A significant new 6pf stamp depicted Baron Wilhelm von Ketteler, Bishop of Mainz (1811-77).(3.28) He was a powerful opponent of Prince Bismarck, the German Chancellor, who sought to assert state control over church schools and clerical appointments and reduce

3.28 6pf and 6 (pf omitted) Wilhelm von Ketteler: from Baden sets 21 June 1948 and November 1948+.

3.30 12pf Friedrich Schiller, 15pf Friedrich Holderlin, 10pf Ravensburg Gate and 16pf Bebenhausen Monastery: from Wurttemberg set 15 May 1947+.

3.29 20(pf omitted) Palatine house: from Baden set November 1948+.

3.31 84pf Lichtenstein Castle and 1m Zwiefalten Abbey: from Wurttemberg set 15 May 1947+.

Roman Catholic influence over political parties. As part of his protest in 1874 von Ketteler forbade diocesan clergy to celebrate Germany's 1870 victory over France at the Battle of Sedan which had led to Bismark's creation of the German Empire. From November 1948 ten values, five of them new, appeared with 'pf' omitted.(3.29)

The initial set for Wurttemberg, begun on 15 May 1947, had 13 stamps. The 2pf, 12pf and 60pf portrayed Friedrich Schiller, and the 3pf, 15pf and 45pf Friedrich Holderlin (1770-1843), born in Lauffen, whose essentially Romantic poetry brought the Greek 'mysteries' to life in fusion with Christian beliefs.(3.30) The 10pf, 20pf and 75pf depicted the historic Ravensburg Gate in Wangen im Allgau, and the 16pf and 24pf Bebenhausen Abbey which after dissolution in 1648 became a school until 1806, a royal retreat until 1918, and in 1946 the meeting place of the publicly elected but French controlled assembly working on a constitution for Wurttemberg.(3.30) The 84pf featured Lichtenstein Castle, rebuilt on ancient foundations in Romantic Gothic Revival style in the mid nineteenth century by Count Wilhelm von Urach, a cousin of the King of Wurttemberg. (3.31) The 1m depicted the Baroque church of Zwiefalten Abbey, most of whose buildings had been a lunatic asylum since dissolution by the French in 1802.(3.31)

When the set was reissued on 21 June 1948 in new colours and new currency values, two new images were included. The 8pf and 30pf depicted the striking Town Hall at Bad Waldsee - a town otherwise known for the German wartime factory striving to develop the Bachem Ba349 Natter, a vertical take-off rocket powered interceptor.(3.32) The 50pf featured Ludwig Uhland

3.32 30pf Bad Waldsee and 50pf Ludwig Uhland: from Wurttemberg set 21 June 1948.

(1787-1862), a Romantic poet and politician fighting for parliamentary democracy in the Kingdom of Wurttemberg.(3.32) From November 1948 ten values, five of them new, appeared with 'pf' omitted.

Several other sets were issued in all three French Zone states, but inscribed with their individual state names. Surtaxed Red Cross sets on 25 February 1949 depicted the named state's coat of arms.(3.33) Identical sets of three portraits of Goethe issued on 12 August 1949 marked the bicentenary of his birth. (3.34)

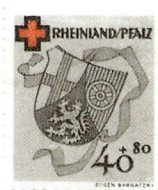

3.33 Red Cross (the three values and Arms): from sets 25 February 1949.

3.35 10pf 1849 Mail coach and 20pf 1949 Bus and aeroplane (from Baden): from sets 17 September 1949.

3.34 20pf+10pf Goethe (from Rheinland-Pfalz): from sets 12 August 1949.

3.36 20pf UPU (from Baden): from sets 4 October 1949.

3.37 4pf+16pf Freiburg granary and 30pf+50pf Fish fountain: from set 24 February 1949.

Identical sets featuring a mail coach of 1849 (10pf) and a modern mail coach, trailer and Douglas DC4 mail plane (20pf) marked the German stamp centenary on 17 September 1949.(3.35) Technically this only applied to the Kingdom of Bavaria as the Kingdoms of Prussia and Saxony began their issues in 1850. Finally identical pairs of stamps issued on 4 October 1949 depicting a globe, olive branch, posthorn and an electrical current (surprisingly not far removed from the Nazi SS insignia) joined the international celebration of the 75th anniversary of the Universal Postal Union.(3.36)

A few other sets were issued only in individual states. In Baden four surtaxed stamps inscribed WIEDERAUFBAU FREIBURG (REBUILDING FREIBURG) and a miniature sheet were issued on 24 February 1949.(3.37) The city had been bombed in error by a squadron of German planes 10 May 1940 and deliberately by the British in November and December 1944. The 4pf+16pf featured the ancient granary, the 10pf+20pf the cathedral, the 20pf+30pf a trumpeting angel from the cathedral, and the 30pf+50pf the ancient fish fountain and basin - used to provide fresh water and on market days to house fish. Freiburg was the French Zone's capital city of Baden.

On 22 June 1949 a single 30pf Baden stamp featuring the host Seehof Hotel on the Bodensee (Lake Constance) marked the International Engineers' Congress in Constance.(3.38) An important item on the agenda was the foundation of an essentially European Federation of National Engineering Associations which was formally established in Paris in 1951.

On 23 August 1949 three Baden stamps portraying a street confrontation and Carl Schurz (1829-1906) marked the centenary of the German revolution of 1848-49.(3.39) Born in the Rhineland, Schurz became a radical journalist and officer in the revolutionary army until escaping after its defeat at Rastatt. He ended up in the USA where he became a Union general in the Civil War, and later a Republican senator and Secretary of the Interior.

On 27 August 1949 a Baden stamp commemorated the centenary of the death of Conradin Kreutzer (1780-1849), Kapellmeister to the King of Wurttemberg and composer of popular songs and the opera Das Nachtlager in Granada.(3.40)

3.38 30pf Seehof Hotel, Lake Constance: 22 June 1949.

3.40 10pf Conradin Kreutzer: 27 August 1949.

3.39 30pf+15pf Carl Schurz and Rastatt revolt: 23 August 1949.

3.41 20pf+30pf St Martin: from set October 1948.

In the Rheinland-Pfalz two surtaxed stamps issued in October 1948, one depicting St Martin dividing his cloak with a beggar, the other St Christopher carrying a child on his shoulders, raised funds for the victims of the huge explosion at I G Farben's chemical plant at Ludwigshafen on the River Rhine on 28 July that year. (3.41) A railway container carrying 30 tons of dimethyl ether failed, and the explosion devastated 74 acres of the plant and its surroundings, killing over 200 people and injuring another 3,800. Other explosions there in 1921 and 1943 had done equal carnage. Two days after the 1948 tragedy thirteen senior I G Farben employees were found guilty of criminal association with the Nazi regime.

3.42 20pf+6pf Skier at Isny im Allgau: from set 11 February 1949.

In Wurttemberg two surtaxed stamps issued on 11 February 1949 supported the first post war German Nordic Ski Championship (the events were cross country, jumping and a combination of both).(3.42) It was held in Isny im Allgau, which features on both stamps, in the far south west of Wurttemberg.

On 4 September 1949 two surtaxed stamps featured the Protestant pastor Gustav Werner (1809-87) whose provision of a refuge and industrial school for orphans in Reutlingen a century earlier grew into the influential and extensive Gustav Werner Foundation for the Bruderhaus (Brother House) named after him.(3.43) The inscription *GUSTAV WERNER HUNDERT JAHRE ZUM BRUDERHAUS CHRISTENTUM DER TAT* possibly translates best as *A HUNDRED YEARS OF GUSTAV WERNER'S CHRISTIAN FRATERNITY IN ACTION.*

3.43 20pf+10pf Gustav Werner: from set 4 September 1949.

THE SAAR

The Saar was a coal rich industrial region in the west of Germany on the border with France and Luxembourg. In 1920 it was occupied, governed and exploited by France under a League of Nations mandate until 1935 when a referendum returned it to Germany until 1945 when it fell into the French Zone. In February 1946 it became the Saar Protectorate, thereby enabling France to exercise economic control but also pursue a policy of winning over the Saarois to eventual French annexation. On 15 December 1947 the Saarland Constitution granted elections and home rule under a French High Commissioner. Its first anniversary in 1948 was celebrated with a pair of suitably inscribed stamps, but the policy failed and in 1957 a referendum returned the Saar to Germany.(3.44)

The Saar used the general issues for the French Zone until January 1947 when a Saar set of 20 German values using six images highlighted the regional economy. Six values featured a coal miner, five sugar beet harvesters, four steelworkers, three Mettlach Abbey, the 84pf Marshal Ney, and 1m the dramatic loop in the River Saare between Mettlach and Merzig.(3.45) The Benedictine Mettlach Abbey was founded in the seventh century, rebuilt in Romanesque style in the thirteenth century and in Baroque style in the eighteenth century, and dissolved in 1802 during the French Revolutionary wars. Soon afterwards it became, and remains, the headquarters of Villeroy & Boch, the ceramic manufacturers.

Marshal Michel Ney (1769-1815) was born in Saarlouis, then a French enclave. Through courage and quick thinking in battle, he rose quickly through the ranks of France's Revolutionary Army, becoming a general in 1799 and marshal in 1804. His rearguard actions in the retreat from Moscow earned him Napoleon's title of 'the bravest of the brave.' After Napoleon's defeat and the impending invasion of France in 1814 Ney demanded his abdication, for which King Louis XVIII made him a duke. However when Napoleon returned after exile in Elba Ney joined him for which change of loyalty he was executed by the royalists after the Battle of Waterloo.

3.46 6f on 24pf Steelworkers, 9f on 30pf Sugar beet harvesters and 20f on 84pf Marshal Ney: from white paper set November 1947+.

On 17 November 1947 thirteen of the values were reissued, first on yellowish paper and then on white paper, overprinted with French values when the currency changed.(3.46)

On 1 April 1948 a new series of local scenes and occupations was introduced. Lower values featured a pair of clasped hands - possibly German and French ones (10c, 60c,1f), a worker in a peaked cap (2f, 3f), a woman and sheaf of wheat (4f, 5f) and a coal miner (6f, 9f).(3.47) Larger stamps with the higher values depicted the chimney of a blast furnace (10f), a foundry (14f), builders (20f) and the front of Mettlach Abbey (50f).(3.48) Three Airmail stamps showed the shadow of an aeroplane flying over the River Saare near Mettlach.

In December 1947 the River Saar burst its banks causing the most severe flooding in 150 years. As part of a massive and long lasting relief campaign, on 12 October 1948 a surtaxed set of five dramatic stamps and miniature sheet showed the floods sweeping through various parts of Saarbrucken and Saarlouis. (3.49) Two years later the region still needed support, and on 20 December 1949 a surtaxed set of five stamps featured

3.44 10f I JAHR VERFASSUNG (1 YEAR CONSTITUTION): from set 15 December 1948.

3.45 8pf Coal miner and 80pf Mettlach Abbey: from set January 1947+.

3.47 1f Clasped hands and 9f Miner: from set 1April 1948.

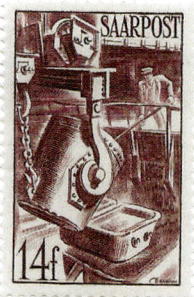

3.48 14f Foundry, 50f Mettlach Abbey and 200f River Saare near Mettlach: from set 1 April 1948.

3.49 6f+4f Floods in St Johann, Saarbrucken: from set 12 October 1948.

are approaching the Ludweiller hostel in the 8f+5f, and the Weiskirchen hostel in the 10f+7f. Both were in the west not far from the French border.

On 2 April 1949 a single stamp featuring scientific instruments marked the foundation of Saarland University in November 1948.(3.52) It had grown out of the medical courses at the state hospital, and became the first post-war European university. As part of France's courtship of the Saar, it received financial support from the French government and academic support from the University of Nancy.

On 25 September 1949 two surtaxed stamps supported Horse Day *(TAG DES PFERDES)*: the 15f+5f showed a mare and foal, the 25f+15f two horses in a steeple-chase. (3.53) The Saar and neighbouring Rheinland-Pfalz had been renowned for the quality of their horse breeding since Duke Christian IV of Zweibrucken financed a royal stud in the mid eighteenth century. Later it became the main Royal Bavarian State Stud. The carefully bred German 'Sport Horse' is still called the 'Zweibrucher'.

From November 1949 an eclectic new definitive set appeared. The lower values depicted scenes and symbols of local industries including the building trade, rolling mills, dumper truck on a slag heap, wagons in a coal

3.50 25f+10f St Thomas of Villanueva heals the sick: from set 20 December 1949.

reassuring themes of healing and intercession. Three were taken from paintings by the Spanish artist Bartolome Esteban Murillo (1618-82) whose enduring popularity lay in his ability to incorporate real people into spiritual scenes. The 8f+2f shows part of his *Moses Striking the Rock*, the 12f+3f *Our Lord healing the Paralytic* and the 25f+10f *St Thomas of Villanueva Heals the Sick*. Throughout his life, successively as friar, court preacher and bishop of Valencia, Thomas of Villanueva (1488-1555) supported the disadvantaged through personal generosity and the provision of education and work.(3.50) The 15f+5f featured the *The Sick Child* by the Dutch artist Gabriel Metsu (1629-67), and the 50f+20f was based on the famous votive image of the Madonna holding the crucified Jesus in the Holy Cross Chapel in Blieskastel in the Saar.

The delights of the Saar dominated the next sets. On 11 January 1949 two surtaxed stamps supported the refurbishment and construction of youth hostels *(JUGENDHERBERGSWERK)*.(3.51) Countryside hikers

3.51 10f+7f Hikers at Weiskirchen: from set 11 January 1949.

3.52 15f Saarland University: 2 April 1949.

GERMANY

3.53 15f+5f Mare and foal: from set 25 September 1949).

3.54 6f Coal wagons, 12f Ceramics, 25f Blast furnace, 60f Countryside around Landsweiler, and 100f Wiebelskirchen: from set 30 November 1949+.

mine, post horn and telephone, and ceramics.(3.54) The 60c featured Ludwig van Beethoven to signify the region's cultural interests. The higher values revealed that not all of the Saarland was industrial. They depicted workers in a foundry (20f) and a blast furnace (25f) but also the factories of Halberg viewed across the valley from St Arnual in Saarbrucken (30f), the strange sandstone 'Giants Boot' in Rentrisch, part of the industrial city of St Ingbert that was heavily bombed in the war (45f), the countryside surrounding the huge coal mine at Landsweiler (60f), and an adult and child sitting on a bench high above the small town of Wiebelskirchen (100f).(3.54) It was the birthplace of Erich Honecker (1912-94) the wartime anti-Nazi, ardent Communist, founder of the Free German Youth in 1946, and later the key figure in the German Democratic Republic.

WEST BERLIN : FROM 1 JULY 1948

On 1 July 1948, soon after the western Allies introduced the Deutsche Mark, the Soviet government withdrew from the four power control of Berlin. The western sectors remained under American, British and French control, and on 1 September 1950 they became a 'land' within the German Federal Republic. On 1 September the 1947-48 Allied Occupation set featuring reconstruction workers and the Dove of Peace was issued with *BERLIN* overprinted diagonally in black. (3.55) These could be purchased with Deutsche Marks or the Soviet Zone's new Ostmarks, the latter representing a significant saving due to its favourable rate of exchange with the Deutsche Mark. However this ceased from 20 January 1949 when red *BERLIN* overprinted stamps replaced the black ones, and were restricted to Deutsche Marks.(3.56) Until 1953 Berlin's stamps were titled *DEUTSCHE POST*: from 1953 *BERLIN* was added.

During 1949 a lengthy set of stamps depicted notable Berlin buildings - with no war damage shown. Berlin's historic glory rather than its Nazi interlude was the aim. The 15pf and 1DM depicted a Douglas C-54 Skymaster Transport flying over Tempelhof Airport - a common sight during the eleven months of the Berlin airlift that ended just a month before this stamp was issued on 17 June 1949.(3.57) The 6f and 50f featured the Reischstag, the parliament building gutted by fire in 1933 thereby giving the Nazis a pretext to arrest opponents and suspend debate. After the war it lay empty until reconstruction and modernisation after German reunification. The 5pf, 25pf and 5DM pictured the Schloss Tegel built in the 1820s by the philosopher, educationalist and diplomat William von Humboldt,

3.55 24pf Bricklayer and harvester with black BERLIN overprint: from set 1 September 1948.

3.56 10pf Sower with red BERLIN overprint: from set 20 January 1949.

3.57 4pf Tempelhof-Schoneberg City Hall, 30pf Kleist Park, 60pf National Gallery, 90pf Technical University, and 1DM Douglas C-54 over Tempelhof Airport; from set 7 May 1949+.

together with his naturalist brother Alexander, as their local home (1767-1835). The university William helped found in Berlin was named after him in 1949. The 20pf, 80pf and 90pf featured Berlin's Technical Academy, originally a gradual amalgamation of historic trade, building, mining and agricultural colleges, that was re-inaugurated in April 1946 as a Technical University. (3.57) The 4pf, 8pf and 40pf pictured the Tempelhof-Schoneberg City Hall.(3.57) Although damaged in the war it became the city hall for West Berlin in 1948 when relations with the Soviet Zone plummeted. In front of it Rudolph-Wilde-Platz was the scene of huge protest rallies during the Russian blockade and Allied airlift. It was here President Kennedy gave his famous speech by the Berlin Wall on 23 June 1963. The 10pf and 30pf pictured the walk-way colonnades at Kleist Park, a large public area that also included the neo-Baroque court house.(3.57) Here the trials took place of the surviving conspirators of the 20 July 1944 plot against Hitler, here the Allies held the first meeting of what became the Nuremberg Trials, and here, too, they decided the division of defeated Germany. The 1pf and 3DM depicted the iconic Brandenburg Gate, now just inside the Soviet Zone although people could still travel freely through it until the Berlin wall was built in 1961. The 60pf showed Berlin's National Gallery, looking much like a Greco-Roman temple, built in the 1870s to reinforce Germany's prestige soon after it was declared an Empire.(3.57) The Gallery ended up in the Soviet Zone, but after some items had been returned by the occupying powers much of the collection was divided between the erstwhile Allies and a new gallery created in the Western Zone. The 2DM depicted the once attractive Gendarmenmarkt in the Soviet Zone, still ruinous in 1949. Flanked by a massive concert hall and the city's French Huguenot Church and German Lutheran Church the former marketplace had been a centre of city life.

In December 1949 three stamps and a miniature sheet portraying an alms plate and a shadowy figure of the Berlin bear raised money, as the inscription said, *FUR BERLINGER WAHRUNGSGESCHADIGTE (FOR BERLINERS DAMAGED BY THEIR CURRENCY).* (3.58) The new Deutsche Mark had protected Germany from hyperinflation whilst creating a stable market economy. Prices had risen and then stabilised as industrial incentives soared, but 'old' private savings had been virtually wiped out at the 10:1 exchange rate. The new set of stamps was part of the temporary relief programme.

Other West Berlin issues in 1949 included a set of seven stamps on 11 April celebrating the 75th anniversary of the Universal Postal Union. Not surprisingly they featured the statue of Heinrich von Stephan (1831-97), whose work standardising the German postal system led him to formulate and promote the far wider UPU.(3.59)

On 29 July three stamps featuring paintings of Goethe and scenes from his Iphigene (10pf), Reineke Fuchs (20pf) and Faust (30pf) marked the bicentenary of his birth.(3.60)

3.58 10pf+5pf Berlin currency relief fund: from set 1 December 1949.

3.59 12pf Heinrich von Stephan and globe: from set 11 April 1949.

GERMANY

3.60 30pf Goethe and scenes from Faust: from set 29 July 1949.

3.61 20pf European Recovery Programme: 1 October 1950.

Although West Berlin continued to issue its own stamps until 1990, in 1950 it joined the American, British and French Zones which had formally become the German Federal Republic the previous year. West Berlin became a significant recipient of American money under the European Recovery Programme (ERP or Marshall Plan - named after General George C Marshall, the US Secretary of State) aimed at modernising industry, rebuilding shattered districts and stemming Communism. A stamp issued on the opening day of the revived Berlin Industrial Exhibition - 1 October 1950 - recognised the ERP's importance. (3.61)

RUSSIAN ZONE : MAY 1945 to 7 OCTOBER 1949

In the Soviet Zone the military government allowed the Higher Postal Directorates *(Oberpostdirections or O.P.D.)* covering Berlin-Brandenburg, Mecklenburg-Vorpommern, Saxony, East Saxony, West Saxony, and Thuringia, to organise their own individual but broadly similar systems. However this occurred gradually, and only after numerous localities had made their own temporary arrangements after the country's surrender. Many lasted a year or more, and a selection are shown here.

Towns across the populous state of Saxony were particularly inventive - as several examples will show. Bad Schmeideberg, Schwarzenberg and Wittenberg-Lutherstadt continued using Hitler definitive stocks but completely blacked out the portrait with simple circular dies which kept the values clear.(3.62)

Other localities were less precise. From 20 May until 30 June 1945 Lobau blackened Hitler's head to a greater or lesser degree with an outer hatched octagon with a Gothic D (for Dresden O.P.D.) in the blackened centre. (3.63) Dobeln did not quite obliterate Hitler's head by overprinting it with the town's name, the date 6.5.1945, and a mesh of linked black dots.(3.64)

Glauchau opted to overprint its supplies of Hitler head definitives with various bars, new values and *KREIS GLAUCHAU (DISTRICT OF GLAUCHAU)*. However Deutsches Reich remained clear until June 1945 when a heavy bottom bar was applied.(3.65)

From 15 June 1945 the famous porcelain centre of Meissen issued Hitler head definitives overprinted *DEUTSCHLANDS VERDERBER (GERMANY'S SPOILER or DESTROYER)*.(3.66) From 31 December 1945 they were replaced by four specially designed surtaxed stamps inscribed *WIEDERAUFBAU (RECONSTRUCTION)*.(3.67) The 5pf+15pf featured housing and viticulture, the 6pf+24pf porcelain, the 8pf+32pf hoisting steel girders, and the 12pf+48pf a wrecked bridge.

In June 1945 Gorlitz, on Saxony's post-war border with Poland, issued two designs inscribed *STADT GORLITZ (CITY OF GORLITZ)*. One was merely an enclosed numeral, the other depicted the city's coat of

3.62 Schwarzenberg: blacked 8pf Hitler definitive: May 1945.

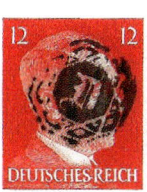

3.63 Lobau: octagon overprinted 12pf Hitler definitive: 20 May 1945.

3.64 Dobeln: mesh overprinted 6pf Hitler definitive: 6 May 1945.

3.65 Glauchau: bar, district and value overprinted 8pf Hitler definitive: from set 2 June 1945+.

3.66 Meissen: Deutschlands Verderber overprinted 12pf Hitler definitive: from set 23 June 1945.

3.67 Meissen: 12pf+48pf Wrecked bridge: from Reconstruction set 31 December 1945.

And early in 1946 in Cottbus in eastern Brandenburg the postal administration recognised the city's surtaxed set featuring an attractive range of detailed drawings of local scenes - the old walls and towers, town hall and market, and streets, parks and riverside.(3.72) Conversely nearby Spremberg contented itself with the simplest of stamps inscribed *GEBUR BEZAHLT (FEE PAID)*, the value and *SPREMBERG*. In February 1946 they appeared overprinted *WIEDERAUFBAU (RECONSTRUCTION)* and a hefty 1 MARK.(3.73)

In due course the *Oberpostdirection* (O.P.D.) Berlin, embracing Berlin and Brandenburg, issued its own highly symbolic set, inscribed *STADT BERLIN POST*, between 3 August and 6 December 1945. Six featured arms of the Imperial eagle and Bohemia's lion (Gorlitz was in Bohemia until 1635).(3.68)

3.68 Gorlitz: 6pf and 12pf: from set 12 June 1945.

The industrial town of Grossbraschen not far from the new Polish border used various local post-marks and labels until settling in August 1945 on a simple set depicting two crossed mining tools, the word *POST* and no place name but with the postal administrator's signature. In December the stamps appeared with the place name and without the signature (3.69), and in January 1946 the town brought out four surtaxed stamps for local reconstruction depicting a miner, glassblower, house building and a briquette and foundry.(3.70)

Finsterwalde in Brandenburg briefly issued a blackened out 1pf Hitler head stamp revalued 6pf, but in February 1946 produced an approved surtaxed set depicting the city hall, coat of arms and the inscription *SANGERSTADT (THE SINGER CITY)*.(3.71) Since the nineteenth century the city had been famous for its singers and folk festival. The stamps appeared imperforate and perforated, in numerous shades and on various papers.

3.69 Grossbraschen: 5pf Crossed mining tools: from set 27 August 1945+, and 40pf: from set 20 December 1945.

3.70 Grossbraschen: 6pf+24pf Uniformed official (Michel says bergmann - miner) (Interestingly he is pointing to the tiny words 'gluck ause' - good luck) and 12pf+28pf Glassblower: from set 20 January 1946.

the historic bear symbol of Berlin in various poses - rampant (5pf), wielding a spade (6pf), on a shield (8pf), carrying a brick (12pf), carrying a plank (12pf) and on the city's coat of arms (20pf). The seventh (30pf) featured an oak sapling growing out of the ruins. (3.74, 375)

The O.P.D. Schwerin, serving Mecklenburg-Vorpommern, issued three commonly used values in several printings and colours between 28 August 1945 and 30 January 1946. The 6pf had no inscription and just the value within a decorated border, while the 8pf featured a ploughman and the 12pf a sheaf of corn outside a granary.(3.76)

However on 21 October 1945 a surtaxed set of three striking woodcut portraits entitled Victims of Fascism harked back to the war.(3.77) The 6pf+14pf featured Dr Rudolf Breitscheid (1874-1944). After a lengthy career as a Socialist politician in the Reichstag he fled to France in 1933 after voting against the Enabling Act giving Hitler plenary powers, but was arrested in 1941 and incarcerated in Buchenwald concentration camp where he died in 1944. The 8pf+22pf depicted Dr Erich Klausener (1885-1934), a senior Prussian interior official and ardent Roman Catholic whose open opposition to the Nazis led to his murder on the 'Night of the Long Knives' in 1934. The 12pf+28pf portrayed

3.74 O.P.D. Berlin: 5pf, 20pf and 30pf: from set 3 August 1945+.

3.71 Finsterwalde: 40pf: from set 16 February 1946.

3.75 O.P.D. Berlin 8pf with special cancellation publicising the 'German Social Democratic Party Conference 19-20 April 1946'. After months of Communist pressure this conference marked the final forced merger of the SDP with the German Communist Party to form the Communist dominated Socialist Unity Party.

3.72 Cottbus: 8pf+4pf Ancient market and 25pf+12pf Old Cottbus stagecoach: from set 17 January 1946.

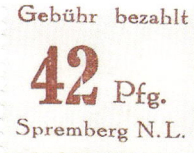 

3.73 Spremberg: 42pf: from set 3 January 1946, and 12pf overprinted Wiederaufbau 1 Mark: from set 25 February 1946.

3.76 O.D.P. Schwerin: 6pf and 12pf: 28 August 1945+.

3.77 O.D.P. Schwerin: 6f+14f Rudolf Breitschied, 8pf+22pf Erich Klausener, and 12pf+28pf Ernst Thalmann: set 21 October 1945.

3.78 O.D.P. Schwerin: 8pf+22pf Sower: from set 8 December 1945+.

3.80 O.D.P Schwerin: 20pf Docks and 40pf Spinning: from set 17 January 1946+.

3.79 O.D.P. Schwerin: 8pf+22pf Schoolgirl in winter: from set 31 December 1945.

Ernst Thalmann (1886-1944), the leader of Germany's militant Communist Party from 1925 to 1933 when he was imprisoned in Buchenwald, and shot in 1944. Interestingly no-one - especially his rival Walter Ulbricht - sought his release under the Russian-Germany pact of 1939-41. All three had post-war monuments, and streets named after them.

In December 1945 three O.P.D. Schwerin surtaxed charity stamps depicting horse ploughing (6pf+14pf), a sower (8pf+22pf) and a reaper (12pf+28pf) also reminded east Germans they were in Communist hands. (3.78) The set was inscribed *JUNKERLAND IN BAUERNHAND (JUNKER LAND IN PEASANT HANDS)*, and referred to the *Bodenreform (Land Reform)* in the Soviet zone whereby all private property over 250 acres was confiscated and allocated to 'new farmers'. Later on these farmers were pressurised to join collectives. Most of the expropriated land had belonged to 'Junkers', the old landed nobility of Prussia, many of whom were imprisoned by the Russians.

On 31 December 1945 another unusual woodcut set inscribed *HELFT DEN KINDERN (HELP THE CHILDREN)* depicting a 'helping hand' cradling a baby (6pf+14pf), a schoolgirl in winter (8pf+22pf) and a boy's head (12pf+28pf) sought funds to relieve the appalling post-war distress.(3.79) People were still starving amidst the ruins.

Finally between 17 January and 25 February 1946 a longer definitive set appeared in both perforated and imperforate formats. Four values featured a factory, scaffolding, docks and fishing boats, and a further six peaceful pictures depicted the far from peaceful rural economy - a village street, windmill, horse plough, a deer, a tractor, and a woman spinning.(3.80)

The O.D.P. Halle serving Saxony-Anhalt issued a definitive set from 10 October 1945 inscribed *PROVINZ SACHSEN (PROVINCE OF SAXONY)* depicting its historic coat of arms of a field of horizontal black and gold stripes crossed with a green crancelin (a stylised 'crown of rue').(3.81) It dated back to the twelfth century when Emperor Frederick Barbarossa draped his rue wreath over the shield of Bernard, Count of Anhalt's as a mark of favour when he created him Duke. Soon, though, Communist style sheaves of corn and crossed hammers topped the full Saxony-Anhalt arms rather than any royal crown or eagle.

Stamps here, too, promoted egalitarian land reform with two inscribed *BODENREFORM 1945 (LAND*

3.81 O.D.P. Halle: 1pf Arms: from set 10 October 1945+.

3.84 O.D.P. Leipzig: 30pf Numeral: from perforated set 9 November 1945+.

3.82 O.D.P. Halle: 6pf Ploughing: from redrawn set 21 February 1946.

3.83 O.D.P. Halle: 42pf+28pf Locomotive engineering works: from set 19 January 1946.

REFORM 1945) featuring fields being ploughed against a brightly rising Socialist sun.(3.82) They were issued perforated and imperforate in December 1945, and redrawn and reissued in February 1946.

The reconstruction programme *(WIEDERAUFBAU)* led to perforated and imperforate versions (on 19 January and 21 February 1946 respectively) of a surtaxed set featuring house building (6pf+4pf), bridge and waterways construction (12pf+8pf) and locomotive engineering (42pf+28pf).(3.83)

O.P.D. Leipzig, serving West Saxony, started with a bland set containing a numeral and *Deutsches Post* inscription issued from 28 September 1945.(3.84)

On 18 October 1945 two innocuous 6pf and 12pf stamps advertised the *MUSTERSCHSAU LEIPZIGER ERZEUGNISSE (SAMPLE SHOW OF LEIPZIG PRODUCTS)*.(3.85) The full Leipzig Trade Fair was not restored until 1946, but the inscription is accurate as the set refers to the Soviet military authority's insistence late in 1945 on a small show of regional goods to stimulate production and interest.

The surtaxed 1946 Leipzig Fair set was marked with the formal title *LEIPZIGER MESSE 1946* and the new double M logo.(3.86) As the pre-war show-ground had been largely destroyed, the Fair was scattered in several venues, including the old town hall and market dating from 1556 featured on the stamps, and the university. Exhibitors came from all four occupation zones and the USSR.

On 7 January 1946 a set of twelve surtaxed stamps featuring florally framed values and the inscription *GEGEN VOLKSNOT VOLKSSOLIDARITAT (NATIONAL SOLIDARITY IN THE NATIONAL EMERGENCY)* supported the Relief Fund.(3.87) The highest value reached 1 Mark in total. The first post-war winter was particularly cold, towns remained devastated, many thousands were malnourished and homeless, many children were orphans, and many Germans remained dependent on relief supplies - and were constantly fearful of the Russian occupiers.

In February and March 1946 a set issued on both watermarked and unwatermarked paper centred on the city of Leipzig itself. The 3pf and 4pf depicted its coat of arms - the lion of the medieval Margraves of Meissen and the vertical blue and gold strips of the medieval Margraves of Landsberg.(3.88) The 5pf and 6pf featured its famous Protestant Church of St Nicholas where Johann Sebastian Bach's *St John's Passion* was premiered

3.85 O.D.P. Leipzig: 12pf Leipzig 'Sample Show': from set 18 October 1945.

3.86 O.D.P. Leipzig: 84pf+66pf Leipzig Fair (Market and Old Town Hall): from set 8 May 1946.

3.87 O.D.P. Leipzig: 6pf Relief Fund: from set 7 January 1946.

3.90 O.P.D. Dresden: 10pf with flaw: from November 1945 printing.

3.88 O.P.D. Leipzig: 4pf Leipzig coat of arms: from watermarked set 12 February 1946.

3.91 O.P.D. Dresden: 6pf+44pf Zwinger pavilion and 12pf+88pf Town Hall: from set 6 February 1946.

3.89 O.P.D. Leipzig: 6pf St Nicholas Church, and 12pf New Town Hall: from watermarked set 12 February 1946.

in 1724.(3.89) The 8pf and 12pf depicted the massive new Town Hall built in a blend of Baroque and Art Nouveau between 1899 and 1905, and the scene of many suicides in 1945 as the Russians neared the city. (3.89)

O.P.D. Dresden, covering East Saxony, got off to an early but controversial start on 23 June 1945 with a simple floral bordered imperforate stamp with 12pf in an inner circle. However as well as saying POST at the top it had the Russian NOYTA (POST) at the bottom, and as this contravened the Allied language agreement it was withdrawn the same day. On 28 June the 12pf appeared with just POST at the top and was followed by eight other values by the end of July. Between November 1945 and January 1946 several different printers, papers and colours were used to replenish stocks.(3.90) Crudely printed, they were issued with varying strengths of colour and often with flaws.

Dresden itself suffered from four massive British and American air raids between 13 and 15 February 1945: the city centre was destroyed, and an estimated 23,000 people killed. Early in March more American raids focussed on factories and the railway yards. The saturation bombing of the city caused lasting arguments about its military and moral justification, especially as the city was crowded with refugees from the east. On 6 February 1946 O.A.P Dresden issued two heavily surtaxed stamps, inscribed BUNDESLAND SACHSEN (STATE OF SAXONY) and WIR BAUEN AUF! (WE BUILD ON!).(3.91) The 6pf+44pf depicted the prominent wall pavilion of the famous Zwinger, a richly decorated area of Baroque pavilions, galleries, gardens and fountains. The 12pf+88pf featured the medieval Town Hall. Both buildings suffered heavy damage, and both were reconstructed much on their original lines within a few years. The Town Hall added a statue honouring all the women who moved millions of tons of wartime debris.

O.P.D Erfurt was responsible for Thuringia. From 1 October 1945 a varied set of eight definitives, plus miniature sheets, featured fir trees (3pf, 4pf and 5pf), a letter and posthorn (6pf and 8pf), Friedrich Schiller (12pf) and Johann Goethe (20pf and 30pf).(3.92) In later life Schiller had settled in Weimar, not far from Erfurt, and with Goethe, who also lived in Weimar with his mistress (later his wife), ensured the Weimar Theatre became renowned for its productions. Attracted by Goethe and the liberal attitude and patronage of the Grand Dukes of Saxe-Weimar-Eisenach, other writers and composers sought out Weimar and the city entered its cultural golden age. In 1919 Weimar achieved a different fame as the seat of the new Republic's National Assembly, and when the Nazis achieved power in 1933 army barracks and concentration camps were built

3.92 O.P.D Erfurt: 4pf Fir trees and 12pf Schiller: from set 1 October 1945+.

nearby. The city was bombed in 1945 and many historic buildings damaged or destroyed, but the city's cultural legacy - and the potential publicity attached to it - meant they became a priority for restoration.

An imperforate miniature sheet inscribed *WIEDERAUFBAUSPENDE (RECONSTRUCTION DONATION)*, priced 7.50 Reich Marks, was issued on 27 March 1946 depicting four of Weimar's celebrated residents in aid of the restoration of the national theatre. (3.93) The 40pf featured the theatre, the 6pf Schiller, the 10pf Goethe, the 12pf the pianist and composer Franz Liszt (1811-86) and the 16pf the poet and playwright Christoph Wieland (1733-1813). After retiring from concert tours, Liszt lived in Weimar from 1848 until about 1861 with Princess Carolyne zu Sayn-Wittegenstein, and afterwards divided his time between Weimar, Rome and Budapest. Much of Wieland's work explored the relationship between the sensual and spiritual, and beauty and the intellect. He was also a professor of philosophy at the University of Erfurt. In 1772 he moved to Weimar as tutor to the children of the Duchess of Brunswick-Wolfenbuttel and remained there for much of his life, not least because the Duchess herself was instrumental in the city becoming a cultural centre.

On 30 March 1946 a heavily surtaxed O.P.D. Erfurt set and miniature sheet inscribed *WIRBAUEN BRUCKEN (WE BUILD BRIDGES)* featured four vital reconstruction projects.(3.94) All the bridges had been partially destroyed by the German army late in the war to stem the Allied advance. Their names appear in tiny print below the frame. The bridge at Saalburg, (10pf+60pf), near the Bavarian border, linked the small town to neighbouring Ebersdorf across the Saale River. The ancient stone Camsdorf Bridge (12f+68pf) linked the centre of Jena across the Saale with its suburb of Weningenjena. The long vaulted autobahn bridge built between 1938 and 1942 shown in the 16pf+74pf crossed the Saale at Goschwitz south of Jena. The 24pf+76pf featured another 1930s autobahn bridge that crossed the Ilm River at Meelingan.

From February 1946 until June 1948 the Soviet Zone used the same stamps as the British and American

3.93 O.P.D Erfurt: Weimar Theatre miniature sheet: 27 March 1946.

zones. After the complete breakdown in relations following the Western Allies introduction of the Deutsche Mark on 18 June 1948 the Soviet Zone went its own way, hurriedly introducing the Ostmark on 24 June and issuing its own stamps. As an emergency measure the 'workers' definitive issue and remaining stocks of other issues were crudely hand-stamped locally with O.P.D. numbers and postal district names to create the only official *Ostmark* stamps.(3.95) There were around 1,900 handstamps from 1,100 postal districts. The overprints were valid for just 17 days - 24 June to 10 July 1948 - when they were replaced with the centrally produced overprint *Sowjetische Besatzungs Zone (Soviet Occupation Zone)* on the 'workers' set and later on some of the 1946 Numeral issue and 1945 Berlin-Brandenburg Bear set.(3.96)

However the Soviet Zone soon issued a set of sixteen definitives depicting eight carefully selected German politicians, artists, writers and scientists. The 2pf and 20pf portrayed the eminent artist and sculptor Kathe Kollwitz (1867-1945) whose works increasingly depicted the sufferings of ordinary people and whose views increasingly became Socialist and Communist in outlook. Only her international reputation saved her from arrest, although not from harassment, by the Nazis.(3.97) The 6pf and 40pf featured the dramatist and novelist Gerhart Hauptmann (1862-1946) who won the Nobel Prize for Literature in 1912, who supported Germany in the First World War and the Republic afterwards, and, like Kollwitz, survived Nazi suspicions only because of the popularity of his socially critical canon of works. The 10pf and 84pf depicted the Marxist politician August Bebel (1840-1913) who founded the Social Democratic Workers' Party of Germany in 1869, led repeated attacks on Bismarck's authoritarianism and Germany's brutal colonialism, and endured several periods of imprisonment. The 16pf and 25pf featured the physician and politician Rudolf Virchow (1821-1902) whose researches led him to become an advocate of radical educational and welfare reform as weapons to combat the prevalence of contagious diseases. His researches also led him to denounce theories about the superiority of the 'Aryan race' long before the Nazis took it up.(3.97) The 15pf and 60pf portrayed the towering German Idealist philosopher Georg Hegel (1770-1831) whose *Elements of the Philosophy of Right* stated that the ideal civil state both subsumes family and civil society and fulfils them: citizens both choose and know their place, and fulfil their obligations knowing their supreme duty is to the state which honours them.(3.97) If the state fails Hegel thought it acceptable that it was destroyed. After Hegel's death, his ideas were used to strengthen both right-wing defenders of a strong ruler and left-wing advocates of a social revolution, including Karl Marx. The 8pf and 50pf featured Marx, the 12pf and 30pf Friedrich Engels, and the 24pf and 80pf Ernst Thalmann, the inter-war leader of the German Communist Party, imprisoned by the Nazis and forgotten by his Party.

Not surprisingly a Soviet Zone stamp marked the 30th anniversary of the violent deaths of Karl Liebknecht (1871-1919) and Rosa Luxemburg (1871-1919) in Berlin after the crushing of the Spartacus uprising.(3.98) The stamp depicted them above a crowd advancing towards the sun of Communism. A Marxist

3.94 O.P.D Erfurt: 10pf+60 Saalburg Bridge and 12pf+68pf Camsdorf Bridge: from set 30 March 1946.

3.95 60pf Miner overprinted 3 Berlin 113 (O.P.D. 3 Berlin, sub-district 113): from series June-July 1948.

3.96 40pf Sower overprinted Sowjetische Besatzungs Zone: from series 3 July 1948+.

3.97 2pf Kathe Kollwitz, 25pf Rudolf Virchow and 60pf Georg Hegel: from set October 1948+.

Social Democratic member of the Reichstag, Liebknecht was imprisoned for vigorously opposing German militarism as the First World War loomed. In 1914, along with Rosa Luxembourg and others, he founded the Spartacus League, the precursor of the German Communist Party, but in 1919 their revolution, although initially widespread and, indeed violent, was brutally crushed by the new German republican government in tacit alliance with the army and right wing militia - the Freikorps. Rosa Luxemburg was also a high profile Marxist Social Democrat and then a Communist, and she, too, had been imprisoned for attacking German militarism and calling for workers across Europe to unite. Along with Liebknecht she was captured after the Spartacus revolt, tortured and shot. They became icons of German left-wing movements to the present day.

On 13 May 1949 a stamp depicting a dove and olive branch appeared inscribed *WAHL ZUM 3. VOLKSCONGRESS 15-16 MAI 1949 (ELECTIONS FOR 3rd PEOPLE'S CONGRESS 15-16 MAY 1949).* (3.99) On 29 May it was reissued overprinted *3. DeutscherVolkskongress 29.-30 Mai 1949*, and the new date was important. There had been two earlier People's Congresses in 1947 and 1948 embracing all Zones but dominated by Soviet Zone representatives who rejected the Marshall Plan, accepted the new border with Poland (and loss of territory), and urged reunification. On 15-16 May Soviet Zone voters elected the crucial Third People's Congress and were presented with a 'Unity List' composed from 'Anti-Fascist Democratic Parties' and dominated by the virtually Communist Socialist Unity Party. Voters had to say Yes or No to the statement *I am in favour of German unity and a just peace agreement. I therefore vote for the following list of candidates for the Third German People's Congress.* Around 95% of people voted and 66% approved the list, although in many areas there was no attempt to operate a secret ballot Later elections ensured 99% of voters voted the 'right way'. The new Soviet Zone/Democratic Republic Congress convened in Berlin on 29-30 May. Everything had been done hurriedly in response to the conversion of the American, British and French Zones into the Federal Republic of Germany on 23 May 1949.

3.98 24pf Karl Liebknecht and Rosa Luxemburg: 15 January 1949.

3.99 24pf Third German People's Congress: 13 May 1949, and overprint: 29 May 1949.

3.100 24pf+16pf and 84pf+36pf Goethe: from set 20 July 1949.

On 20 July 1949 an attractive surtaxed set featured Goethe at various ages based upon famous paintings - as a student by Georg Friedrich Schmoll (6pf+4pf), on tour in Campagna by Johann Heinrich Tischbein (12pf+8pf), as a minister in the Grand Duchy of Saxe-Weimar by Johann Heinrich Lips (24pf+16pf), aged 64 by Joseph Karl Stieler (50pf+25pf), and an engraving shortly before his death by Carl August Schwerdgeburth (84pf+36pf).(3.100) The set celebrated the 200th anniversary of his birth (on 28 August) and in order to claim Goethe as some kind of proto-Communist the Soviet Zone (soon to be the German Democratic Republic) organised a huge festival in Weimar to show the West that German Communists were patriots and cared deeply about their historic culture. The fact that Goethe's early enthusiasm for the French Revolution had turned to utter revulsion of the aggressive autocracy was forgotten. On 22 August 1949 the high profile

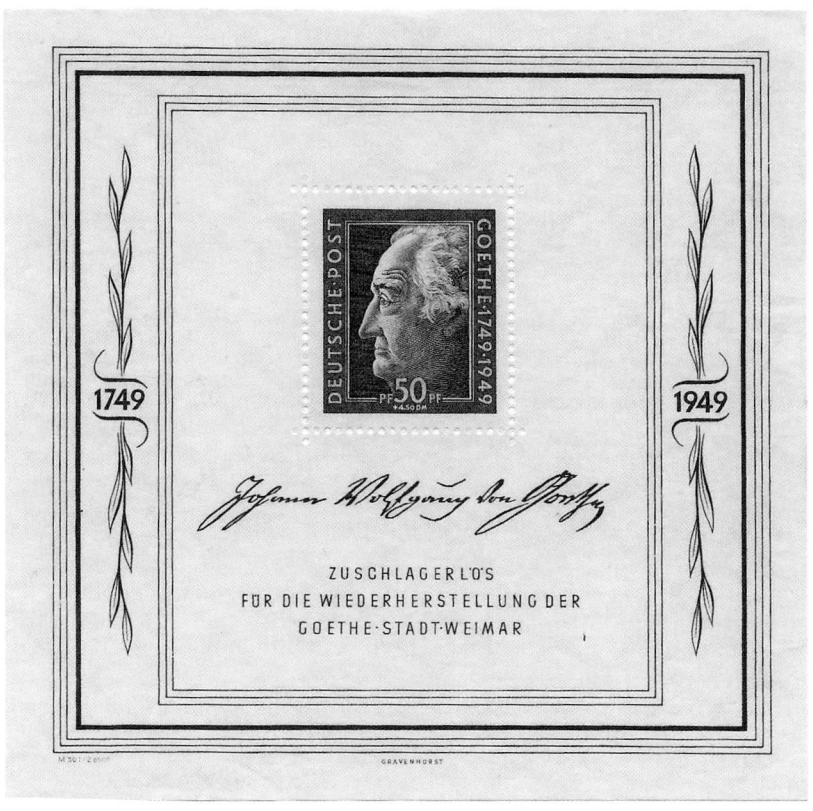

3.101 50pf (+4.50DM) Goethe Festival: 22 August 1949.

3.102 50pf+25pf Italian merchants at Leipzig Fair 1536: from set 6 March 1949.

Festival Week was publicised with a miniature sheet enclosing a perforated 50pf stamp depicting Goethe after the portrait by Ludwig Sebbers.(3.101) The sheet sold for ten times the stamp's value to support the new festival, and its inscription clearly announced *ZUSCHLAGERLOS FUR DIE WIEDERHERSTELLUNG DER GOETHE STADT WEIMAR (NO SUPPLEMENT FOR THE RESTORATION OF THE GOETHE CITY OF WEIMAR)*. A Festival highlight was a huge blazing torch parade of Free German Youth through the streets to the Goethe-Schiller Monument.

And just as the Goethe festivals were aimed at challenging Western cultural events so the Leipzig Fair became a Communist showplace. On 13 May 1949 the Spring Fair was promoted on two large stamps featuring the first fair in the new town hall in 1556 (30pf+15pf), and Italian merchants at the fair in 1536 (50pf+25pf). (3.102) In August 1949 the Autumn Fair was announced with similar stamps featuring, perhaps not surprisingly, Russian merchants attending the fair in 1650 (12pf+8pf), and Goethe visiting it in 1765 (24pf+16pf).(3.103)

THE GERMAN FEDERAL REPUBLIC (WEST GERMANY) AND THE GERMAN DEMOCRATIC REPUBLIC (EAST GERMANY) : 1949

West Germany formally came into being on 21 September 1949. Its first pair of stamps, on 7 September 1949, featured the new Parliament Building under construction in Bonn, the Republic's capital city.(3.104) The democratic sun was shining in rivalry with the Communist sun that adorned many Soviet bloc stamps. Bonn was preferred over Frankfurt and Hamburg because Konrad Adenauer, the new Chancellor, and other key figures believed the far smaller city would send out a clear message that this was a temporary measure until unification was achieved.

On 30 September 1949 the second set, comprising three stamps, highlighted Germany's continuity by commemorating the centenary of its first stamps issued by the Kingdom of Bavaria.(3.105) On 9 October a

3.103 24pf+16pf Goethe at Leipzig Fair 1765: from set 28 August 1949+.

3.104 20pf Bonn Parliament Building: from set 7 September 1949.

3.105 20pf 1849 Bavarian stamp: from set 30 September 1949.

striking stamp marking the 75th anniversary of the Universal Postal Union not surprisingly proudly portrayed Heinrich von Stephan, the nineteenth century unifier of Germany's postal system and instigator of the UPU. The stamp featured him by Berlin's old General Post Office and the Standehaus, the UPU's headquarters in Berne.(3.106)

On 14 December 1949 a surtaxed set inscribed *HELFT DER FREIEN WOHLFARHTSPFLEGE DIE NOT ZU LINDERN (HELP THE FREE WELFARE IN ORDER TO ALLEVIATE THE NEED)* sought to remind everyone that the refugee problem was far from over. An estimated 12 million Germans had fled from or were expelled from Poland, the Baltic States, Czechoslovakia, the Soviet Union, Hungary, Romania and Yugoslavia. In a hard-pressed economy the refugees were not always welcomed or their hardship recognised. In an attempt to trigger greater sympathy with fellow countrymen the stamps featured famous German humanitarian figures who had faced misunderstanding and opposition. The 8pf+2pf portrayed St Elizabeth of Thuringia (1207-31), daughter of the King of Hungary and wife of Ludwig IV, Landgrave of Thuringia.(3.107) Devoted to the care of the sick and poor, as a young widow she endured the harsh regime laid down by her priest and confessor, Konrad von Marburg, and resisted the hostile court's attempts to force a second marriage. The 10pf+5pf depicted the pioneering physician Paracelsus von Hohengeim (c1493-1541). Contemptuous of conventional medicine and convinced of the value of chemicals and minerals in health and healing, he experimented with a variety of substances to cleanse wounds and cure sickness - some sound, some not. Subject to great criticism he was often barred from practice. The 20f+10pf featured Friedrich Froebal (1782-1852) whose holistic approach to child development led to a greater appreciation of the importance of play, the natural environment, practical activities, discussion and motivation in education. (3.107) After crushing the 1848-49 revolutions Prussia and other German states banned his 'kindergartens' as 'atheistic and demagogic.' The 30pf+15pf portrayed Johann Hinrich Wichern (1808-81) who despite enduring contempt and hostility founded hostels and a 'corps of brothers' to educate and train the poor, ex-criminals and the disabled.

3.106 30pf Heinrich von Stephan and UPU 75th anniversary: 9 October 1949.

3.107 8pf+2pf St Elizabeth of Thuringia and 20pf+10pf Friedrich Froebal; from set 14 December 1949.

3.108 50pf UPU 75th anniversary: 9 October 1949.

3.109 12pf Postal Workers Congress: 27 October 1949.

3.110 12pf Stamp Day: 30 October 1949.

East Germany, including East Berlin, was established on 7 October 1949. Its first three issues were all connected with the post. On 9 October 1949 a stamp featuring a carrier pigeon and envelope celebrated the 75th anniversary of the *WELTPOSTVEREIN (UPU)* (3.108). Later that month two stamps depicting a male and female postal worker marked the East Berlin congress that established the International Union of Trade Unions of Postal, Telephone and Telegraph Workers.(3.109) It failed to become truly international as outside France and Italy, where Communist influences remained significant, the only European members were Communist dominated organisations. On 30 October a 'Stamp Day' issue rivalled West Germany's by featuring Bavaria's first stamp in 1849. (3.110)

CHAPTER 4

THE SOVIET UNION

The Bolsheviks seized power during the 1917 October revolution, and under their leader, Vladimir Lenin (1870-1924), they created a one-party Communist state. Joseph Stalin (1878-1953) assumed leadership after Lenin's death in 1924, and steadily consolidated his authority by securing the loyalty of younger party members and the secret police, eroding the position of older colleagues whom he perceived as rivals, and finally engaging in terror campaigns against all real or imagined opponents.

In the 1930s state planning, backed up by savage penalties for lack of effort, boosted industrial output. Two Five Year Plans bore harshly down upon managers and workers alike but coal and steel production soared and there were great improvements in the railway network and arms production. In the countryside state controlled collective farms sought to feed the growing towns and secure export currency but it took the deportation or execution of several million conservative-minded land-owning peasants (the kulaks) before resistance was overcome. Famine stalked vast swathes of land.

As the Communist leadership appreciated, people needed some education as a basis for indoctrination, and the Five Year Plans needed fit and literate workers. Throughout the 1930s millions more children attended schools, girls received the same education as boys, state radio stations and printing houses flourished, and the need for healthy workers meant everyone had access to free medical care and immunisation programmes. The Communist Youth League (Komsomol) was well funded, and provided an energetic corps of political activists.

As Hitler rose to power so Stalin ordered European Communists to work with other left-wing parties to oppose the Nazis while Hitler supported countries such as Hungary and Finland in their suppression of Communist influence. Nevertheless in 1939 when France and Great Britain dithered over an alliance with the Soviet Union to counter German aggression, Stalin agreed a pact with Hitler that effectively signed Poland's death warrant and allowed Stalin free rein in the Baltic States and Finland. Estonia, Latvia and Lithuania were terrorised into 'willing' incorporation into the Soviet Union, although Finland successfully fought a Soviet invasion to a standstill and kept its independence. Soviet forces briefly occupied eastern Poland after Germany invaded from the west, only for Hitler to renege on the pact with Stalin in June 1941 and launch a sudden and devastating attack on Russia. Huge areas were occupied in which German brutality matched that of the Russians in intensity. However after eighteen months of utter devastation German forces were held outside Leningrad and Moscow, and then forced to surrender in Stalingrad. Russia made massive efforts to relocate its threatened factories to safe areas beyond the Urals and Soviet propaganda switched from praise for Communist policies to eulogies of a more universally recognisable 'Mother Russia' and urged loyalty to it. Even the Orthodox Church and various ethnic groups within the Soviet Union were temporarily freed from oppression. From 1943 massive counter-attacks steadily pushed the Germans and their allies back until overwhelmingly strong Soviet army groups crossed into Poland, East Prussia, Slovakia and the Balkans, and finally occupied Berlin in May 1945. Overall the Soviet Union suffered around 26,000,000 military and civilian casualties, and undoubtedly played the greatest part of any nation in the defeat of Germany and its Balkan allies.

For Stalin the war may have ended in 1945 but he had many worries. Numerous towns and cities and much of the urban and rural economy needed rebuilding, and Communist influence in occupied countries needed consolidating. Significant numbers from ethnic minorities within the Soviet Union had joined Nazi military organisations, and Stalin always believed regional nationalism threatened Soviet unity. Millions of Poles, Estonians, Latvians, Lithuanians and Ukrainians were deported to labour camps, and ethnic groups he considered troublesome from the Volga region, Crimea and Turkish border were deported to Siberia or Central Asia. Stalin himself soon replaced 'Mother Russia' as the national symbol of loyalty, and his heroic yet paternal image appeared everywhere - not least on stamps in Poland, Czechoslovakia, Hungary, Romania and Bulgaria as well as the Soviet Union. Although skilled and aggressive generals had led the armies to victory, Stalin ensured they were sidetracked as national heroes and replaced by himself and Communist-inspired ordinary soldiers as the architects of victory.

In May 1945 Soviet armies occupied eastern Germany and Berlin, the Baltic States, Poland, Hungary, Romania and Bulgaria, were present in parts of Austria,

Czechoslovakia and Finland, and were on the doorstep of Greece, Albania and Yugoslavia. Exhausted, Great Britain and France were in no position militarily or politically to engage in warfare with their recent ally, however threatening Stalin appeared, and the USA had shown its hand by halting its forces at Pilsen in western Czechoslovakia and letting Russia occupy Berlin. However Stalin was well aware that the USA's economy was buoyant, its armaments output prolific, and it possessed atomic bombs and a far larger long range bomber force. And the USA had vast sums to invest overseas, and Stalin feared the creation of a league of nations beholden to this powerful outward-looking capitalist democracy. He was fortunate that for a few years the American government believed it could reach acceptable agreements with Stalin, and certainly this was initially so over the German and Austrian occupation Zones. It seems Stalin hoped his control over the eastern Zone might lead eventually to a unified Germany under Soviet influence but of course France, the UK and USA thought otherwise. Although France long remained in fear of a resurgent Germany, the UK and USA welcomed the economic recovery of the amalgamated western Zones and their place in the capitalist world. Not least, it was cheaper than occupying them.

The American sourced Marshall Aid programme helped ensure the regeneration of many struggling European nations, and represented an effective containment of Communist influence. Stalin recognised this, and his satellite countries were required to refuse it and instead they were saddled with Comecon - the Council for Mutual Economic Assistance - whose title masked the reality of their complete economic subjugation to the USSR's needs. At the same time the creation of Cominform, the agency devoted to ensuring all Communist nations and Communist parties elsewhere spoke with Moscow's voice, revealed the growing gulf between West and East. The Cold War began in earnest in 1947.

Lasting damage was done by the USA's attempt in 1948 to introduce the new West German Deutschmark into Berlin where each of the four wartime allies administered a Zone. Fearful of an aggressively capitalist enclave deep in East Germany Stalin believed a blockade of Berlin would quickly lead the Western Allies to cease their interference. In the event the massive Allied airlift led Stalin to back down. Perceiving the USA as the dominant force across the recently united West Germany, Stalin now intensified the USSR's domination of East Germany (the German Democratic Republic), expelled the too independently minded Josif Tito from the Communist circle, and ordered the Communists in Poland, Czechoslovakia and across the Balkans to consolidate their political, economic and cultural control, and eliminate all rivals. (See specific chapters)

At home a propaganda campaign ensured Stalin was presented as the single figure guaranteeing the country's stability and security. The country was closed down to most foreigners, few Russians were permitted to visit the West, and the media dedicated itself to celebrating Russian achievements, both past and present, and ignoring or denigrating those of the West. Scientists, artists, writers and film makers were well advised to work within the pragmatic parameters of state requirements - greater economic production, better armaments and the eulogisation of Communism's liberating force. Nothing 'foreign' should contaminate their work. Tikhon Khrennikov (1913-2007), General Secretary of the Union of Soviet Musicians, and Alexander Fadeyev (1901-56), co-founder of the Union of Soviet Writers, were in thrall of Stalin and promoted every tenet of the country's narrow cultural policy laid down by Andrei Zhdanov (1896-1948), Second Secretary of the Communist Party and its cultural ideologist.

Zhdanov died suddenly in 1948 and on 3 September he received the rare accolade of a stamp marking the passing of a major party figure.(4.1) It was perhaps significant that earlier in the year he had lost all his posts and been banished to a sanatorium when his lack of warmth for the condemnation of Tito had incensed Stalin. However Zhdanov's cultural policy did not die with him.

Although the middle and higher echelons of party functionaries, government bureaucrats, security police and armed forces lived reasonably comfortably, most families lived spartan lives even if they were the beneficiaries of the state's welfare and education programmes. And yet it seems patriotism remained high with victory in the war and possession of a new Russian 'Empire' in the form of the Baltic and satellite states engendering a general sense of pride. The era of revolutionary zeal might not be over in the satellite countries but it was in the USSR. Stability was the aim, with statues of past and present heroes proliferating, and vast new building being erected to symbolise the firm foundations and modernist form of the Soviet state. Numerous towns, streets, and public buildings were renamed after Communist heroes. Conformity was vital and terror ruled, and no-one was free from being betrayed for careless words or lack of effort.

The prolific output of Russian stamps highlighted the country's priorities. A host of sets glorified the nation permanently at arms against external enemies, the Communist revolutionaries who battled to free the people from a stifling authoritarian Tsardom, and the carefully selected Russian 'giants' of science, literature

4.1 40k Andrei Zhdanov: 3 September 1948.

4.2 30k Marshal Kutusov: from set 16 September 1945.

and art showing their works were, in fact, in tune with later Communist ideals. Par excellence, Communist stamps can be relied upon to tell stories.

Medals and the heroic actions of the armed forces dominated sets in 1945 and 1946. Several reasons governed the Soviet Union's determination to flaunt its military strength. It helped keep its satellites submissive, sent warning messages to what it perceived as the potentially aggressive West, and by highlighting the need for a vast military establishment and constantly preaching the threat of external enemies it contributed to keeping its own population committed to the current regime.

The Second World War saw the introduction of many new awards, and significantly several harked back to famous historical figures as part of the patriotic 'Mother Russia' campaign. In May and June 1944 stamps featured the Order of Alexander Nevsky, Order of Suvorov and Order of Kutuzov, all established in July 1942 to reward the strategic skills, resolute leadership and courage of army officers. Alexander Nevsky (1221-63) attained legendary status for his defeat of German and Swedish invaders, Field Marshal Count Alexander Suvorov (c1729-1800) had driven the French Revolutionary armies out of Italy, and Field Marshal Prince Mikhail Kutusov (1745-1813) was the army commander instrumental in defeating Napoleon's invasion in 1812. All were role models for the defence of Russia. On 16 September 1945 the bicentenary of Kutusov's birth was commemorated with two stamps portraying him in full uniform.(4.2)

On 4 January 1945 a set featured six awards, and several were reissued later in the year, and indeed later in the decade, with far higher values.(4.3, 4.4, 4.5) The Order of Bogdan Khmielnitsky, established in October 1943, had three classes for senior officers, junior officers and other ranks who led or performed bravely in successful attacks. Khmielnitsky (c1595-1657) was a Ukrainian Hetman who led a revolt against the vast Polish-Lithuanian Commonwealth, established a separate Cossack state and later accepted the overlordship of the Russian Tsar. The Communists asserted he unified Ukraine with Russia, something Ukrainians have viewed with mixed feelings ever since - especially as many fought, unsuccessfully, for independence after the Bolshevik Revolution. The Order of Ushakov, established in March 1944, comprised two classes for naval officers planning and leading major successful operations. It was named after Admiral Fyodor Ushakov (1745-1817) who won numerous battles against the Turks and then Revolutionary France. The Order of Nakhimov, established in March 1944, also had two classes for naval officers executing successful operations. It took its name from Admiral Pavel Nakhimov (1802-55) who destroyed the Turkish

4.3 1k (blue) Order of Ushakov, and 1k (green) Order of Nakhimov: from set 4 January 1945.

4.4 2r Order of Bogdan Khmielnitsky: from set February 1945+.

4.5 60k Order of Victory, 30k Order of Glory, and 15k Partisan's Medal: from set 4 January 1945.

4.6 60k Order of Lenin, 60k Hero of the Soviet Union, 60k Hero of Socialist Labour: from set 30 April 1946+.

fleet at Sinope and skilfully organised the defences of Sevastopol in the Crimean War.

The Order of Victory, the highest military decoration and replete with rubies and diamonds, was established in November 1943 and awarded only to generals and marshals whose command at the front had contributed significantly to Russian victories. It featured Moscow's Spasskaya Tower and Lenin's Mausoleum. The Order of Glory, also featuring the Spasskaya Tower, was established in November 1943, and had three classes reserved for lower ranks in the army and air force pilots. A recipient received the third class initially, and the second and first class for further acts of bravery. The Partisan of the Patriotic War medal established in February 1943 featured Lenin and Stalin. It had two classes and was awarded to partisans fighting occupying forces.(4.5)

Between April and June 1946 a set of fifteen 60k stamps depicted Soviet medals for exemplary service on the military or domestic front.(4.6) Eight of them reappeared with 1r values on 5 September 1946.(4.7) Several were for exceptional productivity and economic improvements - the Order of the Red Banner of Labour (1928), the Medal for Distinguished Labour (1938), the Medal for Labour Valour (1938) and the Hero of Socialist Labour (1938). One, the Order of the Badge of Honour (1935) was awarded primarily for achievements in science and culture. Others were for the armed forces, including the Marshal's Star (1940), the Order of the Red Star (1930), the Order of the Red Banner (1918 - the earliest Soviet award for military personnel), the Medals for the Defence of Moscow, the Caucasus and the Soviet Arctic (1944), the Medal for Battle Merit (1938), and the

4.7 1r Defence of Moscow, 1r Medal for Distinguished Labour, and 1r Medal for Valour: from set 5 September 1946.

Medal for Valour (1938) for personal courage putting the recipient's life at risk. The other two were the prestigious Order of Lenin (1930), the highest civil decoration for outstanding service, and Hero of the Soviet Union (1934) the highest award for civilians and soldiers for heroic acts.

4.8 20k Motherhood Medal, 30k Order of Maternal Glory, and 60k Order of Heroine Mother: smaller size set 28 July 1945.

4.10 30k Infantry protecting civilians from an advancing tank (inscribed 'Death to the German invaders') from set April 1945.

4.11 60k Civilians welcoming Soviet troops: from set April 1945

4.9 3r Relief of Stalingrad: from set March 1945+.

4.12 60k Red Guards commemoration: April 1945.

4.13 1r Aerial battle over Moscow: from set June 1945.

Between July and December 1945 a set issued in small and large sizes highlighted the state's interest in a higher birth rate after the devastating wartime losses.(4.8) The Maternity Medal, established in July 1944, had two classes - the second for raising five children, the first for raising six. A month later the Order of Maternal Glory was established with three classes for raising seven, eight or nine children. At the same time a special Order of Heroine Mother was created for raising ten children or more which seems to have been awarded to around 430,000 mothers. These awards sought not only to increase the population but to ensure such families were recorded and received enhanced state benefits.

A regular supply of dramatically designed sets kept the heroic image of the armed forces - and thereby the regime itself - to the fore. In March and April 1945 two stamps and a miniature sheet featuring a soldier waving the national flag amidst rubble commemorated the relief of Stalingrad.(4.9) A second set in April featuring a standard bearer (20k), infantry defending wounded civilians from an advancing tank (30k) and infantry charging (1r) celebrated later wartime victories.(4.10) A third set, also in April 1945, celebrated the final liberation of Russian soil with images of an assault by tanks and infantry (30k), people welcoming troops (60k), and a grenade thrower (1r).(4.11)

A fourth issue that month was a single stamp featuring heavy guns and commemorating the achievements of the Red Guards.(4.12) The original Bolshevik Red Guard had comprised local volunteers whose enthusiasm far outshone their training and performance,

4.14 15k Petlyakov-Pe2 bomber, 30k Polikarpov Po-2 biplane, and 50k Lavochkin La-7 fighter in action: from reissued set 26 March 1946.

and when the Red Army was formed after 1918 the Red Guard became the Army Reserve feeding men into regular units. In June 1945 a set of three stamps remembering the Battle of Moscow between October 1941 and January 1942 featured barricades (30k), tanks in Red Square (60k) and an aerial battle in the glare of searchlights (1r).(4.13)

Aviation Day in August 1945 was marked with nine 1r stamps featuring the Air Force in victorious wartime action. They included the Petlyakov-Pe2 and Pe8 TB-7, Ilyushin-Il-4 and Tupolev ANT 60 Tu2 light and heavy bombers, and the Ilyushin Il-2M3 Stormovik, Lavochkin La-7, and Yakovlev Yak-3 and Yak-9 fighters. The ninth plane was the celebrated Polikarpov Po-2 biplane whose versatility enabled it to be used for training, reconnaissance, low level ground attack and rescue work. One female Po-2 pilot, Nadezda Popova was awarded the Order of Lenin, three Orders of the Red Banner, the Order of the Patriotic War and made a Hero of the Soviet Union. The set was reissued with different values on 26 March 1946.(4.14)

On 20 August 1945 the Soviet Union issued an overprinted 3r Order of Victory stamp to mark VE Day which had been on 9 May - as the stamp announced. (4.15) On 23 January 1946 a further three stamps featured the Victory Medal (inscribed For Victory over Germany in the Great Patriotic War 1941-45) and another two a Soviet soldier advancing with a Victory banner - which, like the medal, portrayed Stalin.(4.16) Almost 15 million servicemen and women received the award.

Further sets in 1945 and 1946 kept memories of the war and Soviet military prowess alive. In December 1945 a pair of stamps featuring heavy guns marked Artillery Day (4.17), and a rather fussy set of four stamps celebrated the Home Front with images of tank production (20k), harvesting (30k), aircraft designers (60k) and fireworks over the Kremlin (1r).(4.18) On 23 February 1946 three stamps featuring the parade of tanks and infantry celebrated the 25th anniversary of the Red Army and Navy, and on 8 September 1946 more images of tanks in Red Square commemorated

4.15 VE Day commemoration: 20 August 1945.

4.16 60k Soldier and banner (inscribed 'Long live our victory!'), and 60k Victory Medal: from Victory set 23 January 1946.

4.17 60k Artillery Day: from set December 1945.

4.18 20k Tank production and 30k Food production: from Home Front set 25 December 1945.

4.20 2r Lomonosov and Academy of Sciences, Leningrad: from set June 1945.

4.21 30k Stalin Prize medal: 21 December 1946.

4.19 2r Tanks in Red Square: from 25th anniversary of the Red Army set 23 February 1946, and 30k Tanks in Red Square: from Heroes of Tank Engagements set 8 September 1946.

the heroes of wartime tank engagements.(4.19) On the 30k stamp illustrated in 4.19 the front tank's angled glacis suggests it was the powerful new T-10 with a 122mm gun. Although under development since 1944 it was not in mass production until after this set was issued.

Interspersed with all these issues were sets commemorating the achievements of selected historic figures and institutions. In June 1945 two stamps depicting the original buildings in St Petersburg (Leningrad) (2r) and Moscow (30k) marked the 220th anniversary of the Academy of Sciences founded by Tsar Peter the Great to encourage research.(4.20) In 1917 it was renamed the Academy of Sciences of the Soviet Union and in return for state aid its work concentrated on the needs of the state - notably mineral processing, electrification, industrial expansion, and in wartime the development of armaments, and later the atomic bomb. The Academy's headquarters transferred from Leningrad to Moscow in 1934, and embraced, and controlled, all sciences across all USSR republics. The 2r stamp also featured the Russian polymath and distinguished Academician Mikhail Lomonosov (1711-65). Just a few of his wide-ranging discoveries were the atmosphere on Venus, the chemical conservation of mass, the organic origin of soil, and the land formation of icebergs. The Moscow University, which he founded, was renamed after him in 1940.

The Stalin Prize made expectations clear.(4.21) Established in 1941 it was awarded to scientists, mathematicians, architects, writers and artists whose work had advanced the Soviet Union or the wider cause of Communism. On 21 December 1946 the badge given to winners appeared on a stamp.

Around this time three Academicians were recognised in sets. In July 1945 three stamps portrayed Alexander Popov (1859-1905) whose work on a wireless detector of lightning and the transmission of radio signals in the 1890s paralleled that of Marconi, but it seems without knowledge of each other's research.(4.22) Not surprisingly the Soviet Union championed Popov as the inventor on 7 May 1895 when he demonstrated his detector device on to the Russian Physical and Chemical Society in St Petersburg. However firm evidence is

4.22 60k Alexander Popov: from set July 1945.

4.25 50k Alexander Karpinsky, and 30k Nikolay Zhukovsky: from sets 17 January 1947.

4.24 60k Pafnuty Chebyshev: from set 25 May 1946.

4.26 20k Count Fydor Litke and 60k Nicholai Przhevalsky; from set 27 January 1947.

lacking that he used radio waves for wireless communications before March 1896. Marconi had transmitted messages in the summer of 1895.

On 27 November 1945 a pair of stamps featured Ilya Mechnikov (1845-1916), a Nobel prize winning immunologist who discovered phagocytes - the cells that surround and kill pathogens.(4.23) On 25 May 1946 another pair featured the mathematician Pafnuty Chebyshev (1821-94) whose work on statistics, mechanics, number theory and probability led to him being hailed as the founder of Russian mathematics. (4.24)

Several more followed in 1947. On 17 January two pairs of stamps marked the centenary of the birth of Alexander Karpinsky (1847-1936) and Nikolay Zhukovsky (1847-1921).(4.25) Both had sound Soviet credentials. A geologist and mineralogist, Karpinsky was the Imperial director of mining research from 1885 until 1916, and President of the Academy of Sciences from 1917 until his death. In 1947 the USSR created the Karpinsky Gold Medal for outstanding geological achievements. Zhukovsky was a mathematician and engineer who pioneered the study of aerodynamics, and from 1918 headed the Soviet Central Aero-Hydro-Dynamics Institute.

On 27 January 1947 the centenary of the Geographical Society of the USSR, originally the Imperial Geographical Society, was commemorated with two pairs of stamps. (4.26) The 20k pictured Admiral Count Fyodor Litke (1797-1882) and the Senyavin in which he circumnavigated the world (1826-29) paying particular attention to surveying the Siberian and Alaskan coast and collecting plant, animal and mineral samples. He became President of the Society and also of the Academy of Science. The 60k featured Nicholai Przhevalsky (1839-88) who led four perilous expeditions across central Asia into China. The stamp pictures a breed of horses named after him. Surreptitious rumours circulated during the Soviet era that he was Stalin's father, partly because they looked alike and partly because he was so highly honoured by the state.

On 26 October 1945 two stamps portraying Alexander Herzen (1812-70) marked the 75th anniversary of the death of this major writer who opposed the repression of Tsar Nicholas I, championed the emancipation of the serfs, and sought the common ownership of land, wide individual rights and government by the people.(4.27) Although he believed in a non-interventionist

4.27 2r Alexander Herzen: from set 26 October 1945.

4.28 30k Maxim Gorky: from set 1 8 June 1946.

4.29 60k Lenin as orator: from set September 1945, 50k Lenin: from set 21 January 1947, and 60k Queue at Lenin Mausoleum: from set 21 January 1948.

government once individual rights were protected, with some justification the Soviet Union hailed him as a pioneer of Russian Socialism.

On 18 June 1946 two stamps marked the tenth anniversary of the social realist writer Maxim Gorky (real name Alexei Peshkov) (1868-1936).(4.28) A novelist whose early works highlighted the lives of the desperately poor, Gorky opposed the inequalities and repression of the Tsarist regime and endured imprisonment and exile. Initially friendly with Lenin, later he criticised Bolshevik tyranny and lived in Italy between 1921 and 1931. He was persuaded to return and much lauded, even though his praise for Stalin's regime was soon accompanied by criticisms. His survival as a popular critic during Stalin's purges was remarkable, but no doubt his naive defence of the show trials and the forced labour camps told in his favour.

In September 1945 the 75th anniversary of the birth of Lenin was marked with five stamps portraying him in well-known poses as an orator and writer.(4.29) The 60k is taken from the famous painting of Lenin as an impassioned orator by the 'heroic realist' Russian artist Alexander Gerassimov (1881-1963). Future years marked the anniversary of his death with varying sets depicting his portrait and mausoleum.(4.29) On 7 December 1945 a pair of stamps portrayed Friedrich Engels (1820-95) to mark the 125th anniversary of the birth of the co-author of *The Communist Manifesto*. (4.30) And on 1 April 1948 both Engels and Marx appeared on a pair of stamps to mark the centenary of its publication. (4.30)

On 10 February 1946 a set showing the Arms of the USSR (30k and 60k) and the Kremlin (45k) marked the elections to the Supreme Soviet on that day.(4.31) By the new Soviet constitution of 1936 the Supreme Soviet

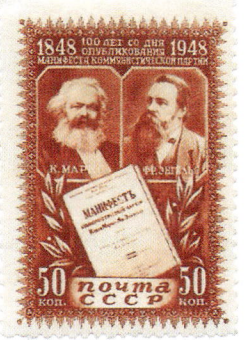

4.30 60l Friedrich Engels: from set 7 December 1945, and 50k Marx and Engels: from set 1 April 1948.

4.31 60k Supreme Soviet elections: from set 10 February 1946.

4.32 30k Arms of Lithuania and 1r USSR: from set 9 February 1947.

4.33 30k 25th anniversary of the USSR: from set 5 July 1948.

4.34 30k 25th anniversary of Soviet postal services: from set 6 November 1946+.

4.35 30k Sochi: from Health Resort set 18 June 1946.

had two chambers of equal powers - the Soviet of the Union (with one deputy for every 300,000 people in the USSR) and the Soviet of the Nationalities (with deputies specifically elected from each constituent republic, autonomous republic and oblast). Voting was by secret ballot and the Supreme Soviet was the lawmaker of the USSR, although in practice there was only one party to vote for and the Supreme Soviet was confined to approving the actions of the Communist Party and the state's governing body, the Presidium. The 1937 election ensured Stalin stayed supreme through the exercise of the Communist Party's terror tactics against any opposition, and in 1946 the Party's glorification of the nation's victory over German, and Stalin's leading role in it, as proof that Communism was a uniquely successful egalitarian system of government ensured his majority was equally overwhelming. On 9 February 1947 similar elections to constituent republic assemblies were marked with a set of 16 stamps featuring their Arms with the far larger seventeenth bearing the Arms of the USSR.(4.32) They included Estonia, Latvia and Lithuania, obliged by overwhelming military force and a campaign of terror to 'request' admission to the USSR in 1940 during the USSR's pact with Germany. On 5 July 1948 the 25th anniversary of the USSR was marked by two stamps depicting its Arms surrounded by joyful people from constituent republics.(4.33)

Soviet domestic achievements were celebrated. The 25th anniversary of the Soviet Union's Postal Service was commemorated between November 1946 and June 1947 with three stamps and miniature sheets.(4.34) The large 15k and 60k featured an array of Soviet stamps (see 1.16) and the smaller 30k featured a famous 1921 stamp showing a noble worker slaying an Imperialist dragon and advancing into the Bolshevik light. The postal services had made heroic wartime efforts to keep service personnel in touch with families, but by 1947 its reconstruction and extension to remote areas was still incomplete.

On 18 June 1946 a set featured four Black Sea health resorts at Sukhumi (15k), Gagra (30k), Sochi (30k) and Novy Afon (45k).(4.35) Hundreds of them were created: many were huge and often built in attractive locations and in striking Constructivist style. The Labour Code in 1922 required workers to attend state sanitoriums in health resorts for most of their annual fortnight's

4.36 30k Gagra: from Health Resort set 10 September 1947.

4.37 15k Girls' school and 30k Female students and banner: from set 11 March 1947.

holiday to ensure their health was maintained. While there, workers were not accompanied by their families and specialists created and monitored each person's regime of callisthenics, spa treatments and diet. There was no alcohol, no gambling and no noisy parties. Some sanatoriums were reserved for the Communist Party elite. On 10 September 1947 ten 30k stamps pictured the sanatoriums at Gagra, Novy Afon, Riga (Latvia), Livadiya (Crimea), Kislovodsk (Caucasus) and two at Sukhumi and three at Sochi.(4.36)

On 11 March 1947 two stamps marking International Women's Day epitomised the Soviet Union's attitude to women.(4.37) The Day had been celebrated by Socialist Parties since the start of the century, but when Soviet Russia made it an annual holiday on 8 March - the date St Petersburg's female textile workers demonstrated against the war in 1917 - most other Socialist and Communist countries followed suit. The smaller stamp depicted girls' education, and the larger one young women marching determinedly behind a banner portraying Lenin and Stalin. Soviet women had the right to education and a vote, both of which were expected to serve the Communist state - and, as we have seen, so was women's fertility.

The regime was careful to include females on other stamps promoting Communism, not least in those celebrating summer camps and the Young Communist League where enjoyable group activities went hand-in-hand with indoctrination. On 26 October 1948 a set promoting the state's summer holiday programme featured uniformed children flying model aeroplanes (30k), gathering around a camp fire (1r), marching along the coast behind a banner (45k), sounding a trumpet (60k) and saluting in front of flags and emblems (45k).(4.38)

A few day's later, on 29 October 1948, a set marked the 30th anniversary of *Komsomol* - Lenin's Young Communist League for those aged 14 to 28.(4.39) After a slow start, especially in conservative rural communities, the League prospered because membership brought rewards in terms of better education and career prospects. Stalin's succession of Five Year Plans engaged young people as both workers and missionaries in numerous projects. Each stamp displayed the Order of Lenin, Order of the Red Banner and Order of the Red Banner of Labour awarded to *Komsomol* as an institution. The 20k featured members on parade, the 25k a girl harvester, the 40k members in Moscow waving a banner, the 50k members at a lecture, the 1r the Orders awarded to *Komsomol*, and the 2r an enthusiastic youth in a factory alongside the inscription *All efforts of Soviet youth for a speedy five-year plan.*

On 21 July 1946 a large single stamp highlighted the state's approach to sport with the national Sports Festival being celebrated with athletes waving constituent republic banners marching behind the USSR's banner and a huge medallion portrait of Stalin. (4.40) Physical culture served primarily as a stimulus to workers health and a doctrinal training ground promoting service to the state. There was no 'sport for sports' sake'. Only in 1952 did the USSR see participation in the Olympic Games as a way of promoting Communism through sporting victories. The 1948

4.38 45k Children saluting and 1r Camp fire: from Summer Vacation set 26 October 1948.

4.39 25k Girl harvester, 1r Awards, and 2r Youthful factory worker: from Komsomol set 29 October 1948.

Stalin, the 10k and 20k the iconic Bolshoi Theatre, rebuilt several times over its 150 years existence, the 15k the massive Moscow Hotel, built in Imperial style by the state in the 1930s to rival any Western hotel, the 50k the former City Hall built in the 1890s in a mixed antique Russian and Neo-Renaissance style, that became the Lenin museum, and the 1r the eye-catching Spasskaya (Saviour) Tower in the Kremlin. In 1936 Stalin had the Imperial two-headed eagle on the top of the Tower replaced with a rotating red star.

In May and June 1947 a stamp featured Moscow's Council Building to celebrate the 30th anniversary of the city's council - the local Soviet.(4.45) From September 1947 a large outpouring of stamps marked the city's 800th anniversary. The first set comprised four stamps from the previous year's Moscow issue, with colour changes, overprinted *800th anniversary of Moscow 1147-1947*.(4.46) The second set depicted the power plant and five grand stations - 'palaces of the

4.40 30k Sports Festival: 21 July 1946.

4.41 20k Motor cyclist: from RSFSR Games set 23 February 1948.

Olympics were ignored, but on 23 February that year two stamps depicting skiing and cross country motor cycling marked the Russian Soviet Federated Socialist Republic's own games.(4.41) A set of stamps on 15 September 1948 encouraging physical challenges depicted running (15k), football (30k), power boat racing (45k) and diving (60c).(4.42) However on the world stage the USSR was more interested in the 1948 World Chess Championship organised by new World Chess Federation. Held in Moscow the event heralded the USSR's domination of world chess and was celebrated by a set on 20 November 1948 featuring its venue, the Trades Union Building (30k and 50k), and the event's chessboard and castle emblem (40k).(4.43)

On 5 September 1946 eight stamps publicised important Moscow buildings, and in doing so reinforced its supremacy over Leningrad - something Stalin was always keen to do as he viewed the well-established and powerful leaders of the USSR's 'second city' as potential rivals.(4.44) The 5k, 45k and 60k pictured the Kremlin Complex, since 1918 the fortress residence of Lenin and

4.42 50k Diving: from set 15 September 1948.

4.43 30k Trades Union Building: from Chess Championship set 20 November 1948.

4.44 15k Hotel Moscow, 20k Bolshoi Theatre, and 60k Kremlin: from set 5 September 1946.

4.45 30k Moscow's Council Building: 30 May 1947.

4.47 45k Sokol and 60k Mayakovskaya Underground Stations: from set 7 September 1947.

4.46 1r Spasskaya Tower with 800th anniversary overprint; from set September 1947.

people' they were termed - on the Moscow Underground system, most of which was completed in the late 1930s. (4.47) Opened in 1938 Mayakovskaya Station was famous for its 34 ceiling mosaics depicting in heroic style '24 Hours in the Land of the Soviets.'

The third was a lengthy set of views, mostly valued 30k or 60k. Several depicted parts of the Kremlin while others highlighted aspects of the city regenerated by Stalin's construction schemes - the Crimea Bridge opened in 1938, Gorky Street and Kaluga Street full of prestigious Soviet buildings, Kazan Railway Station opened in 1940, Kiev Railway Station repaired after the war, and Pushkin Square remodelled after the Soviet demolition of the Passion Monastery. The final stamp featured the city's great towers and walls in part of the painting 'Old Moscow' by the national revivalist artist Victor Vasnetsov (1848-1926)

Despite his aristocratic lineage, the poet Alexander Pushkin (1799-1837) became a Soviet favourite due to his *Ode to Liberty* and other works that led to his exile by Tsar Alexander I. In February 1947 his portrait adorned a pair of stamps to mark the 110th anniversary of his death - in a duel with the rumoured lover of his wife.(4.50)

On 1 November 1948 the 50th anniversary of Moscow Arts Theatre was celebrated with stamps featuring its interior (40k) and its co-founders, Konstantin Stanislavski (1863-1938) who was largely responsible for producing and directing, and the playwright Vladimir Nemirovich-Danchenko (1858-1943) who took all the literary decisions (1r).(4.51) They sought to breakaway from popular melodramas and offer high quality plays: works by Shakespeare, Chekhov, Hauptmann and Ibsen were among their first productions. With Lenin's support the Theatre survived the Revolution and prospered, but in the 1930s its founders succumbed to Stalinist pressure, accepted Socialist Realism as the main criterion of production - and thereby survived the Purges.

On 23 December 1946 two large stamps pictured the reconstruction of the mighty River Dnieper Dam and Hydroelectric Power Station in the Ukraine.(4.52) Accompanied by the First Five Year Plan's massive publicity, construction on the 800 metres dam began in 1927 and electricity was first produced in 1932 but the

4.48 30k Kaluga Street, 30k Pushkin Square, and 1r 'Old Moscow': from set 7 September 1947+.

4.49 1k St Basil Cathedral and 5k government buildings: from set 7 September 1947+.

4.50 Alexander Pushkin: from set February 1947.

4.51 1r 50th anniversary of Moscow Arts Theatre: from set 1 November 1948.

decision was taken to blow it up in 1941 in the face of the German advance. Thousands of unsuspecting civilians were killed by the tidal surge. In 1943 the retreating Germans did further damage but everything was rebuilt between 1944 and 1949. Thousands of prisoners of war and inmates of the gulags toiled on the reconstruction.

On 7 September 1947 a set commemorated the 10th anniversary of the completion of the 80 mile long canal connecting the Volga and Moskva rivers and thereby linking Moscow through Russia's internal waterways to the Black Sea, Caspian Sea, Baltic Sea and White Sea. (4.53) The canal and its accompanying bridges, locks, reservoirs, pumping stations and hydro-electric plants formed part of the Second Five Year Plan. It was constructed between 1932 and 1937, largely by two hundred thousand prisoners from the gulags under the direction of the secret police. The celebratory stamps depict a map (60k), the Karamyshevsky Dam (30k), Yakhromsky Lock (30k), Yakhromsky Pumping Station (45k), a pleasure boat and landing pier on the Khimki Reservoir near Moscow (50k) and Lock No8 (1r).

The initial Dneiper Dam and later Moskva-Volga Canal projects were part of Stalin's early Five Year Plans respectively. Beginning in 1928 these were a series of comprehensive centralised economic schemes aimed at rapid industrialisation and modernisation. They involved fearsome targets for factory and farm outputs,

4.52 60k Restoration of Dnieper Dam and Power Station: from set 23 December 1946.

4.53 30k Karamyshevsky Dam, 50k Khimki Reservoir, and 1r Lock No8: from set 7 September 1947.

and rapid developments in power supplies, transport, education and welfare projects. Every initiative was approached like a military campaign, with medals and advancement as rewards, and all opposition - especially by conservative rural communities - was swept aside. The Fourth Plan, starting in 1945, centred on reconstructing a shattered infrastructure. On 8 October 1946 a set promoted the Plan with depictions of mechanised harvesting (5k), oil rigs and refinery (10k), a coal mine (15k), steel works (20k) and an iron foundry (30k).(4.54) As always patriotic slogans were included - the 10k, for example, announced *Each year we give the country 60 million tons of oil*. A year on, in November 1947, a set of 11 action-packed stamps, issued perforated and imperforate, featured major construction sites, massive foundries and metallurgical works, and factories turning out tractors and combine harvesters. (4.55) Patriotic banners were everywhere and output was everything.

Over the next year or so frequent sets highlighted different aspects of the Plan. On 12 July 1948 it was Agriculture with images of tractors drawing seed drills (30k and 50k) and harvesting cereal (60k) and the arduous work of harvesting cotton (45k and 60k) and sugar beet (30k and 1r).(4.56) The slogans exhorted *The early execution of the five year post-war plan*. On 30 September 1948 it was Livestock with pictures of a groom and horses (30k and 1r) and female dairy farmers (60k) and also Transport with stamps featuring motor vehicles (60k), steam locomotives (30k and 50k) and the liner *Vyacheslav Molotov*, named after the USSR's Minister of Foreign Affairs. (1r).(4.57) Built in 1939 the liner was heavily involved as a transport and hospital ship in the war, and survived although damaged by German mines, bombs and artillery. Her sister ship, the *Josif Stalin*, was airbrushed out of Soviet history for being damaged by mines and gunfire in December 1941 while evacuating Russians from southern Finland and then captured by the Germans.

On 29 August 1948 Miners' Day was celebrated with images of smiling miners (30k), modern extraction

4.54 10k Oil refinery and 15k Coal mine: from set 8 October 1946.

machinery (60k) and the miners firmly Communist emblem of a wreath enclosing a drill and hammers (1r). (4.58) On 14 October 1948 it was Rolled Iron, Steel and Machine Making with images of heavy machinery (60k), blast furnaces (30k and 50k), cauldrons of molten metal (30k and 50k), and rolled steel sheeting (60k and 1r).(4.59) On 24 October 1948 it was not only Coal Mining and Oil Extraction with pictures of a miner and

4.55 30k Harvester, 60k Builders, 1r Foundry, and 1r Tractors: from set November 1947.

4.56 30k Seed drills, 30k Sugar beet harvest, and 60k Cotton harvest: from set 12 July 1948.

4.57 60k Motor vehicles and 1r Liner 'Vyacheslav Molotov': from set 30 September 1948.

4.58 30k Miners and 1r Miners' emblem: from set 29 August 1948.

coal truck (30k and 60k) and oil rigs and tanker train (60k and 1r) (4.60), but also Electrification with pictures of Farkhadsk and Zuevsk Power Stations, both of which were constructed largely by German and Austrian prisoners of war, many of whom were held captive long after 1945.(4.61)

Meanwhile sets glorifying the Bolshevik Revolution and armed forces kept on coming. On 6 November 1946 two stamps, followed in June 1947 by a miniature sheet, marked the 29th anniversary of the Revolution.(4.62) They featured Lenin and Stalin almost deified above a wreathed altar inscribed with the new regime. On 7 November 1947 the 30th anniversary merited six large dramatic stamps.(4.63) Two featured advancing revolutionaries, and the inscription *All power to the Soviets 1917-47* and *30 years of the great Socialist October Revolution*. Two depicted smoking chimneys, factories and goods trains, and two a combined harvester and a lorry full of sacks topped by a banner waving worker under the inscription *The USSR - the country of advanced agriculture*. On 7 November 1948 two 31st anniversary stamps depicted searchlights over Moscow lighting up a celebratory banner inscribed *Long live the 31st anniversary of the great Socialist October Revolution*.(4.64)

May Day was an occasion for outpourings of celebrations of Communism, usually with local games and processions, and often with displays of military might in Moscow targeted largely at international observers. It was commemorated philatelically in 1947 - although belatedly. On 10 June 1947 two stamps featured a joyous procession (4.65), and on 5 June 1948 two stamps depicted a similar event but set against the armed forces assembled in Red Square with the waving banner proclaiming *Long live May 1st - the day of the review of the workers' armed forces*.(4.66)

4.59 60k Heavy machinery production and 1r Rolled steel sheets: from set 14 October 1948.

4.60 60k Mining and 1r Oil refinery: from set 24 October 1948.

4.63 60k Revolutionaries, 60k Harvesting, and 1r Industry: from set 7 November 1947.

4.61 30l Farkhadsk Power Station: from set 24 October 1948.

4.62 30k Lenin and Stalin: from set 6 November 1946.

On 29 February 1947 three stamps featuring a soldier and his medals (20k), a cadet studying (30k), and a soldier, sailor and airman (30k) marked, as the inscription announced, the 29th anniversary of the Soviet Armed Forces.(4.67) On 23 February 1948 three 30k stamps marked XXX depicting a sailor and warship, an airman and light bomber, and a soldier and artillery, commemorated the 30th anniversary.(4.68) The set also included a 60k stamp depicting Marshal Nikolai Bulganin (1895-1975) at a military school. Never a serving soldier, Bulganin was a wartime senior political commissar, and then Minister for the Armed Forces, becoming a General in 1944 and Marshal in 1947. In the 1950s he was Minister of Defence and then Chairman of the Council of Ministers.

The 1948 set was accompanied by a new 60k issue of three 1944 stamps honouring Heroes of the Civil War of 1917-23.(4.69) All three had died young, and mysteriously, and their dramatic lives were easily romanticised. Vasily Chapayev (1887-1919) (60k brown) died when the regiment he was elected to lead was ambushed by White Russian forces near the River Volga. His fame rested largely on a popular novel and film about his exploits, as does that of Nikolay Shchors

4.64 40k Searchlights over Moscow: from set 7 November 1948.

4.65 1r May Day: 10 June 1947.

4.66 30k May Day 5 June 1948.

4.67 20k Soldier and 30k Cadet studying: from set 29 February 1947.

4.68 30k Sailor and 60k Marshal Bulganin: from set 23 February 1948.

(1895-1919) (60k green) who led the 1st Ukrainian Soviet division in campaigns against the independent Ukrainian Republic and Polish armies, and no-one witnessed his death during a confused battle. Sergey Lazo (1894-1920) (60k blue) commanded units in the Far East against Baikalan Cossack, American and Japanese anti-Bolshevik forces. He disappeared after being seized by the Japanese near Vladivostok.

With 1948 witnessing the Berlin airlift and the hardening of the Cold War, and with Stalin increasing his grip on satellite nations while pursuing his disagreement with Marshal Tito of Yugoslavia, the Soviet Union lost no opportunity to continue to publicise it military strength. On 12 September 1948 the face of a determined sailor marked the Navy Day set (4.70), on 25 September stamps featuring tanks in action (30r) and massed on parade (1r) marked Tank Drivers' Day (4.71), and on 19 November two stamps depicting heavy guns saluting in Red Square (Spasskaya Tower is in the background) marked Artillery Day. (4.72)

The formidable Soviet Air Force was far from forgotten. On 1 September 1947 two stamps featuring a Yakovlev Yak-9 fighter plane marked Air Force Day: they were reissued overprinted with a new date on 2 August 1948.(4.73) The formidable fighter, still in use after its successful introduction in the war, was depicted soaring above the striking Air Force flag of bright blue and yellow rays shining from the sun with a red star at its centre and a winged propellor underneath. A similar design was used on a propaganda issue on 10 December 1948 in the middle of the Berlin blockade to highlight Soviet strength and determination.(4.74) The USSR phased out the Yak-9 in 1949 but shrewdly sold many of them as reinforcements to satellite countries.

During 1948 a flurry of stamps honoured selected artists and writers whose works glorified Russia's historic expansion and natural beauty while exposing the denigrating effect of Tsardom on the people's moral and physical welfare. On 15 February 1948 two stamps marked the centenary of the birth of the Realist artist Vasily Surikov (1848-1916) whose house at Krasnoyarsk was being turned into a museum.(4.75) His huge and dramatic paintings centred on blood curdling Russian events such as the conquest of Siberia by the legendary sixteenth century Cossack Yermak Timofeyevich, and the execution of the Streltsy Regiments rebels by an implacable Tsar Peter the Great (reigned 1682-1725).

On 7 June 1948 three stamps marked the centenary of the death of Vissarion Belinsky (1811-48), an influential literary critic whose championship of the ideas of the individual self, based largely on Western European philosophy, led to his attacks on Russian autocracy and serfdom.(4.76) On 4 December 1946 his great friend, the poet Nikolay Nekrasov (1821-77), had been portrayed on two stamps commemorating the 125th anniversary of his birth.(4.77) They shared a deep hatred of serfdom and political repression, and much of Nekrasov's poetry, imbued with humour as well as didactic insight, highlighted what he believed to be the intrinsic moral values of peasants that were tragically eroded by poverty, ignorance and crime. His verse remained popular and was a favourite of Lenin who called him 'a great Russian Socialist.'

On 10 June 1948 three stamps marked the 125th anniversary of the birth of the Realist playwright Alexander Ostrovsky (1823-86) whose numerous plays centred on the virtues and vices of traditional Russian society divided critics but delighted audiences - before and after the Revolution - and popularised the theatre. (4.78)

On 12 June 1948 four colourful stamps featured the artist Ivan Shishkin (1832-98) and two of his detailed landscapes - *The Rye Field* (50k) and *Morning in the Forest* (60k).(4.79) Shiskin, along with Surikov and Repin, were members of the *Peredvizhniki* (Wanderers), a group of Russian Realist artists who viewed Russian life as unique and beautiful if only autocracy, censorship and serfdom were abolished.

On 27 November 1948 two stamps commemorated the works of the architect Vasily Stasov (1769-1848). (4.80) Although he worked on cathedrals and palaces, notably Tsarskoe Selo, his general advocacy of essentially Russian architecture and making utilitarian buildings look imposing resonated with the post-war Soviet leadership. No doubt they liked his imposing Triumphal Gates in St Petersburg and Moscow commemorating,

4.71 *30k Tank Drivers' Day: from set 25 September 1948.*

4.69 *60k Chapayev, Shchors and Lazo: from set 23 February 1948.*

4.72 *1r Artillery Day: from set 19 November 1948.*

4.73 *30k Air Force Day: from set 1 September 1947.*

4.70 *60k Navy Day: from set 12 September 1948.*

respectively, Russian victories over Napoleon in 1812 and the Ottoman Empire in 1828-29. The 1r stamp featured his Imperial style Presidential Palace at Vilnius in Lithuania - since 1945 reduced in status to an officers' centre.

In 1948 two sets cast a warm glow upon two other republics within the USSR. On 25 January 1948 four stamps celebrated the 30th anniversary of the Ukrainian Soviet Socialist Republic with celebratory inscriptions and images of Kiev's state building (30k), the Dneiper dam (50k), a grain harvest and huge granary (60k) and a coal train and power station (1r).(4.81) In fact in 1917 Ukraine tried to break free from over a century of Russian control, but savage internal disagreements and the advancing Red Army led to the creation of the Ukrainian Soviet Socialist Republic. In the 1930s the USSR's economic mismanagement - and possibly deliberate genocide - led to millions starving. In 1941 many Ukrainians welcomed the Germans while others fought them as partisans, and by 1945 the region had lost millions of lives, thousands of villages and towns, and hundreds of factories - and in 1948 recovery was still far from complete.

On 16 October 1948 two stamps inscribed *The founder of modern Armenian literature* depicted the teacher and writer Khachatur Abovian (1809-48), whose novel *Wounds of Armenia* and poems attacking injustice, and promoting free, secular and wide-ranging education, received a hostile reception from Armenian clerics and Tsarist bureaucrats.(4.82) However his literary works and advocacy of friendship with Russia

4.76 60k Vissarion Belinsky: from set 7 June 1948.

4.77 60k Nikolay Nekrasov: from set 4 December 1946.

4.78 1r Alexander Ostrovsky: from set 10 June 1948.

4.74 1r Yakovlev Yak-9 and flag: 10 December 1948.

4.79 1r Ivan Shishkin and 60k 'Morning in the Forest': from set 12 June 1948.

4.75 60k Vasily Surikov: from set 15 February 1948.

4.80 1r Vasily Stasov and Presidential Palace: from set 27 November 1948

4.81 50k Ukraine's state building and 60k grain harvest: from set 25 January 1948.

goods. The 15k and 60k stamps featured heavy industry with the slogan *The fiery cry of Leningrad - the five year plan in four years nationwide* and the 30k the proclamation of the Plan to workers with the slogan *Let's execute Stalin's five year post war plan in four years*. However, although industrialisation intensified, the Plan was unrealistic in its aim of Leningrad rivalling Moscow, and Stalin had no intention of letting the city's

4.82 50c Khachatur Abovian: from set 10 October 1948.

4.83 50k Peter the Great monument and 1r Smolny Institute: from set 10 January 1948.

ensured his recognition by the Soviet Union. In fact Armenia had suffered from Ottoman repression up until the First World war, and then enjoyed a brief period of fragile independence until succumbing to Bolshevik pressure and invasion in the early 1920s.

Perhaps the sets issued on 10 January and 25 June 1948 most belied the political reality of life in the USSR. The January set ostensibly celebrated the fourth anniversary of the relief of Leningrad after enduring its wartime siege, but did so not by honouring its heroic civilian and military defenders, or even its reconstruction efforts, but by pictures of its historic Winter Palace (30k), Peter the Great monument (50k), Peter & Paul Fortress (60k) and Smolny Institute (1r).(4.83) All were legendary places in the wider 1917 Bolshevik Revolution.(4.83) The Smolny Institute, for example, was Lenin's headquarters in 1917 from which the Bolshevik victory was acclaimed that October. And carefully sandbagged, Peter the Great's monument had become a symbol of the city's wartime defiance in 1941.

The June set commemorated the announcement in 1947 of a new Leningrad Development Plan formulated by the influential Communist leaders in the city.(4.84) Since the devastating siege, the 1943-47 Reconstruction Plan had led to considerable rebuilding, especially of housing blocks, and now the new Plan sought to make the city a Western looking international port, regional industrial centre, and large scale producer of consumer

4.84 30k Proclamation and 60k Factories: from set 25 June 1948.

ambitious leaders rival him, even though many were heroes of the terrible siege. In 1949 Stalin's close colleagues accused Leningrad's leaders of attempting to subvert Moscow's economic and political leadership. Several thousand local politicians, managers and intellectuals were arrested, key figures such as Pyotr Popkov and Alexey Kuznetsov tried and executed, and hundreds imprisoned. Henceforth Leningrad was ruled by Moscow's nominees.

And all the time the common definitive series centred on ordinary workers and servicemen - along with the state Arms. In 1947-1948 two values featuring the iconic Spasskaya Tower were added (4.85), and in May1948 the designs were modernised and a a female agricultural worker belatedly included.(4.86)

4.85 1r Spasskaya Tower: 9 September 1948.

4.86 5k Miner, 20k Farm worker, 30k Arms, 45k Scientist, and 60k Soldier: from set 15 May 1948.

CHAPTER 5

FRANCE

After the searing agonies of bitter trench warfare stretching south of Flanders through Artois, Picardy and Champagne to Lorraine and Alsace, in 1918 France's families faced the peace with one and half million dead, around three million injured survivors, and with a chronic national debt and output from farms and factories at a very low ebb. The trauma of war created a national mood of vengeance towards Germany that existed alongside a deep pacifism that centred on a policy of keeping Germany militarily impotent and creating a sense of security behind the massive Maginot line of fortresses along France's eastern border. France's inter-war years were further blighted by chronic political instability with its numerous elections switching between left and right wing governments which were fragile and often internally warring coalitions. The renowned glamour of French fashion, art and design, cinema and theatre did little to mask the national controversies over the national debt, the alarmingly volatile economy, the desirability of rearmament and how to deal with a resurgent Germany.

Hitler's absorption of Austria and dismemberment of Czechoslovakia stoked the fears of yet another German pre-emptive strike, and France trembled when its government joined Great Britain in trying to stop the break-up of Czechoslovakia and then guaranteeing Polish, Romanian and Greek territorial integrity. Hitler treated the warning with contempt and invaded Poland on 1 September 1939. Paranoid France remained purely defensive in its attitude, and only at the eleventh hour did the government of Paul Reynaud try to mobilise its forces when German forces crashed through the Ardennes on 10 May 1940, bypassing the monolithic Maginot Line. A few French and British units fought back vigorously, but most others were swept aside and north-eastern France quickly became a land of terrified refugees, confused troops, dispirited generals and defeatist politicians. On flying visits Winston Churchill sought to encourage French resistance alongside British army, naval and air forces in the region but the discussions broke down on French vacillation, despair and age-old suspicions of British sincerity, and indeed the smallness of the available British forces. Reynaud handed power to Marshal Petain, a hero of the last war, who signed an armistice with Germany on 22 June with the vast majority of the nation's Senate and Chamber of Deputies voting in favour. France had fallen in just six weeks. Germany occupied northern and western France, including Paris and the Atlantic coastline, and re-absorbed Alsace-Lorraine. Petain's government was left with around 40% of France to rule as a German puppet. He found a base at the unremarkable town of Vichy and headed an authoritarian and strongly pro-German government.

As historian Jonathan Fenby has written, 'The legend that, apart from a small group of Fascists and crooks around the geriatric Marshal (Petain), France resisted the Germans for four years is just that' - a legend. Most people merely endured the occupation, and many opponents of the unstable pre-war Republic saw the aged Petain as a national father figure - a view perpetuated on Vichy French stamps. Many approved of his dictatorial regime which harped on family values, rural regeneration, law and order, respect for Roman Catholicism and active anti-Semitism. Among other collaborators, the Legion of French Volunteers against Bolshevism numbered around 6,000 men and fought alongside German forces on the Eastern Front. Vichy propaganda asserted the need for a period of painful national regeneration to restore France to its historic greatness - although Hitler treated the Petain's regime with contempt and swept much of France's food and factory production into Germany. Inevitably living conditions slumped, disease was rife, and the Vichy regime steadily lost support, while at the same time de Gaulle's position in London as the exiled self-appointed head of the French resistance grew steadily stronger. Resistance across France slowly grew in effectiveness in damaging enemy installations and assisting downed aircrew to escape, although German mass executions in reprisal for sabotage severely limited wider support for the partisans. It was only after the Allied invasion in June 1944 when victory seemed assured that resistance groups soared in number. By then Free French forces had bolstered de Gaulle's status by victories against Vichy forces in Gabon and Syria and against German troops in North Africa. Not surprisingly, despite Allied leaders hating his arrogance, de Gaulle made much of France's own struggle to free itself to ensure he became the internationally accepted leader of a totally intact and independent nation. However despite France's claims to the contrary, the nation's glory days and general acceptance as a Great Power were over. The reluctant decision of the USA and Great Britain to include France as an occupying Power in Germany and Austria was more about boosting her morale, cost-sharing and suppressing Communism than recognition of her contribution to victory. France's post-war stamp issues reveal much about the painful emergence of this nation after the war, and its brittle self-image.

French stamps from competing sources were in circulation after the Free French landings in Corsica in September 1943 and the wider Allied landings in Normandy in June 1944 and Provence in August 1944. The Vichy government persevered with its definitive set featuring Marshal Petain and added a new set in April 1944 commemorating his 88th birthday and promising workers' charters.(5.1) Conversely another Vichy set in July 1944 drew upon renowned figures from King Louis XIV's golden age - presumably in a last desperate attempt at visionary political propaganda and fund raising.(5.2)

However as Allied forces advanced after the D-Day landings many Vichy stamps ended up cancelled with celebratory liberation postmarks.(5.3) Others were overprinted 'F.F.I.' by the Forces Francaises de l'Interieur, the resistance fighters who, in 1944, multiplied significantly and worked alongside the Free French Army and other Allied forces.(5.4) They were particularly active in the mountainous south-east,

5.2 4f+6f King Louis XIV: from set 31 July 1944.

 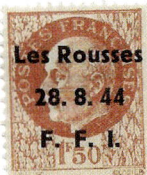

5.4 1f50 Petain definitives (issued 1942) with 1944 F.F.I. overprints.

especially Savoie and Les Rousses in the Jura near the Swiss border. In November 1944 several Vichy definitive stamps were reissued by liberating French forces with the Vichy POSTES FRANCAISES pointedly obliterated by RF in black for the traditional REPUBLIQUE FRANCAISE.(5.5)

Meanwhile the French Committee of National Liberation put on sale in Corsica, then in Provence and finally across liberated France a lengthy definitive set, some values featuring the celebrated Gallic Cock beside de Gaulle's symbol of the Cross of Lorraine, and others 'Marianne', the female symbol of the republic wearing the Phrygian cap of the 1790s revolutionaries.(5.6)

5.1 2f+3f Petain and rural regeneration: from set 24 April 1944.

5.3 10c Mercury (issued 1938) and 40c and 70c Petain definitives (issued 1941) with Lyon liberation cancellation.

5.5 30c 'Mercury' Vichy issue overprinted RF: from set 27 November 1955.

5.8 1f20 Arc de Triomphe: from set 12 February 1945.

5.6 20f Gallic Cock and 3f 'Marianne': from set 1944.

5.9 2f40 'Iris': from set 5 September 1944+.

5.7 5c Arc de Triomphe: from set June 1944.

5.10 4f50 'Marianne': from set 16 September 1944+.

After the Normandy landings a second set featuring the Arc de Triomphe accompanied the Allied advance towards Paris and then Germany.(5.7) It was reprinted in February 1945 with new values in black.(5.8) The Arc de Triomphe commemorated the victories of the French Revolutionary and Napoleonic armies and marked the resting place of France's Unknown Warrior of the First World War. Significantly its frieze included heroic Frenchmen fighting bearded Teuton warriors. On 25 August 1944 General Choltitz, the German commander, surrendered Paris to the Free French General Leclerc and the following day General Charles De Gaulle strode down the Champs Elysees ahead of his forces thereby at least partially assuaging the shame of Germany's similar parade there in 1940. Equally significantly he was asserting his newly assumed role as President of the French Republic's Provisional Government. At this time he had no guarantee that the Allies would not impose their own military rule on a 'collaborationist' France. In the event his assertions that the legitimate French Republic had had a continuous existence under his wartime leadership, his obvious popularity in liberated towns and amongst resistance fighters, and the fact that Stalin ordered the French Communist Party to cooperate with, not challenge, other parties at this time, meant that he faced little opposition.

Later in 1944 a short set re-used a pre-war design of 'Iris', the Classical winged goddess of the rainbow and communication between mortals and the heavens.(5.9) Soon afterwards, and long into 1945, a lengthy set printed in London featured a stately new portrait of 'Marianne' by the noted designer Edmund Dulac, born in France but a naturalised Briton.(5.10) All these symbols of national unity and regeneration actually reflected the generally productive although sometimes strained working alliance between the Communist, Socialist and Christian Democrat Parties on the Committee of National Liberation. It was to last under various premiers until 1947 when the Communists were finally expelled from government as a pre-requisite for France receiving American Marshall Aid.

Alongside Dulac's set, and gradually replacing it during 1945 and 1946, a lengthy all-French designed and printed set eventually reaching 100 francs used three images. Most values contained a third portrayal of 'Marianne', this time as a modern Frenchwoman staring steadfastly into the future. However several values used a slightly redesigned early French stamp featuring 'Ceres', the Classical goddess of agriculture and fertility, while others had a shield emblazoned with the Free French Cross of Lorraine and shattered chains with the date '1944'.(5.11) The set was heralded by a striking

EUROPEAN STAMP ISSUES AND THE AFTERMATH OF THE SECOND WORLD WAR: 1944–1949

5.11 50c France freed, 80c 'Ceres', and 2f 'Marianne': from set 1 February 1945+.

5.13 2f40 Arms of Metz and 4f Arms of Strasbourg: set 5 March 1945, and 4f Liberation of Alsace & Lorraine: 16 May 1945.

5.12 4f 'Marianne' exhorting resistance fighters: 16 January 1945.

5.14 2f Map of French Empire: 17 September 1945.

5.15 10c Arms of Corsica and 60c Arms of Nice.

single stamp in January 1945 celebrating Liberation which featured Marianne astride a winged horse urging France's resistance fighters on to victory.(5.12)

Not surprisingly, no time was lost highlighting victories by Free French forces. On 5 March 1945 stamps featuring the Arms of Strasbourg in Alsace and Metz in Lorraine, and another one on 16 May 1945 portraying joyful young women in regional dresses, celebrated the liberation of Alsace-Lorraine. For centuries France and Germany had bitterly contested the region.(5.13) Strasbourg had been retaken by Free French forces in November 1944, and in the same month Metz was captured after bitter fighting by General Patton's Third Army, but without French involvement. De Gaulle considered the liberation of Alsace-Lorraine so important to national morale and his own popularity that he had threatened to withdraw Free French forces from General Eisenhower's authority unless he sanctioned the French attack on Strasbourg which he considered an unnecessary diversion from the main Allied thrust eastwards. In September 1945 a stamp from April 1940 showing France and its Empire *(LA FRANCE D'OUTRE MER 1945)* was reissued incorporating the Cross of Lorraine.(5.14) Despite many overseas territories serving the Vichy regime, France had regained its Empire, sometimes after severe fighting, just in time to face the rising tide of militant nationalism across Indochina and Africa, notably in Algeria and Madagascar.

In June and July 1946 four stamps featured the Arms of Alsace, Lorraine, Nice and Corsica.(5.15) Resistance fighters had been instrumental in freeing Corsica and Nice from enemy occupation in 1943 and 1944 respectively - although in both instances wisely not before major Allied units were closing in.

A few years later, on 14 May 1949 a stamp celebrating the 600th anniversary of the cession of Dauphiny in the far south-east to France had the additional merit of reinforcing French territorial rights after Italy's wartime annexation of parts of Savoy and Provence.(5.16) Medieval Dauphiny, which centred on Grenoble, was sold by its impoverished ruler in 1349 to the French king at the Treaty of Romans (pictured in the stamp) with the provision that his heir would always be known as the Dauphin - the title of the ruler of Dauphiny.

Several sets reflected other aspects of the immediate post-war world. On 16 May 1945 a surtaxed stamp showing a family leaving its shattered home for a sunlit

5.16 12f France acquires Dauphiny: 14 May 1949.

5.17 4f+6f Postal Employees War Victims' Fund: 16 May 1945.

rural future supported the Postal Employees War Victims' Fund.(5.17) The vital anti-tuberculosis and fresh air campaigns featured on two early post-war stamps - one in May 1945 showing a patient outside in a deck chair (5.18), and the other in July that year featuring children happily playing in the fresh air.(5.19)

5.18 2f+1f Anti-TB Fund: 16 May 1945, and reissue overprinted 3f: 21 February 1946.

In stark contrast, on 13 October 1945 a stamp featured German soldiers by the burning church at Oradour-sur-Glane in mid-west France on 10 June 1944.(5.20) Acting on information by collaborators that a Waffen-SS officer had been captured by the French resistance, a battalion from the 4th SS Panzer Grenadier Regiment retaliated by shooting and burning 190 men in a barn and then killing 247 women and 205 children in the village church. De Gaulle ordered the remains of the village to serve as a memorial, and a new village was rebuilt nearby.

5.19 4f+2f Fresh Air Crusade: 9 July 1945.

On 5 November 1945 a surtaxed set featured four towns and cities devastated in battles.(5.21) The 1f 50+1f 50 pictured Dunkirk, heavily damaged during the famous evacuation of British and French troops in June 1940. The 2f+2f featured Rouen, a German stronghold heavily damaged by Allied bombing in April and August 1944. The 2f40+2f40 featured Caen, largely destroyed by British and Canadian bombardments against a stubborn German defence in July 1944. The 4f+4f featured the historic walled port of St Malo which was almost totally destroyed by American shelling and British naval gunfire in August and September 1944 when the German commander refused to surrender. In all these actions, and elsewhere, thousands of French civilians were killed or wounded. Arguments soon arose regarding whether or not different tactics could have saved countless lives.

5.20 4f+2f Oradour-sur-Glane atrocity: 13 October 1945.

Early stamps from the Provisional Government between June 1944 and October 1946 included several significant historical sets aimed at restoring national pride. On 20 November 1944 a single stamp marked the eighth centenary of the rebuilding of the early Gothic St Denis Basilica in Paris.(5.22) St Denis was a third century missionary and martyr who became a patron saint of the French nation and the basilica was the burial place of many French kings. On the same day a surcharged set supported French cathedrals - whose maintenance was the responsibility of the state, not the Roman Catholic Church.(5.23) The 50c+1f 50 featured the Romanesque facade of Angouleme Cathedral, perhaps chosen as its numerous sculptures possessed apt wartime resonances with the faithful looking towards Christ and the damned suffering their punishments. The 80c+2f 20 featured the thirteenth century Chartres Cathedral, famously saved from destruction by American guns on 16 August 1944 when Colonel Welborn Griffith courageously entered the city

5.21 Devastated towns of Dunkirk, Rouen, Caen and St Malo: set 5 November 1945.

and then the cathedral and rang the bells when he found the Germans were not using the towers for artillery direction and ranging. He was killed later that day. The 1f 20+2f 80 featured Amiens Cathedral whose central portal portrayed the sinners and saved at the Last Judgement, and whose south door had eleven panels commemorating the dead of the First World War. The 1f 50+3f 50 featured the late Gothic Beauvais cathedral that had been badly damaged, along with much of the city, during the German advance on Paris in June 1940. The 4f+6f featured Albi, the brick-built fortress-like cathedral whose construction started in the late thirteenth century as a powerful counter to the Cathar or Albigensian heresy (a belief in a good God and a bad God) which was being savagely suppressed across the region. In 1945 the concern was to punish collaborators and crush memories of the Vichy creed.

A second National Relief Fund set on 6 January 1947 pictured St Julien's Cathedral in Le Mans, St Semin in Toulouse, Notre Dame du Port in Clermont Ferrand, St Front in Perigueux, and Notre Dame in Paris.(5.24) In December 1947, and again in May 1948, stamps featured Conques Abbey in southern France, where the remains of St Foy, a young woman martyred in the fourth century, had attracted numerous pilgrims due to her ability to free those tied down by physical and mental chains.(5.25) The tympanum above the main door contained a fearsome carving of the Last Judgement that paid particular attention to the tortures of Hell. It was reissued in May 1948 in a new colour and higher

5.22 2f40 St Denis Basilica: 20 November 1944.

5.23 50c+1f50 Angouleme Cathedral and 80c+2f20 Chartres Cathedral: from set 20 November 1944.

5.24 3f+2f Notre Dame du Port and 10f+6f Notre Dame de Paris: from set 6 January 1947.

5.25 *18f Conques Abbey: 10 May 1948.*

5.26 *4f Marshal Bugeaud: 20 November 1944.*

5.27 *4f+1f Sarah Bernhardt: 16 May 1945.*

value. Catholic observance remained strong in parts of France, and increasingly so as one went from north to south, and possibly these issues played their multiple parts in unifying the nation, reinforcing traditional values, highlighting France's architectural glories, restoring national pride - and stimulating a new wave of tourism. Many of the religious buildings featured in the sets were on the long established, and commercially profitable, European pilgrimage routes known as the 'Way of St James' leading to his shrine in the Cathedral of Santiago de Compostela in Spain.

Carefully selected figures were commemorated. On 20 November 1944 a stamp portrayed Marshal Thomas Bugeaud (1784-1849) who had been instrumental in the French conquest of Algeria.(5.26) Ostensibly the stamp marked the centenary of his victory at Isly on 14 August 1844 but the stamp (issued several months after the anniversary) was more about signalling and maintaining France's Imperial might. Ironically it could be said to mark the start of rising Algerian opposition that soon erupted into an outright war of independence. On 16 May 1945 a stamp belatedly marked the centenary of the birth of the famous actress Sarah Bernhardt (23 October 1844-1923) whose fame included running a war hospital in Paris during the 1870-71 war against Germany and, as an old but still charismatic woman, making patriotic visits to the Front in the First World War.(5.27) She was a Jew and in a move deeply unpopular with the French during the occupation the Germans changed the name of Paris's iconic Theatre Sarah-Bernhardt to Theatre de la Cite.

On 4 February 1946 two scientists were commemorated in support of two different campaigns. The first was linked to the battle against cancer and featured Henri Becquerel (1852-1908) who discoveries around radioactivity led to his pioneering work on radiotherapy.(5.28) The second stamp portrayed Jean Alfred Fournier (1832-1914), a researcher into venereal disease, and its surtax supported the national Prophylaxis Fund.(5.29) As cases everywhere mounted during the war, it was re-issued in a different colour in

5.28 *2f+3f Henri Becquerel: 4 February 1946.*

October 1947. On 17 November 1948 two other scientists were honoured on stamps when their ashes were interned in the Pantheon, the Paris mausoleum for distinguished citizens. They were Paul Langevin (1872-1946) who created a successful ultrasound submarine detector, and Jean Baptiste Perrin (1870-1940) who proposed that nuclear reactions were the source of stellar energy.(5.30)

War charities continued to be supported by stamp issues. On 11 March 1946 a stamp featuring Les Invalides, the capital's historic home for old and sick soldiers, supported the War Invalids Relief Fund (5.31), and on 8 April a stamp picturing two warships supported naval charities.(5.32) Both vessels, though, had undistinguished careers. The cruiser *Emile Bertin* was damaged by bombs during the Allied Norwegian campaign, and after France's surrender remained at Martinique until rejoining the Allied fleet in 1943-44 to support the invasion of southern France. From 1940 until 1943 the ancient battleship *Lorraine* was idle in Alexandria, and then joined the *Emile Bertin* in bombarding enemy positions in the Mediterranean.

1946 saw sets encouraging tourism along with a series of attractive Airmail stamps. Straddling 1946 and 1947 an Air set featured aeroplanes alongside Iris, the winged messenger of the Gods (50f), Jupiter as an eagle carrying off the beautiful Egine (100f), Apollo and his sun-chariot (200f), and the half man, half horse Centaur (40f).(5.33) In May 1947 a striking 500f Air stamp from a set marking the Universal Postal Union Conference in Paris pictured a seagull soaring over the Seine and Notre Dame. Other stamps in this set ensured Paris was seen at its best for this prestigious event - with striking images of La Conciergerie (4f50), La Cite (6f) and Place de la Concorde (10f).(5.34)

In January 1948 surtaxed Air stamps supporting Air Force charities depicted two celebrated aviators, both of whom died in the war. The first, Antoine de Saint-Exupery (1900-44) (50f+30f), was famous as a writer

5.32 2f+3f 'Emile Bertin' and 'Lorraine': 8 April 1946.

5.29 2f+3f Jean Alfred Fournier: 20 October 1947.

5.33 50f Iris and 200f Apollo: from set 27 May 1946.

5.30 5f Paul Langevin and 8f Jean Baptiste Perrin: set 17 November 1948.

5.31 4f+6f Les Invalides: 11 March 1946.

5.3 500f Notre Dame and the Seine and 10f Place de la Concorde: from UPU Conference set 7 May 1947.

5.35 50f+30f Antoine de Saint-Exupery: from set 19 January 1948.

5.36 40f+10f Clement Ader's Avion III: 23 February 1948.

(notably of the philosophic novel *The Little Prince* and memoir *Wind, Sand and Stars*) as well as a long distance pilot.(5.35) In 1940 he fought against the Germans, then worked towards America's involvement in the war, and finally joined the Free French Air Force only to vanish without a trace on a reconnaissance flight from Corsica. Saint Exupery usually flew a Bloch MB174 but disappeared flying a Lockheed P-38 Lightning, although the aeroplane on the stamp seems to the Douglas DB-7 which was used by the French against the German invasion. The second figure was Jean Dagnaux (1891-1940) (100f+70f), a much decorated First World War fighter pilot, the first to fly across the Sahara, and the founder of several commercial routes in northern Africa. He was shot down over the Aisne in May 1940.

The following month another Air stamp featured the ghostly image of the steam powered bat-like *Avion III* designed by Clement Ader (1841-1925) in the 1890s. It is seen flying above a much later Douglas DB-7.(5.36) Although Ader was lauded in France as the father of aviation (thereby implicitly ousting the Wright brothers) grave doubts always existed over whether his cumbersome machine ever left the ground.

Between 1946 and 1948 a tourist set included Vezelay (5f) and Rocamadour (15f), two historic hilltop villages whose sacred sites had long been places of pilgrimage.(5.37) Others in the set were Brittany's wild Pointe du Raz (20f), luxurious Cannes in the south which held its first Film Festival in 1946 (6f), and the majestic Stanislaus Place in Nancy (25f). Three stamps featured the Luxembourg Palace in Paris (10f, 12f and 15f), a former royal residence that hosted the Paris Peace Conference between 29 July and 15 October 1946.(5.38)

The 10f view of the Luxembourg Place was issued on 29 July 1946, the first day of the Conference, as were two further stamps featuring the release of Doves of Peace. (5.39) Hosting the Peace Conference flattered French pride, and no doubt the same can be said about the 1946 stamp celebrating Paris hosting the first UNESCO Conference (5.40), and the pair of stamps in 1948 featuring the Palais de Chaillot in Paris where the third United Nations Assembly was held which adopted the Universal Declaration of Human Rights.(5.41) The Palais de Chaillot issue might have eased the raw scar if not erased the memory of the humiliating photograph of a triumphant Hitler standing on its terrace in 1940 framed by the Eiffel Tower.

5.37 5f Vezelay and 15f Rocamadour: from set 20 July 1946+.

5.38 6f Cannes and 10f Luxembourg Palace, Paris: from set 20 July 1946+.

On 12 July 1947 a stamp had commemorated Francois Fenelon, Archbishop of Cambrai (1651-1715).(5.42) As no anniversary seems involved, the issue was probably to highlight his liberal views on politics and education, emphasis on the moral responsibilities of rulers, and opposition to religious intolerance. With justification, he could be claimed as an early French proponent of universal human rights

Three other stamps in the late 1940s featured carefully selected images of the war. On 2 August 1947 a surtaxed stamp featured St Nazaire's dockyard and memorial to mark the 5th anniversary of the successful, though costly, British raid using the old destroyer *HMS Campbeltown* to block the entrance to its dry dock - the only one capable of servicing Germany's huge battleship *Tirpitz*.(5.43) Not long afterwards, and perhaps to highlight French sacrifices alongside British ones, on 10

5.42 Francois Fenelon: 12 July 1947.

5.43 6f+4f 5th anniversary of the St Nazaire raid: 2 August 1947.

5.39 10f Dove of Peace released: from set 29 July 1946.

5.44 5f 'Resistance': 10 November 1947.

5.40 10f UNESCO: 19 November 1946.

5.41 18f Palais de Chaillot: from set 21 September 1948.

November 1947 a striking stamp portrayed a resistance fighter about to be shot by a German firing squad.(5.44) By then it was safe to honour, even eulogise, the 'Resistance' as its thousands of members had been peacefully disarmed and represented no political threat. Even the militant Communists had obeyed Stalin's orders to disband. On 3 July 1948 a stamp marked the early death of the national hero General Philippe Leclerc (1902-47), killed in an air crash in Algiers.(5.45) He had defied France's surrender to join de Gaulle and lead the Free French army against Vichy forces in French Equatorial Africa and then German armies in northern Europe. The stamp bears the names Koufra and Strasbourg referring to the famous oath taken by his forces after capturing Koufra in Africa in March 1941 that they would bear arms until their flag flew over Strassbourg Cathedral in Alsace - which it did in August 1944.

5.45 6f General Leclerc commemoration: 3 July 1948.

5.46 10f+6f King Charles VII, 5f+4f Joan of Arc, and 6f+5f Jean Gerson: from set 28 October 1946.

Perhaps for the sake of philatelic continuity, a set supporting the post-war version of the National Relief Fund in October 1946 used a framed portrait design similar to the Vichy charity issues. And in common with the Vichy issues the set highlighted celebrated historic figures, this time from Medieval France.(5.46) The 2f+1f pictured Francois Villon (c1431-c1463), whose disreputable wandering life informed his innovative poetry celebrating the underclasses, often against the courtly ideals. The 3f+1f featured Jean Fouquet (c1420-81), the artist whose works promoted the regality of the hard-pressed French court during the latter part of the Hundred Year's War, and the 4f+43f pictured the diplomat Philippe de Commynes (1447-1511) whose insightful memoirs analysed the machinations of the mutually suspicious Burgundian and French rulers. The 5f+4f pictured the French heroine, Saint Joan of Arc (c1412-1431), whose personal charisma, angelic visitations and military talent reinvigorated French resistance to English domination. She had been canonised in 1920. The 6f+5f pictured Jean Gerson (1363-1429), theologian and Chancellor of the University of Paris, whose life and works sought to unite Christendom by ending the 'Great Schism' of two rival Popes and the destructive feud between the ruling Houses of Burgundy and Orleans. The 10f+6f portrayed Charles VII of France (reigned 1422-61), the ruler inspired by Joan of Arc to continue the successful war against the English. All the figures struggled against the mores, feuds and oppression of their times, including, for some, hostile British intervention in French affairs. By 1946 French animosity was mounting to what the country took to be British and American snubs to their aspirations to reclaim a key place in the international sun. France was excluded from the Allied conferenced at Yalta in 1945, the Americans opposed French (and British) colonialism, and British troops dramatically intervened to stop the French bombardment of Syrian towns in late May 1945 when the people protested against the slow withdrawal of French troops after independence.

Three other issues highlighted France's desire to restore its international standing. On 30 May 1947 a stamp marked the centenary of the birth of Auguste Pavie (1847-1925), the French explorer and diplomat whose life was devoted to furthering French interests in south-east Asia, not least as a rival to British expansion into Burma.(5.47) By 1894 the various treaties he negotiated, sometimes through 'gunboat diplomacy' established French controlled Indo-China. By the time the stamp was issued, however, Pavie's legacy was fast becoming 'a poisoned chalice' as French troops vainly tried to suppress the Vietnamese nationalists. As a French statement of intent the stamp was as outdated as Pavie's achievements.

On 2 May 1949 a stunning stamp commemorated French polar expeditions.(5.48) The clear contender for recognition was Jean-Baptiste Charcot (1867-1936) whose voyages of discovery in 1904-07 and 1908-10 to the Antarctic, and in the 1920s and 1930s to the Arctic, mapped many areas and attracted national attention.

5.47 4f50 Auguste Pavie: 30 May 1947.

5.48 *15f Polar expeditions: 2 May 1949.*

5.50 *10f Claude Chappe and 50f General Ferrie: from set 13 June 1949.*

5.49 *25f Franco-American Amity: 14 May 1949.*

More likely, though, the stamp signalled France's determination to be fully involved in the post-war international agreements over rights to build Antarctic research stations. During this tense period the French built two stations in Adelie Land, and its aptly named naval vessel, the *Commandant Charcot*, conducted high atmospheric research off the coast.

A couple of weeks later a costly 25 franc stamp showing ribbons encircling American and French shields, and an aeroplane and liner between the two, celebrated 'amity' between the two countries. It suited both parties.(5.49) The USA appreciated France's anti-Communist stance at home and in South East Asia, and France welcomed the waiving of its First World War debts and receipt of $2.3 billion in Marshall Aid.

Paris hosted the International Telephone and Telegraph Congress in June 1949, which agreed common regulations. A commemorative set highlighted France's contributions in these fields.(5.50) The 10f pictured Claude Chappe (1763-1805) who pioneered a practical semaphore system using signal masts on high towers which proved valuable during the Napoleonic Wars. The 15f featured Francois Arago (1786-1853) who discovered rotatory magnetism and Andre-Marie Ampere (1775-1836) who invented the solenoid and electric telegraph. The 25f portrayed Emile Baudot (1845-1903) who invented the multiplexed printing telegraph allowing many transmissions over a single line. The 50f featured General Gustave-Auguste Ferrie (1869-1932), an army officer and scientist, who led teams improving radio transmitters and receivers, notably in the First World War. The large 100f had a fine view of the 'Petit Palais' hosting the Congress.

A national referendum and election in October 1945 had confirmed support for a new constitution and sweeping reforms. The immediate post-war Provisional Government, firstly under General de Gaulle (June 1944-January 1946) and then three veteran Socialist ministers in quick succession, saw a decided swing to the left. The new constitution which governed the Fourth Republic from 1947 to 1959 meant the presidency was largely a ceremonial office and rendered the prime minister a vulnerable figure at the mercy of equally unstable and constantly warring political parties. It was the thought of a weak president and over-strong legislature that caused the imperious de Gaulle to retire temporarily from politics. Nevertheless, despite frequent ministerial changes France became heavily engaged in the nationalisation of transport systems, fuel supplies and financial institutions, and implemented wide-ranging improvements in social welfare provision.

Several issues convey this populist swing. On 2 August 1947 a stamp commemorated the sixth world Boy Scout Jamboree in the Forest of Moisson with over 24,000 representatives from across the world, including countries formerly at war.(5.51) Hailed as the 'Jamboree of Peace' the French president made a well-publicised visit. On 19 January 1948 a stamp featured Louis Braille (1809-52) who invented the reading system for the blind named after him.(5.52) Although slow to spread, by the 1930s it was used world-wide. This stamp was surtaxed for charities supporting the visually impaired. On 18 June 1948 a stamp marking the first International BCG Vaccine Conference in Paris pictured Dr Albert Calmette (1863-1933) who with Jean-Marie Camille Guerin (1872-1961) discovered the *Bacillus Calmette-Guerin* used in the TB vaccine named after them.(5.53) At long last mass vaccinations were about to begin.

A single stamp in September 1947 promoted improved roads as the 'milestones of liberty' (5.54) and another in September 1948 commemorated the inauguration of the mighty hydro-electric Genissiat Dam on the Rhone after the wartime delay and damage.(5.55) In February 1949 a set of four highlighted the nation's farmers, fishermen, miners and factory workers, and was probably an attempt to mask the array of violent strikes by transport workers and miners, often part of Communist inspired demonstrations against the government from which the party had been ejected in 1947.(5.56) In the countryside protectionist policies had encouraged an uncontrolled expansion of farming which led in turn to over-production, falling prices and further violent protests.

On 5 April 1948 a lengthy set supported the National Relief Fund while commemorating the centenary of the violent French Revolution of 1848 which deposed King Louis Philippe.(5.57) Ironically, it also opened the way for Louis Napoleon, the nephew of Napoleon Bonaparte, to be elected President and later seize power as Emperor Napoleon III. The 1f+1f portrayed Alphonse de Lamartine (1790-1869), the renowned poet and republican who framed the constitution of the Second Republic in 1848 but alienated support by his basic moderation and pacifism. The 3f+2f portrayed Alexandre Ledru-Rolin (1807-74) whose autocratic Socialism helped divide the revolutionaries, the 4f+2f Louis Blanc (1811-82) the Socialist whose state supported workers' cooperatives proved too extreme for his colleagues, and the 5f+4f Alexandre Martin (nicknamed Albert) (1815-95), initially a Socialist associate of Louis Blanc but later his enemy. Three further stamps featured Pierre-Joseph Proudhon (1809-65) (6f+5f), an advocate of extreme nationalisation, and Louis-Auguste Blanqui (1805-81) 10f+6f) and Armand Barbes (1809-70) (15f+7f) whose destructive invective incensed other revolutionaries as much as the monarchist regime they sought to destroy. Full of opposing ideas, incessantly quarrelsome and inadequate leaders, all of them were failures like the cause they espoused, but in time they were transformed into the romanticised successors of the 1790s revolutionaries and precursors of the republicans who ousted Napoleon III in 1870. The 20f+8f featured Denis-Auguste Affre (1793-1848), Archbishop of Paris, who was shot dead on the city's barricades as he tried to stop the fighting between the rioters and National Guard.

5.51 5f Scouts Jamboree: 2 August 1947.

5.52 6f+4f Louis Braille: 19 January 1948.

5.54 6f+4f Road Maintenance Fund: 10 September 1947.

5.53 6f+4f BCG Vaccine Conference: 18 June 1948.

5.55 12f Genissiat Barrage: 21 September 1948.

5.5 3f+1f Agriculture and 8f+4f Mining: from set 14 February 1949.

5.57 1f+1f Alphonse de Lamartine, 4f+3f Louis Blanc, and 20f+8f Denis-Auguste Affre: from set 5 April 1948.

5.58 18f Francois-Rene, Vicomte de Chateaubriand: 3 July 1948.

5.59 12f Jean Racine: 24 May 1949.

On 3 July 1948 a stamp marked the centenary of the death, in the midst of the 1848 Revolution, of the renowned politician and writer Francois-Rene, Vicomte de Chateaubriand (1768-1848).(5.58) It featured the ageing disillusioned writer and a suitably atmospheric view of his birthplace, the Chateau de Combourg in Brittany. Initially Chateaubriand welcomed the French Revolution of the 1790s, but disgusted at the violence he sailed to North America. Later he joined the French Royalists and returned to the Catholic faith. Already famous as a writer, his *Genius of Christianity* and works criticising Napoleon ensured his great favour under the restored Louis XVIII - until he criticised him. Briefly holding state offices, he veered from ultra-Royalism to moderate Liberal, and refused to support Louis-Philippe in 1830. His later works are full of pessimistic analyses of a corrupt and hedonistic society, but they contributed to his idolisation by young Romantics seeking solace in, and inspiration from, the imagination, idealised Medievalism, emotional nationalism and Byronic heroism.

In May 1949 a stamp marking the 250th anniversary of the death of the playwright Jean Racine (1639-99) signalled his growing re-establishment as a a major literary figure after condemnation for a century or more as a mere courtly writer turning out unhistorical works and tied to superannuated seventeenth century etiquette and conventions.(5.59) Twentieth century audiences proved more appreciative of his complex characters with their evolving thoughts and feelings as representing real people from any century.

Some months later, in November 1949 the National Relief Fund set went back to the eighteenth century - a golden age of French thought and culture even if latterly cut short by the savage revolution against the inequalities of the 'ancien regime'.(5.60) Many ideas of the chosen figures remained relevant to the modern world. The 5f+1f pictured Charles Louis de Secondat, Baron de La Brede et de Montesquieu (1689-1756) the political philosopher who achieved lasting fame for his arguments favouring the clear separation and balance of powers in any constitution between the executive, legislature and judiciary - an issue with which republican France wrestled constantly in formulating its successive constitutions. The 8f+2f featured Voltaire, the non-de-

5.60 National Relief Fund: set 14 November 1949.

Finally the 25f+10f featured Anne-Robert Turgot (1727-81), the statesman whose works upheld the universal advantages of free trade, equitable taxation and an educated populace.

Interestingly in December 1949 a further National Relief Fund set continued this attachment to the 'golden era' with four stamps based upon the bas-relief figures from the grand Fountain of the Four Seasons by the royal sculptor Edme Bouchardin (1698-1762).(5.61) Other bas-relief designs, severely Classical in style, featured on 1949 stamps honouring the French Chambers of Commerce and the Universal Postal Union - although without the inscriptions it would have been hard to determine the purpose of the stamps. (5.62 and 5.63)

5.61 15f+4f National Relief Fund 'Winter': from set 19 December 1949.

5.62 15f Allegory of Commerce: 18 October 1949.

5.63 25f Allegory of UPU: from set 7 November 1949.

plume of Francois-Marie Arouet (1694-1778) whose long list of works upheld civil liberties and savagely criticised the intolerance, rapacity and repression of the monarchy and Roman Catholic Church. He became the hero of many revolutionaries and resistance fighters - including the anti-Fascists. The 10f+3f portrayed Jean-Antoine Watteau (1684-1721) whose atmospheric landscapes, once almost forgotten, influenced the early Impressionists. The 12f+4f pictured the naturalist Georges-Louis Leclerc, Comte de Buffon (1707-88) whose pre-Darwin thoughts on the diversity of the natural world embraced the impact of climate change and evidence of natural degeneration and improvement. The 15f+5f featured Joseph Francois Dupleix (1697-1763) the Governor General of French India and opponent of Britain's Robert Clive. His reputation had been revived a century after his death as France expanded its Empire and three successive warships carried his name. The last was a heavy cruiser scuttled at Toulon in 1940 to avoid seizure by the Germans.

CHAPTER 6

BELGIUM

In May 1940 German armies crashed through the Low Countries into France, quickly over-running Belgium's line of defences and trapping most of its army. After just 18 days of fighting King Leopold III personally surrendered his country and stayed a German prisoner rather than fleeing with his ministers to Bordeaux and then London. His decision was widely criticised as the Germans made much of the civilian government ruling in his name although effectively under German military authority. Throughout the war Belgian definitive stamp issues continued to portray Leopold.

Belgium's neo-Fascist right wing parties actively encouraged collaboration and anti-Semitism in local communities, and promoted membership of the Waffen SS Flemish and Walloon Legions, which reached a total of 15,000 fighting men. Germany absorbed much of Belgian's taxes and produce, the cost of living soared, hundreds of thousands became forced labourers in Germany, and later in the war British and American air raids killed and injured thousands more in attempts to destroy factories and railway junctions. Additional destruction was caused by resistance groups who also ran escape lines for Allied airmen and sought to hide Jewish families during the particularly active persecutions, notably in Brussels and Antwerp.

The Allies afforded the government in exile full recognition, and eventually the Free Belgian forces included an infantry brigade, two fighter squadrons and several small warships. Canadian forces advanced into Belgium on 2 September 1944 and British troops liberated Brussels and Antwerp a few days later. However stubborn German defences held up the Polish, Canadian, American and Free Belgian forces trying to seize the Scheldt estuary and Ghent canal giving access to Antwerp docks until November. And on 16 December 1944 Hitler launched his desperate Ardennes Offensive with a quarter of a million men. The surprise assault failed to reach its target of Antwerp but Belgian towns and civilians suffered badly in the bitter fighting that endured until the Germans retreated at the end of January 1945. And in 1945 more than 2,000 V1 and V2 rockets deliberately targeted cities such as Liege and Antwerp. In the years to follow over 55,000 collaborators were prosecuted. Many were imprisoned and 250 executed, and the impact of the war remained very visible in many towns and across the Ardennes. Out of its bitter wartime experiences grew Belgium's decision to integrate as fully as possible in Europe's post-war military, political and economic agreements. In 1948 it became part of the Benelux Economic Union, and the following year it was a signatory of the North Atlantic Treaty Organisation (NATO).

As early as 10 November 1944, when it seemed Belgium was soon to be free of all German troops, three sets of stamps were issued featuring the letter 'V' for Victory - one was fore-fronted by the Belgian rampant lion, the second overprinted on stamps from the definitive national arms set, and the third printed adjacent to a portrait of King Leopold.(6.1, 6.2) These sets, in common with every Belgian set, included the dual Dutch and French names *BELGIE - BELGIQUE or BELGIQUE - BELGIE*. This was more than a courtesy, as there was constant political, cultural and economic friction between Belgium's Dutch speaking Flemings and French speaking Walloons.

Already, though, King Leopold's brother, Charles of Flanders, had been appointed Regent until Belgium and the Allies decided whether or not the king could continue to reign. It was, perhaps, an indication of the widespread antagonism that in June 1946 a reduction in postage rates led post offices to be authorised to

6.1 2f75 'V' on Lion Rampant: from set 10 November 1944.

6.2 15c 'V' overprinted on Arms series: from set 10 November 1944.

overprint three stamp values bearing his portrait and V emblem with '-10%'. As this example shows, some officials were less than careful about obliterating their king's image.(6.3) And it was the pre-war state arms set, not the royal portrait set, that was extended with several new values from 65c to 1f in 1945.(6.4)

On 1 May 1945, a week before the war officially ended, two large stamps raised funds for the numerous victims of the conflict. One featured their desperate plight, the other hopeful signs of rebuilding homes. (6.5) The pair were reissued in July, specifically on behalf of the Post Office Employees' Relief Fund, in new colours, smaller in size, and with different values.(6.6) The next set that September embraced nine stamps featuring soldiers, resistance fighters, an execution, and a father and child in aid of the Prisoners of War Fund. (6.7) Tens of thousands were returning home to rebuild their lives after internment in Germany.

In December 1945 an early post-war opportunity was taken to encourage a sense of unity by featuring the Coat of Arms of each Belgian province on an anti-TB campaign set.(6.8) Friction between Flemings and Walloons remained high as many Flemings were rural pro-monarchy Liberals or Christian Democrats and most Walloons urban anti-monarchy Socialists. Diplomatically the set carefully scattered the nine Flemish and Walloon provinces among the high and low values. Two further anti-TB sets in December 1946 and December 1947 celebrated a range of Flemish and Walloon towns and their traditional industries.(6.9, 6.10)

Later sets supporting anti-TB funds took a different approach. In December 1948 three small stamps highlighted the international campaign's emblem, the

6.5 1f+30f Victims of war: from set 1 May 1945.

6.6 1f+9f Rebuilding homes: from set 21 July 1945.

6.7 20c+20c Father and child, 75c+50c Prisoner and letter, and 1f50+1f Execution: from set 10 September 1945.

6.3 1f50 King Leopold and V (from set 18 December 1944+) overprinted -10%: from set 2 June 1946.

6.4 1f Arms: from additional values 1945+.

Cross of Lorraine, and two larger ones featured Archduke Albert VII (1559-1621) and his wife Isabella (1566-1633).(6.11) Formerly a Cardinal and Viceroy of Portugal, Albert became military Governor General of the Netherlands in 1595, and then at King Philip II's behest he resigned from the College of Cardinals, married Philip's daughter Isabella, and together they ruled the Hapsburg Netherlands from 1598 until Albert's death in 1621. The Catholic southern provinces were largely peaceful, although years of inconclusive war against the Protestant northern ones only ended with a tense truce in 1609. Nevertheless Albert and Isabella sought overall peace, and eventually secured it, meaning agriculture, industry and trade could recover, the judicial system be overhauled, and the Arts encouraged.

The following December four small stamps pictured wild flowers and five larger ones some more historical figures - all of which reinforced the concept of strong rulers protecting citizens and encouraging peaceful commerce.(6.12) Indeed all five figures possessed domains far exceeding modern Belgium in size and could be said to represent the virtues of large interconnected economies - something many in post-war Europe were considering. The 1f75+25c portrayed the powerful Philip the Good, Duke of Burgundy (1396-1467), under whose rule Belgium prospered economically and culturally. In his never-ending conflict with France, though, he was responsible for the capture of Joan of Arc. The 3f+1f50 portrayed the Holy Roman Emperor, Charles V (1500-58), ruler of Spain and vast swathes of land extending from the Low Countries to Italy. The Low Countries were prosperous, and despite minor revolts most provinces saw the advantage of remaining loyal. The 4f+2f portrayed Maria Christina (1742-98), daughter of Empress Maria Theresa and later Duchess of Teschen, who shared the Governorship of the Austrian Netherlands (including modern Belgium) with her husband on behalf of the

6.10 90c+60c St Truiden and fruit, and 1f35+1f15 Charleroi and mining: from set 15 December 1947.

6.8 10c+15c West Flanders (Flanders) and 1f+75c Hainaut (Walloon): from set 1 December 1945.

6.11 1f+30c Cross of Lorraine, 4f+3f25 Isabella of Austria, and 20f+20f Archduke Albert: from set 15 December 1948.

6.9 1f35+1f15 Ostend and fishing, and 3f15+1f85 Verviers and textiles: from set 2 December 1946.

6.12 1f20+30c Poppy, 1f75+25c Philip of Burgundy, 3f+1f50 Emperor Charles V, and 6f+3f Charles of Lorraine:from set 20 December 1949.

Holy Roman Emperor. Much of the time they sought to counter ill-considered Imperial plans for centralising the control of education, the judiciary and taxation that aroused unrest, and eventually rebellion. The 6f+3f portrayed Prince Charles of Lorraine (1712-80) who was an efficient and popular Governor of the Hapsburg Low Countries. The 8f+4f portrayed the Empress Maria Theresa (1717-80) who fought against all male opposition to become a successful ruler of the vast Holy Roman Empire (including the Low Countries), holding Prussia at bay in major wars, improving military and administrative efficiency, and introducing better education, medical care, and freer internal trade.

In June 1946 a set commemorated the centenary of the important Ostend to Dover mail-boat service.(6.13) It was also a celebration of the post-war resumption of normal services. The set featured three ships under way - the first mail-boat, the *Chemin de Fer* (later renamed *Diamant*) (1f35), the fast record breaking paddle steamer *Henriette-Marie* that was wrecked on a reef in October 1914 (2f25), and the modern twin screw diesel powered *Prince Baudouin* built in 1934 (3f15). The route operated its first purpose-built car ferry in 1949.

The first post-war Belgian airmail stamps appeared in April 1946. *SABENA*, the national airline had started operations in 1923, and in 1930 the first airmail set had featured an early mainstay, the German Fokker F.VIIB. During the war all flights ceased, except to the Belgian Congo. Not surprisingly the 1946 set featured an American aircraft, the Douglas DC-4 OO-DAA ,which flew on *SABENA's* first transatlantic flights to New York that June.(6.14) With the USA as much as Belgium in mind a new pair of airmail stamps was issued in June featuring a paratrooper and inscribed *BASTOGNE IN MEMORIAM*.(6.15) The high surtax contributed towards a monument in the town of Bastogne where in December 1944 a disparate force of American troops in

6.13 3f15 'Chemin de Fer'/'Diamant': from set 15 June 1946.

the Ardennes refused to surrender to the advancing Germans who had encircled the town, and held them off under eventually relieved..

In July 1946 three coordinated sets of three stamps appeared celebrating national figures who fearlessly imperilled their lives by supporting the oppressed. Francois Bovesse (1890-1944) was a politician and government minister from Namur who campaigned for Walloon's cultural and linguistic identity through which he believed national stability could be achieved. Vigorously opposing any official recognition of the right wing neo-Nazi Rexist party, during the war he was imprisoned and then murdered by Rexist collaborators. (6.16) Emile Vandervelde (1866-1938) was a Fleming, a leading figure in the Belgian Labour Party, and as a minister he supported many social reforms, including prisons, trades unions, and women's rights. An ardent Socialist, and a long standing president of the Labour & Socialist International, he totally opposed the destruction of Russia's Socialist-Revolutionary Party by Lenin and the Bolsheviks in 1922. As a result he achieved fame by being mocked in a work by the Soviet poet Vladimir Mayakovsky.(6.17) The third figure was the revered Roman Catholic priest, Father Damien (1840-89) who spent much of his life caring for the lepers on the Hawaiian island of Molokai. Eventually he, too, succumbed to the disease.(6.18) One stamp in each set featured a portrait, the other two symbols of his career - in Bovesse's set it was symbols of patriotism and mourning, in Vandevelde's set it was a miner's family and a sower, and in Father Damien's it was the leper colony and his grave. In 1947 these nine stamps were specially selected to be overprinted with new values and *LUCHTPOST POSTE AERIENNE* to be used at New York's International Stamp Exhibition in preference to the September 1946 airmail stamp - which contained a rather nondescript allegory of Flight.

In August and September 1946 another set equally clearly promoted national self-consciousness and unity but this time with celebrated warriors.(6.19) Somewhat ironically the premium went towards the War Victims' Relief Fund. The 75c+25c featured Pepin de Herstal (c635-714) whose ability led him to become mayor of the palace (essentially the power behind the throne) of Frankish Austrasia embracing modern Belgium and parts of France, Germany and the Netherlands, and then, after further battles, he rose to be Duke and Prince of the Franks. The 1f+50c featured Charlemagne (748-814) whose military and diplomatic skills unified and Christianised (often forcibly) much of western and central Europe leading to the grateful Pope Leo III recognising him as a new 'Emperor of the Romans'. The 1f50+1f featured Godfrey of Bouillon (1060-1100) who inherited, and had to vigorously defend, the Duchy of Lower Lotharingia which embraced the modern Netherlands, central and eastern Belgium and the northern Rhineland. However his lasting fame rested on his reputation as the Crusader who captured Jerusalem and became its Christian ruler. The 3f50+1f50 featured Robert II, Count of Flanders (c1065-1111), another Crusader whose prowess contributed to victories at Antioch, Arqa, Jerusalem and Ascalon. Finally the 5f+45f featured Baudouin (1172-c1205) who inherited Flanders in 1194, recovered Hainaut soon afterwards,

6.16 1f35+2f Francois Bovesse and 1f75+18f Mourning Bovesse: from set 16 July 1946.

6.14 8f Douglas DC-4 OO-DAA: from set 20 April 1946+.

6.15 Illustrated cover with set of Bastogne Memorial Fund stamps issued 15 June 1946 with Bastogne postmark dated 4 July 1946 flown to Washington, USA.

6.17 65c+75c Father Damien and 1f75+18f Damien and leper: from set 16 July 1946.

6.18 65c+75c Emile Vandervelde and 1f35+2f Vandervelde and social reform: from set 16 July 1946.

6.19 75c+25c Pepin de Herstal, 1f+50c Charlemagne and 1f50+1f Godfrey of Bouillon; from set 16 August 1946+.

and laid down a long-lasting legal code before joining the Fourth Crusade. When the Crusaders captured Constantinople Baudouin was elected Latin Emperor, but the following year he was seized and killed by a rival. In November 1946 this stamp was reissued in a different shade to raise funds for the restoration of the historic Chateau de Beaulieu in Brussels, the residence of many illustrious visitors to Belgium, including England's King William III (reigned 1689-1702) and the renowned general in the wars against France, John Churchill, Duke of Marlborough (1650-1722).(6.20)

In September 1947 a second set appeared, similarly devoted to the historic theme of preserving the nation and ensuring its prosperity.(6.21) The 65c+35c pictured John II, Duke of Brabant (1275-1312), who countered French intrigues and was celebrated for his Charter of Kortenberg granting freedoms to towns, promising fair taxation and establishing equity under the law for all citizens. In contrast, England's Magna Carta had limited itself to the barons. The 90c+60c pictured Philippe of Alsace, Count of Flanders (1143-91), who fought numerous diplomatic and military campaigns to preserve his inheritance and ensure it prospered, and took part in two Crusades. The 1f35+1f15 pictured William the Good, Count of Hainaut, Avesnes, Holland and Zeeland (c1286-1337). A warlike defender of his lands, he shrewdly married his four daughters to key rulers, including Philippa who became Queen of Edward III in England. The 3f15+1f85 pictured Notger, Bishop of Liege (c940-1008), who made the city and its environs an ecclesiastical centre with a new cathedral and abbeys, and a celebrated school. The 20f+20f pictured Philip the Noble, Margrave of Namur (1175-1212), who wrestled his inheritance free from Luxembourg, resolved the interminable baronial conflicts, and stabilised the economy.

Belgian painters were celebrated. In April 1949 a 50 franc miniature sheet issued on behalf of national welfare and cultural funds featured three devotional

6.20 5f+45f Baudouin: 15 November 1946.

6.21 1f35+1f15 William of Hainaut and 3f15+1f85 Notger, Bishop of Liege: from set 25 September 1947+.

6.22 90c 'Woman reading', 1f75 'The flute player' and 4f 'Old woman reading a letter': from miniature sheet 1 April 1949.

6.23 1f75 Mary Magdalene: 15 July 1949.

6.24 3f15 Joseph Plateau: June 1947.

works attributed to Rogier van der Weyden (c1399-1464). Born in Tournai, now in Belgium, then in the Netherlands, he rose to become the wealthy and prestigious 'city painter' of Brussels, then a political and cultural centre of the Valois Dukes of Burgundy. The sheet featured his *Madonna & Child, Crucifixion* and *Mary Magdalene*. Another 50 franc miniature sheet that April featured paintings by Jacob Jordaens (1593-1678) who lived and worked in Antwerp. Although he, too, painted altar pieces, the sheet features his more intimate *Woman reading, The flute player* and *Old woman reading a letter*.(6.22)

In July 1949 Bruges hosted an exhibition of the paintings of Gerard David (c1460-1534). Born in Bruges where he mainly worked, David was a highly successful painter of religious scenes, notably for altar pieces. However his fame faded and he was long forgotten until the late nineteenth century and it was only in the twentieth century that his reputation as a master of colour was restored. On 15 July 1949 a stamp marked the exhibition with his image of Mary Magdalene from the reverse side of a wing of his 1505 triptych *The Baptism of Christ*.(6.23) The choice of Mary Magdalene for the stamp, from many other people depicted on the triptych, may well have been made to favour the Roman Catholic Church and send out a message of post-war conciliation and unity.

In June 1947 two relatively modern Belgians were commemorated. The International Film & Belgian Fine Arts Festival was marked with a stamp featuring Joseph Plateau (1801-83), whose pioneering work on visual perception laid the foundations for films.(6.24) One experiment - his phenakistiscope - comprised counter-rotating disks, one of which had a series of repeated but slightly different drawings and the other regularly spaced slits. When the two discs rotated the illusion of motion was created. Two other stamps commemorated the 50th anniversary of the Belgian Antarctic Expedition with pictures of its leader, Adrien de Gerlache de Gomery (1866-1934) and his ship, *Belgica*.(6.25) After crossing the Antarctic Circle in February 1898 the expedition was trapped in thick ice for seven months. Several crew members became insane, and many others suffered from scurvy. Nevertheless, despite very modest scientific

6.25 1f35 Adrien de Gerlache de Gomery and 2f25 Belgica and explorers: set 9 June 1947.

6.27 65c+35c Edward Anseele monument and 90c+60c Anseele and Ghent: from set 21 June 1948.

achievements, this was the age of heroic polar expeditions and Belgium's national pride ensured lavish celebrations greeted the men's return.

In April 1948 a set of four stamps raised funds for Achel Abbey, and another set for Chevremont Basilica and Malines Campanologists' School. Achel Abbey in Flanders, famous for its brewery, dates back to the seventeenth century, but suffered closure and destruction during the French Revolutionary Wars and again in the First World War. A new abbey was started in 1946. Chevremont Basilica near Liege (1f35+1f35) was built as a place of Marian pilgrimage between 1877 and 1899 only to be heavily damaged by German bombardments in 1914.(6.26) Repairs were funded by German post-war reparations, but it was badly damaged again in 1940 and 1944. Reconstruction, largely by German prisoners of war began in 1946. The 65c+65c stamp refers to the story of the seventh century St Begge or Bega, the daughter of Pepin de Landen, the powerful palace mayor of the Frankish king. She married Ansegisel, another powerful courtier, who rebuilt Chevremont castle. Their descendants, probably their grandson, started the Carolingian dynasty of French kings. As a widow Begge founded several chapels and nunneries in the region. After the Second World War the Roman Catholic Church still exercised considerable authority across Belgium, especially in its rural areas. The Church was strongly represented in the powerful centre-leftist Christian Democrat Party which worked in alliance, and ruling coalitions, with the Socialists. However times were changing, endowments were thin on the ground, and both Achel and Chevremont found it difficult to raise funds.

6.26 65c+65c St Begge and Chevremont Castle and 1f35+1f35 Chevremont Basilica: from set 5 April 1948.

In June 1948 a set of four stamps marked the unveiling of a striking statue to the Socialist politician Edward Anseele (1856-1938).(6.27). He created a vast cooperative business to challenge the capitalist system and was the founder of the Belgian Labour Party (recast as the Socialist Party in 1945) which between the wars forced a reforming coalition onto the hitherto dominant Christian Democrats that lasted into the post-war world. The stamps portray him and his home city of Ghent, and his statue there.

In September 1948 two stamps featuring figures representing Liberty and Resistance raised funds for monuments in Liege and Antwerp, each of which endured occupation and substantial damage during both world wars.(6.28) Both cities subsequently erected striking memorials - Liege's featuring two armed resistance fighters in smooth Modernist sculptured format, and Antwerp's a tall single figure blackened and badly scarred but unbroken.

By this date King Leopold III's position remained unresolved. Although he had refused to administer Belgium as the Germans asked, his surrender was deemed unconstitutional by his prime minister and only in 1946 was he officially exonerated from acting treasonably, not least in meeting Hitler. After the war he lived near Geneva, unable to return to Belgium as the Allies and Belgian government feared civil war would break out as feelings for and against him were so strong. It probably did not help his case that in July 1949 four

6.28 10f+10f 'Resistance': from set 4 September 1948.

6.29 3f King Leopold 1: from set 1 July 1949.

stamps of a set celebrating the centenary of Belgian stamps featured his forbear King Leopold I (reigned 1831-65), a much respected international figure.(6.29) The situation was exacerbated in 1950 when a referendum led 70% of Flemings to approve his return but only 42% of Walloons. As this created a seemingly favourable majority Leopold re-entered the country, only for violence and strikes to break out. Under government pressure he abdicated in August 1950 in favour of his son Baudouin.

By then Belgium aspired to a key role in forging European political and economic cooperation, a policy pursued with skill and success by Paul-Henri Spaak, Belgium's Socialist prime minister and internationally respected statesman. Belgium's good transport connections, as epitomised by the stamp (using the latest railways parcel design) in October 1949 celebrating the electrification of the Brussels to Charleroi line, and the particularly striking stamp celebrating the 75th anniversary of the Universal Postal Union in 1949, all signalled its interest in wider economy and political union. (6.30, 6.31) Perhaps, too, its stamp marking the 50th anniversary of the death of the Roman Catholic priest and poet Guido Gezelle (1830-99) in November 1949 subtly signalled the peace-making mood.(6.32) Although Belgium had been often at odds with its neighbour, the Netherlands, Father Gezelle's promotion of the Flemish language in his essentially religious poems made him a revered figure in both countries - whose history was fraught with mutual animosity. In 1948 Belgium had joined with the Netherlands and Luxembourg in the Benelux Economic Union,

Under the European Recovery Programme (the Marshall Plan), from 1948 until 1951 the USA gave Belgium $559,000,000 in grants to promote productivity, and to do so along American lines of innovation and corporatist negotiations with all partners in order to raise productivity and keep wages high. The Belgians largely evaded American business practice but the grants were invaluable in accelerating the revival of road, rail and shipping transport links and modernising farms and factories. No doubt the set of twelve stamps in 1948-49 featuring key aspects of the modern Belgian economy - but also not forgetting traditional lace making - was timed to greet the initial grants.(6.33,

6.30 60f Type 101 electric locomotive (for the electrified Brussels to Charleroi line): 15 October 1949.

6.31 4f 75th Anniversary of the UPU: 1 October 1949.

6.32 1f75+75c Guido Gezelle: 15 November 1949

6.34) No doubt, too, they were intended to promote Belgian exports. In 1951 Belgium was an enthusiastic founder member of the European Coal & Steel Community along with France, Germany, Italy, Luxembourg and the Netherlands. However, despite the strengthening economy and high industrial wages many Belgians outside these relatively privileged workers, and especially in rural areas, remained poor.

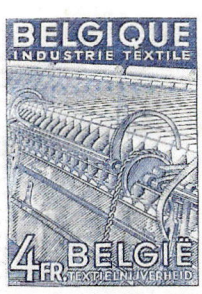

6.33 60c Chemicals, 1f35 Lace, and 1f75 Farm produce: from set 2 February 1948+.

6.34 2f25 Antwerp docks, 4f Textiles, and 6f30 Steel works: from set 2 February 1948+.

CHAPTER 7

LUXEMBOURG

All hopes of Luxembourg remaining neutral in the Second World War were dashed when German forces invaded on 10 May 1940. Grand Duchess Charlotte and her chief ministers fled to France and then Spain before setting up their government-in-exile in London. Luxembourg was reduced to the administrative status of a German province or *Gau*, with the French language forbidden, young men liable for German military or labour service, and Jews increasingly persecuted. A small but vocal collaborationist party urged full incorporation into Greater Germany, as had happened in Austria, and this occurred in 1942. Up until December 1941 Luxembourg stamps were issued overprinted with German values; after that only German stamps were available. As elsewhere, resistance groups were formed, and many other men fled to avoid conscription

Luxembourg was liberated in September 1944, with little German resistance. However, much of the northern part was temporarily reoccupied by the Germans during their Ardennes offensive in December 1944, and witnessed heavy and destructive fighting. Hundreds of civilians died, and thousands more became homeless refugees. After the war many collaborators were imprisoned, and Luxembourg abandoned all thoughts of neutrality and worked actively towards the creation of NATO. There was a seamless return to positions of authority by the pre-war and exiled rightist Christian Social People's ministry of Pierre Dupong and Joseph Beck.

Although in the event somewhat precipitate, 'liberated' Luxembourg issued its first definitive stamps portraying Grand Duchess Charlotte on 6 November 1944.(7.1) On 1 March 1945, after the final expulsion of the Germans, an elaborate set thanked the major victors. The common feature was the Arms of Luxembourg, with 60c+60c showing the ship symbol of

7.2 Thanks to France, the USSR, Great Britain and the USA: Liberation set 1 March 1945.

7.1 1f75 Grand Duchess Charlotte: from set 6 November 1944+.

Paris and the cross of Lorraine, the 1.20f +1.80f a man killing a snake and the Arms of the Soviet Union, the 2.50f+3.50f Britannia and George VI's badge (GRI under a crown), and the 4.20f+4.80f an eagle and the Arms of the USA.(7.2)

During the next few months several stamps were issued bearing the image of the crowned Lion of Luxembourg.(7.3) Alongside them were two striking sets linked to the war. On 4 June 1945, a set and miniature sheet contained various views of the shrine and ancient lime-wood statue of Our Lady of Luxembourg in the city's Notre Dame Cathedral.(7.4)

7.3 1f20 Lion of Luxembourg: from set 15 May 1945+.

7.4 60c+40c Madonna in procession and 2f50+2f50 Madonna over Luxembourg: from set 4 June 1945.

7.5 20c+30c Resistance fighters and 5f+10f Execution: from set 20 December 1945.

7.6 5f Hamm military cemetery and 10f General Patton and the Ardennes: from set 24 October.

Carried in an annual procession during the post-Easter Octave, the Virgin Mary was the duchy's patron saint, and the statue became a symbol of nationhood and hope for many during the war. In a long line of royal gifts to the shrine, Grand Duchess Charlotte had recently presented to it the rosary she used throughout her exile.

In sharp contrast, but also perhaps complementary, that December a starkly illustrated set and miniature sheet promoted the National War Victims' Fund.(7.5) The 20c+30c featured three young men, not all in uniform, with the inscription *FIR ONS JONGEN ZALDOT a MAQUISARD (FOR OUR YOUNG SOLDIER AND MAQUISARD)*. Maquisard referred to resistance fighters, but especially those in the rural bush - the 'maquis'. The 1.50f+1f featured a desperate mother and child, the 3.50f+3.50f an emaciated political prisoner, and the 5f+10f a man shot at the stake. In December 1945 memories were still raw. On 24 October 1947 the Grand Duchy issued a set with two designs honouring General George S Patton, the flamboyant commander of the American Third Army responsible for pushing the Germans out of Luxembourg after their ill-fated Ardennes campaign in December 1944.(7.6) Patton died after a car crash in December 1945 and chose to be buried with Third Army men in Luxembourg's Hamm American Cemetery.

On 25 May 1947 an attractive and informative set promoted the restoration of the ancient Benedictine Abbey of Echternach in eastern Luxembourg.(7.7) It was another reflection on the war and the Grand Duchy's capacity for survival and recovery. In 1944 shelling during the German-American Ardennes battles destroyed part of the basilica and for the sixth time the abbey needed to be rebuilt or heavily restored since its foundation in the seventh century by Pepin of Herstal (c635-714), de facto ruler of the Frankish Empire, and St Willibrord (c658-739), an apostle (originally from Northumbria) to the pagan Frisians and first bishop of Utrecht. It was reconsecrated in 1953.

Several other Caritas (Charity) issues commemorated famous figures linked to the Grand Duchy's history and unique culture. A set in December 1946 marked the sixth centenary of the death of King John the Blind

7.7 1f50+50c Ruined interior of basilica and 25f+25f St Willibrord: from set 25 May 1947.

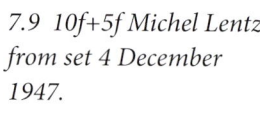

7.9 10f+5f Michel Lentz: from set 4 December 1947.

7.10 3f50+3f50 Edmund de la Fontaine: from set 18 November 1948.

7.8 1f50+50c King John the Blind: from set 5 December 1946.

7.11 2f+1f Michel Rodange: from set 5 December 1949.

(1296-1346) who was King of Bohemia from 1310, Count of Luxembourg from 1313 and one of the electors of the Holy Roman Emperor.(7.8) A major European figure and arbiter of conflicts, John went blind but supported France in the Hundred Years War and died fighting against the English at Crecy. He was buried in Luxembourg but during the Napoleonic Wars his body was taken to Germany from where it was restored to Luxembourg in 1945.

During the late 1940s the annual National Welfare Fund sets featured celebrated Luxembourg writers. In December 1947 it was Michel Lentz (1820-93), who wrote the Grand Duchy's national anthem.(7.9) In December 1948 it was Edmund de la Fontaine (1823-91), known as 'Dicks', another celebrated poet in the Luxembourgish language.(7.10) In December 1949 it was Michel Rodange (1827-76) who relocated the ancient stories of Reynard the Fox into a Luxembourg setting and wove local dialects, character traits and foibles into the numerous animals filling his satirical epic, *Renert*.(7.11)

7.12 4f+15c Jean Antoine Zinnen: from set 5 December 1950.

In December 1950 the set featured Jean Antoine Zinnen (1827-98), the director of Luxembourg's city conservatoire who composed the music for Michel Lentz's national anthem.(7.12)

And as late as June 1950 Luxembourg was still raising funds for its War Orphans Fund through a set of poignant stamps featuring a haunted looking young girl and emaciated mother and child.(7.13)

A scattering of sets paid attention to Luxembourg's landscape and communications as a tourist destination.

7.13 1f20c War Orphans Fund: from set 24 June 1950.

7.14 5f Wing and city view, 10f Wheel and river view, and 50f Engine and castle view: from Air set 7 June 1946.

In June 1946 the first, and for many years the only, post-war Air set was issued, perhaps as a precursor to the establishment of Luxembourg Airlines (later Luxair) in 1948.(7.14) The stamps featured views of the Duchy from the air.

A striking miniature sheet accompanying the National Stamp Exhibition in 1946 featured men working at the Old Rolling Mill at Dudelange, the host city.(7.15) Further views of the Grand Duchy appeared in a wide ranging Tourist Publicity set in 1948 embracing the northern hills and forests of L'Oesling (7f), the River Moselle along the eastern border (10f), the iron ore mines in the south (Le Bassin Minier) (15f) and historic Luxembourg city itself (20f).(7.16) The Grand Duchy's post-war self-publicity was well under way.

Between 1948 and 1958 a second definitive set appeared portraying a more regal, more mature, Grand Duchess Charlotte.(7.17) Her dynasty was safe and her realm steadily prospering.

7.15 50f The old rolling mill at Dudelange: 28 July 1946.

EUROPEAN STAMP ISSUES AND THE AFTERMATH OF THE SECOND WORLD WAR: 1944–1949

7.16 7f L'Oesling, 10f Moselle, 15f Le Bassin Minier, and 20f Luxembourg City: from set 5 August 1948+.

7.17 1f Grand Duchess Charlotte: from set 1948+.

CHAPTER 8

THE NETHERLANDS

The Netherlands remained free and neutral throughout the First World War, and trusted it would do so in any future conflict. However starting on 10 May 1940 German forces pushed aside its outdated army and after Rotterdam was heavily bombed and Utrecht threatened with a similar onslaught the Dutch commander-in-chief surrendered on 15 May. By then Queen Wilhelmina and her ministers had escaped on a British destroyer to establish a government-in-exile in London. The Queen regularly broadcast to the Netherlands and remained a focus of loyalty and symbol of nationhood. In the Netherlands the Germans initially implemented a policy of *Gleichschaltung* (enforced conformity) which proved popular with Dutch businesses as the commercial German market remained open to them but unpopular elsewhere as all non-Nazi parties, publications and institutions were banned. Around 20,000 men served in the two Dutch Waffen-SS brigades while about 3,000 men served in the Dutch Princess Irene Brigade alongside the Allies and others joined American and Canadian units. Several Dutch warships fought with Allied fleets, and the Dutch formed two RAF squadrons.

When Allied forces advanced rapidly to the Dutch border in 1944, there was general rejoicing at the prospect of imminent liberation only for the population to endure months of fighting and shortages as various Allied operations ran into stubborn German resistance. In September 1944 Operation Market Garden liberated parts of the south but failed to cross the Rhine into the north. The Germans defended the Scheldt estuary until October and Walcheren Island until November, and finally opened the dykes to flood Holland in the north. Here the Dutch endured the bitter Hongewinter (hunger winter) until the war ended. Thousands starved to death. The Netherlands had the highest per capita death rate throughout western Europe with 205,000 deaths of which about 107,000 were Jews. Alongside Rotterdam, cities such as Nijmegen, Arnhem and The Hague were badly damaged, and transport systems wrecked. After the war many collaborators were prosecuted and imprisoned, and in 1946 several thousand Germans living in the Netherlands were deported under the 'Black Tulip' programme.

In June 1944, at the time of the D-Day landings, a set of nine stamps featuring Queen Wilhelmina, a soldier, airman, the Dutch cruiser *De Ruyter* and liner *Nieuw Amsterdam* were issued for use initially by personnel on Dutch warships serving with the Allies.(8.1) Further values portraying the Queen were added on 1 April 1946 when the set became available across the Netherlands. Named after a famous seventeenth century Dutch admiral, the *De Ruyter* was completed in 1936, but its seven 5.9 inch guns rendered it less powerful than most other light cruisers of the time. On 27 February 1942 it was sunk along with its sister ship Java by Japanese heavy cruisers in a disastrous encounter off the Java coast. The prestigious 36,000 ton liner *Nieuw Amsterdam* had a far more successful career. Beginning service in 1938 she became a stylish and popular means of crossing the Atlantic. During the war she was requisitioned by the British as a major troop transport, and after the war she was refitted first as a luxury liner and then as a cruise ship. She was not scrapped until 1974.

8.1 2½c Liner 'Nieuw Amsterdam', 5c Cruiser 'De Ruyter', and 20c Queen Wilhelmina: from set 156 June 1944+.

8.2 7½c Liberation: 15 July 1945.

EUROPEAN STAMP ISSUES AND THE AFTERMATH OF THE SECOND WORLD WAR: 1944–1949

The Netherlands' Liberation issue was a single stamp issued on 15 July 1945 featuring a lion battling a dragon. (8.2) It adorned numerous celebratory covers.

Throughout the rest of the decade various definitive issues featured the popular Queen Wilhelmina, culminating in her Golden Jubilee pair on 30 August 1948.(8.3, 8.4) Interspersed with these, however, was a series starting in 1946, mainly for booklets, whose bland abstract design was strangely reminiscent of the wartime wavy line overprints of October 1940 on the pre-war 'carrier pigeon' definitive set.(8.5)

Wilhelmina abdicated on 4 September 1948 in favour of her daughter Juliana who soon appeared on a pair of coronation stamps and then on her own definitive sets. (8.6, 8.7) In May 1950 superannuated stocks of the 7½c Queen Wilhelmina definitive were overprinted '6 (c)' in an emergency shortage when postal rates changed.(8.8)

On 1 May 1946 a set of five stamps featuring a stylish and optimistic emblem of future 'Abundance' raised

8.6 20c Queen Juliana's Coronation: from set 6 September 1948.

8.7 5c Queen Juliana definitive: from set July 1949+.

8.3 1g Queen Wilhelmina: from set 1946, and 6c: from set 1947+.

8.8 6(c) overprint on 7½c Queen Wilhelmina definitive: May 1949.

8.4 20c Queen Wilhelmina's Golden Jubilee: from set 30 August 1948.

8.9 2½c+5c 'Abundance': from set 1 May 1946.

8.5 2½c definitive: from set 1 November 1946.

8.10 5c+5c Child Welfare: from set 1 December 1945.

THE NETHERLANDS

funds for the numerous victims of war.(8.9) However shortages and hardship were widespread, rationing was tight and thousands emigrated to North America and Australia. Successive coalitions between the Catholic People's Party and socialist inclined Labour Party worked towards economic reconstruction, the creation of a welfare state, and integrating the country into new cooperative European and international organisations such as NATO, the Benelux Economic Union and the European Coal & Steel Community. In due course much rested on Marshall Plan funds.

Understandably many surtaxed sets centred upon child welfare charities. In December 1945 a set featured the sad face of a little girl, and exactly a year later a set pictured a happier looking boy on a roundabout.(8.10, 8.11) Inbetween them, in September 1946, a further child welfare set featured the Queen's three grandchildren - Princessses Irene, Margreit and Beatrix. As widely appreciated across the country, the royal family took great interest in child welfare.(8.12)

Later child welfare sets continued in optimistic vein. In December 1947 a set of five featured photographs of a baby's face and a group of sturdy well-dressed children. (8.13) In November 1948 a set of five drawings featured happy and healthy children swinging, swimming,

8.11 4c+2c Child Welfare: from set 2 December 1946.

8.12 Princesses Irene, Margreit and Beatrix: from set 16 September 1946.

8.13 2c+2c Group of children and 10c+5c Baby: from set 1 December 1947.

8.14 6c+4c Boy tobogganing and 10c+5c Girl on swing: from set 15 November 1948.

8.15 5c+3c Summer and 10c+5c Winter: from set 14 November 1949.

canoeing, skating, and tabogganing.(8.14) These two sets noted the surtax in tiny writing at the foot of the stamps. The following year the set pictured children in spring, summer, autumn, New Year and winter, and the surtax was more clearly marked.(8.15) The sets were inscribed *VOOR HET KIND (FOR THE CHILD).* They reflected not only the signs of recovery from the wartime distress but also the significant increase in the post-war birth rate as war weary young adults married and started to look forward, not back.

In August 1947 a set raising money for the Cultural and Social Relief programme featured an eclectic group

97

8.16 Cultural & Social Relief Fund: complete set 1 August 1947.

8.17 2c+2c Ridderzaal and 10c+5c Kneuterdijk Palace: from set 17 June 1948.

of celebrated Dutch figures and, presumably deliberately, used a portrait style previously used during the war. (8.16) The tiny words at the foot of the stamp included the person's name and occupation and the specific surtax ZOMERZEGEL BIJSLAG 2, 2½, 5 CENTS GELDIG T/M 31/12/48 (SUMMER STAMP SUPPLEMENT 2, 2½, 5 CENTS VALID UNTIL 31/12/48). The 2c+2c pictured Hendrik van Deventer (1651-1724), a pioneer of modern obstetrics, and clearly linked to post-war child welfare campaign. The other figures harked back to various Dutch wars and the nation's reaction to threats to its prosperity and integrity. The 4c+2c pictured Pieter Corneliszoon Hooft (1581-1647), a poet, playwright and historian of the recent Dutch wars against Spain. The 7½c+2½c portrayed Johann de Wit (1625-72), the powerful Republican leader of the Dutch United Provinces who brought mercantile prosperity but also costly wars with England and France and was eventually murdered by the mob. The 10c+5c pictured Jean Francois van Royen (1878-1942), the General Secretary of the Dutch State's Post, Telegraph & Telephony Company(PTT). He is remembered for creating the Netherlands Organisation of Artists during the war to counter pressure to form a pro-Nazi artists' organisation. In 1942 he was arrested and imprisoned, accused of opposing the German *Kultuurkamer* which obliged all artists to affiliate to it in order to work. The 20c+5c pictured Hugo Grotius (1583-1645), lawyer, theologian and statesman whose books *On the Law of War and Peace* and *The Free Seas* long influenced European nations, the former by defining the just war and proposing international rules of war, the latter by justifying free maritime trade and rejecting maritime trading monopolies.

In June 1948 the Cultural and Social Relief set pictured state buildings with both a significant history and modern relevance to the restored constitutional monarchy and to the democratically elected government.(8.17) The 2c+2c featured the medieval Ridderzaal (Hall of Knights) in The Hague where the monarch arrived in the Golden Coach to deliver the royal speech before Parliament. The 6c+4c featured the seventeenth century Royal Palace of Amsterdam, used primarily for state functions. The 10c+5c featured the eighteenth century Kneuterdijk Palace in The Hague, formerly a royal palace, then a court trying Second World War collaborators, and afterwards the Ministry of Finance. The 20c+5c featured the Gothic Protestant Nieuwe Kerk (New Church) in Amsterdam where royal investitures and weddings took place.

Preferring to strike a far more populist note, a radically modern Cultural and Social Relief set in May 1949 pictured people at the seaside, hikers in the countryside, campers around a fire, yachts under sail, and harvesters.

In 1950, however, a set of six surtaxed Cultural and Social Relief stamps returned to the war and its aftermath.(8.19) They featured images of an emaciated resistance fighter (as a model for a monument) (2c+2c), the rebuilding of the huge Moerdijk pontoon road and railway bridge destroyed by the German 15th army as it retreated into North Holland in 1944 (10c+5c), and resealing the dykes broken by the retreating Germans (4c+2c). Three others pictured a canal freighter reusing the canals, a new skyscraper representing the rebuilding

8.18 2c+2c On the beach and 5c+3c Hiking in the country: from set 2 May 1949.

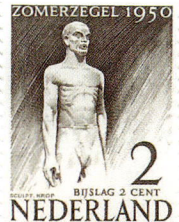

8.19 2c+2c Resistance monument, 4c+2c Resealing dykes, and 10c+5c Repairing Moerdijk Bridge: from set 2 May 1950.

of Rotterdam, and peaceful mechanical harvesting. 1950 also saw a set of five stamps raising funds for the rebuilding of the Netherlands' bombed churches.(8.20) Full recovery took many years.

On 1 August 1949 a set of four surtaxed stamps picturing white and brown hands reaching for a sunflower were issued in support of the Red Cross and the Indonesian Relief Fund.(8.21) This overtly humanitarian issue occurred as four years of fighting between Dutch forces and Indonesian nationalists were coming to an end. Many atrocities had been committed by each side. For three centuries the Dutch had struggled to impose their rule over the East Indies and had engaged in endless wars against local island rulers, but in December 1949 the Netherlands had little choice but to formally recognise Indonesian sovereignty. Ejected by the Japanese during the war, the Dutch had returned in 1945 only to find Indonesians even more determined to be free of foreign rule. The irony of the Dutch suffering under German occupation and then attempting to deny Indonesia its independence was not lost on contemporary commentators.

8.20 20c+5c Good Samaritan and bombed church: from set 17 July 1950.

8.21 30c+10c Hands reaching for sunflower: from set 1 August 1949.

CHAPTER 9

DENMARK

Not surprisingly, with a troubled history of relations with Germany over the contested border provinces of Schleswig and Holstein, Denmark was an enthusiastic member of the inter-war League of Nations, and Hitler's rise to power in 1933 filled it with alarm. In September 1939 Denmark declared itself neutral, but it meant little as on 9 April 1940 German forces crossed the border and within two hours Denmark surrendered.

Initially Germany rule was relatively benign, not least because the Nazis generally accepted Scandinavians as fellow Aryans. The Danish government, parliament and police continued to run the country, King Christian X remained head of state, and the German ambassador became the all-important Reich Plenipotentiary. Most Danes accepted that Germany would win the European war and therefore considered peaceful accommodation was the most realistic and least damaging way forward. The government duly acted in German interests by banning critical newspaper reports, arresting Communists, discouraging violent resistance, redirecting the economy, and demilitarising its armed forces. In return Denmark endured no savage persecution of the Jews, kept its own law courts and avoided harmful currency union with Germany, Indeed for several years Danish businesses did well out of the war with German contracts. About 6,000 Danes (and Germans living in Denmark) joined the *Frikorps Danmark* and fought with German armies on the Eastern Front.

However relations grew increasingly sour between the two countries, not least because the government refused to sign Germany's Anti-Comitern Pact in 1941. Bolstered by thoughts of Germany's ultimate defeat, in the summer of 1943 a series of demonstrations and strikes was followed by the Danish government's refusal to outlaw strikes, tighten censorship or execute saboteurs, after which the Germans dissolved the government and imposed martial law. Resistance groups became more aggressive, and a host of small ships ferried Jewish families to safety in Sweden. By 1944 the hitherto suspicious Allied governments were becoming more confident of Denmark's willingness to show opposition to Nazi rule.

Denmark was liberated in May 1945, and the Social Democrats returned to power. Around 4,000 Danes had been killed as resistance fighters, sailors or civilians, and another 600 in concentration camps. 13,500 were found guilty of collaboration, although embarrassing controversy rages over how far everyone, including the government, had been to some extent a collaborator. A further controversy arose when, in early 1945, the Germans housed in Denmark around 250,000 refugees escaping across the Baltic Sea from the Russian advance into East Prussia. After the German surrender Denmark was left to administer the make-shift camps, and shortages of food and medicine combined with Danish resentment against caring for them at the expense of its own citizens led to an estimated 13,000 deaths.

Danish definitive stamps portraying King Christian had continued to be used during the German occupation with a new design being introduced in 1942 and continuing well into peacetime.(9.1)

Wartime Danish commemorative stamps honoured celebrated historic figures, notably the explorer Vitus Bering and astronomer Ole Romer, and two sets used the Royal family to attract support for Red Cross and Child Welfare funds. One, with issues in November 1939 and December 1940, pictured Queen Alexandrine, the

9.1 10o King Christian X: from set 26 September 1942+.

9.2 5o+3o Queen Alexandrine: 14 December 1940, and 10o+5o Princess Ingrid: 16 April 1941.

9.3 25o+5o Princess Anne-Marie: 10 October 1950.

9.5 1k Arms: from set 11 July 1946+.

9.4 40o King Christian X's 75th birthday: from set 26 September 1945.

9.6 20o Tycho Brahe: 14 December 1946.

9.7 15o King Frederick IX: from set 12 February 1948+.

German-born but nevertheless popular wife of the king. The other, with issues in April 1941 and November 1943, featured Princess Ingrid, the Swedish wife of Crown Prince Frederick, holding Princess Margrethe who became Queen of Denmark on 14 January 1972.(9.2) The next Child Welfare stamp only appeared in October 1950 and portrayed the four year old Princess Anne-Marie, Frederick and Ingrid's youngest daughter who married King Constantine of Greece (who reigned from 1964 until forced into exile by a military coup in 1973).(9.3)

Four months after Germany's defeat a set of three portrait stamps marked King Christian's 75th birthday, and in July 1946 the first stamp - the 1k - appeared in the long lasting definitive series featuring Denmark's Arms.(9.4, 9.5)

On 14 December 1946 a stamp commemorated the 400th anniversary of the birth of Tycho Brahe (1546-1601). An alchemist, astrologer and astronomer, Brahe's lasting fame rests on his concern for exact astronomical measurements. In doing so he refuted the Classical assertion that the heavens were an unchanging realm. In 1572 he studied the appearance of the supernova now known as Tycho's Nova SN 1572. His measurements indicated that comets existed far beyond the Moon, and he recorded the Moon orbiting the Earth and several planets orbiting the Sun, but still believed the Sun orbited the Earth.

Frederick IX succeeded to the throne on 20 April 1947, and definitive stamps portraying him first appeared in February the following year.(9.7) However the first set of his reign, in May 1947, was devoted to the Liberation Fund set up to support humanitarian and educational projects.(9.8) The 15o+5o featured symbols of freedom and victory - a wreath of olive and palm branches, a flaming torch, and a ribbon. The 20o+5c pictured resisters blowing up a railway junction, and the 40o+5o showed the Danish flag rising from the sea.

The following month a set marked the centenary of Danish Railways.(9.9) Building the main lines linking Denmark and Germany through Schleswig and Holstein had been difficult politically and financially but they aided trade to both nation's advantage, not least during the war although the prospect of sabotage, as the previous set highlighted, was ever-present. The 15o pictured *Odin*, Denmark's first locomotive, the 20o an express steam locomotive, and the 40o the modern electric locomotive *Lyntog* and train ferry *Fyn* used between the major islands of Zealand and Funen.

In November 1947 a stamp marked the 60th anniversary of the death of Jacob Christian Jacobsen (1811-87) who founded probably Denmark's most renowned industry - the Carlsberg Brewery near Copenhagen.(9.10) It was named after Jacob's son Carl and the *berg* (hill) on which it was built. Although Stanley Gibbons' catalogue says the Carlsberg Foundation for Scientific Research (mainly into brewing) reached its centenary in 1947 the Carlsberg website confirms the Laboratory started in 1875 and the

Foundation in 1876. However the first Carlsberg brew occurred in 1847.

The Danish monarchy was popular but possessed minimal political authority. From the seventeenth century Denmark possessed an absolutist monarchy but, under increasing pressure from Liberal and populist political parties, in 1849 King Frederick VII (reigned 1848-63) signed a radical new constitution. As he no doubt appreciated, 1848 and 1849 were years when several European monarchies were enduring revolutionary threats to their existence. The constitution gave citizens freedom of speech, worship, association and assembly, and created a system (although only a minority of citizens could vote) whereby the bicameral parliament enacted laws, the government implemented them, and the courts made independent judgements. On 5 June 1949, a hundred years to the day, a single stamp was issued featuring Constantin Hansen's painting of the original National Constitutional Assembly.(9.11) The painting was huge, but the stamp was strangely small for such an important anniversary. June 5th remains a National Holiday.

9.8 Liberation Fund: set 4 May 1947.

9.10 20o Jacob Christian Jacobsen: 10 November 1947.

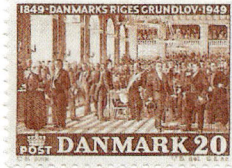

9.11 20o Centenary of Danish Constitution: 5 June 1949.

9.9 Centenary of Danish Railways: set 27 June 1947.

CHAPTER 10

NORWAY

Norway remained neutral in the First World War, and it hoped to remain neutral in any further European conflicts. However its geographical location made this unlikely as both Great Britain and Germany fully appreciated the strategic importance of both the deep water ports along Norway's long western coast and the ease of access through Narvik to Sweden's northern iron ore mines. In the event the German invasion on the night of 8-9 April 1940 pre-empted by a day or so a British invasion ostensibly to defend Norway's neutrality. Superior German planning and military skill overcame Norwegian resistance and the British expeditionary force although the two months of fighting was the longest it had taken Germany to crush any western European country.

King Haakon VII refused to appoint Vidkun Quisling, the leader of Norway's collaborationist fascist party, as prime minister, and had time during the fighting to flee the country with his family. Although Quisling badgered the Germans for political power they had little use for him, and although he became head of state in 1942 it was the Reichkommissar, Joseph Terboven, who made all the key decisions. Norway's economy suffered badly as trade with Germany could not make up the loss of overseas markets, and often there was a risk of famine. Jews were persecuted, and about 15,000 Norwegians volunteered to serve in German combat units. However, unlike Denmark's open flat landscape Norway's mountains and fjords afforded greater opportunities for effective actions by resistance groups - as in tracking the movements of the battleship *Tirpitz* and attacking the heavy water plant at Telemark. The Norwegian government-in-exile in London welcomed around 28,000 of its fleeing countrymen into its numerous small warships which had escaped seizure by the Germans, its four fighter squadrons, and various army units.

Early in May 1945 an interim Norwegian government had prepared itself to take over from the Germans who formally surrendered at midnight on 8 May. The following few days saw Allied soldiers, the royal family and senior government officials return. They were faced with many problems. 10,000 Norwegians had lost their lives in combat or prison. 140,000 refugees and prisoners of war, many of them Russians, were stranded in Norway. 20,000 Norwegians and Germans were given prison sentences for collaboration and war crimes, and 37 executed, including Quisling. Norway's economy was in disarray, and much of Finnmark in the far north abutting the Soviet Union had suffered from the 'scorched earth' programme of the Germans retreating in the face of Finnish and Soviet troops. Conversely the shared adversity and the achievements of the resistance and exiled armed forces raised Norway's self-image, and not surprisingly the 1945 general election returned an actively reforming Labour government, just as in Great Britain. And as in other western European countries, the policy of neutrality was abandoned in favour of joining NATO, creating a modern range of armed services, and keeping a weather-eye on the Soviet Union.

Norway's wartime stamps largely alternated between issues celebrating the country's Viking past, encouraging recruitment to combat units, and commemorating Norwegian figures such as the polar explorer Fridtjof Nansen (1861-1930) and Tyggve Gran (1888-1972, the first person to fly an aeroplane across the North Sea. As well known in Norway, the former became an influential anti-Communist political figure and the latter a supporter of Quisling. Conversely, in January 1943 the Norwegian government-in-exile issued a set featuring King Haakon, an airman, soldiers on skis, merchant ships in convoy, and the destroyer *Sleipner* which had achieved fame for shooting down two German aircraft and capturing two supply vessels during the 1940 invasion before escaping to the UK for service as a convoy escort.(10.1) The final stamp featured the resistance logo *Vi Vil Vinne (We Will Win)* written in secret on Norwegian roads and buildings. The stamps were first used on Norwegian merchant ships and after liberation they went on sale across the country.

Norway's longstanding post-horn and rampant lion symbols continued to be used on definitive stamps during the German occupation and for several years afterwards.(10.2) However on 12 July 1945, the first new commemorative set after liberation portrayed the patriotic poet and playwright Henrik Wergeland (1808-45).(10.3) It was the centenary of his death, and the commemoration was particularly apt because the Nazis had banned any celebrations of his life and works. A fervent devotee of the Norwegian language and culture, Wergeland was equally fervent in his support for the

10.3 10o Henrik Wergeland: from set 12 July 1945.

10.1 5o Destroyer 'Sleipner', 20o Vi Vil Vinne, 30o convoy, and 40o Mountain troops: from set 1 January 1943.

10.4 10o 50th anniversary of Folklore Museum: from set 19 December 1945.

10.2 15o definitive (issued 30 November 1926, cancelled 8 December 1946): from set 1926+.

10.5 15o Honouring Norwegian aircrew trained in Canada: 28 March 1946.

French Revolution of 1830, anti-Semitism, and campaigns for social justice and against repressive government. In his lifetime he was often publicly criticised and barred by publishers for his radical views.

In December 1945 the 50th anniversary of the National Folk Museum provided another opportunity to reinforce national pride and identity after the war. (10.4)

A few months later, in March 1946, a striking stamp honoured the Norwegian aircrew and mechanics trained in Canada during the war.(10.5) A ghostly Viking placed the airmen firmly within the warrior tradition. Many men joined the RAF until Norway's naval and army air forces were united in the Royal Norwegian Air Force in 1944. The English inscription *LITTLE NORWAY TORONTO MUSKOVA* refers to the names given to the initial training camp at Toronto Island Airport, and to Muskova Airport north of Toronto where it moved later in the war.

Norway's war and extensive social distress was recalled, too, in sets raising funds for the Red Cross and National Relief. On 22 September 1945 a close-up eye-catching portrait of a Red Cross sister was used (and repeated in 1948 overprinted 25o+5o), and on 4 March 1946 a National Relief set featured the popular Crown Prince Olav (1903-91) in army uniform.(10.6, 10.7) By 1939 he was an experienced senior officer and in exile he had remained in close touch with Free Norwegian forces.

Olav's father, King Haakon VII (1872-1957), was equally highly respected for his resistance to the Germans and his constitutional role as a hard-working symbol of national unity. He featured on a set of four high value stamps in June 1946, and a single stamp on his 75th birthday, 2 August 1947.(10.8, 10.9) In that year a public subscription raised all the funds to buy a royal yacht. In 1950 new definitive stamps portraying King Haakon appeared - the first since 1918.(10.10)

10.6 20o+10o Red Cross Sister (80th anniversary of the International Red Cross): 22 September 1945.

10.8 1½k King Haakon VII: from set 7 June 1946.

10.7 30o+10o Crown Prince Olav: from set 4 March 1946.

10.9 25o King Haakon's 75th birthday: 2 August 1947.

On 15 April 1947 a handsome and informative set marked the tercentenary of Norway's Post Office but most of the eleven stamps commemorated far wider ranging events and people. Accumulatively they showed how enterprising and outward looking Norway had been over the centuries - and could be so again. They were a remarkable indicator of national resolve as Norway emerged from the trauma of war.

10.10 80o King Haakon: from set 18 December 1950.

Three centred on communications.(10.11) The 5o portrayed Hannibal Sehested (1609-66), a nobleman who found time during a tempestuous military, diplomatic and courtly life to reform Norway's fiscal system and establish a self-funding postal service for all citizens. Government mail went free, but everyone else was charged. Shown alongside him is medieval Akershus Castle in Oslo and, as many Norwegians would know, it was here that the Germans executed Norwegian resisters and the Norwegians executed Vidkun Quisling. The 10o pictured an early 'postal-peasant', the name given to runners and riders carrying mail. The 45o featured the first Norwegian locomotive, the British built Caroline. With Norway's mountainous terrain and preference for coastal and fjord transport the country's first line out of the capital, Oslo, only opened in 1854. However huge engineering projects led to several lines linking major cities with ports such as Bergen and Trondheim.

Three stamps celebrated Norway's illustrious seafarers and explorers.(10.12) The 30o pictured Cleng Peerson (1783-1855) and the *Restauration*, the emigration ship which took the first Quakers and likeminded groups to settle in the USA. The 50o pictured Svend Foyn (1809-94), the whaling magnate and inventor of the harpoon gun, and his *Spes et Fides*, the first steam powered whaler. The 55o featured the polar explorers Fridtjof Nansen (reclaiming him as a national hero rather than a right wing politician) and Roald Amundsen (1872-1928) and their ship *Fram*. In November 1910 Amundsen famously beat Captain Robert Scott to the South Pole. Nansen was not only a celebrated Arctic explorer but also an oceanographer of note, promoter of the League of Nations, and winner of the 1922 Nobel Peace Prize for his work on behalf of refugees.

Five more highlighted Norway's struggles for independence and nationhood.(10.13, 10.14) The 15o celebrated Admiral Peter Tordenskiold (1690-1720) who destroyed the vital supply ships of King Charles XII of Sweden at the Battle of Dynekilen in 1716 thereby frustrating the Swedish invasion. Numerous statues honoured him. The 25o celebrated the statesman Christian Falsen (1782-1830) who framed the Norwegian Constitution that ensured Norway would not endure the absolutist rule of Sweden's monarch once

10.11 5o Hannibal Sehested, 10o 'Postal peasant' and 45o Early locomotive: from set 1 5 April 1947.

10.13 15o Admiral Tordenskiold, 25o Christian Falsen, and 40o 'Constitutionem': from set 15 April 1947.

10.12 30o Cleng Peerson, 50o Svend Foyn, and 55o Fridtjof Nansen and Roald Amundsen: from set 15 April 1947.

celebrated the wild northern landscape and its people. (10.15) On 15 June 1948 two stamps featured Axel Heiberg (1848-1932) on the centenary of his birth. A wealthy financier he had funded Norwegian polar expeditions and the ship *Fram*, and endowed statues to the controversial modernist playwright Henrik Ibsen (1828-1906) and to the equally controversial radical writer Bjornstjerne Bjornson (1832-1910), a great admirer of Henrik Wergeland. The stamps, though, centred, on Axel Heiberg's creation of the economically vital Norwegian Forestry Company *(DET NORSKE SKOGSELSKAP)*.(10.16) On 9 May 1949 a set of stamps commemorated the centenary of the birth of Alexander Lange Kielland (1849-1906) whose satirical novels

they became united in 1814. The dramatic 40o featured the famous Norwegian paddle steamer *Constitutionem* which provoked a riot in Christiana (Oslo's earlier name) in 1829 when the Swedish authorities sought to suppress the Norwegian crowd greeting it on the anniversary of the signing of the Norwegian Constitution. The Swedish king had banned any anniversary celebrations. The poet Henrik Wergeland (see 10.3) was a key figure among the celebrants who were assaulted. The two highest values portrayed King Haakon. The 60o pictured his coronation in Niadaros Cathedral with Queen Maud in 1906, and the 80c pictured the cheering crowds outside Oslo Town Hall on his return from exile on 7 June 1945.

Other post-war issues sought to raise national pride and self-confidence by highlighting selected famous figures whose common links were the beneficial changes they promoted for the Norwegian people. On 1 July 1947 a stamp marked the tercentenary of the birth of the Lutheran pastor and poet Petter Dass (c1647-1707). His hymns remained in use for centuries while his magical stories enriched Norwegian folk-lore, and topographical poem *Trumpet of Nordland* famously

10.14 60o Coronation of King Haakon and Queen Maud, and 80c Return of King Haakon from exile: from set 15 April 1947.

10.15 25o Peter Dass: 1 July 1947.

sympathised with the down trodden at the hands of bigoted priests, sadistic teachers and despotic employers.(10.17)

On 8 October 1949 Norway issued a particularly meaningful stamp in the set marking the 75th anniversary of the Universal Postal Union.(10.18) The larger than usual 10c contained a compass with eight segments, each one of which contained images of people, products and buildings around the world.

Norway was an early member of the United Nations and a founding member of NATO, and it received considerable Marshall Aid whilst always conscious it shared a northern border with the powerful USSR. Its Labour government avidly encouraged economic growth and welfare reforms and, as its UPU stamp succinctly highlighted, peaceful co-existence was its highest post-war priority.

10.16 80o Axel Heiberg: from set 15 June 1948.

10.18 10o 75th anniversary of the UPU: from set 8 October 1949.

10.17 25o Alexander Kielland: from set 9 May 1949.

CHAPTER 11

FINLAND

From 1809 Finland was a grand duchy within the Russian Empire until it declared independence in December 1917 during the Russian Civil War, crushed its own Communists, and seized Russian Eastern Karelia abutting Lake Lagoda in the south and the Arctic port of Petsamo in the far north. Relations with Russia remained tense, especially as Lake Lagoda was not far from Leningrad. Under the Soviet-German Pact of August 1939 it was agreed that Finland would be part of the Russian sphere of interest. Soviet forces duly invaded Finland in November 1939 with complete re-annexation as the aim. However the Finns fought back skilfully and successfully, but despite the Russians suffering huge losses their inexhaustible numbers eventually told and in March 1940 a peace treaty pushed Finland out of Karelia.

Soon afterwards, however, Finland and Germany found themselves allies. When Hitler launched Operation Barbarossa in June 1941 German troops were permitted to advance through Lapland in the far north while Finnish and German troops advanced towards Lake Lagoda in the south. A desperate Stalin sought peace but Finland refused to abandon its conquered territory. With Russia heavily engaged elsewhere, the Finnish defensive positions held until June 1944 when a sudden massive Soviet onslaught pushed the Finns back to the lines of the 1940 treaty. In a peace agreement Finland ceded much of Karelia, several islands in the Gulf of Finland, and also the rich mining region around Petsamo in the far north. Although exhausted, Finland was obliged to go to war against Germany and help clear Lapland of German troops - an obligation that led to the Germans devastating 'scorched earth' retreat into northern Norway.

After the war the Allies classified Finland as an ally of Nazi Germany but its fortunes rose rather than declined. Finland had been dependant on Germany for much of its food, fuel and weaponry and although it refused to sign the Tripartite Pact with Germany, Italy and Japan it did sign the Anti-Comintern Pact against Communism. Nevertheless uniquely among Hitler's allies, Finland retained its democratic government, kept its army outside German control, and it did not persecute Jews. It did, though, house Soviet prisoners of war, and also Russian civilians in Karelia, in appalling conditions, and many died. It was fortunate that in 1945 it was the only European country bordering Russia not occupied by it. And it was perhaps also fortunate that its war was limited to the Soviet Union and not against any European democracies. Although burdened with war crime trials and also reparation payments to the Soviet Union, in due course the amount was reduced. In 1946 Juho Paasikivi (1870-1956) became president, and despite his hostility to Bolshevik intervention in Finland when he was prime minister in 1918 he recognised the need to reduce tension and establish mutually advantageous relations. In 1947 Finland signed a treaty of 'friendship, cooperation and mutual assistance' with the Soviet Union which both sides honoured, and in marked contrast with Soviet practice elsewhere, Finland remained a democracy with a capitalist market economy. A single but dramatic stamp issued on 2 June 1947 with the logo PAX marked the event, and symbolically pictured the god Ilmarinen, the mythical 'great smith' in the Finnish epic the Kalevala using his plough to cultivate a field beset by vipers.(11.1) A little earlier, in March 1947, Paasikivi himself was honoured with a stamp. (11.2)

Officially neutral, 'Finlandization' became a way of life, and was generally defined as 'bowing to the east without mooning the west'. The country preserved and strengthened its national identity by embracing and integrating strong local traditions and pursuing stabilising centrist economic and social welfare programmes. Nevertheless Finns remained resolutely proud of their wartime sacrifices, military prowess and success in preserving their independence. The country's post-war stamps reflect this pride, and as the noted

11.1 10m Ilmarinen ploughing: 2 June 1947.

11.2 10m President Paasikivi: 15 March 1947.

11.3 30k Postal motor coach: 10 February 1947.

11.4 15m Hannes Gebhard: 2 October 1949.

December 1944 a National Relief Fund stamp aptly featured a flower blooming by a shattered tree trunk. (11.7) On 2 May 1945 a Red Cross Fund set repeated a 1941 design, with the date '1945' added, depicting a builder, farmer, mother and child, and blue and white national flag.(11.8) On 7 January 1946 another surtaxed Red Cross set recalled the importance of the rural economy with striking images of men logging, fishing and harvesting, and women butter-making.(11.9) The images implicitly promoted the physical as well as economic benefits of a healthy outdoor life, as well as publicising the importance of smallholders and rural workers who still numbered 50% of the electorate.

The rural and maritime economy was highlighted in other philatelic ways. On 19 September 1946 a stamp featuring a ship sailing past Uto Lighthouse and the perilous Aland Islands marked the 250th anniversary of the Swedish King Charles XII decreeing the charter for the Finnish Pilotage Institution.(11.10) Although the charter was important in creating a recognised profession, Finland's lengthy and dangerous coastline meant that pilots, handing down knowledge from father to son, had earned a living along it for hundreds of years before this. On 1 November 1947 a single stamp

11.5 15m Olavinlinna Castle: 4 September 1945.

11.6 7m Lion rampant: from new issue 20 January 1947+.

graphic designer Aarne Karjalainen was responsible for many sets they possess an immediately recognisable 'Finnish' quality. Examples of his work were the minutely detailed motor postal bus stamps of 1946 and 1947 (11.3) and the bust of Hannes Gebhard (1864-1933) on the 1949 stamp marking the 50th anniversary of his founding of the Finnish Cooperative Movement. (11.4) Probably his most famous design was for the classic stamp depicting the medieval Olavinlinna Castle, first issued in 1930 and reissued with new values in September 1945 and March 1949.(11.5) Fought over by Russia and Sweden and finally becoming part of south-east Finland, since 1912 the huge castle had been the setting for the summer Savonlinna Opera Festival. The design was also part of the 1930 Finnish definitive set comprising a few pictorial values spread amongst the majority featuring the fearsome rampant Finnish lion wielding its sword. The series remained in use well after 1945.(11.6)

Not surprisingly after the wartime traumas Finnish health, culture and regeneration were to the fore. On 1

11.7 3m50+1m50 National Relief Fund: 1 December 1944.

11.8 1m+25p Builder and 3m50+75p Mother and child: from Red Cross set 2 May 1945.

11.9 3m+75p Butter making and 10m+2m50 Logging: from Red Cross set 7 January 1946.

11.10 8m Uto Lighthouse: 19 September 1946.

11.11 10m Sower: 1 November 1947.

11.12 9m Lake, trees and papermill: from set 15 June 1949.

11.13 5m 50th anniversary of Labour Movement: from set 16 July 1949.

picturing a hand sower marked the 150th anniversary of the Central League of Agricultural Societies. This placed its foundation in 1797 when Sweden rule Finland and the Swedish elite looked down upon the Finnish peasants.(11.11) However, although the peasants had owned only small plots of land they were free, not serfs, and from this put-upon class Finnish historians track the fervent nationalism and agrarian parties that evolved in the nineteenth century. The economic importance of Finland's extensive forests was reflected in its hosting of the Third World Forestry Congress in June 1949. A pair of stamps picturing aspects of the timber trade marked this significant international event which had been long delayed from its original date in 1940. (11.12)

In July 1949 a pair of stamps featuring a girl with a flaming torch and man with a hammer marked the 50th anniversary of Finland's Labour Party. It had been founded in historic Turku in 1899 after several years of depression, discontent and strikes.(11.13) The Party had changed dramatically in its history. In 1903 it adopted a socialist agenda and became the Social Democratic Party. In the Civil War of 1918 the party was defeated both militarily and politically in its aims of creating a Soviet-style socialist republic, and after years in the wilderness it became more nationalist and democratic during the war, and significantly anti-Communist in outlook, especially after 1945. Popular but not enough to gain power, post-war Soviet proximity and influence led other major parties to avoid entering any coalition with the Social Democrats - who avidly advocated the acceptance of American funds.

On 10 May 1948 a further Red Cross set switched attention to four national figures from pre-independence

11.14 Red Cross: set 10 May 1948.

days.(11.14) The 7m+2m pictured Fredric Pacius (1809-91) who wrote the music for the poem *Vart land* which later became the Finnish national anthem. It was written by the Lutheran pastor Johan Ludvig Runeberg (1804-77) who featured on the 12m+3m stamp and whose many poems eulogised the steely resolve and Christian faith of Finnish peasants in the hardest of times. The 20m+5m pictured Fredrik Cygnaeus (1807-81), professor, poet and historian, who encouraged patriotism, but also the exclusively peaceful expressions of it, in generations of students. Featured on the 3m+1m, Zachris Topelius (1818-98) was an academic who wrote novels popularising Finnish history when it was part of Sweden's greatest age under King Gustavus Adolphus in the seventeenth century.

Zachris Topelius wrote a poem that was put to music by Jean Sibelius (1865-1957) in 1899 called *Breaking the Ice on the River Oulu* that became a metaphor for Finland's aspirations of freedom from Russian domination. Sibelius's compositions such as *Finlandia, the Karelian Suite* and other works inspired by his native country and its sagas, notably the Creation myth *Karevala*, ensured his standing as Finland's most renowned composer, and cultural publicist. Not surprisingly a stamp marked his 80th birthday in December 1945.(11.15) In May 1945 another much respected 80 year old - former President Kaarlo Stahlberg (1865-1952) - had been honoured with a stamp on his birthday.(11.16) An ardent republican and architect of the constitution, he became Finland's first president (1919-25) and dealt skilfully with the warring internal factions as well as with neighbouring Russia and Sweden and also introduced much needed social reforms.

The practice of honouring Finnish linguistic and cultural achievements when the country was under the authority of Sweden (c1150-1809) or Imperial Russia (1809-1917) was extended in October 1948 to two stamp commemorating Michael Agricola (c1510-57). He was the translator of the New Testament into Finnish who, with the Swedish King Gustav Vasa's support, promoted the Protestant Reformation and became the first Lutheran bishop in Finland. (11.17) On 13

11.15 5m Jean Sibelius: 8 December 1945.

11.16 3.50 President Stahlberg: 16 May 1945.

11.17 12m Michael Agricola: from set 2 October 1948.

11.18 15m Centenary of Helsinki Technical High School: 13 September 1949.

September 1949 a stamp marked the centenary of Helsinki's prestigious Technical High School which had been founded by the Russian Tsar Nicholas I as Grand Duke of Finland. In 1878 it became a polytechnic, and achieved university status in 1908.(11.18) By implication the stamps acknowledged both Sweden and Russia were capable of sympathy with Finnish aspirations - when it suited them.

In May 1949 the Red Cross set featured the long established national habit of taking saunas.(11.19) Traditionally wood was gathered for a fire, as featured in the 5m+2m, which then heated large stones in a fireplace upon which water was thrown to produce steam. This heated the enclosed cabin sufficiently for people to take off their clothes and imbibe the atmosphere, as pictured in the 9m+3m and 15m+5m. Often people then took a cold swim or shower, as pictured in the 30m+10m. Saunas became both a health and social amenity, reminiscent of the Roman baths, and were popular in Germany after German soldiers experienced them during the Second World War.

Just as saunas were seen as mentally and physically beneficial, so the healthy and socially unifying effects of games were fostered as reflected in a succession of stamp issues. In April 1945 five surtaxed stamps

11.21 8m Athletes and wreath: 1 June 1946, and 10m Athletes and flag: 2 June 1947.

11.22 5m+1m Nurse and children: from set 2 September 1946.

11.19 15m+5m Sauna cabin and 30m+10m Taking the cold plunge: from set 5 May 1949.

11.20 1m+50p Wrestling and 4m50+2m25 Skiing: from set 16 April 1945.

featured wrestling, vaulting, running, skiing and javelin throwing in a set supporting the national Sports Fund.(11.20) In June 1946 and June 1947 stamps picturing male and female athletes aspiring to victory marked the first two post-war National Games.(11.21) As a noted sportsman in his younger days, President Paasikivi did much to encourage them.

Finland also issued many sets linked to the international campaign against tuberculosis. Although Robert Koch had identified the TB bacillus in 1882 and the BCG vaccine was first used in 1921, immunisation took another thirty years to be generally accepted. Most countries concentrated on the practice of isolating patients in a sanatorium where rest, good food, cleanliness, fresh air and gentle chest exercises would effect a cure - which it did in some but far from all cases. On 2 September 1946 a pair of stamps supporting the Anti-TB Fund pictured a nurse and doctor caring for children.(11.22) They were re-issued on 1 April 1947 with overprinted higher values.(11.23) All the campaign stamps carried the universal emblem of the Cross of Lorraine.

On 15 September 1947 a set of five campaign stamps featured Alli Paasikivi, the President's wife and noted health campaigner, and various exercises suitable for child patients.(11.24) On 13 September 1948 three of the stamps featuring exercises were reissued surcharged with higher values.(11.25) On 2 June 1949 the TB Relief

Fund set featured flowers - anemones (5m+2m), traditionally said to ward off sickness and bad luck, roses (9m+3m), long used in herbal and folk remedies, and coltsfoot (15m+5m), often used in medicines to treat respiratory problems.(11.26)

Other stamps from the period, attractively detailed in their composition, commemorated the founding of key institutions and the ancient charters of Finnish cities. On 1 April 1947 a stamp celebrated the 60th anniversary of Finland's Postal Savings Bank and on 21 August 1947 another stamp marked the 150th anniversary of its earlier manifestation, the Savings Bank Association.(11.27)

On 3 December 1946 two stamps commemorated the 600th anniversary of the granting of a royal charter to the city of Porvoo on the southern coast east of Helsinki. (11.28) Its later claim to fame was the Diet of Porvoo in 1809 when Sweden ceded Finland to Russia and Czar Alexander I granted it a constitution as an autonomous Grand Duchy. The city centre is renowned for its streets of medieval buildings. On 14 December 1946 a stamp marked the 400th anniversary of Tammisaari, a city and castle set amidst an archipelago on the southern coast.

11.26 9m+3m Rose: from set 2 June 1949.

11.27 10m Beehive Savings Bank emblem: 1 April 1947, and 10m Cornfield and Savings Bank Association emblem: 21 August 1947.

11.23 8m+2m Doctor and child, overprinted 10+2: from reissued set 1 April 1947.

11.24 12m+3m Alli Paasikivi and child patient: from set 15 September 1947.

11.28 8m Bridge and view of Porvoo: from set 3 December 1946.

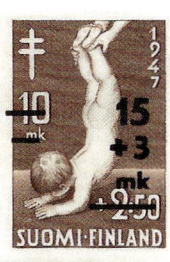

11.25 10m+2m50 Infant exercise, overprinted 15+3m: from reissued set 13 September 1948.

11.29 8m Old harbour at Tammisaari: 14 December 1946.

(11.29) On 15 October 1948 a stamp commemorated the bicentenary of Suomenlinna a strategically important fortress and community straddling eight small islands off Helsinki.(11.30) Originally named Sveaborg, it was proudly renamed Suomenlinna (Castle of Finland) after independence in 1918. When Russian-owned it famously withstood bombardment by the Royal Navy during the Crimean War of 1854-56.

In July 1949 a stamp marked the tercentenary of the small town of Kristiinankaupunki on the west coast. (11.31) It was chartered in 1649 by the Swedish Governor General Count Per Brahe (1602-80), a statesman long admired by Finns for his encouragement of commerce, farming, education, and creation of a postal service. The town (originally Kristinestad) was named after Queen Christina of Sweden (reigned 1632-54). Cultured and forward-looking but extravagant and unconventional, Christina refused to marry, became a Roman Catholic and abdicated - and lived on until 1689).

On 6 and 13 August 1949 single stamps marked the tercentenary of two other cities owing their charters to Count Per Brahe and Queen Christina - the trading and fortress city of Lappeenranta about thirty miles from the south-eastern Russian border (11.32), and the old harbour town of Raahe on the Gulf of Bothnia, later developed as an iron and steel centre.(11.33) Most of these places became profitable tourist centres, and not surprisingly the stamps highlighted their attractive harbours, churches and centres. The significance of tourism was reflected in the stamp issued as early as November 1947 featuring the haunting ice smoothed hills and forests of Koli in eastern Finland and marking the 60th anniversary of the country's Tourist Society. (11.34)

11.30 12m Sailing ships and King's Gate at Suomenlinna: 15 October 1948.

11.31 15m Kristiinankaupunki harbour and town: 30 July 1949.

11.32 5m Lappeenranta: 6 August 1949.

11.33 9m Raahe: 13 August 1949.

11.34 10m Hills of Koli: 1 November 1947.

CHAPTER 12

POLAND

In the late eighteenth century Poland's days as a great kingdom ended in a humiliating series of partitions and eventual oblivion at the hands of its grasping neighbours Imperial Russia, the Kingdom of Prussia and the Austrian Empire. For more than a century hopes and dreams of resurgence as an independent nation led to patriotic revolts and violent repression until a free Poland finally re-emerged at the end of the First World War when all three of its historic aggressors were in complete disarray. However throughout the 1930s a resurgent Germany and Soviet Union looked covetously upon their former Polish lands. In 1939 Poland believed France and Great Britain would defend its independence and therefore resisted all pressure from Hitler to surrender Danzig or any other territory. In August, though, the Soviet-Nazi Pact was signed, and Poland's fate was sealed. Its army was surprised by the massive German attack in the west on 1 September. France and Great Britain did nothing except launch a few disappointing air raids, and once Germany had occupied the western half of Poland the Soviet Union attacked from the east on 17 September. Warsaw was bombed into submission, and Hitler and Stalin agreed a border along the River Bug. Germany sought to crush the Polish nation and its culture, and large areas in the west were annexed to the Reich. Around a million Poles were deported eastwards and replaced by German settlers. The Soviet Union had around twenty months to

1949 Map of post-war Poland and Czechoslovkia. The thinner red lines show Poland's dramatic shift westwards after the war with part of pre-war eastern Germany ceded to Poland, and part of pre-war eastern Poland ceded to the USSR. The thinner green line outlines Carpathia-Ukraine, formerly part of Czechoslovakia, but now in the post-war Soviet Union.

impose its savage will on the eastern Poles, whom it treated as traitors to the Bolshevik revolution, before Germany launched Operation Barbarossa against its erstwhile ally in 1941. Hitler continued his policy of airbrushing Poland out of existence by placing most of the east formerly held by Russia in occupied zones called *Reichskommissariats Ostland* and *Ukraine* (using German stamps overprinted *Ostland* or *Ukraine*) keeping the western region firmly within Germany (using ordinary German stamps) and creating a central part contemptuously termed the *General Government* administered from Cracow (using *General Government* issues). Jews were herded into ghettoes and many sent to extermination camps. Poles everywhere were ruthlessly used as forced labourers, property was plundered, most produce was transported to Germany or the Eastern Front, and disease and hunger was ever present. Over five million Poles died.

Although wartime Polish resistance to the Germans and Russians was fierce despite the savage reprisals, there were some Poles who possessed strong Communist views and cooperated with the Russians. Polish Communists in the General Government and western Poland were ready to spread their views whilst opposing the Germans. As the resistance movement grew in strength it became increasingly divided between those fighting for Poland's place within an idealised version of international Communism and those seeking a return to the fully independent pre-1939 state of affairs.

In September 1939 a completely new Polish government-in-exile was established in London, and ran the nationalist resistance movement - termed the Home Army - in occupied Poland. It campaigned to re-establish pre-war Poland with additional territory taken from eastern Germany and East Prussia. The Soviet Union thought otherwise, and as the war went on so did Winston Churchill who urged the government-in-exile to reach agreement with Stalin - but in vain. Stalin had made it clear at the wartime conferences between the Allied leaders that eastern Poland, the area Russia had seized in 1939, would remain his, and that he sought 'a friendly Poland'.

Hundreds of thousands of Poles fought against Germany in several theatres of war. The large well-trained Polish II Corps, formed partly of escapees from German occupation and partly soldiers released from Soviet prisoner of war camps, fought with the Western Allies in the Middle East and then in Italy, at Monte Cassino in 1944 where they made the final successful attack on the German stronghold, and at Ancona and Bologna in 1945. Exiled Poles also staffed 15 fighter squadrons and several Polish warships. They made a significant contribution to Allied victory. Polish exploits

12.2 75g Polish troops at Tobruk and 80g General Sikorski (prime minister-in-exile and commander-in-chief) and troops in Middle East: from set 1 November 1943.

12.1 1z Saboteurs and 1z50 Printing underground newspapers: from set 1 November 1943.

12.3 1z Wellington bomber and Hurricane fighters (from set 15 December 1941) overprinted Monte Cassino 18.V.1944 and G.80: from commemoration set 27 June 1944.

12.4 45g Monte Cassino and 2z Lieutenant General Anders (Commander of the Polish II Corps): from first Polish Forces in Italy set 1946.

12.5 5c, 50c, 60c, 80c and 5l Polish Forces in Italy (two with Honour the Four Freedoms overprints): from second set 1946.

at home and abroad were pictured on three sets of stamps issued by the Polish government-in-exile (on 15 December 1941, 1 November 1943 and 27 June 1944) which were allowed on mail from Polish ships and, on certain days, from military camps in Britain.

In 1946 the Polish II Corps landed in Great Britain and gradually demobilised. Some months earlier two sets of primarily publicity stamps commemorated their wartime achievements. The first, in Polish currency, featured Monte Cassino (45g), Ancona (55g), Bologna (1z) and the army commander Lieutenant General Wladyslaw Anders (2z).(12.4) Their use was restricted to letters sent by II Corps personnel stationed in Italy. The second set, in Italian currency, was sold in official Polish Post Offices (*Poczta Osiedli Polskich*) in Trani and Barletta in south-east Italy to aid the War Rescue Fund.(12.5) The 15c and 1l featured a medal and bars from the Polish national anthem, the 30c and 60c angels and the Madonna and the pointed inscription *Queen of the Polish Crown we flee under your protection*, the 50c and 3l an eighteenth century and modern soldier and the inscription *From Italian soil to Poland*, the 80c and 10l uniform badges and map showing Trani and Barletta, and the 5l a soldier and his family needing help. The second set was also sold overprinted *Honour the Four Freedoms* in several languages and President Roosevelt's signature. Freedom of speech and worship, and from want and fear, had been the theme of Roosevelt's 1941 State of the Union address, and they became part of the United Nations Declaration of Human Rights. Most Polish servicemen opted to stay in the United Kingdom, or emigrate elsewhere, rather than return to Russian controlled Poland.

Throughout the war Polish Communist underground groups rivalled nationalist groups for membership and recognition by all the Allies. The Warsaw Uprising of August 1944 starkly revealed the mounting conflict over the post-war control of any restored Polish state. It was launched by the nationalist Polish Home Army in order to pre-empt the arrival of Soviet forces but against the advice of the Polish government-in-exile that rightly judged it too early. The German response was swift and savage and Stalin made only token gestures of support as he watched many anti-Communist resistance fighters perish and Warsaw further punished by bombing and massacres. On 3 February 1945 the Polish government-in-exile issued a stamp in support of survivors, although

12.6 1z+2z Warsaw uprising survivors' relief fund: 3 February 1945.

12.7 25g White Eagle and 50g Grunwald Memorial: set 13 September 1944.

12.8 25g White Eagle overprinted 1z 31.XII.1943 K.R.N. 31.XII.1944: 31 December 1944.

12.9 25g White Eagles overprinted 2z P.K.W.N. 31.XII.1944 and 3z 31.XII.1944 R.T.R.P.: 15 January 1945.

by then Communist authority was uppermost in Poland itself.(12.6) Indeed by then Soviet forces aided by the Polish First and Second Armies, recruited from Polish prisoners of war in Soviet camps and others willing to fight under Russian senior officers against the Germans, were well on the way to controlling the country.

From September 1944 a series of issues by the Moscow controlled Polish Workers Party which fundamentally had turned itself into a government-in-waiting marked its takeover of the increasingly extensive liberated parts of the country. It based itself in the recently freed east Polish city of Lublin. On 13 September a 25g stamp displayed the Polish White Eagle emblem, and a 50g featured the Grunwald Memorial in Cracow.(12.7) Significantly the white eagle had had its centuries-old royal crown removed for the stamp. The memorial to the great Polish-Lithuanian victory over the Teutonic Knights at Grunwald in 1410 was a vast stone block topped by a statue of King Wladyslaw II Jagiello of Poland and Lithuania (c1362-1434) completed on the 500th anniversary of the battle in 1910. Not surprisingly the Germans destroyed it in 1940, but in January 1945 the decision was made to rebuild it. And not surprisingly, the stamp featured the side panel showing Ulrich von Jungingen, the Teutonic Knight's Grand Master, lying at the feet of Vytautas, Grand Duke of Lithuania.

The White Eagle stamp was reissued several times with various overprints that reflected the progressive Communist takeover as the Germans retreated. To some, no doubt, the issues heralded a welcome new era while to others they confirmed one oppressor was being replaced by another. On 31 December 1944 the White Eagle stamp appeared overprinted *1z 31.XII.1943 K.R.N. 31.XII.1944* signifying the creation of the *Krajowa Rada Narodowa* (the Homeland National Council) which ignored the government-in-exile and declared itself the vehicle for managing internal affairs - in alliance with the Soviet Union - until liberation and elections.(12.8) On 15 January 1945 the stamp appeared twice more. One was overprinted *2z P.K.W.N. 31.XII.1944* to mark the KRN creating the *Polski Komitet Wolnosci Narodowej* (Polish Committee of National Liberation), which existed between July and December 1944, and the second was overprinted *3z 31.XII.1944 R.T.R.P.* to highlight the date the PKWN became the *Rzad Tymczasowy Rzeczpospolitej Polskiek* (Provisional Government of the Republic of Poland).(12.9)

The Soviet Union's grip on Poland became firm early in 1945. On 12 February ten White Eagle stamps of 13 September 1944 were reissued with overprints celebrating the western advance of the Soviet army accompanied by assorted nationalist and Communist forces. Each stamp was overprinted 3z, the name of a city and the date in January it was liberated. Kielce was

12.10 25g White Eagle overprinted Radom 16.1.1945 3z: from set 12 February 1945.

12.11 15g Romauld Traugutt: from set 7 September 1944.

dated 15th January 1945, Radom the 16th, Czestochowa and Warszawa the 17th, Krakow and Lodz the 19th, Gniezno the 22nd, Bydgoszcz the 23rd, Kalisz the 24th and Zakopane the 29th.(12.10) The Soviet armies had been aided by the Polish Home Army, a vast array of partisan units loyal to the government-in-exile, but on 19 February 1945, with much of Poland free of German troops, it was disbanded and disarmed under rigorous Soviet control. The way was free for the Communists. In due course many opponents were deported or executed in the chaos of liberation. Stalin ensured it was the pro-Communist Polish First and Second Amies forces, often led, and always closely watched by Soviet officers that formed the core of the post-war Polish army. Even here, units were purged of those deemed of doubtful loyalty.

As an international cover-up of its ultimate intentions, the Provisional Government ensured it contained a temporary sprinkling of Liberal and Socialist members alongside the Communist majority, and launched a popular reformist manifesto. In April 1945 it signed a treaty of friendship and cooperation with the Soviet Union. Support grew, the title changed to the Provisional Government of National Unity and in June 1945 it was formally recognised by the USA, UK and other European countries.

The Polish government-in-exile was furious but impotent. It had lost all influence with the Western Allies whose own influence over Polish affairs was minimal. While the Western Allies and the Soviet Union debated the new Polish borders, within Poland anti-Communists movements were crushed, and their members imprisoned or executed. In the end the Soviet Union incorporated eastern Poland, and Poland was compensated with German territory east of the Rivers Oder and Neisse, and parts of Pomerania, Silesia and East Prussia. The entire country shifted to the west - much as it was in Medieval Europe. Around 8,000,000 Germans fled or were deported, and around 3,000,000 Poles moved westwards from the Soviet Union's newly acquired territory.

Poland's stamps reflect the dramatic changes in the country's fortunes, and not least the repeated attempts to ensure the Communist take-over was perceived as the ultimate success of the people's revolts against repressive rulers over the centuries. The myth of liberation, independence and restored nationhood was thus preserved.

While the Polish government-in-exile's stamps had severely limited circulation, by September 1944 the Lublin based Committee of National Liberation was issuing stamps for use across all liberated Polish territory. In addition to the White Eagle ones already mentioned, on 7 September three stamps shrewdly featured national heroes. The 25g pictured Romauld Traugutt (1826-64) who led the 1863 Polish insurrection against Imperial Russia and was eventually betrayed and hanged.(12.11) The 50g pictured Tadeusz Kosciuszko (1746-1817) who fought against England in the American War of Independence, and against Russia in 1792 War of Partition, and led the 1794 Polish uprising against Tsarist Russia. The 1z pictured Jan Henryk Dabrowski (1755-1818) who served under Kosciuszko in 1794 and after the Polish partition he led the Polish Legion under the Napoleon in the hope that once victorious over Austria and Russia the French Emperor might restore Poland.

The Moscow led Polish Communists went to great lengths to ensure Poland's history of revolt against Imperial Russian autocracy reinforced their cause - namely, the beneficence of the revolutionary Soviet Union in freeing the country from Nazi domination. The issues also made it seem the Communists favoured

12.12 50g Tadeusz Kosciuszko overprinted 5zl and 24.III.1794: 9 April 1945.

12.13 3z Kosciuszko memorial in Lodz: 1 July 1945.

12.15 10z 115th anniversary of the 1830 revolt: 29 November 1945

12.14 5z 535th anniversary of the Battle of Grunwald: 16 July 1945.

12.16 6z 83rd anniversary of the 1863 revolt: 22 January 1946.

Polish nationalism. On 22 January 1945 Romauld Traugatt and the 1863 revolt were remembered on its 82nd anniversary with a white eagle stamp overprinted 5zl and the exact date *22.I.1863*. On 9 April 1945 the 50g Kosciuszko stamp was reissued overprinted *5zl* and *24.III.1794* to mark his oath of allegiance to the Polish rebellion. (12.12) On 1 July 1945 a stamp featured his memorial in Lodz. It had been another Polish monument destroyed by the Germans.(12.13) And on 16 July 1945 a stamp featuring a montage of the images on the Grunwald Monument commemorated the 535th anniversary of the battle. (12.14) The impact of these Polish heroes at this time meant the unusual anniversaries - 82nd, 151st and 535th - were well worth celebrating

On 29 November 1945 a dramatic stamp combined a statue of the renowned King of Poland, John III Sobieski (1629-96), who defeated the Ottoman Turks outside Vienna in 1683 with images of soldiers of 1830 to mark the 115th anniversary of the 1830 *Powstanie Listopadowe* (November Uprising) against Imperial Russian occupation.(12.15) A couple of months later, on 22 January 1946 a dramatic image of a flag waving insurgent marked the 83rd anniversary of the 1863 revolt.(12.16)

Proletarian figures were particularly favoured philatelically. On 10 March 1946 a dramatic stamp featuring the vigorous defence of a barricade honoured the estimated 5,000 Poles from Poland, the rest of Europe (mainly from the French and Belgian coalfields)

12.17 3z+5z Polish volunteers in the Spanish Civil War: 10 March 1946.

and the USA who fought in the Republican International Brigade against General Franco's Nationalists in the Spanish Civil War of 1936-39.(12.17) The inscription is *PAMIECI WALK W HISZPANII BRYGADY POLSKIEJ IM JAROSLAWA DABROWSKIEGO (IN MEMORY OF THE POLISH JAROSLAW DABROWSKI BRIGADE IN SPAIN)*. Many were members of the Communist Party, and although vilified by the pre-war Polish government they were hailed as heroes by the post-war People's Republic which ostentatiously awarded medals to the survivors. The brigade took its name from the left-wing hero Jaroslaw Dabrowski (1836-71) who had been arrested for plotting the Polish 1863 revolt, escaped

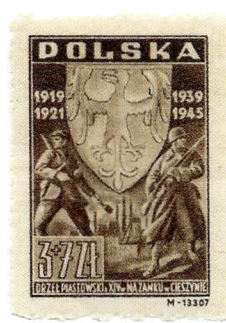

12.18 3z+7z Silesian Uprisings (1919-21, 1939-45): 2 May 1946.

prison, and fled to France where he died on the Paris barricades in 1871 as a leader of the defeated revolutionary Communards.

On 2 May 1946 a single stamp recalled an event embracing Polish nationalism, German aggression and Soviet liberation. It featured a Polish insurgent of 1919-1921, a Russian soldier of 1939-1945 and the spread eagle emblem of Silesia.(12.18) The inscription *ORZET PIASTOWSKI eXIVw NA ZAMKU CIESZYNIE (THE XIVth CENTURY PIAST EAGLE AT CIESZYN CASTLE)* refers to the castle of the medieval Piast rulers of the Polish Duchy of Teschen which guarded the Silesian Olza River and border. Between 1919 and 1921 Polish nationalists violently confronted the German forces striving to retain Upper Silesia and its rich mining areas in the aftermath of the First World War. The region had been part of medieval Poland but most of it had become Prussian in 1742. After several Polish uprisings had been crushed by Allied forces, in 1921 the League of Nations awarded most of the mineral rich territory to Poland. In 1939 Germany quickly retaliated by occupying Silesia, expelling most Poles, bringing in German settlers, and building Auschwitz concentration camp. After liberation by Soviet forces in 1945 most of Silesia became Polish, and the Germans were duly expelled or deported to the USSR.

In March 1945 two stamps highlighted Germany's wartime atrocities and impending defeat. On 9 March a stamp showing a flag waver and war victim highlighted the liberation of Warsaw by the Russian and Polish armies (12.19), and on 15 March a stamp featuring a factory landscape commemorated the liberation of Lodz.(12.20) Before they retreated the Germans had deliberately turned Warsaw into a wasteland, and the German controlled factories at Lodz had been worked by thousands of Jews herded into the vast ghetto.

Cracow had been the German headquarters of the General Government, and it merited a set of five stamps on 10 April 1945.(12.21) They bore the liberation date 19-I-1945, and three featured memorials to the Battle of Grunwald (50g), to the patriot Tadeusz Kosciuszko (1z) and to the mathematician and astronomer Nicolaus Copernicus (1473-1543) (3z). The others pictured the elegant Cloth Hall (2z) and vast Wawel Castle (5z), the seat of the Polish president - and then Hans Frank, the infamous German Gauleiter who was tried at Nuremberg and hanged in October 1946.

Although Poland's brief war against the Soviet Union in 1939 was airbrushed out of history, sets interwove recent memories of Poland's war against Germany with typical Soviet-style issues celebrating proletarian events. On 22 July 1945, the date claimed as the first anniversary of liberation, a stamp pictured the Polish eagle flying free from its chains over the new Communist-style manifesto.(12.22) The date was important as it referred to the Committee of National Liberation, with Stalin's

12.19 5z Liberation of Warsaw: 9 March 1945.

12.20 1z Liberation of Lodz: 15 March 1945.

12.21 1z Kosciuszko Memorial and 5z Wawel Castle: from set 10 April 1945.

approval, signing its ostensibly liberal manifesto for government in agreement with the Union of Polish Patriots (fundamentally the Polish Communist Party) on 22 July 1944. In July 1945 the Allied leaders at the Potsdam Conference confirmed Poland's new borders, another cause for Communist celebration.

On 1 September 1945 a dramatic stamp, heavily surtaxed to support public sanatoriums, marked the sixth anniversary of the week-long Polish defence of Westerplatte in the Bay of Danzig (Polish Gdansk) against bombardment by the veteran German battleship *Schleswig-Holstein,* waves of dive-bombers and landings by marines. (12.23) It had opened the Second World War. Two weeks later, on 15 September 1945, the liberation of Gdansk that March was marked by three stamps featuring the medieval crane tower (1z), Stock Exchange (2z) and High Gate, whose ancient inscription read 'Justice and piety are the foundations of all states.' (3z).(12.24) The previous day a surtaxed stamp had featured Gdansk's ancient and modern cranes and a figure of a soldier saluting a fallen flag bearer.(12.25) The inscription *CZESC POLEGLYM W GDANSKU POCZTOWCOM (ESPECIALLY THE POSTAL WORKERS LOST IN GDANSK)* referred to the 57 Polish Post Office workers in Gdansk who held off repeated German attacks for fifteen hours on 1 September 1939. Eventually surrendering, the survivors (except four who escaped) were executed by the Germans as illegal combatants. The central panel of the stamp was a preliminary design for the Post Office memorial which, although amended, kept the two main figures.

To German fury, the Peace Treaty in 1919 had given Poland access to the sea at Gdansk via a corridor of ex-German territory that left East Prussia isolated from the rest of Germany. Enthusiastic Poles founded the Maritime & Colonial League to encourage seamanship and overseas trade. With government support it popularised ship building and sea-going careers,

12.24 3z Gdansk High Gate: from set 15 September 1945.

12.25 3z+12z Memorial to the fallen in Gdansk: 14 September 1946.

12.22 3z First anniversary of liberation: 22 July 1945.

12.26 50g+2z HMS Dragon and 1z+3z 'Dar Pomorza': from set 24 April 1945.

12.23 1z+9z Sixth anniversary of the defence of Westerplatte: 1 September 1945.

12.27 3z+7z Festival of the sea: 21 July 1946.

12.28 1z50 Royal castle (with overprint), 3z St John's Archcathedral, and 10z Holy Cross Church: from sets 15 October 1945+ and 17 January 1946.

including in the Polish Navy, and probably its most famous action was collecting five million zlotys to build the famous submarine *Orzel* that escaped the Germans to serve with the Royal Navy. The Maritime League (*Liga Morska*) was revived in 1944 - with 'Colonial' omitted - and on 24 April 1945 a surcharged set supported the new initiative.(12.26) The 50g+2z featured the wartime British light cruiser HMS *Dragon* crewed by Poles, the 1z+3z the fully rigged training ship *Dar Pomorza* (the first vessel to sail around the world under the Polish flag in 1934-35), the 2z+4z two naval ensigns, and the 3z+5z the ancient and modern crane towers at Gdansk. On 21 July 1946 Polish maritime interests were further supported through a surcharged stamp inscribed SWIETO MORZA (FESTIVAL OF THE SEA) showing a map of Poland's new post-war coastline.(12.27)

Between October 1945 and January 1946 the utter devastation across Warsaw was publicised by six stamps showing selected religious and secular buildings before and after the war, including the Royal Castle (1z 50), St John's Archcathedral (3z), City Hall (3z 50), General Post Office (6z), War Ministry (8z) and Holy Cross Church (10z). Each of these historic buildings had been destroyed in deliberate acts of German reprisal after the 1944 Warsaw uprising. The set was reissued on 17 January 1946 overprinted WARSZAWA WOLNA 17 Styczen 1945-1946 (WARSAW FREE 17 January 1945-1946).(12.28)

Issued on various dates in 1946, the first post-war Airmail set showed a twin engined Lisunov Li-2 flying over the ruins of Warsaw.(12.29) The widely used Li-2 was a Soviet version, built under licence, of the American Douglas DC3. LOT, the Polish Airline, had been re-established as a state enterprise the previous year. On 1 September 1948 a surtaxed stamp supporting Warsaw's reconstruction showed Route W-Z passing by the ruins of the Royal Palace and heavily damaged St Anne's Church with new tower blocks in the background.(12.30) In 1949 the foundations of St Anne's were hurriedly strengthened as the Route W-Z excavations had severely weakened them.

Three more stamps in April and May 1946 and another in 1947 reinforced German inhumanity and the repercussions of war. The first celebrated the 600th anniversary of the northern trading city of Bydgoszcz on the confluence of the Rivers Vistula and Brda.(12.31) Poles would have known it had been held by Germany from 1772 until 1920 (as Bromberg) until transferred to a reconstituted Poland in 1920. After 1939 it had witnessed thousands of executions of Poles and Jews. The second was inscribed MAJDANEK OBOZ SMIERCI 1941-1944 (MAJDANEK DEATH CAMP 1941-1944) and showed a cloaked skeleton hovering over the camp.(12.32) Built near Lublin it had housed and killed tens of thousands of Jews, other Poles and Russian prisoners of war. On 9 May 1946 a stamp marking the first anniversary of peace pictured advancing infantrymen rather than any hopeful signs of peace itself except the distant sun. And significantly a Red Cross Fund stamp issued as late as 1 June 1947 pictured a wounded soldier supported by a nurse being welcomed home by his son.(12.34) Many prisoners of war and forced labourers were still being repatriated, or awaiting it - some from Germany, but many from the USSR.

12.29 15z Lisunov Li-2 flying over ruins of Warsaw: from Air set 5 March 1946+.

12.30 15z+5z Route W-Z at Warsaw's Royal Palace and St Anne's Church: 1 September 1948.

12.32 3z+5z 'Death' over Majdanek concentration camp: 29 April 1946.

12.31 3z+2z River traffic at Bydgoszcz: 19 April 1946.

12.33 3z First anniversary of peace: 9 May 1946.

anniversary of the National Liberation Committee's manifesto promising a secret ballot, land reforms, free education, economic recovery and higher wages whilst also denouncing the government-in-exile. From left to right it portrayed Edward Osobka-Morawski (1909-97), a Socialist briefly tolerated as prime minister (1945-47)

Interspersed with these grim reminders, Communist Poland's stamps hailed the triumph of the proletariat. On 16 June 1945 a surtaxed stamp featuring the Town Hall in Poznan marked the Postal Employees' Congress there.(12.35) Significantly the ancient Polish city had been part of Prussia and Germany between 1793 and 1918, then part of Poland amidst the expulsion of Germans, and then reabsorbed into Germany between 1939 and 1945 amidst the persecution of Jews, expulsion of Poles, and the destruction of much of the city in a last ditch defence against Soviet forces. In 1945 all remaining German civilians were expelled and the city became Polish again. The heavily damaged Town Hall was rebuilt between 1945 and 1954.

On 18 November 1945 a surtaxed stamp highlighting proletarian comradeship marked the Polish Trades Union Congress *(Kongres Zwiazkow Xawodowych)* (12.36) No doubt the unions already realised their task was to be the subservient intermediaries bringing the needs of the state to the hearts and minds of their members. On 22 July 1946 a stamp marked the second

12.34 5z+5z Red Cross Fund: 1 June 1947.

12.35 1z+5z Postal Employees' Congress in Poznan: 16 June 1945.

by the Communists until they were secure in power, Boleslaw Bierut (1892-1956) successively Communist President of the State Council and President of Poland (1944-52), and Marshal Michal Rola-Zymierski (1890-1989) a Polish-born Russian NKVD agent and head of the repressive Polish Commission of State Security. The stamp reappeared on 4 February 1947 overprinted +7 (z) and *SEJM USTAWODAWCZY 19 I 1947 (LEGISLATIVE PARLIAMENT 19 I 1947)* to mark the opening of the new parliament after the violence, corruption and fraud of the election had given the Communists and their hapless Socialist allies 394 of the 444 seats.(12.37)

On 1 December 1946 a surtaxed set appeared inscribed *W PIECDZIESIECIOLECIE RUCHU LUDOWEGO (THE FIFTIETH ANNIVERSARY OF THE PEASANT/PEOPLE'S MOVEMENT.)* (12.38) Probably it was issued on the initiative of Jozef Putek (1892-1974) who was a senior figure in the pre-war People's Party (also known as the Peasant Party) that supported the Communists and was Post Office Minister from 1946 until 1948. From left to right each stamp featured Stanislaw Stojalowski (1845-1911), a controversial priest and journalist, member of the Austrian State Council and early promoter of the emerging Peasant Movement; Jakub Bojko (1857-1943) and Jan Stapinski (1867-1946), both founder members

12.38 5z+10z Fiftieth anniversary of Peasant Party/Movement: from set 1 December 1946.

12.39 10z Peasant Party/Movement Congress: from set 26 November 1949+.

of the Peasant Movement and key figures in the pre-war People's Party who served in the Austrian State Council and then the Polish Parliament until the mid 1930s; and Wincenty Witos (1874-1945) who served three times as Polish Prime Minister in the 1920s, and co-founded the pre-war People's Party. In 1947 it was consigned to oblivion by forced amalgamation with the United People's Party - the 'front name' of the hitherto separate Communist Peasant Party that already was in the Communist controlled ruling coalition. In November and December 1949 a set picturing a tractor and worker marked the Congress of the United Peasant/People's Movement *(KONGRES JEDNOSCI RUCHU LUDOWEGO)* - by then an entirely subservient entity. (12.39)

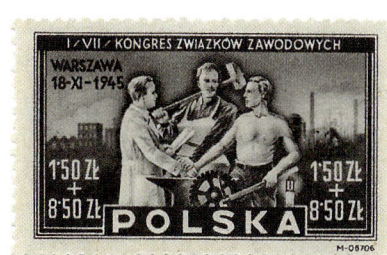

12.36 1z50+8.50 Trades Union Congress: 18 November 1945.

12.37 3z Second anniversary of the manifesto overprinted +7 SEJM USTAWODAWCZY 19 I 1947: 4 February 1947.

On various dates in 1946 stamps featured Bedzin Castle in Upper Silesia (5z), Lanckorona Castle not far from Cracow (6z) and Duke Henryk IV's effigy at St Cross in Wroclaw (10z).(12.40) Their link is tenuous and and the set's overall purpose vague, and most other historic sets stuck to obviously revolutionary themes. Both castles were long past their heyday as residences and fortifications, but they were in lands ruled by Henryk IV (c1258-90), known as Probus (Righteous), who was Duke of Silesia at Wroclaw and High Duke of Krakow. He spent much of his short life defending his Polish lands and seeking to expand them while also finding time to encourage industry and commerce. Probably the stamp recalled his desire to consolidate his Polish territory, and notably Silesia, but no doubt it recalled also the bizarre Nazi disinterment of his body to

12.40 5z Bedzin Castle, 6z Tombstone of Henryk IV, and 10z Lanckorona Castle: set 13 August 1946+.

12.42 5z Wojciech Boguslawski, Helena Modrzejewska, and Stefan Jaracz: from set March 1947+.

12.41 1z, Jan Matejko, Jacek Malczewski, and Josef Chelmonski: from set March 1947+.

prove his 'Germanic' rather than 'Slavic' features. In the event the body disappeared and the results are unknown.

Between March and May 1947 eight stamps featured sixteen carefully selected Polish cultural figures. They were reissued between May and October that year in different colours. Both sets appeared perforate and imperforate. And in June 1948 they were issued again in a miniature sheet. The figures lived at a time when Poland was unhappily and restlessly partitioned between the Russian, German and Austro-Hungarian Empires, and many of their works reflected and inspired the rising tide of opposition to Imperialist repression. The set helped interpret the wartime liberation as the time Poland finally regained its freedom with the help of Russia, itself fully liberated from Tsardom by the Communists.

Four stamps featured three figures each. The 1z featured Jan Matejko (1838-93), an internationally renowned artist whose works glorified Poland's past at a time of discontent at Russian rule, Jacek Malczewski (1854-1929) a neo-Romantic who glorified the Polish countryside and people, and transposed many Classical and Biblical themes into Polish contexts, and Josef Chelmonski (1849-1914) who created vast paintings of Polish rural life and customs.(12.41)

The 5z portrayed Wojciech Boguslawski (1757-1829), an enterprising director of Warsaw's National Theatre and its touring company, Helena Modrzejewska (1840-1909), a celebrated Shakespearian and tragic actress working in the USA and London as well as Poland, and Stefan Jaracz (1885-1945), an actor and producer famous for portraying the disadvantaged, and later imprisoned by the Germans.(12.42)

The 6z pictured Aleksander Swietochowski (1849-1938), a Positivist writer promoting education, scientific inquiry, economic development and equality of rights, Stefan Zeromski (1864-1925), a novelist within the pre-independence Young Poland movement, and Boleslaw Prus (birth name Aleksander Glowacki) (1847-1912) whose articles and novels reflected his Positivist outlook by arguing that the cause of independence was better served by cultural, scientific and economic development than violent revolt.

The 15z featured Stanislaw Wyspianski (1869-1907), a poet, painter and playwright closely associated with the aspirations and frustrations of the Young Poland movement, Juliusz Slowacki (1809-49), a Romantic writer and revolutionary, whose works explored the conflict between good and evil, notably in his interpretation of Polish history, and Jan Kasprowicz (1860-1926), a gifted translator of international works and Young Poland poet and playwright.

Four other stamps contained a single figure. The 2z portrayed Adam Chmielowski (1845-1916). After losing a leg in battle during the 1863 uprising he fled the

12.43 Adam Chmielowski (Brother Albert): Winter Relief issue 21 December 1947.

12.44 3z Frederic Chopin: from set March 1947+.

12.45 10z Marie Curie: from set March 1947+.

The 20z pictured Adam Mickiewicz (1798-1855), a Romantic writer regarded as Poland's greatest poet. Several of his major works inspired the early nineteenth century Polish revolutionaries, especially his epic *Pan Tadeusz* which intertwines the story of two feuding families with a revolt against the local Russian garrison. Adam Mickiewicz, Frederic Chopin and Julius Slowacki were pictured on further issues on 5 December 1949 (12.46), and ten days later Michiewicz appeared with Alexander Pushkin, his Russian contemporary and friend, on a shrewdly designed stamp marking Polish-Russian Friendship Month.(12.47)

A separate stamp, issued in March 1947, featured Emil Zegadlowicz (1888-1941).(12.48) He was a major figure in the literary avant-garde in pre-war Poland as a poet, novelist, translator, theatre manager, radio programmer and early Polish Expressionist. However his left-wing views brought him many enemies, and he was particularly hounded by the Roman Catholic Church. The stamp pictures the gatehouse to his estate and mansion (not his house itself) at Gorzen Gorny in southern Poland.

12.46 10z Adam Mickiewicz, 15z Frederic Chopin, and 35z Julius Slowacki: set 5 December 1949.

country, became a successful artist, returned to Cracow and devoted his life to the poor. Inspired by St Francis of Assisi he became Brother Albert and in 1888 founded the 'Servants of the Poor' and in 1891 the Albertine Sisters. This stamp was re-issued in violet in a smaller format on 21 December 1947 and priced 2z+18z in aid of Winter Relief *(Pomoc Zimowa)*.(12.43)

The 3z portrayed Frederic Chopin (1810-49), the composer of numerous mazurkas, waltzes, nocturnes, polonaises, preludes and sonatas.(12.44)

The 10z pictured Marie Curie (born Maria Sklodowska) (1867-1934) who, with her husband, and for long after his death in 1906, developed and refined the theory of radioactivity, identified new elements and trialled the radio-active treatment of neoplasms.(12.45)

12.47 15z Adam Mickiewicz and Alexander Pushkin: 15 December 1949.

12.48 5z+15z Emil Zegadlowicz: 1 March 1947.

12.49 15z Chainbreakers and 60z Engels and Marx: from set 15 March 1948+.

Interspersed with all the sets harking back to the Polish revolutionaries and the recent war were stamps promoting key themes in Communist society. On 10 October 1946 a surtaxed set and miniature sheet supported Polish education and the International Bureau of Education *(MIEDZYNARODOWE BIURO WYCHOWANIA)* established in 1925 that became linked to UNESCO in 1946. During the war the Bureau and Red Cross provided thousands of books for prisoners of war. The inscription on the 3z+22z highlights the supply of elementary school books, the 6z+24z features the library courtyard of the Jagiellonian University in Cracow, and the 11z+19z pictures Gregor Piramowicz (1735-1801), the author of *The Duties of a Teacher*, and founder of the Jesuit Education Commission and the Society for Elementary Books.(12.52) After 1945 numerous schools and colleges were built across Poland as a matter of urgency, teacher training became a priority, and education became free, compulsory, state controlled, wide in scope and uniform in content. The Polish Roman Catholic Church remained actively anti-Communist, and despite (or because of) its popular

Four stamps issued between 15 March and 15 July 1948 linked past revolutionary figures to present 'freedoms'. The inscription *WIOSNA LUDOW (THE SPRING OF THE PEOPLE)* poignantly, or cynically, refers to the people's hopes dashed in 1848 but realised in 1948. The 15z featured a modern man breaking his chains to begin ploughing, while the 60z portrayed the writers Friedrich Engels (1820-95) and Karl Marx (1818-83), co-authors of *The Communist Manifesto* with its call for the 'forcible overthrow of all existing social conditions.'(12.49)

The other two stamps concentrated on the nineteenth century revolutions the set ostensibly commemorated. Depicted on the 30z, both General Henryk Dembinski (1791-1864) and General Jozef Bem (1794-1850) led Polish forces in the 1830-31 uprising, and Hungarian forces in the 1848-49 revolution. Each won several battles but were ultimately overwhelmed by vastly superior numbers, and forced into exile. Both are Polish and Hungarian national heroes.(12.50)

Three figures featured on the 35z. Stanislaw Worcell (1799-1857) was a well-born utopian Socialist, key participant in the 1830-31 uprising, and member of several revolutionary societies. Father Piotr Sciegienny (1801-90) was imprisoned and barely escaped execution in the 1840s for encouraging peasants and clergy to join independence organisations. Edward Dembowski (1822-46) was another upper-class utopian socialist: he was killed by Austrian troops while leading a procession during the ill-fated Cracow uprising of 1846.(12.51)

12.50 30z General Henryk Dembinski and General Jozef Bem: from set 15 March 1948+.

12.51 35z Stanislaw Worcell, Father Sciegienny, and Edward Dembowski: from set 15 March 1948.

12.52 6z+24z Jagiellonian University library courtyard: from set 10 October 1946.

12.53 25g White Eagle overprinted in support of the National Ski Championship: 21 February 1947.

12.55 15z International Youth Conference in Warsaw: 8 August 1948.

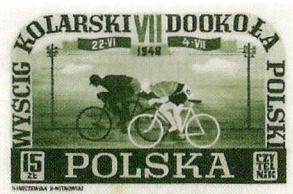

12.54 15z Warsaw-Prague cycle race: 1 May 1948, and 15z Circuit of Poland cycle race: 22 June 1948.

support its historic role as a major force in education dramatically declined. And the Communist government remained suspicious of the Jagiellonian University's teachings, and closed it down in 1954.

Health, sport and youth activities were key Communist themes. On 21 February 1947 the White Eagle stamp appeared again, this time overprinted with a surtax and inscription supporting the 22nd National Ski Championship in Zakopane *(XXII MISTRZOSTWA NARCIARSKIE POLSKI 1947)*.12.53 A stamp on 1 May 1948 marked the Warsaw to Prague international cycle race *(MIEDZYNARODOWY BIEG KOLARSKI)* and a set on 22 June marked the 7th Circuit of Poland cycle race *(WYSCIG KOLARSKI DOOKOLA POLSKI)* which was soon to achieve international status and attract professional teams.(12.54) The main aim of both races, though, was to attract competitors from across Soviet controlled countries in order to highlight Communist sport, competitiveness and prowess.

On 8 August 1948 a stamp picturing youthful silhouettes set against a globe marked the International Youth Conference in Warsaw that year. The lengthy circular inscription translates as *Young people join in the fight for a permanent peace* - a common Communist cry against British and American 'Imperialist aggression'. The lower inscription reads *SWIATOWA FEDERACJA MTODZIEZY DEMOKRATYCZNEJ (THE WORLD FEDERATION OF DEMOCRATIC YOUTH)* This international organisation had been founded in London in 1945, but the western democracies quickly perceived it, with justification, as an organisation increasingly manipulated by the Soviet Union and other national Communist Parties for the transmission of their ideology.(12.55) As the Cold War got colder the organisation was left with mainly young people from socialist countries but it attracted some from movements fighting apartheid such as in South Africa or right-wing dictatorships such as in Cuba.

On 16 December 1948 the scourge of tuberculosis in Poland, as everywhere else, resulted in a lengthy set of surtaxed stamps.(12.56) To raise maximum funds four stamps featured different young children and each one was available with ten different publicity labels - including, as here, one saying *BCG SZCZEPIONKI - TO RATUNEK PRZED GRUZLICA (THE BCG VACCINE - IS A RESCUE FROM TUBERCULOSIS)*

On 20 August 1947 a striking set featured key workers in heroic proletarian poses - a steelworker and hammer (5z), harvester (by hand, not machine) (10z), fisherman (15z) and coal miner (with pick axe) (20z).(12.57) On

12.56 6z+4z Anti-TB Fund: from set 16 December 1948.

12.57 Occupations: set 20 August 1947.

12.58 6z 'Oliwa' and 35z 'General M Zaruski': from set 22 June 1948.

12.59 15z Fifth anniversary of the Warsaw Ghetto Uprising: 19 April 1948.

12.60 15z Exhibition of Recovered Lands: from set 15 July 1948

22 June 1948 a Merchant Marine set featured the mixed cargo-passenger ship *Oliwa* under construction (6z) (named after the Polish naval victory over the Swedes in 1627), an unnamed freighter in dock (15z), and the cadet ketch *General M Zaruski* (35z), built with Maritime League funds in 1939. This was named after a popular supporter of youthful seamanship, and renovated after the war - and still sails.(12.58) The inscription reads *SWIETO MO RZA (HOLIDAY OF THE SEA)*. One wonders how many Poles remembered that the elderly General Mariusz Zaruski (1867-1941), a talented sportsman, sailor and soldier, had been arrested by the Russians after their 1939 invasion of Poland and died of cholera in prison in 1941. One wonders, too, how many Poles who saw the haunting stamp issued on 19 April 1948 portraying a female insurgent and a fallen colleague which commemorated the fifth anniversary of the Warsaw Ghetto Uprising remembered that the Soviet army, not far away, had done virtually nothing to help them.(12.59)

On 15 July 1948 a set showed a searchlight shining over Wroclaw's Centennial Hall which hosted the Exhibition of Recovered Lands *(WYSTAWA ZIEM ODZYSKANYCH)* between July and October.(12.60) This was a massive propaganda event staged by the Communist government to celebrate the German provinces centred on Poznan (German Posen) and Wroclaw (German Breslau) awarded to Poland after the war as compensation for the eastern lands absorbed by the Soviet Union. The numerous exhibits celebrated regional industrial and rural workers, and sought to assure the one and a half million visitors that the Recovered Lands were inherently Polish as they had been part of the medieval Kingdom of Poland. This was largely true of Poznan, but less so of Wroclaw which had been part of medieval Bohemia and Hungary as often as it was part of Poland.

On 6 October 1948 a stamp picturing an express train below a clock-face marked the European Railway Timetable Conference for long distance passenger trains held that year in Cracow.(12.61) It was an essential mainland European meeting held annually since 1872, although with gaps during the two world wars. No doubt the significant shifts in national borders since the end of the war complicated the restoration of railway networks and provision of efficient timetables.

12.61 18z European Railway Timetable Conference: 6 October 1948.

12.63 3z and 5z Trades Union Congress: from set 31 May 1949.

On 8 December 1948 a set publicised the Congress of Working Class Unity *(KONGRES JEDNOSCI KLASY ROBOTNICZEJ)* with images of workers clutching banners (5z), Engels, Marx, Lenin and Stalin (15z) and workers alongside a portrait of Ludwik Warynski (1856-89) who was hailed in post-war Poland as the founder of Polish Socialism (25z).(12.62) A fervent advocate of his egalitarian ideas Warynski was hounded from country to country by Imperial Russian and Austro-Hungarian police until finally dying of tuberculosis in prison. Such Congresses were devoted to intensifying the mythology of the proletariat as the leading social force, to promoting expressions of optimism and joy at successful Communist achievements and developments, and to creating the determination to ensure 'peaceful' Communism prevailed over aggressive Western Imperialism. The set was reissued on 15 December in different colours and with the date *XII 1948* instead of *8 XII 1948* as the Congress lasted several days.

Equally determined and enthusiastic figures featured on the 31 May 1949 set marking the Trades Union Congress *(KONGRES ZWIAZKOW ZAWODOWYCH)*

12.64 35z President Bierut: from set 14 October 1948+.

12.62 5z Workers waving banners and 25z Ludwik Warynski and marchers: from reissued set 15 December 1948.

in Warsaw. The inscriptions *SOCJALIZM (SOCIALISM)* (3z), *PRACA (WORK)* (5z), and *POKOJ (PEACE)* (15z), effectively summed up much of the agenda.(12.63) Between October 1948 and May 1949 the first set of nine stamps portraying the firmly established President Bierut had appeared (12.64). Bierut reappeared on 22 July 1949 in a set marking the fifth anniversary of the National Liberation Committee and exalting the independence and prosperity of the Polish Communist state.(12.65) His portrait on the 15z was inscribed *PIEC LAT POLSKI LUDOWEJ* which may be freely translated as *FIVE YEARS OF POLISH POLAND*. The 10z showed Route W-Z passing through a restored part of Warsaw, and updated the view on the 1 September 1948 Warsaw Reconstruction stamp. The 35z featured the new 335 metres high radio mast at Raszyn which replaced and improved the mast destroyed in the war.

On 30 December 1948 three costly Airmail stamps and a miniature sheet appeared honouring Franklin D Roosevelt (1882-1945) (80z), President of the United States from 1933 until 1945, along with two celebrated Polish patriots who fought alongside the American colonists in the War of Independence from 1775 to 1783.(12.66) Probably their target consumers were

12.65 Fifth anniversary of National Liberation Committee: set 22 July 1949.

12.66 Honouring President Roosevelt, Tadeusz Kosciuszko and Kazimierz Pulaski: set 30 December 1948.

collectors rather than airmail customers, but their presence contributes to the story of post-war Poland and its changing identity. The 120z portrayed Tadeusz Kosciuszko (1746-1817), previously mentioned in this chapter, who was a friend of Thomas Jefferson and became a brigadier general in George Washington's army, and the 100z pictured Kazimierz Pulaski (1745-79) who created the Pulaski Cavalry Legion, led it in several battles and died leading a charge against the British at Savannah in Georgia. Both became American and Polish national heroes. After the First World War President Woodrow Wilson advocated Polish independence but in 1945 Roosevelt pragmatically abandoned the Polish government-in-exile and quickly recognised the Russian supported government in Warsaw. The USA attempted to maintain warm relations with Poland in the later 1940s as it seemed the USA and a Communist state maintaining the guise of a coalition could avoid a diplomatic breakdown. By the end of 1948, though, President Bierut was heading an administration increasingly subservient to Moscow, and relations with the West were soon to freeze.

CHAPTER 13
CZECHOSLOVAKIA

Czechoslovakia was created in 1918 from parts of the defunct Hapsburg Austro-Hungarian Empire, notably Austria's Bohemia and Moravia and Hungary's Slovakia and Galicia. During the First World War well-respected and high-profile nationalists such as Edvard Benes, Tomas Masaryk and Milan Stefanik had fostered support from the Allies. They had been aided by the distinguished war record of the Czechoslovak Legion - a powerful force of Czech and Slovak volunteers whose battle-hardened units fought against their historic Austro-Hungarian overlords and Germany in Russia, Italy and France. However, despite securing independence the country was far from unified. The Czechs and Slovaks had different histories and cultures, and many Germans, Poles and Hungarians hated the new borders that trapped them inside Czechoslovakia.

The predominantly German Sudetenland encircling Bohemia in the west provided Hitler with the means of eventually dismembering Czechoslovakia. Effectively abandoned by France and Great Britain, and surrounded by hostile Germany, Poland and Hungary, the Czech government had little choice but to cede the Sudetenland to Germany under the Munich Agreement between Germany, France, Great Britain and Italy in September 1938. In March 1939 Hitler occupied Bohemia and Moravia, Slovakia became a loyal German puppet state under the nationalist priest, Father Josef Tiso, and Hungary quickly annexed the far eastern province of Carpatho-Ukraine. On stamps, and elsewhere, *Ceskoslovensko* disappeared to be replaced by *Bohmen und Mahren (Deutsches Reich)* in the west and *Slovensko* in the east. In Prague a puppet government under Emile Hacha recognised German occupation as a 'protectorate', industry and agriculture were redirected towards German needs, rationing was soon introduced, the Jewish population virtually annihilated, and any resistance crushed. The assassination of SS *Obergruppenfuhrer* Reinhard Heydrich, Deputy Reich Protector of Bohemia-Moravia by British trained Czechs in 1942 led to hundreds of deaths and the destruction of the villages of Lidice and Lezaky. By then several thousand had fled to join units linked to Allied armed forces, and resistance groups were steadily growing.

Edvard Benes organised a government-in-exile in London, but although he supported the Western Allies he deliberately promoted friendship with the Soviet Union in tacit recognition of the failure of France and Great Britain to protect the country in the 1930s. In 1943 he concluded a treaty of friendship with Stalin in the hope that an independent Czechoslovakia could be restored, and he offered Czech Communist exiles hopes of key posts in government.

Throughout 1943 and 1944 opposition stiffened against Tiso's pro-Nazi rule and the waste of Slovak lives on the Eastern Front. In August 1944 discontented army units rebelled in the 'Slovak Uprising' and although joined by resistance fighters from Poland and Bohemia-Moravia the Germans ruthlessly crushed it. However in late October 1944 Soviet armed forces, assisted by Czech and Romanian units, advanced into Carpatho-Ukraine in the far east of Slovakia. Here only a minority of the mixed population of Slovaks, Hungarians, Germans and Ruthenians favoured returning to Czechoslovakia, especially as Benes wished to deport Hungarians and Germans. The local Communists triumphed and, out-manoeuvring the Czech government-in-exile's mission to re-establish control, successfully created 'a national council' that voted to seek admission to the Ukrainian Soviet Socialist Republic. For a short time both sides strengthened their claims by issuing postage stamps. (13.1) Under severe pressure, in the late autumn of 1945 Czechoslovakia formally ceded Carpatho-Ukraine to the USSR, and Czechs and Slovaks there were given the choice of Czech or Soviet citizenship.

The Western Allies eastward advance stopped at Pilsen in west Bohemia. In May 1945 Edvard Benes took control of a reunited Czechoslovakia, and immediately secured Allied agreement to deport all Sudetenland and other Germans except a minority who were clearly anti-fascist or married to ethnic Czechs. Just under a million went to Germany's Soviet Zone and

13.1 60f National Council of Carpatho-Ukraine: from second set summer 1945.

13.2 Repatriation Fund: set 15 October 1946.

13.3 5k Kosice issues: Soldier and Czech Arms: from set 26 March 1945, and 9k Soviet-Czech clasped hands and map: from set 2 April 1945+.

13.4 1k Bratislava issue: Linden leaf and Arms: from set 30 April 1945+.

13.5 500h Prague issue: Linden leaves: from set 23 May 1945+.

13.6 6pf Germany definitive overprinted 1kc C.S.R. Pravda Vitezi in Cheb, and 1.20k Bohemia-Moravia definitive overprinted Posta Ceskoslovenska 1945 in Olomouc: both May 1945. Pravda Vitezi (Truth Prevails) was Czechoslovakia's motto created by Tomas Masaryk in 1918.

a million and a half to the American Zone. More than 20,000 died in suicides or through ill-treatment linked to the deportations. Thousands of Hungarians also lost their property, and neither they nor the Germans received any compensation. In a huge programme, much of their land was redistributed to Czech peasants. At the same time thousands of Czechs and Slovaks began returning home from exile, forced labour or active service. In October 1946 a set of surcharged stamps highlighted and supported the resettlement programme (as did refugee funds in the UK and elsewhere).(13.2) Three pictures of families in national costume told the story along with three inscriptions - *Odisli ste* (You left), *Zustali ste nast* (You stayed firm) and *Vratili ste sa* (You are back).

On 26 March 1945 the first three stamps inscribed once again CESKOSLOVENSKO had been issued in a set from liberated Kosice in eastern Slovakia featuring a soldier in a starred Russian helmet alongside the Czechoslovak Arms.(13.3) Soon afterwards four other values more diplomatically portrayed Czech and Russian hands clasped against a sunlit map of reunified Czechoslovakia.(13.3) Further west in Bratislava, from April 1945 a new set featured the Czech Arms and a sprig of linden leaves.(13.4) On 23 May a set inscribed Ceskoslovensko hurriedly issued in Prague used the linden leaves design from the Bohemia-Moravia Protectorate set of 1939-40.(13.5) These sets superseded all wartime issues, and notably Slovakia's Tiso and Bohemia-Moravia's Hitler head definitives. Many of these that had been overprinted unofficially with various celebratory designs by post offices as towns had been liberated.(13.6)

On 18 August 1945 a set of 16 stamps portrayed eight wartime heroes.(13.7) Stanislav Zimprich (25h and 2k50), Alois Vasatko (50h and 5k) and Mieczyslaw Adamek (60h and 10k) were pilots who gave their lives serving in Czech squadrons of the RAF. Another pilot,

13.7 40h Jozef Gabcik, 2k Capt Otaker Jaros, and 5k Alois Vasatko: from set 18 August 1945.

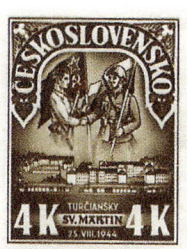

13.8 1k20 'Grief' and 2k40 Flame of Remembrance: from set 10 June 1947.

13.9 2k Banska Bystrica, 4k Turciansky, 4k50 Sklabina, and 5k Strecno: from set 29 August 1945.

Lieutenant Jiri Kral (30h and 3k) was killed in 1940 in the Battle for France, and Captain Frantisek Novak (10h and 1k50) also died in 1940 in France as a flying instructor. Captain Otaker Jaros (20h and 2k) was killed combatting German tanks at Sokolovo in 1943 in the First Czech Army alongside the Red Army, and was awarded the 'Hero of the Soviet Union'. Captain Pravoslav Ridky (5h and 1k) was killed in North Africa in 1943 in a Czech unit fighting in the British Army. Most famous of all, Jozef Gabcik (40h and 4k) was a Slovak parachutist trained in Great Britain who, with Jan Kubris, assassinated Heydrich in Prague. Both were trapped and died in the basement of the Church of St Cyril & St Methodious. On 10 June 1947 a haunting set symbolising Grief and Remembrance marked the fifth anniversary of the German massacre of over 180 men at Lidice, and the deportation to concentration camps of 300 women and children, in retaliation for the assassination.(13.8)

Soon afterwards, on 29 August 1945, a set duly honoured the first anniversary of the ill-fated Slovak Uprising.(13.9) The 4k50 pictured Sklabina where partisans first raised the Czech flag on 21 August, a week before the formal uprising. The village was to suffer badly from German reprisals. The 4k pictured a Russian and Slovak partisan greeting each other at Turciansky, and had the date 25 August. The 2k featured Banska Bystrica where the uprising fully broke out on 29 August - the date history records. The Germans were quick to counter-attack with overwhelming force and although some Communists did rally to the cause, most obeyed Stalin's order to remain independent and bide their time. He had longer term aims in mind. Some British and American aid got through, but any Soviet supplies largely reinforced Communist groups. The 5k featured a partisan at Strecno where the mountains and gorges witnessed bitter partisan battles with the Germans. The 1k50 pictured the flags of Czechoslovakia, the USA, UK and USSR. By the date of the set the heavy Communist presence and propaganda were already ensuring the spread of a favourable, if not entirely accurate, account of the event.

On 5 July 1945 three stamps had pictured Tomas Masaryk (1850-1937) the pre-war Czech statesman and President from 1918-35, and another three values joined them on 5 March 1946.(13.10) They were

13.10 2k Tomas Masaryk: from set 5 July 1945+.

13.12 1k20 Tenth anniversary of death of Tomas Masaryk: from set 14 September 1947.

important early post-war issues as he was the pre-eminent figure in Czechoslovakia achieving independence and, once achieved, maintaining it in the face of internal and external threats. Similar dangers surrounded President Benes when he was restored to office in 1945.

From October 1945 an increasingly long definitive set featured the three national heroes - Tomas Masarayk, President Edvard Benes (1884-1948) who had led the government-in-exile, and the Slovak-French General Milan Stefanic (1880-1919).(13.11) Stefanic's short but tumultuous life embraced fame as an astronomer, French general, Czech Minister of War, organiser of the Czech Legions, close colleague of Masaryk and Benes, and successful international diplomat. He was killed in 1919, in a never satisfactorily explained incident flying over territory contested by Czechoslovakia and Hungary not far from Bratislava. In 1945, and for a while afterwards, Masaryk's reputation remained high, and Benes managed to hold onto power - again for a while. Two stamps marked the tenth anniversary of President Masaryk's death on 14 September 1947. (13.12) Another set portraying President Benes appeared on 28 October 1946 marking Independence Day (in 1918), followed by a third set on 15 February 1948 - just a few months, however, before his resignation. (13.13)

13.13 Edvard Benes: 3k: from set 28 October 1946 and 5k from set 15 February 1948.

13.14 7k40 Hodonin: from set 3 August 1946, and 10k Zvolen Castle: 28 August 1949.

In 1946 stamps featured views of Brno and Hodonin and, in 1949, Zvolen Castle.(13.14) Although they were in the attractive style of the pre-war views set there was no other attempt to promote national sights in this post-war period. Indeed, other factors probably governed these three issues. Brno was hosting a national philatelic exhibition, Hodonin was ex-President Masaryk's birthplace, and Zvolen had been a key centre in the 1944 Slovak National Uprising.

Several other stamps recalled the nation's past and present struggles, and the links between them. The date in 1946 selected for two pre-Communist stamps showing St Gorge slaying the dragon marking the first anniversary of liberation was 5 May, the date in 1945 that resistance fighters and the people of Prague rose against the Germans, rather than 9 May when Soviet forces entered the capital after the Germans had left. The accompanying miniature sheet was, rather

13.11 80h Milan Stefanic, 1k60 Edvard Benes, and 15k Tomas Masaryk: from set 28 October 1945+.

13.15 4k+6k First anniversary of liberation: miniature sheet from set 5 May 1946.

13.16 2k40 Jan Kozina memorial: from set 28 November 1945.

13.17 1k20 Karel Borovsky: 5 July 1946.

13.18 5k St Adalbert (Vojtech): from set 23 April 1947.

cryptically in the complex circumstances, inscribed *PRAVDA VITEZI (TRUTH WINS) KVETEN (MAY) 1945-1946* (13.15) The Allied commander, General Eisenhower, had decided against advancing beyond Pilsen and supporting the uprising, much to the bitter regret of many Czechs. It was perhaps doubly significant that on 28 November 1945 two stamps had commemorated Jan Sladky Kozina (1652-95) who was executed in Pilsen for leading a peasants' revolt, and became immortalised as a resistance figure in later stories and Karel Kovarovic's opera.(13.16)

And just a couple of months after the 'first anniversary of liberation' issue a stamp featured the 90th anniversary (rather than wait for the centenary) of the death of Karel Havlicek Borovsky (1821-56), a long-remembered writer, publisher and political activist who sought Czech freedom from Hapsburg repression in the heady days of European revolutions in 1848 and ended up persecuted and imprisoned.(13.17) On 23 April 1947 a set of three stamps commemorated the 950th anniversary of the martyrdom of St Adalbert (Czech name Vojtech: c956-997), a reforming Bishop of Prague and missionary to the pagan Baltic Prussians who killed him.(13.18)

Slovak patriots were not entirely forgotten. On 19 October 1947 two stamps marked the 150th anniversary of the birth of Stefan Moyses (1797-1869), the renowned Bishop of Banska-Bystrika and chairman of *Matica slovenska*, the pioneering Slovak cultural institution. He headed the 1861 Slovak deputation to the Emperor Franz Joseph submitting the *Memorandum naroda slovenskeho (Memorandum of the Slovak nation)* asking (in vain) for Imperial recognition of a national identity and equality.(13.19) It paved the way for the struggle for independence in 1918.

On 14 November 1945 two surcharged stamps supported the World Student Congress in Prague. (13.20) This event, along with one in London, resumed the pre-war work of the Confederation Internationale des Etudiants and prepared the way for the establishment of a new organisation, the International Union of Students, in 1946. Countries across the world were represented and so were all shades of political, social and educational opinion. Interestingly the featured student is wearing the French revolutionary Phrygian cap. The Union and its Congresses soon became the target of both Soviet and American political infiltration.

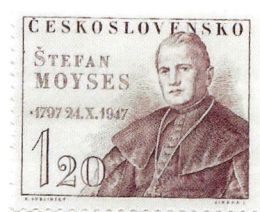

13.19 1k20 Stefan Moyses: from set 19 October 1947.

13.20 2k50+2k50 World Student Congress, Prague: from set 14 November 1945.

13.21 4k World Festival of Youth & Students, Prague: from set 20 July 1947.

13.22 9k Captain Novak, 20k Bratislava, and 24k Prague: from Air set 4 July 1946+.

13.23 4k 'Two Year Plan': from set 1 January 1947.

On 20 July 1947 two stamps marked the month-long First World Festival of Youth and Students at the vast Strahov Stadium in Prague.(13.21) The organising body, the World Federation of Democratic Youth, chose Czechoslovakia in memory of the Lidice massacre and the German oppression of thousands of young Czech protesting in 1939 against the occupation. 17,000 young people from 71 countries attended the Festival and Anatoli Novikov's *Song of Democratic Youth* was sung for the first time. The Federation's first General Secretary, Alexander Shelepin, was an avid Communist and ensured the organisation was critical of everything British and America. With Russian backing the Federation became an obvious vehicle for Soviet propaganda, and most future festivals were staged in Communist countries and scorned by most western governments - but not by all their youthful citizens.

The Czechoslovak State Airlines resumed operations after the war, and Air stamps in June and July 1946 featured Lockheed Constellations flying over Prague and Bratislava.(13.22) The June stamp commemorated the first Prague to New York flight, and several of the 1946 set pictured the war hero Captain Frantisek Novak and the British Westland Lysander he flew on missions. The stamps were reissued surtaxed in September 1949, but by then the Communist government was suspending many international flights and Western countries were placing embargoes on the sale of aeroplanes and spare parts. Czechoslovakia was reduced to using updated Russian Ilyushin Il-14s.

On 1 January 1947 two stamps adorned with symbols of industry, agriculture and learning marked the start of the government's 'Two Year Plan' of investment and development economic, but they marked, too, the final stages of the Communist take-over.(13.23) In 1945 Benes had wanted a liberal democracy, as did the Western Allies, but in the May 1946 elections the Communist Party won 38.7% of the vote, no doubt helped by strong anti-German feelings, the pre-war betrayal of the West, and a new sense of Pan-Slav solidarity. Benes stayed president but Klement Gottwald became prime minister and the Communists took the key interior, justice, finance, information and agriculture ministries. Significantly, on 26 October 1947 two dramatic stamps featuring a young women with broken chains escaping to freedom celebrated the 30th anniversary of the Russian Revolution.(13.24)

Although the coalition parties in government publicly called themselves the National Front, rows raged over nationalisation, taxation of the rich, public

13.24 2k40 Thirtieth anniversary of the Russian Revolution: from set 26 October 1947.

13.25 8k Death of Edvard Benes: 28 September 1948.

13.26 1k50 Thirtieth anniversary of independence: from set 28 October 1948.

died on 3 September 1948, and on 28 September a single stamp devoid of an inscription marked his passing.(13.25) Once the Communists seized total control, both he and Tomas Masaryk were vilified as historic enemies of the state. Not surprisingly Independence Day in October 1948 featured Communist inspired stamps with a sturdy worker and his family staring steadfastly into the future.(13.26)

On 14 May 1948 a grim stamp featuring armed insurgents celebrated the discontented Czechs and Slovaks a hundred years earlier who fought successfully for land reforms and the final abolition of serfdom.(13.27) It was essentially a peasants revolt against the landowners who sought to perpetuate their legal grip on peasants despite serfdom being an inefficient means of production and superannuated as a social system. Even though after 1848 the 'freed' peasants had to compensate landlords for their new holdings, this historic proletarian struggle played perfectly into the hands of the Communists.

13.27 1k50 Centenary of the abolition of serfdom: 14 May 1948.

sector pay rises and above Marshall Aid. The crisis came soon after Soviet pressure had led to the rejection of Marshall Aid. The non-Communist ministers made a fatal mistake and resigned en-bloc on 20 February 1948 in protest at the interior minister barring non-Communists from senior police positions. Instead of the expected scandal and paralysis obliging the Communists ministers to resign too, the Communists seized all the vacant ministry buildings together with those of opposition parties. Mass demonstrations led by Communist activists led the ailing President Benes to give in rather than assert his still considerable authority, and on the 25 February Gottwald filled all the ministries with either Communists or their ultra-Socialist allies. Many non-Communist politicians fled the country along with thousands of others fearing the Communist backlash. Benes resigned on 7 June 1948 rather than sign the new constitution promising nationalisation and effectively limiting freedom of speech. However a new electoral law allowed a general election with a single list of candidates and in June Gottwald became president of the new 'people's republic' which then set about establishing tightly controlled collective farms and purging the armed forces, Roman Catholic Church and political parties of all suspected opponents. Benes

Two sets of stamps in March and June 1948 promoted the 11th *Sokol* Congress and Games in Prague. The *Sokol* (English: *Falcon*) movement was founded in Prague in 1862 to promote physical, moral and mental training exercises based upon the Classical idea of 'a healthy mind in a healthy body'. It became hugely popular and increasingly associated with Czech and Slav nationalism. Huge *Slets* (English: *Flocking of birds*) were held every few years embracing mass gymnastic displays, literary events and dramatic productions. Although permitted, they were viewed with suspicion by the Austro-Hungarian authorities, and after flourishing in the 1920s and 1930s they were suppressed by the Nazis. As part of the post-war *Sokol* revival, the March 1948 set featured an allegory of athletes paying homage to the Republic (13.28), and the June set portrayed two major *Sokol* figures.(13.29) Josef Scheiner (1861-1932) (1k50 and 2k) was a politician and publicist of the anti-clerical, anti-aristocratic Young Czech movement prior to 1914. From 1918 he worked closely with Jindrich Vanicek (1862-1934) (1k and 3k), the influential leader of the Czech *Sokol* movement from 1892 to 1930 who had integrated the *Sokol* philosophy

13.28 5k 'Athletes pay homage to the Republic': from set 7 March 1948.

13.31 3k+1k Father and child: from set 18 December 1949.

13.29 2k Josef Scheiner and 3k Jindrich Vanicek: from set 10 June 1948.

13.32 1k50 Frantisek Palachy (left) and Frantisek Rieger: from set 20 June 1948.

and regime into the post-1918 Czech army. Tens of thousands participated in the 1948 *Slet*, and although by then the *Sokol* movement possessed a strong Socialist element both its independence and nationalist overtones proved unpalatable to Gottwald's regime. It was rigorously suppressed to be replaced by an imported Soviet model of centrally controlled child welfare, youth culture and sport.

On 18 December 1948 the first surtaxed Communist Child Welfare set featured a mother and child, and a boy and girl, enjoying the natural world.(13.30) No doubt Gottwald's government was following the Soviet Union's wartime Family Edict of 1944 which encouraged child-bearing, offered state support to mothers with young families, and encouraged children's participation in activities largely directed by the state. A second set featuring a mother, father and children appeared in December 1949.(13.31)

13.30 3k+1k Young girl and birds: from set 18 December 1948.

During the anti-Hapsburg revolutions of 1848-49 a popularly elected constituent assembly of Germans and Czechs within the Hapsburg Empire met at Kromeriz in Moravia to pressurise the Emperor into agreeing to become a constitutional power-sharing monarch. It got nowhere. Once the Empire recovered from the various revolutions, largely by force of arms (with Russian help), it stayed virtually absolute. However the brave if naive attempt evoked two stamps celebrating its centenary in June 1948. They portrayed Frantisek Palacky (1798-1876), an early leader of the Czech National Party and advocate of a Czech kingdom within a federal Austro-Hungarian Empire. A major cultural historian, he was a towering figure in the Czech National Revival. By his side was his son-in-law Frantisek Ladislav Rieger (1818-1903) who was his successor as leader of the National Party working with, but also frequently frustrated by, the conservative Catholic Church and nobility.(13.32)

On 27 August 1948 three stamps marked the Slovak involvement in the 1848-49 revolutions.(13.33) The 1k50 portrayed Jozef Hurban (1817-88), the 3k Ludovit Stur (1815-56), and the 5k Michal Hodza (1811-70), all of them Slovak national revivalists, major literary figures and civil rights activists. All of them were members of the first Slovak National Council seeking greater Slovak recognition, even autonomy, within the sprawling Hapsburg Empire. In principle, and to a degree in practice, they supported the 1848-49 revolution against the Hapsburgs but at the same time opposed the Hungarian military and political figures leading it who had little sympathy with Slovak

13.33 *Centenary of Slovak insurrection: set 20 June 1948.*

aspirations. Their fears were justified. When Hungary finally achieved internal autonomy in 1867, Slovakia remained firmly under its repressive control.

On 7 April 1948 a set celebrate the 600th anniversary of the renowned Charles University in Prague, founded by and named after the Holy Roman Emperor Charles IV.(13.34) Two stamps show the emperor's crowned head, and two show him kneeling before the haloed figure of St Wenceslaus, the martyred Duke of Bohemia (c911-935) and patron saint of Czechoslovakia. Charles IV was revered by many as 'Father of the Nation' alongside Frantisek Palachy and Tomas Masaryk. Many Czechs would have remembered the student riots, arrests and closure of the university by the Germans in 1939. Academic freedom had been restored in 1945, but 7 June 1948 saw the departure of President Benes and the triumph of Gottwald, and soon after this set was issued the Communist regime began its purge of the university's personnel and courses.

13.34 *1k50 Emperor Charles IV and 3k Charles kneeling before St Wenceslas: from set 7 April 1948.*

13.35 *5k President Gottwald miniature sheet: from set 23 November 1948.*

On 28 October 1948 the first stamp appeared in a set featuring President Gottwald, and a similar stamp and a miniature sheet soon followed to mark his 52nd birthday on 23 November that year. Playing the populist card, the miniature sheet's inscription read *Be even more united and determined, and your will will be the law in this land*. With shrewd reference to continuity and the nation's history, it also featured the 'Greater Arms' of Czechoslovakia, formulated in 1920, featuring the arms of Bohemia, Moravia, Slovakia, Silesia, Tesin Silesia, Opava, Ratibor, and Carpathian Ruthenia, and the motto *PRAVDA VITEZI (TRUTH TRIUMPHS)*. (13.35)

Two more stamps inscribed UNOR 1948 (FEBRUARY 1948), one with Gottwald's now familiar portrait, the other a photograph of him addressing a crowd - celebrated the first anniversary of his government on 25 February 1949.(13.36) To ram home the tight Moscow connection, they were interspersed with stamps on 11 December 1948 cynically commemorating the fifth anniversary of Benes's wartime treaty of friendship with Russia (13.37), on 21 January 1949 marking the 25th anniversary of Lenin's death (13.38), and on 21 December 1949 celebrating Stalin's 70th birthday. (13.39)

13.36 3k President Gottwald addressing a crowd: from set 25 February 1949.

13.37 3k Fifth anniversary of alliance with Russia: 11 December 1948.

13.40 1k Jan Sverma, 2k Julius Fucik, 4k Jiri Wolker, and 8k Alois Jirasek: from set 20 March 1949+.

13.38 5k 25th anniversary of the death of Lenin: from set 21 January.

13.39 3k Stalin's 70th birthday: from set 21 December 1949.

1949 saw a proliferation of stamps hammering home Communist ideology within the context of selected Czechoslovak history and culture. During 1949 a set of six highlighted carefully selected Czechoslovak writers., all of whom challenged oppression whether under the Austro-Hungarians or the Nazis.(13.40) The 50h pictured Pavol Hviezdoslav (1849-1921), poet, Slovak radical and member of the Revolutionary National Assembly in 1918; the 80h Vladislav Vancura (1891-1942), a Czech novelist, screenwriter and Communist resistance fighter executed by the Germans; the 1k Jan Sverma (1901-44), a Slovak Communist journalist and friend of Klement Gottwald, who died leading units in the Slovak Uprising; the 2k Julius Fucik (1903-43), a Czech Communist underground journalist executed by the Germans; the 4k Jiri Wolker (1900-24), poet, playwright and founder member of the Czechoslovak Communist Party; and the 8k Alois Jirasek (1851-1930), many of whose folk-historical novels reflect the oppression of the Czech people. He was a celebrated literary figure, and prominent member of the pre-war Czech right-wing National Democratic Party, but this Communist inspired set attempted to embrace him as a proto-revolutionary patriot. Julius Fucik's wartime articles describing an optimistic Communist future became required reading in all Czech schools.

By 1949 Gottwald's government was implementing the doctrines of Andrei Zhdanov, Stalin's cultural commissar, that 'anti-people modernism' had no place in Communist artistic circles. Only works reflecting positively on life in a Socialist society were to be tolerated. The Czech Communist musician Miroslav Barvik (1919-98) became the country's dictatorial arbiter of acceptability ensuring, in his catchphrase, 'the composers go with the people.' Two composers and a writer appeared on stamps in 1949. On 4 June it was Bedrich Smetana (1824-84), the celebrated Czech composer whose work *Ma Vlast (My Fatherland)* in the 1870s highlighted Bohemia's history, culture and landscape. As a young man he had written marches supporting the 1848 Czech uprising against the Hapsburgs.(13.41) He is portrayed alongside Prague's National Theatre where for a time he was principal conductor. Two days later it was the Russian poet Alexander Pushkin (1799-1837) whose bitter *Ode to Liberty* and ensuing exile under Tsar Alexander I, and verse play *Boris Goduno* highlighting Tsarist

13.41 5k Bedrich Smetana: from set 4 June 1949.

13.42 2k Alexander Pushkin: 6 June 1949.

13.44 1k50 Female farm worker and 3k Workers and banner: from set 24 May 1949.

13.43 3k Frederic Chopin: from set 24 June 1949.

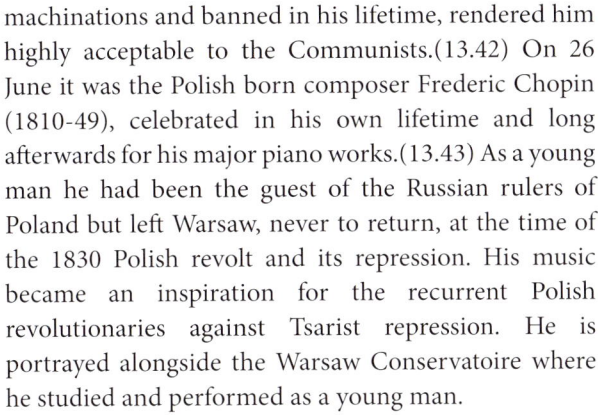

13.45 1k50 Medieval miners and 3k Modern miner: from set 11 September 1949.

machinations and banned in his lifetime, rendered him highly acceptable to the Communists.(13.42) On 26 June it was the Polish born composer Frederic Chopin (1810-49), celebrated in his own lifetime and long afterwards for his major piano works.(13.43) As a young man he had been the guest of the Russian rulers of Poland but left Warsaw, never to return, at the time of the 1830 Polish revolt and its repression. His music became an inspiration for the recurrent Polish revolutionaries against Tsarist repression. He is portrayed alongside the Warsaw Conservatoire where he studied and performed as a young man.

On 24 May 1949 three striking stamps featuring male and female workers and enthusiastic rallies marked the ninth Congress of the Czechoslovak Communist Party. (13.44) Banned in 1938 the party went underground and in 1939 many of its leaders fled to Moscow where the nucleus of the post-war party reconvened. Although important as a show-piece, the Congress met only every five years, the central Committee met only twice a year, and effective day-to-day responsibility lay with the Politburo, and notably with the party leader as head of state. Czech miners appeared on three stamps on 11 September 1949 ostensibly commemorating 700 years of mining and 150 years of protective legislation. The inscription was *DEN HORNIKU 11.IX 1949 (THE MINERS 11.IX 1949)*. In reality it might just as well have signalled the state's assumption of control of production and working conditions, and its hurried post-war exploitation of the country's mineral reserves, notably uranium.(13.45)

Similarly the stamps featuring carpenters and mechanics marking the Second All Union Congress (*II Vseodborovy Sjezd*) in Prague in December 1949 masked the subservience required of trades' unions as instruments of state policy.(13.46) On 20 August 1949 two stamps had marked the 50th Sample (Trade) Fair in

13.46 1k Second All Union Congress: from set 11 December 1949.

13.48 1k50+1k Red Cross Fund.

13.47 1k50 50th Sample (Trade) Fair, Prague: from set 20 August 1949.

Prague, now also beholden to the state's rigid control of industry.(13.47) And, significantly, the pair of surtaxed Red Cross stamps issued on 18 December 1949 featured doves of peace. No doubt this suited *Cominform*, the Soviet Union's policy disseminating body, which was aggressively promoting the concept of 'world peace' as a means of discrediting the allegedly warlike 'Imperialist' anti-Communist policies of the West.(13.48) The transformation of Czechoslovakia was nearing completion.

CHAPTER 14

AUSTRIA

In late 1918 the vast Austro-Hungarian Dual Monarchy straddling central Europe disappeared suddenly and forever. Its two key components, the Empire of Austria and Kingdom of Hungary, were defeated and dismembered, leading to the creation of several new independent countries. The small new Republic of Austria was barely sustainable economically, and in the early 1920s suffered hyperinflation which was eventually resolved by international loans and new taxes, but at the price of unemployment, reduced public services, loss of social benefits, and violent demonstrations. All this fractured the early coalition governments and the national political scene. Left and right parties moved further apart, and both created paramilitary forces - just as in Germany - and used them ruthlessly against each other. In 1932 Engelbert Dollfus of the right wing Christian Social Party became Chancellor, and moved quickly towards a centralised, even Fascist, state but one that rejected all thoughts of absorption into Germany. In 1933 he manipulated a coup whereby parliament was indefinitely postponed and he assumed dictatorial powers. All attempts to reverse the situation were frustrated by armed force, and extreme parties such as the Communists and National Socialists (Nazis),

14.1 *The end of an era. Cover and stamps marking the 88th anniversary of the Austrian Post Office and the end of Austria's independent existence. The upper stamps are the Berlin (left) and Vienna (right) printings of the Austrian plebiscite stamps issued on 8 April 1938. The lower pair featuring a nosegay and the zodiac are the Austrian Christmas issue of 12 December 1937, and were the last Austrian stamps until 1945. The Innsbruck postmark is dated 10 April 1938, the date of the plebiscite,*

although growing in strength, were banned. Dollfuss was assassinated in 1934 by Nazi sympathisers, and Kurt Schuschnigg of the right wing Fatherland Front took over. He, too, opposed German annexation which, by 1934, was already high on Hitler's agenda.

Over the next two years Hitler alternately courted and cajoled Austrian politicians into accepting union (*Anschluss*) but without success. However, the Austrian Nazi Party grew in number and influence, and many others admired Germany's growing economic strength and international standing. In 1936 Schuschnigg signed a treaty with Germany promising to follow Hitler's lead in foreign affairs. Under mounting internal and external pressure, in 1938 Schuschnigg called a referendum for 13 March on the issue of an *Anschluss*. Fearing an unfavourable outcome manipulated by Schuschnigg, Hitler issued an ultimatum - hand over all power to the Austrian Nazi Party or face invasion. The Austrian government caved in, and on 12 March German forces crossed the border to be met by cheering crowds, and Hitler was enthusiastically welcomed in Braunau, his Austrian birthplace. Karl Renner, the leader of the Social Democratic Party, and Cardinal Innitzer, Archbishop of Vienna, supported the *Anschluss* and probably a majority of Austrians agreed with them. Intense Nazi propaganda and an absence of opposition had helped a plebiscite on 10 April record 99.7% in favour.(14.1) Austria was renamed *Ostmark* until 1942 when it became *Alpen-und Donau-Reichsgau* (the Alpine and Danubian Gau). Austrian men became liable for conscription, the economy was integrated with that of Germany, Jews were savagely persecuted, and many Austrians participated in war crimes. 13,600 Austrians were imprisoned after the war, and thousands more lost their jobs under the de-nazification programme.

On 28 March 1945 American troops entered Austria and on 13 April Soviet forces took Vienna but the western Allies prevented the Russians occupying the whole country. In May 1945 Austria was divided into four zones of Allied occupation, as was Vienna, and this lasted until 1955. The Four Power Allied Control Council retained ultimate authority, although as early as June 1946 the new Republic of Austria's parliament was granted significant decision making powers. *De facto* independence was soon achieved, and Austria was to have a relatively easy readmission to European society. Despite the evidence to the contrary, as early as 1943 the Moscow Declaration signed by the UK, Soviet Union and USA included a clause accepting Austria as 'the first free country to fall a victim to Hitlerite aggression', and aiming 'to see re-established a free and independent Austria.' Both major Austrian parties had embarrassments to hide - the Christian Socialists for

14.2 *8pf German 1941 definitive overprinted Osterreich: from set 2 May 1945, and 12pf with added bar: from set 18 May 1945.*

14.3 *10pf German 1941 definitive overprinted Osterreich between vertical lines: from set 22 May 1945.*

their support of the dictatorship in 1933 and the Social Democrats for their support for *Anschluss*. For twenty years after the war the urban support for the Social Democrats (renamed the Socialist Party) matched almost exactly the rural support for the Christian Socialists (renamed the People's Party). However instead of tension and chaos there emerged a series of peaceful coalitions with agreed divisions of senior and junior posts throughout the national government and regional administrations. It was known as *Proporz* - 'shared representation'. Key reasons for this dramatic change in attitudes were, first, the tacit acceptance that it was in no-one's interest to do anything that would recall recent past events, and, second, the closeness to Austria of the Red Army and three Communist neighbours, Yugoslavia, Hungary and Czechoslovakia.

As early as October 1945 the Allies accepted that Karl Renner, the veteran Social Democrat, had created an acceptably stable cross party provisional government dedicated to democracy, neutrality and independence, and gave it official approval. Elections in November revealed little support for the Communists, and Stalin duly showed little interest in Austria. As historian Tony Judt has noted, a 'collective amnesia' protected Austria from post-war recrimination. Vast amounts of American aid alleviated the 1945-46 famine, and then supported the nation's reconstruction, ultimately in the Western camp although officially strictly neutral.

Since *Anschluss* only German stamps had been used, and in April 1945 these started to appear with Hitler's head partially or completely obliterated by post offices

14.4 German stamps from 1942 National Goldsmiths' Institute, 1942 European Postal Congress and 1944 'Brown Ribbon' Horse Race sets overprinted Osterreich and new values and Deutsches Reich/Grossdeutsches Reich obliterated: from set 13 June 1945.

14.6 5m Arms of Austrian Republic: from definitive set 3 July 1945+.

14.7 1s+10s Allegory of the returning homeland: 10 September 1945.

14.5 30pf German 1941 definitive overprinted with bar, lines and oblique Osterreich: from set 21 June 1945+.

using a variety of unofficial marks - often made by circular inked corks. In the Russian Zone, from 2 May 1945 the Hitler portrait definitive series continued in use with *Osterreich* obliquely overprinting the Fuhrer's face. Belatedly, from 18 May an additional bar obliterated the words *Deutsches Reich*.(14.2) A May printing in Graz, briefly in the Russian Zone before transferring to the British Zone in July, used an overprint comprising vertical bars each side of *Osterreich* to deface the portrait on the Hitler definitive set.(14.3) On 13 June the Russian Zone resorted to old stocks of Third Reich commemorative stamps with overprints obliterating *Deutsches Reich* and amending the values.(14.4) Later that month Hitler's portrait on seven definitives was almost completely obliterated by numerous vertical lines and *Osterreich* in oblique lettering. (14.5)

Finally from 3 July 1945 a new long set appeared for the Russian Zone featuring the republic's national arms adopted in 1919 of a red and white shield and a black eagle crowned with a tower and clutching a hammer and sickle.(14.6) The tower stood for the cities, the hammer for urban labourers, and the sickle the farmers, and did not signal any Communist associations. The broken chains on the eagle's legs had been added in 1945 as a sign of freedom from Nazi domination. On 10 September 1945 a new stamp, surtaxed for much-needed welfare charities, pictured a man staring into an idealised landscape but surrounded by chains which once again signalled the relief from oppression, and perhaps the precarious nature of freedom.(14.7)

Stamps used German pfennigs and marks until the Allies introduced an Allied military schilling in the summer of 1945, and this was replaced by an Austrian schilling in December. With inflation soaring, in 1947 the currency was revalued in a painful attempt to limit the money in circulation, and stabilise prices and wages.

From 28 June 1945 a set of innocuous stamps featuring a post-horn topped by an edelweiss and using Allied military groschen and schillings was issued in the British, French and American zones.(14.8)

Starting on 24 November 1945 the republic issued its own first set comprising numerous views of the country's mountains, lakes, forests, parks, resorts and historic buildings. There was one industrial site, Erzberg iron ore mine.(14.9) The stamps were attractive, non controversial, and set the scene, literally, for the country to reinvent itself as a peace-loving pastoral nation and tourist theme park.

Although Austria did not join the United Nations until 1955, when the occupying forces departed, on June 1946 the 30g (brown red) view of Neusiedler Lake

14.8 20g Post-horn and edelweiss; from definitive set 28 June 1945+.

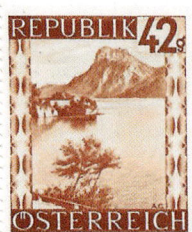

14.9 4g Erzburg mine, 8g Vienna Town Hall Park, 42g Traunstein, 70g Badgastein, and 3s Heiligenblut: from set 24 November 1945+.

14.10 30g Neusiedler Lake as issued, and with United Nations Charter overprint: 25 June 1946.

14.11 12g Schafberg and Lake Wolfgang as issued, and with the conference of the Society for Promotion of Cultural and Economic Relations with the Soviet Union overprint: 26 September 1946.

14.12 1s+1s Dr Karl Renner: from set 7 August 1946.

14.13 1s Thirtieth anniversary of the Austrian Republic: 12 November 1948.

was reissued overprinted with a map of the world, Austria's Arms and *26. Juni 1945*, the date when the United Nations' Charter was signed by the first fifty countries.(14.9) The stamp was an adroit signal of intent, and so was the 12g view of the Schafberg mountain and Lake Wolfgang reissued on 26 September 1946 overprinted with flags, a globe and an inscription marking the conference of the Society for Promotion of Cultural and Economic Relations with the Soviet Union.(14.10)

On 7 August 1946 a set picturing Dr Karl Renner (1870-1950) flanked by Austrian provincial shields commemorated the first anniversary of his government, and in doing so also marked Austria's increasing responsibility for its future.(14.12) Although Renner

14.14 5g+3g Nazi dagger striking Austria and 2g+3g Austrian Arms rising from burning swastika: from set 16 September 1946.

14.16 70g St Ruprecht's Church, Vienna: 30 October 1946.

had favoured union with Germany in 1919 and again in 1938, his ardent Socialism, absence from politics during the war, political acumen in uniting parties and realistic view of Austria's future ensured his return to government in 1945 where he was briefly prime minister (27 April-20 December 1945) and then president (1945-50) until his death. His prestige and career straddling fifty tumultuous years meant he was chosen also to feature on the stamp celebrating the 30th anniversary of the Austrian Republic issued on 12 November 1948.(14.13)

The campaign to distance Austria from Nazi contamination culminated in September 1946 with eight surtaxed stamps supporting a national Anti-Fascist Exhibition highlighting the period 1938 to 1945 as one of outright German oppression.(14.14) Inscribed *Niemals Vergessen (Never Forget)* the lurid designs included a Nazi dagger striking a map of Austria in 1938 (5g+3g), hands stretched behind barbed wire (12g+12g), St Stephen's Cathedral in flames (8g+6g), a broom sweeping away Nazi symbols (6g+4g), a hammer breaking a Nazi column (42g+42g), hands strangling a snake (30g+30g), a hand in triumph by an Austrian banner (1s+1s) and the Austrian Arms arising Phoenix-like from a burning swastika (2g+3g). These eight stamps were permitted by the Allies but a further two were not allowed - one featuring the banned SS lightning emblem striking a map of Austria, and the other a grinning skeleton removing a mask of Hitler's face.

A far more attractive surtaxed set in December 1946 raised funds for the extensive repairs necessary to Vienna's St Stephen's Cathedral.(14.15) It had been founded by Duke Rudolf IV (reigned 1339-65 and pictured on the 3g+12g stamp), but the fire that caused the roof to collapse in April 1945 had not been started by the Germans as implied on the anti-fascist set. The German officer charged with reducing the cathedral to rubble deliberately disregarded his commander's order. However fires raging from nearby looted shops as the Russians entered the city could not be contained and they spread to the cathedral. The altar, pulpit, organ, a tower and spire are featured on the 12g+48g, 6g+24g, 30g+1s20, 1s+5s and 2s+10s respectively, and statues of St Stephen the martyr and the Madonna and Child on the 8g+32g and 10g+40g. The ancient carving of Anton Pilgram (c1460-c1516), the sculptor of the pulpit and statues, was portrayed on the 50g+1s80, and the tomb of the Austrian Duke and first Hapsburg Holy Roman Emperor, Frederick III (reigned 1452-93) on the 5g+20g. His inclusion in the set owed much to his creation of the Diocese of Vienna but perhaps also slyly

   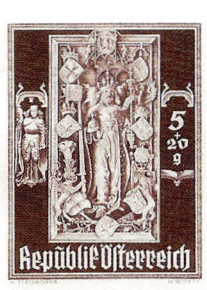

14.15 3g+12g Duke Rudolf IV, 1s+5s north-east tower, 50g+1s80 Anton Pilgram, and 5g+20g Frederick III's tomb: from set 12 December 1946.

to the initials A.E.I.O.U. he famously had inscribed on his possessions which were said (although without proof) to stand for *Alles Erdreich ist Osterreich untertan (All the world is subject to Austria)*. It could hardly have been coincidence that a few weeks earlier, on 30 October 1946 a stamp featuring St Ruprecht's Church, reputedly the oldest in Vienna, proudly commemorated the 950th anniversary of the first recorded use of the name 'Osterreich'.(14.16) St Ruprecht's Church had a plaque marking Frederick III's visit that included the initials A.E.I.O.U.

Several sets in 1946 and 1947 highlighted Austria's attractive scenery, peaceful pastimes and cultural history. In October 1946 and June 1947 surtaxed stamps featuring horses and riders supported the prize fund for Vienna's prestigious Grand Prix horse race.(14.17) Many Austrians would have recalled that in 1943 and 1944 stamps supporting this race had been labelled *Deutsches Reich*. They might also have recalled the *Deutsches Reich* stamps of 1941 promoting the historic Vienna Fair *(Wiener Messe)* when, on 23 March 1947, an entirely Austrian set promoted the post war revival of the grand event. Eight stamps featured the country's rural harvest, logging, factories, mines, oil wells,

14.19 2s Gmund, 5s Limestone column 'Torsaule', and 10s St Charles Church, Vienna: from set 5 May 1947+.

textiles, foundries and hydro-electric power.(14.18) However at this time Austria's extensive oil industry was firmly in Soviet hands, and remained so until 1955. The Russians also plundered many factories.

An Air set in 1947 provide another opportunity to showcase celebrated sights scattered across the country. They included the ancient windmill at St Andra (50g), Roman arch at Heidentor (1s), Gmund on the Vienna to Prague railway (2s), Hinterstoder ski resort (3s), Pragraten in the mountainous Tyrol (4s), Torsaule, the limestone peak in the Berchtesgaden Alps, (5s) and the stunning Baroque St Charles Church in Vienna (10s).(14.19) There was, perhaps, something symbolic in featuring St Charles Church which the Emperor Charles VI began in 1713 as a thank-offering after a plague. Perhaps, too, many Austrians would have recalled that in 1944 Allied bombing obliged Ferdinand Porsche's engineering offices to be transferred from Stuttgart to Gmund.

14.17 60g+60g Austria Grand Prix horse race fund: from set 20 October 1946, and 60g+20g Vienna Prize horse race fund: 29 June 1947.

14.18 3g+2g Harvesting, 18g+12g Oil wells, and 60g+20g Hydro-electric power: from set 23 March 1947.

   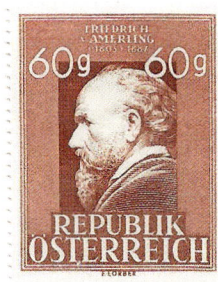

14.20 12g Franz Schubert, 18g Franz Grillparzer, 40g Anton Bruckner, and 60g Friedrich von Amerling: from set 31 March 1947+.

14.21 1s Johann Strauss (the younger): 3 June 1949.

14.22 30g Johann Strauss (the elder): 20 September 1949.

Celebrated Austrians from the nineteenth century, all of them cultural rather than military or political figures, featured on a set of seven stamps issued at long intervals between February 1947 and September 1949.(14.20) The 12g pictured the composer Franz Schubert (1797-1828), who was born, worked and died in Vienna, and increasingly admired a century and more after his death. The 18g pictured Franz Grillparzer (1791-1872) whose poetic plays, full of complex human desires and emotions, made him the most celebrated Austrian dramatist of his day, and as such he became Austria's national poet soon after the Second World War. The 20g pictured Carl Michael Ziehrer (1843-1922), a popular composer whose essentially cheerful waltzes, polkas and marches epitomised Vienna's legendary heyday. His great rival in both output and popularity, Johann Strauss (the younger) (1825-99), had to wait until 3 June 1949 for a commemorative stamp on the 50th anniversary of his death.(14.21) The 40g (chocolate) pictured Adalbert Stifter (1805-68) whose poems and stories were concerned with people striving, rarely successfully, for moral purity in their lives set within the luxuriously described Austrian landscapes. The 60g pictured the Imperial court painter Friedrich von Amerling (1803-87), renowned for his portraits of the aristocracy and wealthy middle classes in what was

14.23 1s Karl Millocker: 31 December 1949.

increasingly seen as a Romanticised period in Austro-Hungarian history. Added last, a new 40g (green) pictured Anton Bruckner (1824-96) whose symphonies, often received lukewarmly in his lifetime, became popular in the twentieth century as expressions of the Austro-German *zeitgeist*, the spirit of the age. Adolf Hitler's strong approval of his works did not mar their post-war popularity in Austria - but might explain the late appearance of the stamp. In due course further single stamp issues commemorated other cultural figures, including Johann Strauss (the elder) (1804-49) on 20 September 1949 (14.22), and on 31 December 1949 Karl Millocker (1842-89) whose international fame rested on his popular operetta *Der Bettelstudent (The Beggar Student)*.(14.23)

14.24 10g+5g Abbey at Melk and 35g+15g National Library, Vienna: from set 20 June 1947.

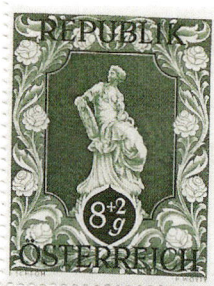 

14.25 8g+2g Providentia Fountain, 30g+10g 'Egeria', and 60g+20g 'Girl in a Straw Hat': from set 20 June 1947.

Schonbrunn Palace (30g+10g). Perhaps *Egeria* was chosen out of dozens of statues at the palace because she taught Numa Pompilius, Romulus's successor as king of Rome, to earn the favour of the Gods by performing honourable and pious acts and thereby ensure the prosperity of the state. By association, a new Austria was in being.

The war returned with a vengeance in a surtaxed set supporting the Prisoners of War Relief Fund issued between 30 August and 9 September 1947.(14.26) Over one and a quarter million Austrians served in Hitler's forces, and about 335,500 became prisoners of the Western Allies and 160,000 of the Russians. The set was timed to coincide with the first prisoners held by the Soviet Union arriving back in Austria on 12 September 1947. Most Austrians held by the other Allies had been released much earlier. Stalin had used prisoners of war as forced labourers rebuilding his shattered cities, but promised all prisoners would be repatriated by 1949. The promise was not kept, and although large anti-Communist protests broke out the fate of many thousands of missing soldiers was never resolved. The set switched from harrowing images of a prisoner of war behind barbed wire (8g+2g), receiving a letter (12g+8g), and being approached by a sinister hooded visiter (possibly disease or death) (18g+12g) to more hopeful ones of the man embracing his family (35g+15g), sowing corn (1s+40g), and being welcomed back to a factory (60g+20g). It was significant that the picture of the ex-prisoner embracing his family shows other men still imprisoned in the background.

In June 1947 a further beautifully designed set supporting the National Art Exhibition Fund highlighted Austrian Art treasures.(14.24) Three featured historic buildings - the stunning Benedictine Abbey high above Melk recently returned after confiscation by the state in 1938 (10g+5g), Vienna's Belvedere Palace, home of the Hapsburg rulers, that suffered bomb damage in the war (20g+10g), and the National Library in Vienna which housed not only the old Imperial collection but also numerous items looted during the war (35g+15g). (14.24) Seven stamps concentrated upon single items of Austrian Art.(14.25) Among them were Friedrich von Amerling's painting *Girl in a Straw Hat* (60g+20g), Georg Donner's early eighteenth century Providentia Fountain in Vienna with figures symbolising parts of the extensive Austrian Empire (8g+2g), and Wilhelm Beyer's statue of the nymph *Egeria* at the Well House Fountain at Vienna's

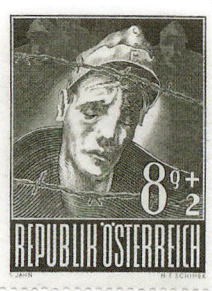 

14.26 8g+2g Emaciated prisoner of war, 18g+12g Sinister camp visitor, and 35g+15g Reunited family: from set 30 August 1947+.

14.27 Prisoners of War Relief Fund: set 17 August 1949.

Deliberately well-timed no doubt, on 17 August 1949 a very different Prisoners of War Relief Fund set was issued.(14.27) Austrian industry was benefitting from Marshall Aid, the coalition government was stable, high level discussions regarding independence looked promising, and Austrian Communists, although still vocal, had little support from Stalin. This new set sent out comforting messages of Austria's conservatism. Highlighting Austria's illustrious past, and optimistic present, it pictured four Coats of Arms but without any inscription. The 40g+10g featured the seal of Duke Frederick II (1211-46) who was held to be the instigator of the country's red and white shield. It might have been significant for the set that he was also a successful warrior against the incursions of the eastern Mongols. The 60g+15g Arms celebrated Austria's growing territorial power culminating in a later Duke Frederick's elevation to Holy Roman Emperor (Frederick III) in 1452. The 1s+25g pictured the Baroque Arms design of 1600 when Austria was engaged in a lengthy war against the Ottoman Empire at the height of its power. The 1s60+40g pictured the current Arms which embraced the historic heartlands of Lower and Upper Austria.

Interestingly - in light of this emphasis upon Imperial Austria - a few days earlier on 9 August 1949 an unusual stamp marked the millenary of the birth of St Gebhard (c949-995). Born in Hohenbregenz Castle he was the youngest son of Count Ulrich of Bregenz, whose title later became one of dozens held by the Hapsburg Austrian emperors until 1918. Gebhard became Bishop of Constance, founded Peterhausen Abbey, and was renowned for ensuring ordinary working people and the poor in his diocese were treated justly and fairly.

On 21 November 1947 the schilling was revalued and new banknotes issued. On 10 December sixteen of the early Views set were reissued in plain vermillion or violet.(14.29) Although they had the same value tablets as before, the new schilling was worth three of the old ones. Starting on 1 June 1948 and lasting into 1952 another new set of 37 attractive definitive stamps featured young women wearing historic costumes from Austria's provinces.(14.30, 14.31) Some costumes were simple, some elaborate, some rural and some urban - such as those from nineteenth century Vienna. The shrewdly chosen set reflected the entirely non-confrontational attitude of Austria, its essentially

 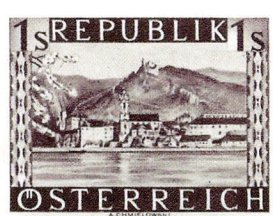

14.29 3g Lermoos and 1s Durnstein: from set 10 December 1947+.

14.28 30g St Gebhard: 9 August 1949.

14.30 3g Tirol Inntal and 90g Steiermark Mittelsteier: from set 1 June 1948+.

14.31 2s40 Kitzbuhel and 10s Vienna 1850: from set 1 June 1948.

14.33 30g+10g Crocus and 1s40+70g Edelweiss: from set 14 May 1948.

14.32 10g+5g Bridge, 45g+20g Railway yard, and 80g+40g Oil wells: from Reconstruction set 18 February 1948.

inward looking celebration of its regions and traditions, and its diverse attractions as a tourist destination. This feminine portrayal of the state was very different to France's strident image of Marianne.

Indeed four other attractive Austrian sets at this time furthered the nation's calm, peaceful yet productive image - although in each case they sought funds for hard-fought campaigns. The first, on 18 February 1948, was inscribed *Wiederaufbau* (Reconstruction) with ten surtaxed stamps showing on-going work on a war damaged bridge, aqueduct, quarry, dock, railway, flats, factory, oil wells, mountain road and Vienna's Parliament House.(14.32) No mention was made of the war, but most Austrians would remember the air raids and battles. Vienna and Innsbruck were the most heavily bombed Austrian cities under the Allied attacks of 1944. In 1945 towns in Lower Austria and Burgenland endured the Russian advance westwards towards Vienna, and the capital was further damaged during fighting there between German SS Panzer units and the Russian army. Russian atrocities followed during the occupation, and the Russians also seized many factories and oil wells, notably those around Vienna.

On 14 May 1948 a set of ten anti-tuberculosis stamps featured Austrian wild flowers - an anemone, crocus, primrose, pasque flower, rhododendron, wild rose, cyclamen, gentian and the national flower, the edelweiss. (14.33) Held to be the symbol of national purity and courage, the mountain edelweiss was appropriated by Hitler as his favourite flower.

On 15 June the 80th anniversary of Austria's Artists' Society provided the opportunity to showcase its headquarters, the Vienna *Kunstlerhaus* (Artist House) (20g+10g), and six of its early members.(14.34) The 30g+15g portrayed the artist Hans Makart (1840-84) who won celebrity status with his sumptuous interior designs and brilliantly coloured historical paintings.

14.34 20g+10g Vienna Kunstlerhaus, 50g+25g August von Siccardsburg, and 60g+30g Hans Canon: from set 15 June 1948.

The 40g+20g portrayed the sculptor Karl Kundmann (1838-1919) who immortalised several key Hapsburg figures. The 50g+25g depicted the architect August von Siccardsburg (1813-68) who co-designed the Vienna State Opera with Eduard van der Null. The 60g+30 featured the painter Hans Canon, the pseudonym of Johan Strasiripka, (1829-1885) whose commissions included members of the royal family and the huge *Circle of Life* in Vienna's Natural History Museum. The 1s+50g portrayed William Unger (1837-1932), an award winning etcher and professor of graphic arts in Vienna. Finally the 1s40+70g featured the architect Friedrich von Schmidt (1825-91), the designer of numerous Gothic churches and Vienna's Town Hall, and ennobled by the Emperor Franz Joesph.

And on 6 August a surtaxed set of views of Salzburg Cathedral supported the substantial renovation it needed after an Allied bomb penetrated the central dome in 1944.(14.35) Founded by St Rupert in 774, the cathedral was rebuilt from 1181, and again in elaborate Baroque style in the seventeenth century by order of Salzburg's powerful prince-bishop. It became internationally famous as the site of Wolfgang Amadeus Mozart's baptism in 1756. One of the stamps featured Salzburg's historic St Peter's Abbey, also founded by St Rupert, to which the monks had recently returned after ejection following the Anschluss.

A scattering of single stamp issues over the immediate post war years continued to highlight past achievements while not forgetting Austria's acceptance into the post-war international community. On 5 November 1947 the centenary of Austria's electric telegraphic communications was commemorated with an image of tape circling the globe.(14.36) Various systems had been trialled earlier in the nineteenth century, but it took the invention of a robust and reliable magneto powered telegraph by Charles Wheatstone in the early 1840s and Friedrich Gerke's improvements to the Morse Code some years later before long distance transmissions were satisfactorily achievable commercially. By the 1850s, though, most nations - including the vast Austrian Empire - had effective networks, with military needs uppermost in mind. And not surprisingly, in October 1949 Austria issued a set of three special stamps celebrating the 75th anniversary of the Universal Postal Union, with a compass enclosing a letter and posthorn (40g), a relief showing children holding a wreathed '75' (60g) and a wreathed female head, probably representing Iris, the Greek goddess of communications (1s).(14.37)

On 16 January 1948 a surtaxed stamp featuring the Olympic flame supported Austrian entries to the Fifth Winter Games in St Moritz, Switzerland, that year. It was the first after the war and beset by financial

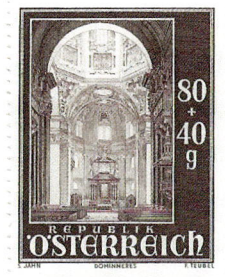

14.35 60g+30g St Peter's Abbey, 80g+40g Salzburg Cathedral, and 1s+50g Salzburg Cathedral and Castle: from set 6 August 1948.

14.36 40g Centenary of the telegraph: 5 November 1947.

14.37 40g 75th anniversary the the UPU: from set 8 October 1949.

14.38 1s+50g Fund supporting Austrian competitors in the Winter Olympic Games: 16 January 1948.

difficulties. Austria won a gold, three silver and four bronze medals, coming a commendable seventh out of 28 competing nations.(14.38) On 25 June 1949 a stamp signalled Austrian interest in Esperanto, the international language created in 1887 to promote world peace and understanding.(14.39) Although both Hitler and Stalin suppressed support, and no country ever embraced it, it grew as an international means of communication and symbol of harmony. The stamp featured the Esperanto Star, and possibly marked a national congress in Vienna. The world congress that year was in in Bournemouth.

On 14 May 1949 another stamp marked Austria's emerging place in the sun by highlighting UNICEF (the United Nations International Children's Emergency Fund).(14.40) The stamp featured a child welcoming the UNICEF dove against the United Nations logo in the sky. It had been founded in December 1946 to provide immediate aid in war torn countries, and later expanded to address longer term needs. In April 1949 Austria issued a set of four surtaxed Child Welfare Fund stamps inscribed *Gluckliche Kindheit* (Happy Childhood) with children praying at Christmas, holding a hare, seated by a Birthday Cake and watching for St Nicholas with gifts symbolised by apples in a boot.(14.41) Many Austrians had endured hunger and indeed food riots a few years earlier, and in 1949 Marshall Aid was still propping up and modernising the economy. Christmas, and a further Austrian claim to fame, had been poignantly recalled in December the previous year with a stamp featuring Father Joseph Mohr and Franz Gruber, the writer and composer of the carol *Silent Night, Holy Night* on the 130th anniversary of its first performance in Oberndorf's parish church.(14.42)

14.40 1s UNICEF: 14 May 1949.

14.41 1s+25g Boy and birthday cake and 1s40+35g Girl at prayer: from set 13 April 1949.

14.42 60g Father Joseph Mohr and Franz Gruber: 18 December 1948.

14.39 20g Esperanto Congress in Vienna: 25 June 1949.

CHAPTER 15

ITALY

In 1861 most, but not quite all, of the disparate states in Italy were united under King Victor Emmanuel II of Piedmont-Sardinia after several decades of revolts and major wars, and much international diplomacy. The struggle was called the *Risorgimento (Rising Again)* and Italian nationalists later extended it to embrace the restoration of all Mediterranean lands once part of the Roman Empire. By 1914 Italy had taken Libya from the Ottoman Turks, angered Greece by occupying the Dodecanese islands, and had its sights on Albania and Austria-Hungary's Dalmatian coastline. After a year of neutrality, in 1915 Italy joined the Allies enticed by promises of annexing Austro-Hungarian territory, but for long after 1918 it nursed a deep seated grudge that whilst its casualties topped a million men it was merely awarded Trieste, Istria and south Tyrol in the peace settlement.

In the years after the First World War Italy was anarchic with widespread economic distress and social unrest. In urban areas workers' councils and strikes proliferated, and Communist support intensified. However in 1922 it was the popular nationalist Benito Musssolini whom King Victor Emmanuel III (reigned 1900-46) appointed as prime minister, and over the next few years his Fascist Party eliminated the opposition while initiating genuine social reforms, and cultivating the extended *Risorgimento*. In 1935 Mussolini annexed Ethiopia, in 1939 he occupied Albania, and in 1940 he invaded Greece - but only to be rescued by German forces from a catastrophic defeat. For a time Italian and German forces fought as allies in north Africa, across the Balkans and in Russia. However Italy was very much the junior partner in terms of equipment, ability and success, and soon after the Allies landed in Sicily on 10 July 1943 the rising war-weariness and disenchantment with Mussolini led the Fascist Great Council to disown him and the king to arrest him. General Pietro Badoglio became prime minister and immediately banned the Fascist Party and signed an armistice with the Allies.

However the Germans had not finished with Italy. They successfully occupied much of the country and with skill and determination long held up the Allied advance from the south. They rescued Mussolini from prison, and established him in a puppet Italian Social Republic based at Salo near Brescia on Lake Garda embracing much of central and northern Italy. All the while Italy descended into civil war with some Italian units joining Mussolini and the Germans, others joining the Allies, and yet more forming roaming anti Fascist resistance groups, often with strong pro-Communist sympathies. On 3 September 1943 Allied forces crossed from Sicily to the mainland, and having fled south to Brindisi the king and his prime minister followed the painfully slow Allied advance. However from the armistice onwards, the king's writ was always subject to Allied agreement.

As a result, for eighteen months or so Italy had several sources of stamps. On 17 September 1943 the Allies

15.1 50c Allied Military Government: from set 17 September 1943.

15.2 20c, 35c and 50c Imperial Series overprinted Governo Militare Alleato: set 10 December 1943.

15.3 50c Romulus, Remus and she-wolf: 30 December 1943 printing.

introduced an intentionally innocuously patterned set printed in the USA inscribed *Allied Military Postage* that was briefly used in Sicily before the new pro-Allied civil government got under way.(15.1) On 10 December 1943, while battles still raged, three low value Italian definitive stamps from the 1929-42 Fascist Imperial Series were overprinted *GOVERNO MILITARE ALLEATO (ALLIED MILITARY GOVERNMENT)* for the restricted mail - limited to censored postcards and business letters in open envelopes - allowed in the liberated southern city of Naples.(15.2) There was little concern that the king's portrait was semi-obliterated, but such was the rush that the lower corners retained the fasces - the axe in a bundle of rods carried by ancient Roman magistrates from which Mussolini's Fascists took their name. On 30 December 1943 the Allies permitted Marshal Badoglio to issue a new general 50c stamp featuring the legendary wolf suckling Romulus and Remus - and perhaps signalling Italy's new beginning.(15.3) This first appeared in Bari on the southern Adriatic coast and gradually spread into other liberated regions. A second printing on unwatermarked paper and with slightly different perforations appeared the following May.

Initially Mussolini's Italian Social Republic used the pre-war Imperial Series stamps with their fasces emblems. However in December 1943 the newly formed and powerful *Guardia Nazionale Repubblicana (National Republican Guard)* sought tighter control of the Social Republic's postal system and its revenue, and several Italian stamps appeared overprinted G.N.R. at Brescia. The overprints appeared in slightly different formats. Internal controversy surrounded the decision, which appeared to place the Guardia in supreme authority, and the overprints ceased after a few days.

In January 1944 the Social Republic issued an assortment of Italian stamps heavily overprinted with a fasces and *REPUBLICA SOCIALE ITALIANA* - the first time Mussolini's puppet state had been named on stamps.(15.4) They included five Imperial series

15.5 *25c King Victor Emmanuel III+war propaganda label of August 1942 overprinted G.N.R.: from set February 1944+.*

definitives, the 1942 propaganda set of 25c, 30c and 50c King Victor Emmanuel stamps with labels picturing the army, navy, air force and militia at war, and an array of Postage Due, Parcel Post, and Express Delivery stamps.

The following month, February 1944, the G.N.R. reappeared on most of the Imperial Series definitive, war propaganda and Air stamps, allegedly to prevent speculation in the original overprinted issue.(15.5) They were printed in Verona. Most likely the sudden changes, and the numerous printing errors, were the result of the tensions and confusion endemic within the puppet state.

From 5 June 1944, despite all the internal chaos and external threats, the Social Republic thought it important to design and issue its own stamps. Seeking to garner conservative and Catholic support, several values pictured famous churches, all of them victims of the war. (15.6, 15.7) Both the venerable St Ciriaco's Cathedral in Ancona (5c) and St Mary of Grace in Milan (1L 25 and 3L) had been extensively damaged by Anglo-American bombing, and the vast Abbey at Monte Cassino (10c and 1L) lay reduced to rubble as a blood soaked battleground between the German defenders and advancing Allies. The 25c featured Rome's Basilica of St Lorenzo, an early martyr and champion of the poor, which lost its renowned frescoes in an air raid. Two different 20c stamps pictured the Merchants' Court (Loggia dei

15.4 *50c, 75c, 1L25 and 2L50 (Express Letter) King Victor Emmanuel III from Imperial Series of April 1929-42 variously overprinted with fasces and/or REPUBLICA SOCIALE ITALIANA: from series 22 January 1944.*

Mercanti) in Bologna, a city that had strongly supported Mussolini and where, in November 1944, Fascist and German forces defeated a partisan uprising. The 30c pictured a drummer boy calling the citizens to arms (all'armi), and the 50c featured the allegorical Italia holding a fasces. The 1l 25 Express Letter stamp pictured Palermo Cathedral with its array of Arab, Norman, Gothic and Classical styles - another victim of Allied air raids in the lead up to the Sicilian landings. Finally in December 1944 a set marked the centenary of the execution of the anti-Hapsburg Italian revolutionaries, Attilio and Emilio Bandiera.(15.8) They had hoped to stir up rebellion in Calabria but few responded and they were betrayed, arrested and shot. Nevertheless stories of their martyrdom helped rally international support for the *Risorgimento*.

Across liberated Italy selected runs of definitives from the Imperial Series redrawn without fasces appeared from late 1944 into 1945 and 1946, sometimes on unwatermarked paper and sometimes on paper with a winged wheel watermark.(15.9, 15.10) A few even used King Victor Emmanuel's portrait as the monarchy still remained in place - precariously.

In April 1945 new Postage Dues appeared which were similar to the pre-war issues but without the fasces inserted into the Royal Arms.(15.11) In 1947 a new dull looking Postage Due set merely featured the values within a frame.

15.8 2L50 Attilio and Emilio Bandiera: from set 6 December 1944.

15.9 10c Emperor Augustus and 60c Italia without fasces from Novara unwatermarked issue: May 1945+.

15.6 5c St Ciriaco's Cathedral, 20c Loggia dei Mercanti, and 25c St Lorenzo Basilica: from set 1944+

15.10 60c King Victor Emmanuel III and 1L Julius Caesar without fasces from Rome watermarked issue: May 1945+.

15.7 1L Monte Cassino Abbey, 1L25 St Mary of Grace, and 1L25 Palermo Cathedral: from set 1944+.

15.11 60c Postage Due with fasces in Arms; from set 3 February 1934, and 25c without fasces: from set April 1945.

15.12 CLN souvenir cover with (from top left) 1L75 and 2L Imperial Series stamps, a 75c Imperial Series overprinted with fasces and Italian Social Republic, and six Italian Social Republic stamps overprinted C.V.L. GARBAGNATE MILANESE 25-4-1945 and cancelled on 28 April 1945.

It took until the very end of April 1945 for the Germans and the Italian Social Republic to be defeated. The *Comitati di Liberazione Nazionale* (CLN) (*National Liberation Committee*) was an organisation set up by various resistance groups, largely in northern Italy, in February 1944 to oust the Germans and crush the Social Republic. It managed to keep political divisions across the resistance groups at bay, liaise successfully with Allied forces and French and Yugoslav resistance groups, and secure funds through a Swiss based network of supporters. From early June 1944 the multi-party *Corpo Volontari della Liberta (CVL) (Voluntary Corps of Freedom)* coordinated the actual resistance campaigns under the auspices of the CLN. It operated with full sanction of the Allies and the interim Italian government, nominally Royalist but subordinate to Allied authority. The various resistance groups were forged into regular military units under the CVL in early 1945 and, to the surprise of many, in June that year peacefully handed in their weapons and dissolved their units.

During early Spring 1945 the Social Republic verged on collapse, until finally on 25th April - known henceforth as Liberation Day - Allied and CVL forces routed the last Germans and Italian Fascists. A few days later a resistance group captured and executed Mussolini. Numerous communities overprinted Social Republic stamps with CLN or CVL and their place names and often added the date 25 April 1945. Examples include *Comitati di Liberazione Nazionale MACCAGNO, C.L.N. Savona, C.L.N. Ponte Chiasso, C.di'L.N ACONA 25-4-1945, C.L.N. SESIO CALENDE 25-4-1945,* and *PIACENZA CLN*. Most were celebratory souvenirs on unaddressed CLN envelopes; few stamps were used for ordinary mail. One CLN/CVL cover, though, came from Garbagnate Milanese dated 28 April 1948, the day Mussolini was shot.(15.12)

During the chaos of May 1945 general recourse was made to redundant 20c and 30c Social Republic stamps, and overprints blocked out the logo and added *Poste Italiane* and new values.(15.13) Also in May the pre-war 40c Concessional Letter stamp was re-issued with the fasces obliterated, but in August as things settled down it was redrawn without the fasces.(15.14) In August a new Express Letter stamp appeared featuring Italia instead of the king.(15.15) Also in August the twin Parcel Post stamps (one side the stamp, the other the

15.13 20c Loggia dei Mercanti and 25c St Lorenzo Basilica Social Republic issues with fasces barred and retitled and revalued: from set 3 March 1945+.

15.14 10c Concession Letter with fasces in Arms: 7 January 1930, 10c overprinted with new Royal Arms and 40c: May 1945, and 1L with Royal Arms redrawn without fasces: from set August 1945+.

15.15 5L Express Letter: August 1945.

15.16 2L Parcel Post with fasces: from set April 1927+, and 1L with fasces obliterated: from set August 1945.

15.17 60c Dante Alighieri (Pneumatic Mail): 22 October 1945.

receipt) appeared with the fasces obliterated, and only in December 1946 were these starting to be replaced by a completely new post-horn design.(15.16)

Although several countries had developed pneumatic mail systems whereby letters are transported through pressurised air tubes - usually across major cities - Italy was the only country to issue special pneumatic mail postage stamps. In October 1945 the two stamps of the 1933 issue were redrawn to replace *REGNO D'ITALIA* with *ITALIA* and the new fasces-free Arms.(15.17) The stamps continued to feature the poet and philosopher Dante Alighieri (1265-1321) (60c) and astronomer and engineer Galileo Galilei (1564-1642). (1L40)

Slowly and painfully the Allies had fought their way up Italy, and the German surrender became effective on 2 May 1945. After a couple of short-lived Allied controlled civil administrations the strong pro-Catholic and anti-Communist Alcide de Gasperi (1881-1954) became prime minister in December 1945. Italy's rural and urban economies were in ruins and the country bitterly divided between left and right wing parties. Nevertheless the 1946 general election confirmed de Gasperi and the Christian Democrat in power in a pragmatic alliance with the minority Socialist and Communist parties. Tainted by his support for the Fascists, King Victor Emmanuel III had transferred his powers to his son Umberto in June 1944 and finally abdicated on 9 May 1946. Umberto became king, only to depart on 13 June after a national referendum voted

15.18 5l European Recovery Plan: from set 30 May 1949.

in favour, although far from overwhelmingly, of a republic. A Constituent Assembly got to work drafting a new constitution establishing a parliamentary democracy. As 1947 progressed there was the attraction of Marshall Aid becoming a reality which the Communists opposed as Imperialist bribery but which proved irresistible to the Christian Democrats. Indeed Italy was unique in issuing a set of stamps on 30 May 1949, to celebrate Marshall Aid (otherwise known as the European Recovery Plan).(15.18) They featured a shipwright and ship - both desperately needed.

In 1947 all Communists were expelled from government, largely as a result of the USA pouring money into Italy's welcoming right wing parties and initiating a massive publicity campaign fearing the country's very active Communist Party would succeed in drawing the volatile country into the Soviet Union's sphere of interest. At the height of his powers, de Gasperi remained in office until 1953 and introduced much needed reforms in health insurance, social housing, unemployment benefits and pensions. The Paris Peace Treaty in 1947 finally ended Italy's age of *Risorgimento*. It lost its colonies of Libya, Ethiopia, Eritrea and Somaliland, although it governed Somaliland as a United Nations Protectorate until 1960. It also recognised the independence of Albania, and ceded the Dodecanese Islands to Greece. Italy also lost the Adriatic peninsula of Istria, including Fiume and Pola, which with Zara and parts of Gorizia were ceded to Yugoslavia.

As soon as possible after the war all images linked to the past were replaced. The first new - and lengthy - peacetime set was issued on 1 October 1945 with further values appearing until January 1948.(15.19) The seven images agreed between the Allied occupiers and Provisional Government signalled the country's realignment towards reconstruction, family welfare and greater social justice. Ancient emperors and recent monarchs were conspicuously absent. Four showed a blacksmith's hammer breaking chains, presumably those of Fascism binding the nation. As the Italian surrender had been followed by an official change of allegiance the Allied victory could be proclaimed as Freedom. Six pictured a hand holding a flaming torch, the traditional emblem of education and enlightenment, and symbolising the nation's new direction. Four pictured a sapling being planted and two a sapling supported by a stake, signs of the nation's healthy regeneration. Two larger stamps with higher values featured an allegory of Peace - a figure much like the Statue of Liberty arising out of a shattered tree trunk that nevertheless was successfully putting out healthy new branches. Four stamps and the larger 100 lira portrayed the Scales of Justice framing a working father alongside his wife who was clasping their young child. They encapsulated the triple aims of Justice, Work and Health for all.

Also on 1 October 1945 the first stamps were issued in a new high value Express Letter set.(15.20) One image featured the winged foot of Mercury, messenger of the Gods, and the other a Classically inspired torchbearer and horse.

15.20 5L Mercury and 10L Horse and torchbearer (possibly the god Eubeleus): from set 1 October 1945+.

15.19 1L Planting sapling, 2L Supporting sapling, 4L Flaming torch, 5L Scales and family, and 50L Peace: from set 1 October 1945+.

15.21 5L Swallows and 50L Caproni Campini N-1: from Air set 1 October 1945+.

15.22 6L Wireless mast, 10L Ship's aerial, and 20L Heinkel He 70: from set 1 September 1947.

15.23 300L Douglas DC-2 flying over Rome: from set 16 February 1948+.

Finally the 1 October 1945 saw the first five of nine Air stamps.(15.21) Two images were used: one showed an aircraft flying through two ghostly clasped hands, the other three barn swallows flying along the coast. The aircraft was a Caproni Campini N-1, an experimental jet aircraft that Italy made much of during the war before it was superseded in performance by the German Heinkel He 178 (that had in fact flown in secret before the N-1). The N-1 never flew in combat, but helped pave the way for future jet travel.

The airline *Alitalia* was established in September 1946 and funded 60%/40% by the Italian government and British European Airways. Its first flights were in May 1947 using a Fiat G.12 Alcione domestically, and the four engined Savoia-Marchetti SM.95 from Rome to Oslo. On 1 September 1947, when transatlantic flights had begun, a new Air set was issued which, the set's inscription stated, marked the 50th anniversary of successful wireless communications.(15.22) Two stamps pictured wireless aerials on land, two stamps aerials on ships, and two stamps the Heinkel He 70 'Blitz', a modest 1930s German passenger aircraft that was one of the first to be equipped with reliable radio communication. The Italian Guglielmo Marconi (1874-1937) is generally credited with building the world's first successful wireless transmitter and receiver in 1896, and transmitting over the sea (the Bristol Channel) in 1897. Another Air set issued between February and September 1948 pictured a Douglas DC-2 flying over Rome.(15.23) This aircraft seems to have been operated by the independent *Avio Linee Italiane (ALI)*, not *Alitalia*.

On 31 October 1946 an attractive set of views and paintings of medieval Italian republics reinforced the fact that the monarchy had ended that summer, while at the same time reinforcing the glories wrought by republican rule.(15.24, 15.25) The designs made a dramatic change from Classical imagery. The 1L featured the St Andrew's Cathedral in Amalfi, the capital of the maritime trading republic known as the Duchy of Amalfi which flourished in the tenth and eleventh centuries. The 2L featured the facade of the Romanesque Church of San Michele in Foro in the Republic of Lucca which maintained its independence for nearly 500 years after gaining its charter in 1160. The 3L featured the figure of Peace from Ambrogio Lorenzetti's early fourteenth century frescoes, *The Allegory of Good and Bad Government*, in Siena's council hall. It was the heyday of the Republic of Siena which flourished from 1125 until defeat by Florence and Spain in 1555. The 4L pictured the Palazzo Vecchio, the fortified council chamber, in Florence, the centre of a powerful, if turbulent, republic from 1115 until the 1530s when the Medici became hereditary Dukes.

15.24 1L Amalfi, 2L Lucca, 3L Siena, and 4L Florence: from set 31 October 1946.

15.25 5L Pisa, 10L Genoa, 15L Venice, and 20L Oath of Pontida: from set 31 October 1946.

The 5L looked over the rooftop of Pisa Cathedral, built in the maritime republic's 11th and 12th century prime. The 10L featured the powerful Doge of Genoa receiving embassies. An aggressive and wealthy banking and maritime trading republic from the 11th to 18th centuries, Genoa was essentially a republic although the elected Doges (from 1399) gathered increasing authority. The 15L featured an allegory of Venice as the inheritor of Imperial Roman might and wealth. The Venetian Republic lasted from 697 until 1797, although its prime was in the Middle Ages. Here, too, the Doge was powerful but he ignored the patrician 'Great Council' and other elected bodies at his peril. The 20L featured the central part of Amos Cassioli's 1885 painting of the legendary *Oath of Pontida* in 1167 when Milan, Parma, Lodi, Ferrara and Piacenza swore to unite against the ravages of the Emperor Frederick Barbarossa (reigned 1155-1190).

Siena was central to another set on 1 March 1948 commemorating the 600th anniversary of the birth of St Catherine of Siena (1347-80).(15.26) The set was a timely one by the Christian Democrat government, now rid of any Communists in ministerial posts. Raised in Siena, visions led Catherine to an ascetic religious life and helper of the poor. With a group of followers and a growing reputation as a mystic favoured by God, she travelled throughout Italy preaching peace between city-states and working towards a settlement between the rival Popes of the period. Her influence was considerable, although not always successful in achieving accord. She was canonised in 1461 and widely venerated. The set pictures her giving a cloak to a beggar

15.26 3L St Catherine and beggar and 5L St Catherine and Cross: from set 1 March 1948.

15.27 30L Proclamation of the new constitution: from set 12 April 1948.

15.28 4L Uprising at Padua and 10L Defence of Vicenza: from set 3 May 1948.

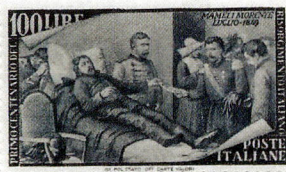

15.29 12L Gaspari, hero of Curtatone and 100L Death of Goffredo Mameli: from set 3 May 1948. (For 3L and 6L stamps in this set see 15.52 below).

(3L), dictating a letter or prayer (30L), carrying the Cross and message of Peace (5L and 100L), and extending her arms and message to all of Italy (10L and 200L). The 100L and 200L were Air stamps.

On 1 January 1948 Italy's long awaited new constitution took effect, and rather belatedly on 12 April the event was marked by two stamps portraying a muscular mason inscribing tablets of stone - possibly with intended Biblical and/or Roman overtones. He is carving the word *LEX (THE LAW)*.(15.27) Overtly avoiding both Fascism and Communism the constitution established an elected bicameral Parliament consisting of the Chamber of Deputies and the Senate, guaranteed the protection of private property and private enterprise, and confirmed every citizen's right to vote, education, health care, work, union membership, and freedom of speech and worship.

Soon afterwards, on 3 May 1948, no less than twelve different stamps celebrated the various Italian revolts in 1848-49 against Bourbon and Hapsburg domination. (15.28) They featured huge paintings of the dramatic events although most are hard to identify in the small single colour images. The 3L featured the rising in Palermo, Sicily, against the Bourbon rulers which helped incite revolts in Lombardy-Venetia against the Austrian Hapsburgs. The 6L showed revolutionaries storming the Porta Tosa, the east gate of the city of Milan, the 4L featured the brief but violent revolt in Padua in Veneto centred on the university, and the 8L pictured local rebels proclaiming the Venetian Republic which other north-eastern provinces such as Padua, Vicenza and Udine immediately joined. The 20L shows the Austrian retreat from Bologna. The 12L portrayed the Italian gunner, Gasperi, a hero of the battle of Curtatone on 29 May 1848 which the Austrian General Radetzky eventually won through overwhelming numbers. The 15L portrayed another hero, Giuseppe Cipriani, who rallied retreating colleagues to help ensure the hard-won Italian victory at Goito - the day after the defeat at Curtatone. However Austrian numbers eventually told in this region's campaign, and the 10L pictured the brave but forlorn defence of Vicenza against Radetzky's assault. The 30L featured Brescia in Lombardy where the revolutionaries held out for ten days against the Austrians. Its fall left the Venetian Republic fatally exposed. The 50L portrayed Giuseppe Garibaldi (1807-82), the charismatic Italian hero, who rallied the revolutionary forces of the Roman Republic (the former Papal States) to resist - ultimately in vain - the French army's attempt to restore the Pope. The 100L was reserved for Goffredo Mameli (1827-49), a poet and fervent revolutionary who was killed in the siege of Rome. His *Il Canto degli Italiani (The Song of the Italians)* became the lyrics of Italy's national anthem. Interestingly the set highlights the republican virtues of the revolutionaries and makes only one reference to the key figure of Charles Albert, King of Sardinia and Duke of Savoy (1798-1849, reigned 1831-48). The 5L stamp depicts him granting the liberal Albertine Statute in 1848 which became the Italian constitution until 1947, but his sympathies with the revolutionaries, desire for unification, and provision of an army were crucial to the challenge to Austrian rule. He abdicated after his defeat by the Austrian at Novara in May 1848 and was succeeded by his son Victor Emmanuel II who became king of Italy in 1861.

Several other issues reinforced the virtues of republicanism and the heroic revolutionaries of the past. In September 1948 the new 35L Express Letter stamp featured the 1848 rising in Naples, then part of the Bourbon Kingdom of the Two Sicilies. And on 18 May 1949 a single 100L stamp commemorated the centenary of the short-lived Roman Republic that sought to replace the Pope's authoritarian regime governing the extensive mid-Italian Papal States. The republicans tried to liberalise education and the press, reform prisons and guarantee freedom of worship but the attempt foundered in the face of the French army that besieged the city and restored the Pope. The stamp featured the vast seventeenth century fortress of Villa Medici del Vascello in Asti, south-east of Turin. (15.30) Defended by republicans led by Giacomo Medici (1817-82), a colleague of Giuseppe Garibaldi, it was the Roman Republic's last desperate bastion of defence against the French.

15.30 100L Villa Medici del Vascello (Centenary of the Roman Republic): 18 May 1949.

15.31 20L Guiseppe Mazzini: 1 June 1949.

15.32 20L Vittorio Alfieri: 4 June 1949.

15.33 20L Lorenzo de'Medici: 4 August 1949.

15.34 20L Domenico Cimarosa: 28 December 1949.

On 1 June 1949 a stamp honoured Guiseppe Mazzini (1805-72) the intellectual champion of the early Risorgimento and founder of the militant *Young Italy* movement.(15.31) An uncompromising republican during the 1848-49 revolution and long afterwards, he refused any involvement in the Italian monarchy governing the unified country in 1861. The stamp featured the statue topping his monument in Rome that was officially unveiled in 1949 to link with the centenary of the Roman Republic. On 4 June 1949 a stamp marked the bicentenary of the birth of the poet Vittorio Alfieri (1749-1803), many of whose works denounced absolutism and declared liberty to be a universal right.(15.32) A such he became a romantic hero of the *Risorgimento*.

On 4 August 1949 a stamp marked the 500th anniversary of the birth of Lorenzo de' Medici (1449-92), often called 'the Magnificent' - as on the stamp. A survivor of the brutal politics of medieval Italian states, he became *de facto* ruler of the Florentine Republic through his wealth and manipulation of the council. He was the lynchpin of the Italic Alliance of states keeping France and the Holy Roman Empire at bay, and patron of numerous scholars and artists such as Leonardo da Vinci and Sandro Botticelli.

On 28 December 1949 a stamp marked the birth bicentenary of the composer Domenico Cimarosa (1749-1801).(15.34) His numerous operas brought him international fame, but while living in Naples his openly liberal stance during its occupation by troops of the revolutionary French Republic in 1799 led to imprisonment when the Bourbon monarchy returned. He escaped execution through the intercession of

15.35 20L Gaius Valerus Catallus: 19 September 1949.

15.36 15L Gaetano Donizetti: 23 October 1948.

15.37 20L Voltaic pile and 50L Count Volta: set 14 September 1949.

15.38 20L Milan Trade Fair venue: 12 April 1949.

15.39 20L Levant Fair at Bari: 16 August 1949.

admirers of his works, including Lady Hamilton and, ironically, the ultra Conservative, but deeply cultured, Cardinals Fabrizio Ruffo and Ercole Consalvi.

Other stamps in 1948 and 1949 commemorated an eclectic range of historic and modern personalities and events. Just once, on 19 September 1949, a single stamp harked back to Classical times by marking, howbeit rather vaguely regarding dates, the bimillenary of the death of the poet Gaius Valerus Catullus (c84-c54BC). (15.35) Probably he was accorded the honour for his many lyrical poems exploring the emotions, notably the complexities of love, and because he was an influential Roman who largely (he was briefly on the staff of the governor of Bithynia) lived his life outside the brutal world of late Republican politics. He adorned the Republic rather than dishonouring it.

The centenary of the death of the operatic composer Gaetano Donizetti (1797-1848) was commemorated on 23 October 1948.(15.36) His comedies such as *L'elisir d'amore* and *Don Pasquale*, and historical dramas such as *Anna Bolena, Roberto de Devereux,* and *Lucia di Lammermoor* remained popular internationally. He took full advantage of the contemporary fascination with Tudor England, and with brooding romantic Scotland as popularised by Sir Walter Scott.

On 14 September 1949 two stamps featured Count Alessandro Volta (1745-1827) and his 'Voltaic pile' of alternate zinc and copper discs separated by felt spacers all soaked in the salt water which formed the electrolyte. (15.37) This was the first electric battery that supplied a continuous current to a circuit. He invented it in 1799, which explains the date of the stamps, although it was not made public until 1800. Volta is shown in what appears to be a Roman toga reflecting the Classical *Tempio Voltiano (Temple of Volta)* opened in 1928 in Como where he died.

Other sets highlighted reconstruction, economic recovery and international connections . On 12 April 1949 a stamp marked the post-war revival of the prestigious international Milan Trade Fair (15.38). It was first held in 1906 just after the opening of the Simplon Tunnel between Italy and Switzerland. On 16 August 1949 a particularly distinctive stamp marked the 13th Levant Fair which had been established in 1930 at Bari on the Adriatic coast. It sought to encourage trade across the Mediterranean and Middle East and revitalise the depressed economy of southern Italy. (15.39) After a wartime gap between 1940 and 1946 the Levant Fair resumed business in 1947. The stamp featured the large purpose-built exhibition centre on the shoreline and what looks like a medieval three masted carrack in full sail.

On 12 April 1949 Venice's 25th Biennial International Art Exhibition was celebrated with four particularly artistic stamps featuring city sights - a decorative

15.40 20L Winged lion emblem and state galley and 50L lion on St Mark's Column: from set 12 April 1949.

15.41 20L World Health Organisation emblem: 13 June 1949.

pinnacle (5L), the Campanile and bellringers (15L), the winged lion flag and the state galley *Bucentaur* (20L), and the lion on St Mark's Column (50L).(15.40) In the 1930s the event had become a wide-ranging festival embracing music, cinema and theatre as well as art.

On 13 June 1949 a stamp featuring a globe and the serpent entwined staff of Aesculapius, the God of healing, marked the coup of Rome hosting the Second Congress of the World Health Organisation (WHO). (15.41) It had been created by the United Nations the previous year. Its initial tasks were to tackle the global issues of TB, malaria and sexually transmitted diseases.

On 1 October 1948 a stamp marked the reopening the ancient wooden pontoon bridge (Ponte Vecchio) at Bassano del Grappa in northern Italy that had been destroyed by partisans in February 1945.(15.42) The stamp pictured the bridge and also an Alpine trooper in accordance with the unproven story that because many of the company's workmen repairing the bridge wore the distinctive quilled hat of the wartime Alpini Corps, and were ex-members, it was the Alpini Corps itself that rebuilt it. The celebrated architect Andrea Palladio (1508-80) had designed the original Ponte Vecchio, and he featured on a stamp issued on 4 August 1949. It commemorated the 400th anniversary of his architecturally ground-breaking rebuilding of Vicenza Basilica with its two tiers of Classical marble columns and rounded arches.(15.43)

On 19 September 1949 a stamp commemorated the construction of a Bailey bridge on the piers of Florence's Holy Trinity Bridge which had been destroyed by the retreating Germans in August 1944.(15.44) The stamp pictured the bridge before its destruction; it was not rebuilt until 1958.

On 8 June 1949 an innocuous stamp featuring Trieste's San Giusto Cathedral contained in small letters the important inscription *ELEZIONI DI TRIESTE 12 GIUGNO 1949 (TRIESTE ELECTIONS 12 JUNE 1949)*. (15.45) The stamp referred to the prolonged struggle between Italy and Yugoslavia over ownership of territory encircling the northern end of the Adriatic Sea. Yugoslavia is the next chapter in this book, but the story is best told as a whole in this one. Since the collapse of the Austro-Hungarian Empire in 1918 much of the region had been seized by Italy. After Italy's

15.42 15L Bassano bridge and Alpini workman: 1 October 1948.

15.43 20L Andrea Palladio and Vicenza Basilica: 4 August 1949.

15.44 20L Holy Trinity Bridge, Florence: 19 September 1949.

ITALY

Map of the Gulf of Venice c1949 showing the italian region of Venetia Giulia, the free state of Trieste (encircled in red), and the loss of the Istrian Peninsula and Fiume to Yogoslavia.

surrender in 1943 Trieste and its hinterland ostensibly fell within the Italian Social Republic but in practice was held by German forces as part of their Operational Zone of the Adriatic Littoral. The area suffered from heavy Allied bombing and CNL partisan attacks culminating in occupation by Yugoslav forces on 1 May 1945. For forty days the Yugoslavs hunted down all opponents - notably anti-Communist Italians and Slovenes, and fleeing Serbian and Croatian collaborators - killing many, until agreeing to leave under Allied pressure. Subsequently Trieste along with Gorizia, Udine and surrounding western territory, plus the enclave of Pula, fell under joint British and American military administration and was termed Zone A. Zone B, the eastern region stretching north past Postumia (Postojna) and across the Istrian peninsula to Fiume (Rijeka) remained under Yugoslav military rule. Stamps from both administrations, but notably Yugoslavia, proliferated. Relations remained tense.

In Zone A the ancient regional name of Venezia-Giulia was perpetuated with numerous Italian stamps being overprinted *A.M.G. V.G. (Allied Military Government Venezia Giulia)*. These included many definitives from the pre-war Imperial Series and post-war Reconstruction set, the 1945 Air set and 1946 Express Letter pair.(15.46)

During the initial occupation, and for some weeks afterwards, the Yugoslavs used several provisional overprints on, largely, Italian Social Republic stamps. On 15 June 1945 a dozen were briefly available postally overprinted *1.V.1945 TRIESTE TRST* with the Communist star and new values.(15.47)

15.45 20L Trieste's San Guisto Cathedral and elections: 8 June 1948.

15.46 60c Italia, 25c Enlightenment, and 1L Airmail overprinted A.M.G. V.G.: from set 22 September 1945+.

15.47 Italian Social Republic 30L Drummer, 50L Fascist allegory, 1L Monte Cassino, and 3L St Mary of Grace, Milan overprinted variously 1.V.1945 TRIESTE TRST and star and new values: from set 15 June 1945.

15.48 75c King Victor Emmanuel III with Italian Social Republic overprint, and overprinted again sideways with ISTRA 6L: from set 1 July 1945.

15.49 Italian Social Republic 75c Drummer and 1L25 Palermo Cathedral overprinted 3-V-1945 FIUME RIJEKA and star and higher values: from set 26 July 1945.

15.50 0.50L Donkey, 2L Duino Castle, 5L Vladimir Gortan's birthplace, and 30L Solkan Viaduct: from second issue 11 February 1946+.

Four stamps (two of which were Imperial Series definitives) were introduced on 1 July 1945 for regional circulation overprinted *ISTRA* and new values (15.48), and eight Social Republic stamps appeared on 26 July 1945 overprinted *3-V-1945 FIUME RIJEKA* together with a star, rising sun and new values.(15.49)

Between 15 August 1945 and 24 December 1945 an eclectic Yugoslav set inscribed *Istria Littoral Slovenia* in Italian and Slovenian supplanted the less than clear overprinted stamps. Many values in the new well-targeted set featured aspects of regional rural life - grapes (0.25L), tuna fishing (20L) a donkey (0.50L), an olive branch (1L50) and ploughing (10L). Others featured damaged houses being rebuilt (1l50), the striking Roman amphitheatre at Pula (4l), Duino Castle on the cliffs overlooking the Bay of Trieste (2L), the Solkan Viaduct, the world's longest stone arch railway bridge (30L), and the birthplace of the Istrian anti-Fascist Vladimir Gortan (1904-25) shot by the Italians after a protest meeting (5L). They were reissued between 11 February and 7 March 1946 in different colours (15.50), and both sets appeared overprinted *PORTO (POSTAGE DUE)*.

On 8 February 1947 two Yugoslavian stamps - the 9d young woman and flag from 1945-47 partisan set and the 1946 0.50d Official stamp - were issued overprinted with ten different values between them, and the legend *VOJN UPRAVA JUGOSLAVENSKE ARMIJE (YUGOSLAV ARMY MILITARY ADMINISTRATION)* (15.51). It signalled a change in international diplomacy and regional borders.

In February 1947 the Paris Peace Treaty awarded all former Italian territory in the 1945 Zone B plus an eastern slice of Zone A to Yugoslavia. It came into effect in September. However the Treaty turned Trieste and a

15.51 9d Female partisan and 0.50d Official overprinted VOJN UPRAVA JUGOSLAVENSKE ARMIJE and 2L and 50L respectively: from set 8 February 1947.

15.53 8L Chain breaking (from set 1 October 1945+) overprinted A.M.G. - F.T.T. with posthorn 1948 TRIESTE (marking Trieste Philatelic Exhibition): 8 September 1948.

15.52 3L Palermo uprising and 6L Storming Porta Tosa, Milan (from set 3 May 1948) overprinted A.M.G. - F.T.T.: from set 1 July 1948.

15.54 100L Villa Medici del Vascello (18 May 1949) overprinted A.M.G. - F.T.T.: 30 May 1949.

strip of land to its west and east into the Free Territory of Trieste, but it was never really free as the Allied Military Government administered the new north-western coastal strip - confusingly still termed Zone A - including Trieste itself. The Yugoslav army ran the new south-eastern Zone B which included part of Istria. This politically awkward situation lasted until 1954 when Zone A became Italian and Zone B joined Yugoslavia (as did three additional villages south of Trieste). Countless stamps signalled the division and tensions. Between 1947 and 1954 Zone A used a succession of Italian definitive and commemorative sets overprinted *A.M.G. - F.T.T. (ALLIED MILITARY GOVERNMENT FREE TERRITORY OF TRIESTE)* in various styles, colours and sizes.(15.52, 15.53, 15.54)

In Zone B the Yugoslav government issued a series of sets tailored to the region and accommodating to local public opinion. The first marked the Communist Labour Day of *1 May 1948*, and comprised 100L stamps featuring a dancer with a hoop issued in se-tenant strips of three inscribed 1 May 1948 and *Military Administration of the Free Territory of Trieste* in Slovene, Italian or Croat.(15.55) A stamp featuring the clear political message of clasped hands and a hammer and sickle marked Labour Day in 1949. (15.56)

Other Yugoslav issues featured local scenes and events. On 23 May 1948 a Red Cross stamp appeared revalued 2L, and this issue and all succeeding ones reduced the lengthy territorial and administrative title *Yugoslav Army Military Administration of the Free Territory of Trieste* to *V.U.J.A. S.T.T.* (or commonly *VUJA STT or STT VUJA)*. On 17 October 1948 a pair of Air stamps marked an economic exhibition, or trade fair, in the important port of Koper (in Slovenian) that week. Known as Capodistria in Italian, the Yugoslav occupation was already pressurising many Italians to leave.(15.57)

On 1 June 1949 three images adorned various values of an Air set of seven stamps. They were a flying boat landing near fishermen hauling in nets, a passenger plane flying over a man driving a laden donkey, and a gull flying over chimneys.(15.58) Soon afterwards the currency switched from Italian to Yugoslavian, and the set was reissued on 5 November 1949 overprinted *DIN* (Dinar).(15.58) Just before then, as an interim measure a range of 1945 Yugoslav stamps featuring Marshal Tito and wartime partisans in action were issued from 15 August overprinted *STT VUJA*.(15.59) No doubt they ensured everyone in Zone B appreciated Yugoslavia's ultimate aim for it - and indeed after numerous issues inscribed *STT VUJA*, on 26 October 1954 Zone B became part of Yugoslavia.

Two sets of stamps first issued in 1944 remained on sale until 1952 from the small Italian enclave of

15.55 se-tenant, Labour Day: 1 May 1948.

15.56 10L Labour Day: 1 May 1949.

15.57 50L Economic Exhibition in Koper/Capodistria: from set 17 October 1948.

15.58 2L Aeroplane over man and donkey and 5L Seaplane and fishermen: from Yugoslav currency set 5 November 1949.

15.59 1d Partisans, 2d Marshal Tito, and 9d Female partisan and flag (from Yugoslav set 8 October 1945+) variously overprinted STT VUJA: from set 15 August 1949.

Campione on the mountainous shore of Lake Lugano. It had ended up completely surrounded by Swiss territory in the early sixteenth century when Pope Julius II had transferred the region of Ticino from the bishop of Como to Switzerland in gratitude for support in war. However Campione itself was not included, and remained isolated right through the nineteenth century wars of Italian unification and every border settlement. In 1943 Campione supported Italy's break with Germany, and even remained free from Mussolini's Social Republic. However when Allied stamps could not be obtained from southern Italy in 1944 and 1945 it printed its own for local use and mail to Switzerland.

The first set featured the Arms of the House of Savoy of which King Victor Emmanuel III was the head. The attractive and carefully thought out second set featured views more closely connected with local people.(15.60, 15.61) The 0.05f showed the commune and lake, the 0.30f a view of Campione, and the 0.20f the simple Baroque parish church of St Zenone facing the town square by the lake. The 0.10f featured the grander Church of Santa Maria dei Ghirli high on a terrace above the lake. 'dei Ghirli' refers to the builders and sculptors from the locality who spent months away from home, like 'Ghirli - swallows. The 0.40f pictured Romanesque Modena Cathedral later embellished by masons from Campione, one of whom designed the octagonal cusp topping the main tower (left on the stamp) - allegedly to ensure it exceeded the height of Bologna's tower. The 1f featured the Romanesque Basilica of Santa Maria Maggiore in Bergamo clearly showing on the far left one of the elaborately decorated

15.60 0.20f St Zenone and lake and 0.40f Modena Cathedral: from set 7 September 1944.

15.61 0.60f Cansignorio della Scala's tomb, Verona and 1f Basilica of Santa Maria Maggiore, Bergamo: from set 7 September 1944.

porches created by Giovanni da Campione in 1353. The 0.60f contained a panel from the richly carved tombs of the ruling Della Scala family (known as the Scaligeri) in medieval Verona. The Gospel figures come from the tomb of Cansignorio della Scala designed by Bonino da Campione around 1375.

From 1952 Campione used Swiss stamps for Swiss mail and Italian stamps for Italian, and either nation's stamps for international mail.

CHAPTER 16

YUGOSLAVIA

In 1918 a Kingdom of the Serbs, Croats and Slovenes was created, and renamed Yugoslavia in 1929, although the new title barely concealed the ethnic jealousies, sectarian tensions and political assassinations that wracked the fragile new country. In 1939 the Serbian ruling classes favoured a western alliance, the growing Fascist Ustase party in Croatia was pro-German, and the banned Communist Party looked to Moscow for guidance. Yugoslavia joined the Axis alliance in March 1941 only for a military coup to reject it. In retaliation German, Italian and Hungarian forces immediately invaded Yugoslavia, conquering it in ten days.

Yugoslavia disappeared. King Peter fled to Great Britain, never to return. Germany annexed northern Slovenia, and Italy took southern Slovenia along with Kosovo, much of the Dalmatian coast, and Montenegro. Croatia, which also included Bosnia, became a puppet Axis state administered by the Ustase, and Serbia was directly controlled by Germany. Hungary annexed several small provinces along its borders, and Bulgaria took much of Macedonia and western Thrace, and part of eastern Serbia. They all issued stamps avidly publicising their regional administrations and eulogising their achievements.

Unfortunately King Peter's four sets between 1943 and 1945 meant little because their use was limited to stamp collectors and Yugoslav merchant ships working with the Allies. One featuring Peter himself marked the second anniversary of his coming of age and assumption

Map of Post-War Yugoslavia, Hungary, Romania and Bulgaria. It shows the reversion of Hungary's borders to those before 1938, notably the return of Northern Transylvania to Romania, and also Romania's loss of Bukovina and Bessarabia to the USSR and Southern Dobruja to Bulgaria. It shows, too Yugoslavia's post-war possession of former Italian territory abutting the Free Territory of Trieste.

16.1 2d Petar Njegos, 4d Vuk Karadzic, 5d Josip Strossmayer, and 10d Djordje Petrovic (Karadorde): from set 1945.

16.2 1L25 Chiefs taking oath (from Montenegro occupation set 9 May 1943) overprinted 5L Democratic Federation of Yugoslavia: from Cetinje set 1 March 1945

of power, the second was the first set overprinted *CRVENI KRST (RED CROSS)* and a surtax, and the third portrayed historic figures to mark the 25th anniversary of the country's creation. The last set was reissued overprinted '1945' to mark the Allied victory - which coincided with Marshal Tito's *de facto* seizure of power.(16.1)

As we shall soon see - in 16.27, 16.29 and 16.30 - just two or three years later Tito's government found opportunities to issue its own stamps honouring three of the six figures in the exiled government's final sets. These were the poet and prince-bishop Petar Njegos of Montenegro (1813-51) on the 2d, the Serbian philologist Vuk Karadzic (1787-1864) on the 4d, and the Croatian Bishop Josip Strossmayer (1815-1905) on the 5d. The others selected by the government in exile were the Croatian writer and publisher Ludovit Gaj (1809-72) (3d), the Slovenian poet Valentin Vodnik (1758-1819) (1d), and Djordje Petrovic (Karadorde) (1768-1817) (10d), the Serbian revolutionary against Turkish rule who founded the Karadordevic dynasty. In addition Valentin Vodnik's pupil, France Preseren, who was considered Slovenia's greatest poet appeared on a Yugoslav set in 1949 (see 16.31). It suited Tito to hijack the cultural initiative, encourage nationalism, and foster regional achievements rather than animosities.

During the war two powerful underground groups had emerged. The Chetniks were largely nationalist and royalist, and drawn primarily from Serbia and its army, and initially they were the only resistance organisation recognised by the Yugoslav government-in-exile and the Western Allies. The Partisans were Communist led and drew additional support from republicans, socialists and liberals right across the defunct kingdom, and were supported by the USSR. Other localised partisan groups had the ultimate independence of Slovenia, Macedonia and Montenegro uppermost in mind. Ambushes and sabotage became common as did savage German, Bulgarian and Hungarian reprisals; atrocities were common on all sides. Within a year the Chetniks had turned against the Partisans and started to collaborate with the Germans against them, although still receiving Allied arms drops. However despite regular Axis campaigns against them, by the summer of 1943 the Partisans controlled much of the northern and western parts of the old kingdom. That September Allied intelligence led the western Allies to switch their support to the Partisans led by Josip Broz Tito (1892-1980). They formally recognised his National Liberation Army, and also the new Yugoslav government-in-waiting formed jointly from Tito's Communists and some members of the royalist government-in-exile. The question of whether Yugoslavia would be a monarchy or republic was left open - except in Tito's own mind.

In 1944 Tito's forces grew to 750,000 or more, organised into four huge armies. In that year the Slovene and Macedonian groups placed themselves under Tito's command, and in due course Bulgaria switched sides and joined in the expulsion of Axis forces. On 8 October 1944 Soviet troops crossed into Yugoslavia, and together with the Bulgarians and Partisans steadily drove the German and Croatian Ustase forces northwards towards Slovenia and then Italy and Austria. Casualties were numbered in tens of thousands on each side. Germany surrendered on 8 May, but the following weeks saw bloody battles around Banja Luka as Serbian Chetniks, now keen to prove their Allied credentials, fought Ustase units wanting a free state of Croatia. Tens of thousands of both Serbs and Croats fleeing from the

16.3 3k Osijek Church (from Croatia set 1941+) with Split Democratic Federation of Yugoslavia overprint: from set 1 March 1945+, and 25b Mount Ozalj with Zagreb overprint: from set 20 June.

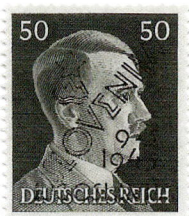

16.4 50pf Third Reich definitive (from set 1 August 1941+) overprinted SLOVENIA JUGOSLAVIA 9.5.1945 and star: from Maribor set 15 June 1945.

Partisans surrendered to the British on the Austrian border only to be handed over to Tito's ex-Partisans now forming the new Yugoslavia Army. Most were executed or imprisoned.

As the primary liberator of Yugoslavia Tito enjoyed widespread popularity that was probably enhanced by his immediate post-war purge of Nazi collaborators and probably not diminished by his a purge of those termed political dissidents. New inmates were crowded into the old Nazi and Ustase concentration camps across Yugoslavia. Although Tito was an orthodox Marxist the absence of Soviet forces in the country (except the far north-east), and a large loyal army, permitted him significant independence from the dictates of Stalin. Early on Tito firmly rejected Stalin's call to create joint-stock companies which was his way of rebuilding Russia's shattered economy by draining the resources of its satellites. By and large Stalin abided by his agreement with the Allies not to support the Greek Communists but Tito enthusiastically backed them, partly with an eye on gaining access to the Aegean Sea via Macedonia. In 1947-48 a massive falling out occurred between Tito and Stalin over Tito's wider plans for a Balkan/Danube confederation embracing Yugoslavia, Bulgaria, Albania and Greece. Such independent action, and greater satellite togetherness, was intolerable to Moscow, and Stalin imposed a crippling trade embargo as well as isolating Tito politically. In defiance Tito purged all pro-Stalin associates, established trade links with the West, and fostered a new nationalist spirit across Yugoslavia while also allowing major internal regions (the federated republics) a modicum of cultural liberty. As elsewhere in Communist states, though, the draconian collectivisation of farms proved a disaster resulting in low production, uncooperative peasantry, local revolts and savage repression.

Between October 1944 and June 1945 the major political and ethnic regions of the pre-war Kingdom of Yugoslavia reissued supplies of various wartime stamps variously overprinted but all confirming membership of the new Democratic Federation of Yugoslavia. On 20 October 1944 Serbia overprinted Hungarian stamps with a star, *Yugoslavia* in Cyrillic and the date 8 X 1944. They emanated from Senta which Hungary had seized in 1941 until liberation on 8 October 1944. On 1 March 1945 Italian occupation stamps were overprinted in Cetinje in Montenegro with a star and *Democratic Federation of Yugoslavia* in Cyrillic.(16.2) In Croatia wartime Croatian stamps were issued in Split from 1 March 1945 overprinted with a star, new value and *Demokratska Federativna Jugoslavija*, and on 20 June 1945 another issue in Zagreb followed suit but with a differently designed overprint.(16.3) On 28 April 1945 a further overprint variant from Mostar on wartime Croatian stamps marked Bosnia and Herzegovina joining the federation. And in Slovenia on various dates in June 1945 German stamps were overprinted *SLOVENIA, JUGOSLAVIJA*, 9.5.45 in Ljubjana and Maribor, and Hungarian stamps similarly overprinted in Murska Sobota.(16.4) Some regional issues had been overprinted with Croatian *kuna* values while others kept the wartime Italian and German currencies.

As early as December 1944 Tito's emerging nation hurriedly reissued five of the 'Monasteries' set, originally issued by German controlled Serbia, overprinted with *Democratic Federation of Yugoslavia* in Cyrillic, a surtax to help steady the Yugoslav *dinar*, and the new national emblem.(16.5) The emblem comprised ribbons entwining two ears of corn enclosing five torches flaming together surmounted by a red star. Although hard to see, inscribed on the ribbon is the date 29-XI-1943, the day of the wartime Second Session of the Anti-Fascist Council for the National Liberation of Yugoslavia (AVNOJ) which declared the new country

16.5 3d Ljubostinja Monastery (from Serbian set 10 January 1942+) overprinted Democratic Federation of Yugoslavia with Arms and +2: from set 14 December 1944+.

16.6 10d Postage Due (from Serbian set 1 July 1943) overprinted Democratic Federation of Yugoslavia with Arms: from set 25 December 1944, and new 20d Postage Due; from set 13 February 1945+.

16.7 2d Marshal Tito: from currency revaluation definitive set 19 May 1945+.

16.8 3d Bosnia-Herzegovina's Arms and 10d Yugoslavia's Arms: from set 29 November 1948.

16.9 2d St Prohor Pcinjski: 2 August 1945.

would be a federal republic. The five torches represented the individuality and unity of the five constituent republics - Croatia, Macedonia, Montenegro, Serbia and Slovenia. The overprints also appeared on reissued Serbian Postage Due stamps until in February 1945 newly designed Yugoslav Postage Dues had the national emblem as its impressive centrepiece. (16.6) At the same time a new definitive set featured the emblem alongside Tito himself.(16.7) The intensification of the cult of the great leader in both war and peace was underway. The new Postage Due and Tito portrait designs continued through 1945 and the painful but vital revaluation of the currency in May. One dinar now equalled 10 occupation ones.

There was no sixth torch within the country's emblem for Bosnia-Herzegovina until 1963. However on 29 November 1948, a set of celebrating the fifth anniversary of the federated republic gave each component republic, including Bosnia-Herzegovina, a stamp featuring its Arms. A far larger and higher value stamp was reserved for the national Arms.(16.8)

The heritage and legitimacy of the fledgling Communist regime was not forgotten, however, with a stamp on 2 August 1945 commemorating the first meeting of the Communist delegates to the Anti-Fascist Assembly for the Liberation of Macedonia exactly a year ago.(16.9) They had gathered in the midst of war in the chapel of the ancient St Prohor Pcinjski Monastery on the Serbian border with North Macedonia to declare an independent Macedonian state although after much controversy, and pressure and manipulation by Tito's supporters, the Assembly eventually supported federation. Plentiful stories of the victimisation and execution of dissidents filtered out of Macedonia long afterwards. Tito secured the western part of Macedonia for Yugoslavia, but the break with Stalin and the defeat of the Greek Communists wrecked Tito's plans for a Balkan federation. During August 1949 the fifth anniversary of the liberation of Macedonia from the savage wartime Bulgarian occupation was marked by three stamps. The 3d depicted partisans passing St

16.10 3d Partisans at St Prohor Pcinjski and 5d Workers with hammer and sickle: from Air set 25 August 1949.

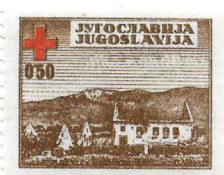 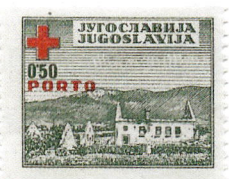

16.12 50p Obligatory Tax: Red Cross Fund 1 January 1947, and 50p Postage Due (Porto): Red Cross Fund 1 January 1947.

16.11 1d+4d Partisans carrying wounded colleague and 2d+6d Child: Red Cross Fund set 15 September 1945.

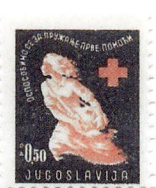 

16.13 50p Obligatory Tax: Red Cross Fund 1 October 1948, and 50p Obligatory Tax: Red Cross Fund 5 November 1949.

16.14 1d50+1d 'BGC Vaccine Defeating Tuberculosis' and 5d+3d 'Fight Against Tuberculosis':from set 1 April 1948.

Prohor Pcinjski Monastery, the 5d workers holding a hammer and sickle, and the 12d the Arms and flags of Yugoslavia and Macedonia.(16.10) The set was also issued as an airmail set overprinted *AVIONSKA POSTA*.

In 1945 the restored but ravaged country had numerous victims of war needing urgent aid. On 15 September 1945 two surtaxed stamps supported the Red Cross (using four regional languages). One featured a sad looking child, the other partisans carrying a wounded colleague to safety.(16.11) On 1 January 1947 two stamps - one postage, one postage due *(PORTO)* - were issued featuring a roofless house, and their 50p value tablets represented a temporary obligatory postal tax on behalf of the Red Cross.(16.12) The scheme was re-introduced on 1 October 1948 and again on 5 November 1949, with different stamps featuring busy nurses.(16.13) On 1 April 1948 three different surtaxed stamps, one of which pictured the BCG vaccine, promoted the anti-TB campaign.(16.14)

The new Yugoslavia possessed a controversial wartime legacy of armed resistance, but Tito quickly triumphed its liberation as exclusively a clean-cut Communist achievement. Starting in October 1945 a long set appeared whose values adroitly interspersed a portrait of Tito with scenes of wartime partisans.(16.15) Not surprisingly at a time of shortages the set appears on a variety of papers and in a variety of shades. Some show partisans tracking through mountains, others two riflemen firing from cover, a young woman partisan marching with a flag, and a view of the small town of Jajce in central Bosnia where the AVNOJ delegates had met in October 1943. On 20 October 1945 a stamp featuring Russian and Yugoslav flags marked the exact day in 1944 when Yugoslav partisans and Russian and Bulgarian forces finally liberated Belgrade.(16.16) (By then most Bulgarian units had switched sides from Germany to Russia - see Chapter Nineteen)

YUGOSLAVIA

16.15 2d Tito, 5d Jajce, 6d Female partisan, 16d Partisans in mountains, and 20 Riflemen in action: from set October 1945+.

16.16 2d+5d First anniversary of the liberation of Belgrade: 20 October 1945.

The first post-war general election was held on 11 November 1945 and only the candidates from the People's Front representing the Communists and their allies were named on ballot papers. In the hostile atmosphere opposition parties, notably the royalists, withdrew from the contest. Officially votes for other candidates could be placed in another ballot box but as this allowed the police to identify the voters the People's Front received 85% of the vote. On 29 November 1945 the Constituent Assembly abolished the monarchy, the country became the Federal People's Republic of

16.17 Miniature sheet with 9d and 20d 'Industry' and 'Agriculture' stamps inscribed 'Convening the Constituent Assembly' with Arms and dates Jajce 29-XI-1943 and Belgrade 29-XI-1945: issued and cancelled 29 November 1945.

179

Yugoslavia and the six federated states became Peoples' Republics. For a time the country was a model of Communist orthodoxy with a centrally controlled urban and rural economy, strict production targets, ever-present police force, and tightly controlled trades' unions. On 29 November, too, an adroitly prepared miniature sheet and set of stamps inscribed in Cyrillic and Roman scripts with the country's new name featured statues of a young workman holding a hammer and a young woman holding a sheaf of corn.(16.17) They represented Industry and Agriculture, the immediate targets of the new state, and they stood, as though taking an oath, with their hands on a book placed on an altar inscribed *State Constitution 29-XI-1945*.

On 9 May 1946 an unusual set of three stamps marking the first anniversary of the defeat of Fascism featured a protective circle of soldiers - some leading pack animals, some in a river boat, some driving a waggon - around the red star of the Communist state.(16.18)

Subsequent sets highlighted key aspects of the centralised Communist state while at the same time remembering the cultural identity of the federalised republics. In 1946 the ancient Zagreb Fair was reconstituted as a state controlled entity and the first post-war international exhibition of goods was held in

16.18 5d First anniversary of victory over Fascism: from set 9 May 1946.

16.19 5d Zagreb Fair: from set 8 April 1948.

16.20 2d50+2d50 Telecommunications Congress: from set 10 May 1946.

16.21 1d50+1d Volunteer Workers Railway Reconstruction Fund; from set 1 August 1946.

16.22 5d+2d Juvenile Labour Organisations' Relief Fund; from set 25 September 1947.

1947. Many Croatians, and no doubt many others, may have remembered that a few years earlier the exhibition ground had been a Ustase transit camp for Jews. On 8 April 1948 a set of three stamps featuring a map of Yugoslavia and symbols of industry and agriculture publicised the 1948 Fair.(16.19)

On 10 May 1946 a surtaxed set depicting radio masts and telegraph poles supported the first national Telecommunications Congress.(16.20) On 1 August 1946 a surtaxed set aptly inscribed *OMLADINSKA PRUGA (YOUTH RAILWAY)* supported the volunteer workers helping reconstruct the war damaged railway network.(16.21) The stamps featured the national flag waving behind a young woman clutching a spade aloft and urging on a young man pushing a loaded wheelbarrow. On 25 September 1947 another surtaxed set featuring young railway workers near a modern industrial town supported the state's Juvenile Labour Organisation Relief Fund.(16.22) No doubt the harsh conditions took their toll. As in most Communist countries older children were encouraged, and often pressurised, into joining state organisations mixing social activities with political indoctrination and patriotic participation in labour schemes. Coercion and rewards went hand in hand. They were expected to encourage, and even indoctrinate, the older and possibly less ardently enthusiastic workers.

On 15 December 1949 four stamps featuring locomotives marked the centenary of the railways in the regions forming Yugoslavia, although it was not the centenary of Yugoslavia's National Railways as this had only existed from 1929 until 1941, and from 1945. At other times the lines had been owned by private

YUGOSLAVIA

16.23 2d Early steam locomotive and 10d Electric locomotive: from set 15 December 1949.

16.24 Bilingual pairs: 2d Aeroplane over historic Kalimegdan Terrace, Belgrade and 20d Aeroplane over Dubrovnik: from set 21 April 1947.

16.25 5d Yacht 'Krajina' passing under Sava Railway Bridge, Belgrade: from set 30 July 1948.

companies or states such as Austria-Hungary or independent Serbia. Prior to 1870 the first lines were built in Slovenia to link central Hapsburg lands with key Adriatic ports. The 2d stamp shows an early steam locomotive, almost certainly of Austro-Hungarian lineage. The 3d features a later steam locomotive, and 5d and 10d diesel and electric locomotives respectively. (16.23) However other than in the north and around Belgrade the country still had few railway lines in 1949, and the diesel and electric locomotives were more a philatelic statement of future intent than actual motive power experienced by more than a tiny minority of passengers.

On 21 April 1947 colourful stamps marking the inaugural flights of JAT *(Jugoslovenski Aerotransport)* that month featured a twin engined aeroplane flying over Belgrade and Dubrovnik.(16.24) The upper fuselage blister seems to identify it as an Ilyushin II-4 DB-3, originally a Soviet bomber developed in the late 1930s and heavily used in the war. There is no evidence JAT flew any of these aircraft, but initially it used a few American Douglas DC-47s, the famous Dakota. Perhaps it was impolitic to feature these. After the split with the Soviet Union in 1948-49, Yugoslavia was isolated internationally, the airline was reduced to domestic flights, and fuel and spare parts were hard to obtain, until an agreement was reached with Swissair and relations with the West eased.

Although by July 1948 Tito's relations with Stalin were decidedly frosty, Yugoslavia stood firm with the USSR and its new satellites bordering the mighty River Danube on opposing the American, British and French attempts to reinstate the pre-war international freedom of navigation along the waterway. On 30 July 1948 a set of four stamps pointedly featuring the former royal yacht *Krajina*, now used by President Tito, passing under Belgrade's old Sava Railway Bridge marked a much-publicised conference in Belgrade where the Communist states used their majority to establish a new and exclusively Eastern European River Commission.(16.25) Built in Germany in 1928 for King Alexander of Yugoslavia, the *Krajina* was seized by the Croatian Fascists after the German invasion and presented to King Boris of Bulgaria, then a rather reluctant ally of Hitler. In 1945 it found its way back to Belgrade,.

There was a succession of complimentary issues celebrating cultural aspects of each republic. On 22 September 1946 two stamps marked the centenary of the birth of Svetozar Markovic (1846-75), a radical Serbian writer and political activist whose vigorous opposition to the repression of popular opinion by the ruling Obrenovic family led to his arrest, harsh imprisonment and early death.(16.26)

16.26 2d50 Svetozar Markovic: from set 22 September 1946.

16.27 1d50 Music and Serbian long necked lute (sargija) and 2d50 Vuk Karadzic: from set 27 September 1947 (See also 16.1 for government-in-exile issue).

16.28 1d Charles Bridge, Prague, 2d50 Victor Monument, Belgrade, and 5d Spasskaya Tower, Moscow: from set 8 December 1946.

On 27 September 1947 a set celebrated the work of the internationally renowned philologist Vuk Karadzic (1787-1864) in preserving Serbian folk songs, reforming the modern Serbian language, creating the first Serbian dictionary and (less of interest to the new regime), publishing in 1847 a Serbian translation of the New Testament.(16.27)

On December 1946 Yugoslavia had issued a set of five stamps featuring five capitals marking the Slavic (not Slav) Congress in Belgrade chaired by Tito. The 0.5d featured a silhouette of Sofia's theatre, the 1d Charles Bridge in Prague, the 1.50d the monument to King Sigismund III Vasa in Warsaw, the 2.50d the Victor (not Victory) Monument in Belgrade, and the 5d Moscow's Spasskaya Tower.(16.28) Pan-Slavism, the closer union of Slavs linguistically, culturally and politically, which had attracted huge attention when the Balkan states were emerging from Ottoman and Hapsburg rule gained no post-war support from Stalin or the obedient leaders of satellite states. Small separate states suited Stalin perfectly. Although the 1942 wartime Congress, the first since 1910, had seen Stalin actively promote Pan-Slavism as the means of energising the fight against the Nazis and their collaborators, and the 1946 event discussed Tito's ideas on federation, something Albania and Bulgaria initially supported, the idea remained still-born. There were no more Slavic Congresses until after the collapse of Communism in the 1990s.

On 28 July 1948 a surtaxed set marked the 80th anniversary of the Yugoslav (more accurately the South Slav) Academy of Sciences and Arts. An 80th anniversary, rather a centenary, is unusual but the set should be seen as one of a series deliberately highlighting Slav culture as a political gesture.(16.29) The Academy was established at Zagreb in Croatia as a body dedicated to preserving Slav culture within the Austrian Empire, but with the ultimate aim of securing greater autonomy for Croatia. The Emperor Franz Joseph sanctioned it in 1866, and under the three figures portrayed on the stamps the Academy quickly became a major teaching, research and publishing centre. The 4d+2d pictured Bishop Josip Strossmayer (1815-1905) of the wealthy Roman Catholic diocese of Bosnia and Syrmia in Croatia, and also leader of the Croatian People's Party, who was elected the Academy's patron, not least because he had been instrumental in its foundation and funding. The 2d 50+1d portrayed Franjo Racki (1828-94), a priest, historian and member of the Croatian legislative assembly, who was elected president. The 1d 50+0d 50 featured Djura Danicic (1825-82) who was a noted Serbian philologist but, as a promoter of Croatian and Serbian linguistic unity, served two lengthy terms as the Academy's secretary-general. In due course Serbian and Bulgarian Academies were created to promote their particular regional identities, and although the Croatian Academy prospered it did so increasingly as a Croatian,

16.29 4d+2d Bishop Josip Strossmayer: from set 28 July 1948 (See also 16.1).

16.31 10d France Preseren: from set 8 February 1949.

16.30 2d Petar II Petrovic-Njegos and 5d 'Wreath of Mountains': from set 8 June 1947 (See also 16.1).

16.32 12d Lovrenz Kosir and 15d Kosir, his birthplace and inscribed label: from set 21 August 1948.

not wider South Slav, initiative. It survives to this day through two world wars and all the intervening conflicts.

On 8 June 1947 a set commemorated Petar II Petrovic-Njegos (1813-51), Prince-Bishop of Montenegro and his epic poem *Wreath of Mountains* published in 1847. (16.30) It centred on the alleged massacre in the early eighteenth century on the order of Metropolitan Danilo I Petrovic-Njegos (Petar's ancestor) of Montenegrins who had converted to Islam. The verses explore numerous issues, notably the ethical values and ethnic identities of the perpetrators and victims, the dissonance between fighting for individual and national rights, and the moral and political consequences of Danilo opposing the Turks and promoting Montenegrin unity. Petar II's reign was dominated, too, by the constant struggle to bring law and order to his principality and wrestle autonomy from the Turkish Sultan, but the reason for the inclusion of the set was probably his concern to unite Balkan Slavs while preserving local customs and rights. The *Wreath of Mountains* became one of Yugoslavia's national epics.

On 8 February 1949 it was the turn of Slovenia when three stamps portrayed the Romantic poet France Preseren (1800-49) on the centenary of his death. (16.31) His lyrical verse combined his personal unhappiness with the loss of friends and an unrequited love with what he saw as the unhappiness of Slovenia subjugated by the Hapsburgs. Typical was his *The Baptism on the Savica* exploring issues of individual and collective identity, and despair and hope, based upon the story of the forced conversion to Christianity of the pre-Slovene settlers of Carinthia. By the twentieth century he had become Slovenia's national poet.

On 25 August 1948 the 80th anniversary of the death of Lovrenz Kosir (1804-79) was marked by four stamps portraying him, and one large Air stamp featuring an aeroplane flying over his birthplace.(16.32) He was a Slovenian in the Imperial Austrian civil service, and had a claim to be the inventor of the postage stamp as in 1836 he had proposed the use of adhesive postmarks signifying the pre-payment of postage rates. It is possible he got the idea from James Chalmers in Scotland who had designed stamps in 1834/35 but did not publicise his scheme until 1838. Kosir's idea was not accepted but long after his death both Austria and Yugoslavia enthusiastically promoted his claim. The airmail stamp went so far as to have an unusual publicity label attached to it saying in Slovenian and French: *In commemoration of Lovrenz Kosir, ideological creator of the first postage stamp in 1836. Born 26 July 1804 in Lusa, Republic of Slovenia, Yugoslavia.* Probably this unusual 80th anniversary was chosen to remind the world of Kosir's claim by the time the 75th anniversary of the Universal Postal Union was celebrated in 1949, the following year.(16.33)

Interspersed with these cultural issues were sets emphasising national well-being. Several sets promoted physical training and sports meetings, reflecting the general Communist interest in highly disciplined activities and a healthy working population. The group displays and parade of athletes waving banners on the set issued on 15 June 1947 inscribed *DAN FISKULTURNIKA (DAY OF GYMNASTICS)* promoting the Federal Sports Meeting that month looked much like any other Communist display and obligatory demonstrations of loyalty.(16.34)

A gymnast appeared on a set on 5 September 1947 marking the country's participation in the unofficial Balkan Games held in Romania.(16.35) The official Balkan Games only recommenced in 1953. Tito's early enthusiasm for a Balkan Federation meant Yugoslavia actively encouraged such Pan Slav events, although Stalin was less than keen on anything that might threaten his authority. On 10 September 1948 a surtaxed set featuring a shot putter, hurdler and pole vaulter

16.35 2d50+0.50d Balkan Games 1947: from set 5 September 1947.

16.36 5d+2d Balkan Games 1948: from set 10 September 1948.

16.33 5d Transporting mail by coach, train and aeroplane: from set 8 September 1949.

16.37 3d Fifth Yugoslav Communist Party Congress: 21 July 1948+.

16.34 1d50 Mass physical training and 4d Parade of athletes: from set 15 June 1947.

promoted the recreation of the official *BALKANSKO SREDNJE EVROPSKE IGRE U ATLETICI 1948 (BALKAN CENTRAL EUROPEAN ATHLETICS GAMES 1948)* but it was too late as by then the USSR and its satellite nations had ostracised and isolated Tito. (16.36) In response Yugoslavia realigned itself as a neutral country and accepted Marshall Aid. In the event the 1948 Balkan Games were abandoned due to lack of funds, and nervousness about Stalin's clear lack of interest.

Significantly, a little earlier - 21 July to 3 August 1948 - a set of typical Communist stamps picturing a young man and woman striding purposefully forward clutching a banner marked the Fifth Congress of the Yugoslav Communist Party. It was the first Congress since the war, and its main function was to support

Tito's action against Stalin and condemn *Cominform's* (the Soviet Union's Information Bureau) accusation that Yugoslavia was abandoning Marxism.(16.37)

And perhaps equally significantly on 20 March 1949 two stamps picturing skiers and the ski jump at Planica in Slovenia marked the International Ski Jumping Games there that month.(16.38) Most competitors came from Yugoslavia – including Janez Polda, who enhanced national pride by winning one event and being runner-up in another – but it attracted entrants from Sweden, Finland, Switzerland, Italy and Austria. Yugoslavia was signalling its cautious interest in positive contacts with the wider Western world. Until 1949 not all stamps had FNR *(FEDERALNA NARODNA REPUBLIKA) (FEDERAL PEOPLE'S REPUBLIC)* preceding *YUGOSLAVIA* in the title, but henceforth these all important proletarian initials were not forgotten. Indeed straddling 1949 and 1950 numerous stamps from the 1945-47 set featuring the wartime partisans were reintroduced overprinted with F*NR JUGOSLAVIJA* and new values thereby adroitly highlighting the initial battles to create the republic and the new struggle to maintain its independence. (16.39)

16.38 10d Planica ski jump: from set 20 March 1949.

16.39 8d Female partisan and 20d Partisans in the mountains overprinted FNR JUGOSLAVIJA and new values: set 19 December 1949+.

CHAPTER 17

ALBANIA

The son of a feudal chieftain, Ahmet Muhtar Zogolli became president of Albania and then pronounced himself King Zog I in a coup in 1928. Although ruthless and authoritarian he improved the economic infrastructure of the desperately poor country but largely through tying Albania to crippling Italian loans and Mussolini's increasing intervention in its internal affairs. In April 1939 Mussolini invaded Albania, largely to match Hitler's invasion of Czechoslovakia. Zog fled, and the country became an Italian protectorate. When Italy surrendered in 1943 German forces swiftly took over.

Before the war the Communists failed to secure much support in a largely agrarian and Muslim society, and against an ever-watchful security police. However two future principal players, Enver Hoxha and Mehmet Shehu, led the small wartime Communist Party and became active resistance fighters against the Italians, and later the Germans. In 1942 the National Liberation Army was formed at the invitation of the Communists. Led by the Communists, it directed the actions of all groups agreeing to join, whether Communist or not. Vicious guerrilla campaigns took place, usually against Axis troops but sometimes against Albanians in the overtly anti-Communist National Front which often worked in tacit partnership with Axis forces. Indeed in 1943 the National Front formed a fragile government, formally neutral in stance, but with German sanction and support - something of which the Communists made significant political capital as the war ended.

However by the end of November 1944 Hoxha's forces numbering over 70,000 members had liberated all of Albania from German control and many Albanian partisans had assisted Tito free parts of Yugoslavia. The surviving National Front units were ruthlessly crushed. The Albanian Communist Party was ready to seize power, and not surprisingly it dominated the supposedly openly elected Anti-Fascist Council of National Liberation that elected Enver Hoxha as the 'provisional' prime minister. All Italian and German property was seized, all overseas debts cancelled, many businesses nationalised, and the great estates of many tribal chiefs divided up among poorer tenants and peasants. An election in December 1945, accompanied by one-sided propaganda and terror tactics, was limited to candidates favoured by the Democratic Front, the successor to the National Liberation Front, and duly confirmed the Communists in power. Early in 1946 the National Assembly abolished the monarchy, declared a people's republic, and adopted a Soviet style constitution.

In due course the Communists purged all moderates and a Russian style centralised economy was introduced covering all industries, agriculture and foreign trade. Relations with neighbouring Yugoslavia, which had been bad until the war, dramatically improved - for a few years. In 1945 Albania conceded the hitherto contested region of Kosovo to Yugoslavia, and the following year the two countries signed a trade deal that integrated the two economies. Albania was desperate for foreign aid and technical support, and Tito supplied both, leading to modernised factories, enhanced production and a better transport system.

However in 1947 relations soured again, this time over suspicions that Yugoslavia was effectively absorbing Albania and profiteering at its expense. This led to conflict and instability within Albania's Communist Party, and initially sparked another round of purges by Hoxha against critics of his pro-Tito policies. However within a year all agreements with Yugoslavia were rescinded, and Hoxha shifted to side with Stalin against Tito's independent thinking. Emerging unscathed from the internal chaos and blood-letting Hoxha went on to ensure Yugoslavia was condemned as Albania's national enemy - along with the western democracies. Albania now became dependent on Soviet aid and expertise, and Hoxha duly intensified his rigid Stalinist regime and joined the Communist Bloc's Council for Mutual Economic Assistance. The situation stabilised until 1958 when Hoxha switched his allegiance to China in protest against the USSR's 'de-Stalinisation' programme which he saw as a potential threat to his own position.

In 1945 a flurry of hurriedly and heavily overprinted wartime stamps celebrated the new state. On 4 January 1945 nine of the Italian occupation stamps were overprinted with higher inflationary values and *QEVERIJA DEMOKRAT. E SHQIPERISE 22-X-1944 (THE DEMOCRATIC GOVERNMENT OF ALBANIA 22-X-1944)*.(17.1) On 10 July 1945 the second anniversary of the wartime formation of the first major battalions of what became the People's Army was commemorated with stocks of a 1930 Albanian set ironically commemorating the second anniversary of

17.1 Italian occupation 15q King Victor Emmanuel III (from set August 1939+) overprinted QEVERIJA DEMOKRAT. E SHQIPERISE 22-X-1944: from set 4 January 1945.

17.2 2q Lake of Butrinto (from King Zog Second Anniversary of Succession set 1 September 1930) overprinted 1943 1945 U.N.CL. SHQ 10 KORRICK, red star and new value: from set 10 July 1945.

17.3 25q+15q anti-TB Fund (from set 1 April 1943) overprinted with QEVERIJA DEMOKRAT. E SHQIPERISE, border, Red Cross, JAVA E K.K. SHQIPTAR 4-11 1945 and 2f+1f: from set 4 May 1945.

17.4 20q Labinot, 40q Bridge at Berat, and 3f Permet: from set 28 November 1945.

17.5 60q Bridge at Berat (from set 28 November 1945) overprinted QSAMBLEJA KUSHTETUESE 10 KALLNUER 1946: from set 10 January 1946.

17.6 30q Labinot (from set 28 November 1945) overprinted REPUBLIKA POPULLORE E SHQIPERISE: from set 1 July 1946.

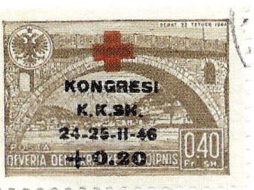

17.7 40q bridge at Berat (from set 28 November 1945) overprinted KONGRESI K. K. SH. 24-25. II.46, +0.20 and Red Cross: from set 16 July 1946.

Zog's accession overprinted with new values, a star, the dates *10 KORRIK 1943-1945* and *U.N.CL. SHQ. (USHTRIA NACIONAL CLIRIMTARE SHQIPERIA: Trans 10 JULY 1943-1945 ALBANIAN NATIONAL LIBERATION ARMY)*.(17.2)

The much needed services of the Red Cross were supported in May 1945 with the 1943 anti-TB set virtually obliterated by a heavily bordered overprint of the new state's name, rays from a large Red Cross, surtax, and the inscription *JAVA E K.K. (for Krygit te Kuj) 4-11 MAJ 1945 SHQIPTAR (ALBANIAN RED CROSS WEEK 4-11 MAY 1945)*.(17.3)

On 28 November 1945 the first specially designed post-war set featured three highly regarded wartime sites.(17.4) The 20q and 30q featured Labinot where the first national conference of Albania's Communist Party was held, largely to create a better organised liberation army. The 40q and 60q featured the Bridge at Berat, the village where 60 Muslim and Christian families famously hid Jews from German persecution. The 1f and 3f featured Permet where, in May 1944, the Anti-

Fascist Council of National Liberation was created to administer liberated territory.

This important set was later reissued three times with overprints that did not obliterate the images. The first, on 10 January 1946 celebrated the election of the Constitutional Assembly (QSAMBLEJA KUSHTETUESE) on that date.(17.5) The second, on 1 July 1946, marked the proclamation of the new People's Republic of Albania (REPUBLIKA POPULLORE E SHQIPERISE).(17.6) The third, on 16 July 1946, was surtaxed in support of the Albanian Red Cross Congress (KONGRESI K. K. SH. 24-25. II.46).(17.7)

Most other sets throughout the 1940s glorified the achievements of the state and reinforced the Communist victory over Fascism. Significantly a striking set on 8 March 1946 highlighted the Congress of the Women's International Democratic Federation.(17.8) Founded the year before in Paris, the set's globe, dove and olive branch signalled the organisation's anti-Fascist dedication to world peace as well as concern for family welfare and women's rights. However it was soon banned in France after which it relocated to East Berlin and was widely perceived in the West as a front for Communist propaganda. Notwithstanding this view, under both King Zog and Enver Hoxha Albanian women - at least in the few cities, if not in practice amongst rural tribes - enjoyed a right to education, vote, divorce, and independent careers.

In common with other Balkan countries Albania welcomed the possible revival of the Balkan Games as a way of promoting both national unity and closer Slavic collaboration. In 1946 Tirana, the capital, hosted an unofficial Balkan Games (17.9), and in that year Albania's football team scored a notable triumph by winning the Balkans Cup.

Soon after the war 5 May became Albania's Martyrs' Day, the day to remember those killed in the war - or at least the Communist ones. It was the birthday of Qemal Stafa (1920-42), featured on a set issued on that day in 1947, who was one of the youthful founders of the Albanian Communist Party. A political activist, he was trapped and killed near Tirana by the Italians.(17.10)

On 10 July 1947 the fourth anniversary of the formation of the People's Army merited four individually inscribed stamps.(17.11) The 16q, dated 1942, featured early partisans led by Hasim Zeneli, 'a hero of the nation', killed in battle with the Italians in 1943. The 20q portrayed Enver Hoxha as a wartime partisan alongside Vasil Shanto, killed in a skirmish

17.10 20q Qemal Strafa: from set 5 May 1947.

17.8 40q Women's International Democratic Federation Congress: from set 8 March 1946.

17.9 1q Balkan Games: from set 6 October 1946.

17.11 16q Hasim Zeneli and partisans, 20q Enver Hoxha and Vasil Shanto, 28q partisans on the march, and 40q Vojo Kushi: set 10 July 1947.

17.12 8l NLA troops hurling grenades: from set 10 July 1948.

17.15 1l Armed war invalids: 17 November 1947.

17.13 5l Soldier and map of Albania: from set 10 July 1949.

with the Germans in 1944. The marching column on the 28q commemorates the inauguration on 15 August 1943 at Vithkuj of the first brigade of the National Liberation Army (NLA) under Mehmet Shehu. The 40q featured Vojo Kushi, another early Communist killed by the Italians in 1942 near Tirana and honoured by both Yugoslavia and Albania.(17.11) The pair of fifth anniversary stamps on 10 July 1948 featured NLA troops hurling grenades and marching on parade (17.12), and three stamps on the sixth anniversary on 10 July 1949 pictured a soldier against a map of liberated Albania.(17.13)

Interspersed with these sets were yet more that recalled the heroic days of the war. On 16th September 1947 a pair of stamps pictured the (later ruined) Peza conference building outside Tirana in which, exactly five years earlier, the Communists successfully unified most of the various partisan groups in the National Liberation Movement and Army.(17.14) On 17 November 1947 a congress of war invalids was marked by a single stamp featuring badly wounded soldiers - but still armed and struggling to fight.(17.15)

17.16 1l50 Burning village, 2l50 Soldiers ready to fire, and 12l Column of infantry: from set 29 November 1947.

17.14 2l Ruined conference building at Peza: from set 16 September 1947.

117.14 2l Ruined conference building at Peza: from set 16 September 1947.

On 29 November 1947 five dramatic stamps commemorated the third anniversary of liberation with images of a burning village (1l 50), riflemen ready to fire (2l 50), machine gunners ready to fire (5l), a mounted soldier trudging through the snow (8l), and a column of infantry in the winter countryside. (12l).(17.16) And in 1949 the fifth anniversary of liberation set featured bitter street fighting (3l and 8l) and a triumphant partisan holding a flag in the light of a shining star (2l 50 and 5l).(17.17)

Four other sets reflected key aspects of Hoxha's regime - the need for better communications and control of the countryside and his desire to slavishly imitate Stalin's version of a communist state.

In 1945 Albania had no standard rail services, but Hoxha recognised the need for the key Adriatic port of Durres to be well connected. On 16 May 1947 a set celebrated the thousands of members of the Albanian Labour Youth Union, both male and female, assisted by young volunteers from Bulgaria and Yugoslavia, who were constructing the new railway line from Durres to Elbasan. By November 1947, within a year, the first 43 kilometres to Pequin were opened.(171.8) On 1 June 1948 an action packed set pictured the youthful workers digging out the track of the Durres to Tirana railway ahead of an approaching passenger train adorned with the Communist star.(17.19) Sixty eight kilometres long, the line connected the two most important cities in Albania, and was constructed within two years with minimal mechanical aid. Once again Yugoslav volunteers took part, but only until Hoxha's split with Tito. Hoxha's regime prohibited private vehicle ownership and only one railway line - a freight link with Montenegro - ever crossed the national borders.

Hoxha attempted to make Albania self-sufficient in food production largely through willing or forced collectivisation. Landowners large and small lost their holdings in the mass nationalisation programme, and much land was granted to peasant communities who also benefited from the abolition of their debts. In return wages were strictly controlled and local production targets levied. Thousands of Communist volunteers spread the virtues, and demands, of the new regime to the villagers. Any sign of a market economy was instantly suppressed. On 17 November 1947 a set celebrated the initiative with a strikingly realistic set featuring peasants presumably gathering for a collective discussion (1l 50), being addressed at a meal (2l), rejoicing at a dance (2l 50), and being visited by a surprisingly friendly soldier (3l).(17.20) Deliberately designed as a set of photographs, the stamps were no doubt hailed as evidence of Hoxha's radical changes being welcomed by village communities who were still able to enjoy enjoyed their age-old traditions. Indeed the land transfer was welcomed, but the gradual enforcement of collectivisation and the creation of state farms worked by low wage labourers were not.

17.18 28q Men and women building the Durres to Pequin railway: from set 16 May.

17.19 8l Building the Durres to Tirana railway: from set 1 June 1948.

17.20 1l50 Peasants' meeting, 2l Mealtime address, 2l50 Celebratory dance, and 3l Soldier's visit: set 17 November 1947.

 *17.21 8l Labour Day: from set 1 May 1949.*

 *17.23 12l Enver Hoxha: from set 16 October 1949.*

17.22 4l Albanian-USSR friendship: from set 10 September 1949.

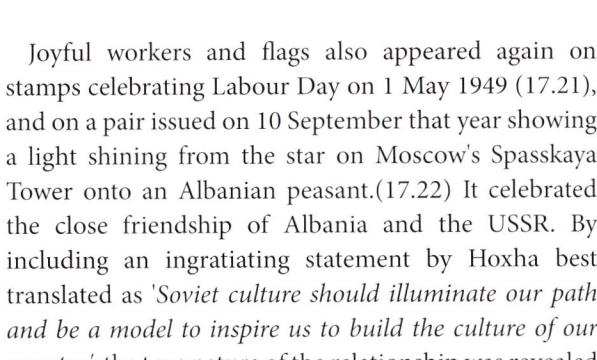 *17.24 5l Joseph Stalin: from set 21 December 1949.*

Joyful workers and flags also appeared again on stamps celebrating Labour Day on 1 May 1949 (17.21), and on a pair issued on 10 September that year showing a light shining from the star on Moscow's Spasskaya Tower onto an Albanian peasant.(17.22) It celebrated the close friendship of Albania and the USSR. By including an ingratiating statement by Hoxha best translated as '*Soviet culture should illuminate our path and be a model to inspire us to build the culture of our country*', the true nature of the relationship was revealed to all.

On 16 October 1949 a set portrayed Enver Hoxha (17.23), and not surprisingly on 21 December 1949 a set pictured an authoritative but benign Joseph Stalin on his 70th birthday.(17.24) At this time Albania was entirely dependant on Russian aid and technical expertise, and in return Hoxha intensified replicating Stalin's ruthless regime in Albania. Welfare projects and political indoctrination went hand in hand: the health care system improved to turn out fitter workers, and the increased number of schools ensured young adults were equipped with the requisite skills and beliefs to further the Socialist state.

CHAPTER 18

HUNGARY

In 1918 the Hapsburg Kingdom of Hungary collapsed along with the Hapsburg Austrian Empire, and in the ensuing chaos various parts were occupied by Romanian, French and Czech forces. Amidst the confusion Hungary became a short-lived Democratic Republic and then a short-lived brutal Soviet Republic under Bela Kun. Late in 1919 the ex-commander-in-chief of the Austro-Hungarian navy, Admiral Miklos Horthy, led a right wing nationalist coup with Allied diplomatic support. The Allies pressurised the Romanian army to withdraw and Horthy duly purged the Communists and other left wing groups. Hungary returned to being a *de jure* constitutional monarchy, but as the Hapsburg King Karl IV was barred from returning as monarch Horthy remained a permanent Regent with almost complete freedom of action. However social conditions barely improved, the country endured hyperinflation followed by the depression of 1929 which blighted trade, caused mass unemployment and laid the country open in the 1930s to Germany influence. Hungary resented the post-war loss of Transylvania to Romania, much of upper Hungary to Czechoslovakia, and parts of the south to Yugoslavia, and Horthy responded favourably to German and Italian entreaties and bribes. In 1938 Hitler sweetened Hungary by restoring southern stretches of Czechoslovakia and in 1939 Horthy annexed Carpatho-Ukraine. In 1940 Hitler pressurised Romania to grant northern Transylvania to Hungary. Soon afterwards Hungary joined the Axis powers and its armies fought alongside the Germans in the invasion of Yugoslavia and the Soviet Union.

Catastrophe followed as Hungarian forces in Russia were torn to pieces by the Russians, especially at Stalingrad. In 1944 Horthy sought an armistice with the western Allies, only for German forces to occupy Hungary, restrict Horthy's authority, and instal a puppet government. The war continued. Hitler threatened Hungary with occupation by the hated Romanians, Slovaks and Croats if resistance grew, but when Soviet forces crossed into Hungary in September 1944 Horthy desperately sought peace with Moscow, only to be imprisoned by the Germans and replaced by the brutal regime of the neo-Nazi Arrow Cross Party. Hungary's armies continued to fight vigorously alongside the Germans against the Soviet invaders and their new Romanian allies (see next chapter), but were savagely mauled defending Budapest between December 1944 and February 1945. By early April 1945 Hungary was free of German control but occupied by the Russians. Half a million Hungarian Jews and 300,000 Hungarian soldiers perished in the war, and perhaps another half a million Hungarians, including 150,000 ethnic Germans, were deported to Russia in 1944 and 1945.

As early as December 1944 a Hungarian 'interim assembly' met at Debrecen with Stalin's approval to elect a provisional government headed by Bela Miklos, a former general who had fought alongside the Germans but later turned against them. In March 1945 the German puppet government of Hungary was ejected and the Regency replaced by the provisional government. In the elections of November 1945 the Hungarian Communist Party received only 17% of the vote and the Independent Smallholders' Party (ISP) 57%, but the Soviet army commander, Marshal Voroshilov, forced the ISP to form a coalition administration with several Communists holding key ministries. On 1 February 1946 the Kingdom of Hungary was formally abolished and the Second Republic proclaimed (The First Republic had been the brief Communist one in 1919.) The Soviet army stayed in occupation thereby easing the Communist task of eliminating opponents - Prime Minister Ferenc Nagy (of the ISP) resigned and fled in May 1947 to avoid arrest - crushing dissent, launching massive propaganda campaigns, curbing the influence of the churches, and forcing though the nationalisation of industries. The Hungarian stamp marking the Paris Peace Treaty in February 1947 featured Peace in the form of a young woman in the sun holding sheaves of corn and gazing at

18.1 60f Peace Treaty: 22 September 1947.

18.2 1f Prince Arpad, 2f King Ladislas I, 3f Miklos Toldi, 4f Janos Hunyadi, 5f Pal Kinizsi and 6f Miklos Zrinyi: from set 1 January 1943+.

18.3 8f Ferenc Rakoczi, 10f Andras Hadik, 12f Artur Gorgey, 20f St Stephen's Crown, 24f the Madonna, and 30f St Margaret: from set 1 January 1943+.

a dove offering her a sprig of olive.(18.1) Hungary's borders returned to those of 1938 meaning all its acquisitions from Czechoslovakia and Romania were lost. Stalin had little interest in such grievances, and far more in identifying Communism with the popular cause of peace and castigating Great Britain and the USA as Imperialist aggressors.

The Peace Treaty stamp was delayed until September 1947, just after the August election. Despite widespread fraud it only increased the Communist vote to 24%, but at Moscow's behest any pretence at democratic processes disappeared. By June 1949 terror tactics meant the leaders of other parties had fled, been imprisoned - including President Zoltan Tildy (of the ISP) - or forced to merge with the Communists. Having achieved full control the Hungarian People's Republic could be declared in August 1949 and a Stalinist constitution adopted. The Soviet army was never far away in its vast camp at Baden, near Vienna.

When Hungary's military fortunes were in alarming decline in 1943 and 1944 a lengthy set aimed to improve morale with portraits of famous rulers and military figures from across the centuries. Early heroes included Prince Arpad (c845-c907) (1f), the legendary leader of the Magyar tribes settling in the region, and King Ladislas I (c1040-95) (2f) who extended the kingdom, secured its borders, and was deemed a saint. The Middle Ages were recalled by Miklos Toldi (c1320-90) (3f), whose military exploits were woven into folk tales, and his name given to a Hungarian tank, Janos Hunyadi (c1406-56) (4f), an aristocratic warrior who held the Turks at bay, and was father of Matthias Corvinus, and Pal Kinizsi (1432-95) (5f), a successful general serving King Matthias Corvinus against the Turks. From later centuries there were Miklos Zrinyi (1620-64) (6f), who fought the Swedes and Turks to preserve Hungary within the Hapsburg Empire, Ferenc Rakoczi II (1676-1735) (8f) who led a brave but ill-fated peasant uprising against the Hapsburgs, and Andras Hadik (1710-90) (10f) a Hungarian general in the Austrian Hapsburg army who skilfully out-manoeuvred the Prussians to capture Berlin in the Seven Years War of 1756-63. Finally there was Artur Gorgey (1818-1916) (12f), the brilliant revolutionary general in the 1848-49 Hungarian uprising. Several higher values pictured the Madonna or St Stephen's Crown, the symbol of Hungarian autonomy, and in January 1944 a new 30f featured St Margaret (1242-70), the daughter of King Bela IV who forsook her royal life to become a nun with many miracles of healing linked to her name. She had been canonised in November 1943.(18.2, 18.3)

These stamps were to have an unexpected and demeaning future, as did the set on 1 August 1944 commemorating six famous Hungarian women. They included St Margaret (24f), St Elizabeth of Hungary (1207-31) (20f), another princess who became a nun and carer of the sick; Elizabeth Szilagyi (1410-83) (30f), the wife of John Hunyadi and fiercely protective mother of King Matthias Corvinus; Dorothy Kanizsai (c1478-c1531) (50f), the aristocratic founder of schools and famous for giving a Christian burial to the hundreds of Hungarians killed by the Turks at the Battle of Mohacs in 1526; Zsuzsanna Lorantffy (1602-60) (70f), who with her husband, the Prince of Transylvania, introduced Calvinism to the region, and Ilona Zrinyi (1643-1703) (80f) who defended her husband's castle of Palanok for three years against an Imperial Austrian army before joining him in exile.(18.4)

The stamps possess a poignancy stemming from the battles the heroic figures fought against jealous enemies within their own country as well as outside it. Hungary was not saved from defeat in 1945, and the sets reappeared several times as easily available platforms for various overprints associated with the country's changing political structure and increasingly chronic inflation. Often the portrait was obscured by the surface tinting as well as the heavy overprint. On 1 May 1945 - the Communist May Day - thirteen of the 1943 famous people set appeared on both yellow or blue surface tinted paper and overprinted *1945 apr 4 FELSZABADULAS (LIBERATION)* and higher inflationary values.(18.5) The date 4 April 1945 was the official end of the Soviet offensive in Hungary, although some Hungarian units fought on alongside the Germans in Austria and Bavaria.

On 1 June 1945 all nineteen famous people stamps appeared on surface tinted paper overprinted 1945 and generally higher values in black or red, as did the famous women set. These comprised the First Provisional Issue.(18.6, 18.7)

18.5 1f Prince Arpad, 24f the Madonna and 1p St Stephen's Crown from set 1 January 1943+ overprinted 1945 apr 4 FELSZABADULAS (LIBERATION) and higher values: from set 1 May 1945.

18.6 5f Pal Kinizsi, 8f Ferenc Rakoczi, and 12f Artur Gorgey from set 1 January 1943+ overprinted 1945 and new values.

18.7 30f Elizabeth Szilagyi and 50f Dorothy Kanizsai from set 1 August 1944 overprinted 1945 and similar values.

18.4 20f St Elizabeth, 24f St Margaret, 30f Elizabeth Szilagyi, 50f Dorothy Kanizsai, 70f Zsuzsanna Lorantffy, and 80f Ilona Zrinyi: set 1 August 1944.

18.8 10f Andras Hadik and 80f St Stephen's Crown from set 1 January 1943+ overprinted 1945 and higher inflationary values: from set 18 July 1945.

18.9 20f St Elizabeth and 30f Elizabeth Szilagyi from set 1 August 1944 overprinted 1945 and higher inflationary values: from set 18 July 1945.

Soon afterwards, on 18 July 1945, ten of the famous people and four of the famous women stamps appeared, once again on surface tinted paper, but this time with much higher inflationary values. In June, for example, the 8f was overprinted 60f, but in July it was 5p (pengo). These were the Second Provisional Issue.(18.8 18.9)

A set issued on 20 March 1944 to mark the 50th anniversary of the death of the internationally feted Hungarian revolutionary leader, Louis Kossuth (1802-94) also suffered overprinting but in a worthy cause and without obscuring the main characters, especially the national hero himself.(18.10) Briefly de facto ruler of Hungary during the 1848-49 revolution, Louis Kossuth's desire for an independent Hungary led to bitter disagreement with his key general, Artur Gorgey, who favoured autonomy within the Hapsburg Empire. In the event Kossuth's extremism led Tsar Nicholas I of Russia to intervene on Austria's behalf. Under great pressure Kossuth resigned, and Gorgey surrendered rather than face military annihilation. The dramatic set featured Kossuth welcoming a family (4f) inspiring a meeting (30f), his army advancing with banners waving and drums beating (20f), and his portrait (50f). It reappeared on 23 July 1945 with coloured surfaces carefully overprinted *BEKE (PEACE)* and additional inflationary values and a surtax with the inscription *A NEPFOISKOLAKERT (FOR PEOPLE'S COLLEGES)*. Many schools had been destroyed or damaged in the war, but the new government sought to renovate them and replace the traditional system based upon social class with a universal one. It was a slow process, especially as colleges for higher education were so few. Most schools remained church schools, but they worked under increasing critical pressure until 1948 when all were nationalised.

Four overprinted stamps from the famous people and famous women sets appeared on 8 November 1945 with values from 40 pengo to 100pengo. By January 1946 the pengo had utterly collapsed, and many of these stamps appeared three more times on 14 January, 1 February and 1 May 1946 overprinted to show a particular postal item which was charged at the rapidly rising rate for the day.(18.11, 18.12, 18.13) Amongst these Inflation Provisionals 'Hl.' or 'Helyi level' was a local letter, 'Hlp.' or 'Helyi lev.-lap' a local postcard, 'Ajl.' or 'Ajanlas' a registered letter, 'Tl.' or 'Tavolsagi level' an inland letter, 'Tlp.' or 'Tavoslagi lev.-lap' an inland postcard, 'Any.' or 'Nyomtatv 20gr.' light printed matter, and 'Cs.' or 'Csomag' parcel post - with the weight up to 5kg or 10kg

18.10 4f and 20f from Kossuth set as issued 20 March 1944, and 30f and 50f overprinted BEKE, A NEPFOISKOLAKERT and additional values and surtax: from set 23 July 1945.

EUROPEAN STAMP ISSUES AND THE AFTERMATH OF THE SECOND WORLD WAR: 1944–1949

18.11 1f overprinted Any.1, 4f overprinted Tlp.1, and 20f overprinted Ajl.1: from set 14 January 1946.

18.12 4f overprinted 1945 10 filler, and Tl.2., 20f overprinted 1945 8 pengo and Hlp.2, and 12f overprinted Ajl.2: from set 1 February 1946.

18.13 8f overprinted 1945 60 filler and Nyomtatv. 20gr., 18f overprinted Tavolsagi level, and 20f overprinted Helyi lev.-lap: from set 1 May 1946.

18.14 Four thousand and 800 thousand pengos: from set 18 February 1946+.

18.15 1 million and 50 million pengos: from set 1 May 1946+.

18.16 100 million and 50,000 million pengos: from set 24 May 1946+.

18.17 500 thousand million pengos: from set 27 June 1946.

18.18 1 million million and 500,000 million million pengos: from set 3 July 1946+.

added. The first and second issues used the abbreviations with '1' or '2' 'added to them, and the third issue used the full item description. Some appeared overprinted twice - first with 1945 and new value and later with the inflationary postal item.

From February 1946 a succession of short-lived sets raced to keep pace with surging inflation. Between 18 February and 15 April a set picturing a mounted postman and horn featured values from four thousand pengos to 800 thousand.(18.14) Between 1 and 20 May a set featuring the crown-less Hungarian Coat of Arms adopted by Louis Kossuth, but with additional proletarian sheaves of corn, ranged from one million to 50 million pengos.(18.15) From 24 May to 18 June that year another set featuring the 'Kossuth' shield surmounted by a post-horn went from 100 million to 50,000 million pengos.(18.16) On 27 June three stamps enclosing a simplified shield within a posthorn went up to 500 thousand million pengos (18.17), and between 3 and 13 July a long set picturing a dove and letter ran up to 500,000 million million pengos.(18.18) By then prices were doubling every 15 hours.

The alarming situation was tackled with the creation of the government's *adopengo* or 'tax pengo' on 1 January 1946 which slowly stabilised the currency as it managed to retain at least some of its value against the discredited pengo which fell into disuse. On 15 July 1946 it was deemed safe enough for a set of four stamps featuring steam locomotives, an electric locomotive and a railcar to be printed with static values between 10,000 and 40,000 tax pengos to mark the centenary of Hungarian railways.(18.19) The track, rolling stock, bridges and stations destroyed during the war were being replaced or rebuilt as a matter of urgency. The first electrified section opened in October 1945. In mid July 1946 a set using the shield and posthorn design appeared with values from 5,000 to five million 'tax pengos'.(18.20) On 1 August 1946 the filler and forint were introduced - technically at a rate of of one forint to 4x1029 old pengos. The first new currency set was issued between 1 and 14 August with the filler values featuring a male industrial worker and the forint values a female harvester.(18.21)

Alongside these inflationary issues the coalition government issued several special sets reinforcing its anti-Fascist pedigree and radical left-wing policies. The

18.19 10,000ap 4-2-0 Steam locomotive 'Heves' made by John Cockerill & Co 1846 and 30,000ap Overhead electric powered locomotive: from set 15 July 1946.

18.20 5,000ap and 5,000,000ap: from set 16 July 1946+.

18.21 12fi Male worker and 1.40fo Female harvester: from new currency set 1 August 1946+.

18.22 1p+1p Endre Bajcsy-Zsilinszky: 27 May 1945.

first, on 27 May 1945 honoured Endre Bajcsy-Zsilinszky (1886-1944), a nationalist politician and newspaper editor consistently opposing German expansion and aggression until his arrest by the Gestapo and execution in December 1944.(18.22)

On 6 October 1945 eight stamps in a National Relief Fund set featured sixteen people executed as Communists or anti-Fascist fighters, or both.(18.23, 18.24) It was a clear indictment of Admiral Horthy's regime, and its successor, the Arrow Cross Party given power by the Germans in 1944-45. Among them was Imri Sallai and Sandor Furst (2p+2p), founder members of the Hungarian Communist Party, who were executed in July 1932; Lajos Kabok and Elijah Monus (3p+3p), both prominent union leaders and Social Democrats killed by Arrow Cross squads in January 1945 and November 1944 respectively; Ferenc Rozsa and Zoltan Schonherz (10p+10p), both prominent Communist

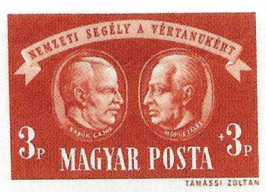

18.23 2p+2p Imri Sallai and Sandor Furst and 3p+3p Lajos Kabok and Elijah Monus: from set 11 September 1946.

18.24 10p+10p Ferenc Rozsa and Zoltan Schonherz and 15p+15p Vilmos Tartsay and Jeno Nagy: from set 11 September 1946.

opponents of the Horthy regime who died in prison or were executed in 1942; and Vilmos Tartsay and Jeno Nagy (15p+15p), officers in the anti-Fascist Magyar Front betrayed and executed by the Arrow Cross in December 1944.

On 11 September 1945 a set publicised the First International Trade Union Congress in Paris in October. (18.25) Attended by representatives from 55 countries, it built upon a preliminary meeting in London to create the World Federation of Trades Unions in a bold attempt to ensure workers everywhere never had to endure servility under totalitarian regimes again. Each stamp carried a symbol of a trade - hammer and anvil, winged locomotive wheel, trowel and bricks, plough, telephone wires and carrier pigeon, technical compasses, and a clerk's pen and book. However the WFTU soon came under the control of state controlled Communist trades unions which resulted in the creation of the opposing International Confederation of Free Trade Unions in 1949. On 29 June that year Hungary marked the 1949 WFTU Congress in Milan *(SZAKSZERVEZETI VILAGSZOVETSEG II KONGRESSZUSA)* with four stamps featuring a group of workers and the WFTU banner.(18.26) The Cold War ended most proletarian cooperative ventures.

Between 9 November 1945 and 5 February 1946 a set of fifteen values symbolised National Reconstruction - both politically and economically - with a mighty worker triumphantly freeing himself from his chains over an anvil emblazoned with the new crown-less Arms of Budapest.(18.27) The city's famous chain bridge is in the background. Avidly promoted by the Hungarian patriot and reformer, Count Istvan Szechenyi (1791-1860), it was designed and built by English and Scottish engineers, and opened on 20 November 1849 amidst great celebration - not least because it symbolised Hungarian unity by linking the two sides of the capital, Buda and Pest, across the Danube. Blown up in January 1945 by the retreating Germans, two miniature sheets on 15 May 1948 heralded its reopening on 20 November 1949 - its exact centenary. A further celebratory set and miniature sheet was issued on that day.(18.28)

On 12 February 1946 two stamps inscribed *HUNGARICA RESPUBLICA* announcing the Second Republic (formally declared on 1 May) featured a woman carrying a torch, ears of corn and the 'Kossuth' Shield, and a man with broken chains, striding optimistically into the future.(18.29) And on 1 May 1946 soaring inflation did not stop four stamps

18.25 2p Symbols of railway workers and 10p Engineers: from set 11 September 1945.

18.26 40f Workers and WFTU banner: from set 29 June 1949.

18.27 120p National Reconstruction: from set 9 November 1945+.

18.28 1fo60 Buda-Pest Chain Bridge: from set 20 November 1949.

18.29 3,000p Second Republic: from set 12 February 1946.

18.32 8fi Gyorgy Dozsa, 10fi Antal Nagy de Buda, and 12fi Tamas Esze: from set 15 March 1947.

18.30 1 million+1million pengos 75th anniversary of the first Hungarian stamps: from set 1 May 1946.

18.33 1fo Sandor Petofi, 2fo Endre Ady, and 4fo Attila Jozsef: from set 15 March 1947.

celebrating the 75th anniversary of the first Hungarian stamps. They featured a lion with a hammer and broken chains holding the new republic's Coat of Arms in the form of a book.(18.30) No opportunity was lost to hammer home the populist and liberating nature of the new regime and yet give reassuring signs of the historic continuity of the nation. Hungary became a Hapsburg Kingdom in 1867 (as part of the Austro-Hungarian 'Dual Monarchy') but the first stamps for ordinary mail printed in Budapest dated from 1871.

On 7 September 1946 a set of three surcharged stamps picturing a young peasant woman holding ears of corn publicised ORSZAGOS PARASZTNAPOK (NATIONAL PEASANTS DAY).(18.31) By then a massive land reform was underway with several thousand large estates owned for centuries by aristocratic families or the Churches broken up into peasants' holdings or earmarked for state, municipal or communal purposes. The set may have been linked to a national agricultural fair as some catalogues say, but more likely it celebrated the rapid completion of the massive transfer of land. For many more years, though, the lack of tools, equipment, loans and capital investment severely impeded agricultural production.

18.31 30fi+30fi Peasant woman and ears of corn: from set 7 September 1946.

On 15 March 1947 a Freedom Fighters set celebrated Liberation - in the form of the Communist triumph over Horthy, the Germans, the Arrow Cross and all other opponents. The shrewd use of portraits of past revolutionaries made the current regime seem like the final success of the age-old protest movements.(18.32, 18.33) The first three were Gyorgy Dozsa (1470-1514) (8fi) who was executed after leading an unsuccessful peasants' revolt against Hungary's landed aristocracy, Antal Nagy de Buda (d.1437) (10fi) who won battles but lost the war and his life in an earlier peasants revolt, and Tamas Esze (c1666-1708) (12fi) who led part of Ferenc II Rakoczi's army in the anti-Hapsburg Hungarian uprising of 1703-11. The 20fi and 30fi featured Ignac Martinovics (1755-95), a Franciscan friar beheaded in Budapest as a Jacobin revolutionary and James Batsanyi (1763-1845), a poet imprisoned for supporting Martinovics. The 40fi pictured Louis Kossuth, and the 60fi Mihaly Tancsics (1799-1884), an ardent radical writer and supporter of the 1848-49 revolution. Two of Hungary's greatest poets featured next. The revolutionary poetry of Sandor Petofi (1823-1849) (1fo), especially his *Nemzeti Dal (National Song)* and *Az Apostol (The Apostle)*, led to his elevation as a national poet. This status was also accorded Endre Ady (1877-1919) (2fo) who highlighted the cruel realities of the

18.34 60f Sandor Petofi: from set 31 July 1949.

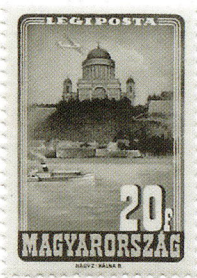

18.35 20fi Esztergom Cathedral, 70fi Palace Hotel, Lillafured, 3fo Lake Balaton, and 5fo Parliament Building and Louis Kossuth Bridge: from set 5 March 1947.

peasants' world compared with that of the wealthy elite, and sought a fairer Hungary. The 4fo featured Attila Jozsef (1905-37), an early Communist and evocative poet of the proletariat struggling against oppression.

Sandor Petofi merited two more portrait stamps on 31 July 1949 to mark the centenary of his death.(18.34) He disappeared, and was presumed killed, fighting against the Russians in the Battle of Segesvar during the final weeks of the Hungarian revolt in 1849.

From 1947 several sets promoted government initiatives as well as ideologies. Lengthy Airmail sets were calculated to attract funds. On 5 March 1947, a year after the Hungarian-Soviet Civil Air Transport Company *(MASZOULET)* was set up - as a joint stock company, no doubt working in the USSR's favour - a set promoted eight famous Hungarian sights carefully selected to resonate with the new regime.(18.35) The two engined passenger aeroplane seen on the stamps was probably a Lisunov Li-2, the Soviet variant of the Douglas DC-3. The 10fi pictured Sopron's Loyalty Tower, so named because the ancient border city chose to be in Hungary, not Austria, in a plebiscite in 1921. Esztergom Cathedral (20fi) was the centre of Roman Catholicism in Hungary and the anti-Nazi Cardinal Josef Mindszenty (1892-1975) was its archbishop. The set was issued a year before the Communist attacks on the Church when, ironically, Mindszenty achieved even greater international fame for his opposition to them. The 50fi featured Budapest's Emperor Franz Joseph Bridge that had been repaired after war damage and renamed Liberty Bridge. The vast pre-war luxury Palace Hotel in Lillafured (70fi) became a wartime hospital for Russian soldiers and then a workers' holiday resort run by the National Council of Trades Unions. Two stamps reflected the country's longevity. Vajdahunyad Castle in Budapest (1fo) had been built as a wooden castle reflecting various Hungarian styles to celebrate the country's millenary in 1895/96, and was later rebuilt in stone as a popular attraction and agricultural museum. Now a tourist attraction, Visegrad Castle (1.40fo) was a genuinely ancient fortress overlooking the Danube, and the summer residence of King Matthias Corvinus (1443-90). By 1947 Lake Balaton (3fo) was a popular destination for subsidised excursions by trades unions but many Hungarians would have remembered the area as a final battleground between German and Hungarian armies striving to stem the Soviet advance in March 1945. The 5fo featured Budapest's Parliament Building and the recently repaired Louis Kossuth Bridge.

Two other Airmail sets appeared on 15 May and 16 October 1948. The first featured ten world-wide inventors and explorers, the second ten famous writers. No doubt as airmail stamps they attracted international collectors, thereby raising revenue, and the sets included figures representing the USA (Robert Fulton, Thomas Edison, Edgar Allan Poe, Mark Twain), Great Britain (George Stephenson, William Shakespeare, Lord Byron), Germany (Johannes Gutenberg, Count Ferdinand von Zeppelin, Johann von Goethe) France (Louis Bleriot, Victor Hugo, Voltaire), Italy (Christopher Columbus) and Norway (Roald Amundsen). However notables closer to home were included. The May set included the Hungarian inventor David Schwarz (1850-97) alongside Count Zeppelin on the 6fi as he had built, but not managed to fly, a hydrogen filled aluminium airship in the 1890s. Rumours persisted that Count Zeppelin benefited greatly from his work, not least by purchasing his patent from his widow. The May set also featured the Hungarian Kalman Kando (1869-1931) (30fi), often recognised as 'the father of the electric train' for developing the powerful three phase AC motors and generators, and the rotary phase converter.

18.36 6fi David Schwarz and Count Zeppelin, 30fi Kalman Kando, and 40fi Alexander Popov: from set 15 May 1948.

 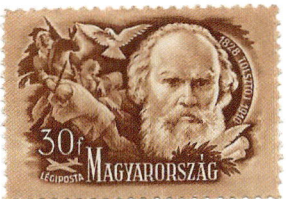 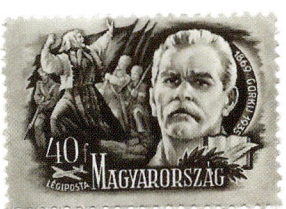

18.37 2fi Voltaire, 30fi Leo Tolstoy, and 40fi Maxim Gorki: from set 16 October 1948.

It also diplomatically included Alexander Popov (1859-1906) (40fi), the Russian physicist whom the Soviet Union asserted was the first to develop a working radio receiver, basically as a lightning detector.(18.36) In 1945 the Soviet Union declared 6 May that year as Radio Day (a custom still kept) to mark the 50th anniversary of his experiment.

The October set included the Hungarian poet and revolutionary Sandor Petofi (10fi), and the internationally renowned Russian writers Leo Tolstoy (1828-1910) (30fi), a fervent critic of a repressive state and church, and Maxim Gorki (1868-1936) (40fi), an early Bolshevik, friend of Lenin, critic of later repression, and exile in Italy until finally accepting restoration to Soviet favour under Stalin.(18.37)

In-between the two sets, on 27 July 1948 a stamp marked the centenary of the birth of another Hungarian physicist, Baron Lorand Eotvos (1848-1919) whose 'Eotvos pendulum' measured the density of underlying rock and whose wider work on gravity informed Einstein's theory of relativity.(18.38) And on 6 June 1949 the 150th anniversary of the birth of Alexander Pushkin (1799-1837), the Russian poet, playwright and novelist, was commemorated with a stamp inscribed *A NAGY OROSZ KOLTO (THE GREAT RUSSIAN POET)*. It portrayed him with a manuscript and flaming torch. An accompanying miniature sheet contained a stamp showed him writing together with a label depicting young people marching under a banner and an extract of verse trusting his ideas lived in the hearts of people. (18.39) Although not a revolutionary, Pushkin angered Tsar Alexander I sufficiently with his *Ode to Liberty* to be exiled and closely watched.

Not surprisingly a set of eleven stamps issued between 15 March and 27 July 1948 marked the centenary of the

18.38 60fi Lorand Eotvos: 27 July 1948.

18.39 1fo+1fo Alexander Puskin and 1fo+1fo Puskin writing and label: 6 June 1949.

18.40 10fi Printing press, 20fi General Bem's sword, 40fi Independence Flag, 60fi Petofi's cry, and 1fo 'Kossuth Shield': from set 15 March 1948+.

1848-49 revolution.(18.40) The six images included the Independence Flag with its 'Louis Kossuth' shield and red and green 'wolf teeth' edge (8f and 40f). It was not quite the 1848 flag as the stamp included the oak and olive branches framing the shield which were only added to certain flags in the twentieth century. Four higher values, 1fo to 4fo, featured the dates 1848 and 1948, the 'Kossuth Shield' and a sprig of olive, the symbol of peace. The 10f featured a printing press, ironically with the inscription SZABADSAJTO (FREE PRESS) and the 30f and 60f Sandor Petofi's cry TALPRA MAGYAR HI A HAZA! (RESTORE OUR HUNGARIAN HOMELAND!) The 12fi showed a dove flying from a barred window, and the 20fi featured a 1848 shako, bugle and a sword marked BEM referring to the Polish and Hungarian hero General Jozef Bem (1794-1850) whose skill for long held the Austrians and Russians at bay during the revolution until finally overwhelmed at the Battle of Segesvar, where Sandor Petofi disappeared, on 31 July 1849.

On the domestic front several issues reinforced Communist policies and relations with the Soviet Union. On 16 May 1947 four heavily surtaxed stamps picturing doctors using syringes (8fi+50fi) and X-rays (12fi+50fi), a nurse comforting a child (20fi+50fi) and a returning prisoner of war (60fi+50fi) raised funds for welfare organisations.(18.41) Many soldiers fighting for Germany and captured by the Russians endured lengthy captivity in the USSR as useful political hostages and cheap sources of labour.

On 29 October 1947 the 30th anniversary of the Soviet Union and the Hungarian-Soviet Cultural Society saw three surtaxed stamps supporting its funds, probably for the recently completed Liberty Statue (60fi+60fi).(18.42) This stood 14 metres high on a massive 26 metre stone pedestal on a hill in Budapest. Its inscription said it was erected *'by the grateful people of Hungary'* in remembrance of the 'liberating Soviet heroes'. The other two stamps made the situation crystal clear by featuring Lenin and Stalin - the first time they had appeared on Hungarian stamps.

Stamps marked other important Communist events. On 17 October 1948 a stamp with figures representing industry, agriculture and culture marked the 17th Hungarian Trades Union Congress. It was the year in which the Communist Party fully flexed its muscles, and trades unions fully appreciated their role was to support, not criticise, the Communist Party's policies. (18.43) The Communist obsession with Savings Banks

18.41 20fi+50fi Nurse and child and 60fi+50fi Returning prisoner of war: from set 16 May 1947.

18.42 60fi+60fi Liberty Statue, and 1fo+1fo Stalin: from set 29 October 1947.

18.43 30fi Trades Union Congress: 17 October 1948.

18.44 40fi Savings Day: from set 31 October 1947.

18.45 60fi+60fi International Women's Day: 8 March 1949.

18.46 40fi and 60fi Thirtieth anniversary of the first Hungarian Soviet Republic: 19 March 1949.

led to two stamps with the beehive emblem and bank headquarters on 31 October 1947.(18.44)

On 8 March 1949 a surtaxed stamp picturing a radiant female farm worker supported International Women's Day *(NEMZETKOZI NONAP)*. It was an event day that pre-dated the Bolshevik Revolution of 1917 but afterwards was increasingly associated with Communist regimes and their recognition of the importance of gaining the support of women.(18.45)

On 19 March 1949 the 30th anniversary of Bela Kun's short-lived but bloody Hungarian Soviet Republic (22 March to 1 August 1919) in the aftermath of the First World War was commemorated as a heroic initiative. The two stamps reproduced stamps he had issued in 1919 featuring Karl Marx and Sandor Petofi, but added the Russian flag and scenes of Communist marchers. (18.46) The inscription and dates *A MAGYAR TANACS KOZTARSASAG EMLEKERE 1919-1949 (IN MEMORY OF THE HUNGARIAN REPUBLIC 1919-1949)* implied the 1919 Republic stayed in the national consciousness and thereby paved the way for the current regime. Kun had operated under direct orders from the Kremlin, but after the violent rejection of his savage regime he had fled to Moscow to end up a victim of Stalin's purges in the 1930s. In 1949 this sympathetic issue could not have made the nature of the current regime clearer - ideological Bolshevikism with a thin veil of liberal nationalism. Within a few months the veil was finally withdrawn.

On 14 August 1949 five stamps and a miniature sheet marked the 2nd World Festival of Youth *(VILAGIFJUSAGI ES DAIK TALALKOZO)* held in Budapest attended by 20,000 participants from 82 countries.(18.47) The fortnight's festival was launched in 1947 by the International Union of Students as a vehicle for democracy and peace, but quickly became seen in the West as an instrument of worldwide Communist propaganda. The stamps give a flavour of this with the 20fi featuring young faces from different continents, the 30fi showing their clenched fists, the 40fi a young Asian breaking free from chains (the Communist revolution in China was in 1949), the 60fi young people marching behind a banner (as featured on many Communist sets), and the 1fo young workers with hammer and sickle waving a book/manifesto and the bright light of Communism clarifying the way forward. Notwithstanding Western governments' criticisms, the movement did resonate with young people seeking freedom from European colonial rule.

The Hungarian People's Republic was established on 18 August 1949, and a 60fi stamp on 20 August marked the proclamation that the Communist controlled parliament had adopted a Soviet-style Constitution. (18.48) It considered itself the heir of Bela Kun's republic of 1919. Two further values (20fi and 1fo)

18.47 30fi Clenched fists, 40f Breaking chains, and 1ft Workers and manifesto: from set 14 August 1949.

18.48 60fi Arms of the Second Republic: from set 20 August 1949.

18.49 1ft Stalin's 70th birthday: from set 21 December 1949.

appeared on 26 September. Large in size and brightly coloured they featured the new national emblem in proletarian Soviet style and were inscribed *1949 VIII 20 MAGYAR NEPKOZTARSASAG (HUNGARIAN PEOPLE'S REPUBLIC)*.

As First Secretary of the Working People's Party Matyas Rakosi (1892-1971) now embarked upon a ruthless purge of rival colleagues and dissidents and modelled his despotic rule, until ousted in 1956, on that of Stalin in the USSR. And duly, on 21 December 1949 Stalin's 70th birthday merited three stamps bearing his portrait. (18.49)

CHAPTER 19

ROMANIA

Romania had fought with the Allies against Germany and Austria-Hungary in the First World War, and afterwards was ceded Transylvania, Bessarabia and Bukovina. However twenty years later the Balkans became a Russian 'sphere of interest' under the Russian-German Pact of August 1939, and all Romania's territorial acquisitions were lost in 1940. The Soviet Union obliged it to return Bessarabia and northern Bukovina, and Germany forced it to cede northern Transylvania to Hungary, and southern Dobruja to Bulgaria. These humiliations, coupled with disgust at his disreputable life style, led Romania's King Carol II to flee the country in September 1940 in favour of his son, the youthful King Michael. However power lay with the new prime minister General Ion Antonescu, the right wing political parties and the Iron Guard paramilitary association. In November 1940 Romania joined the Axis powers - Germany reigned supreme and accommodation seemed Romania's only hope for survival and the restoration of lost territory. When the Iron Guard staged its own coup in January 1941 Antonescu, now known as *Conducator (Leader)* brutally crushed it.

For a time Romania successfully outshone other Balkan states in supporting the Nazis against the Soviet Union and Hitler duly restored Bessarabia and Bukovina to it and allowed it to occupy Russian territory between the Bug and Dniester. Romanian troops working alongside German ones systematically ravaged the countryside and persecuted the Jews, killing tens of thousands. The war remained popular until disaster struck at Stalingrad, casualties mounted, and Soviet armies began to advance westwards. Romania had supplied the Axis war effort with huge quantities of oil, grain and machinery but by 1943 the vast Ploiesti oil fields and key railway junctions were under increasing Allied air attack. In August 1944 Soviet forces crossed the eastern border into Romania despite the determined German and Romanian resistance. Later that month King Michael, drawing support from the army and opposition politicians, overthrew Antonescu, negotiated an armistice with the Allies, and declared war on Germany. A German counter attack around Bucharest was successful resisted, although Stalin cannily delayed his own confirmation of the armistice until his troops were well into Romania. For a brief period some Romanian units were fighting the Germans and others the Russians. Ultimately the Romanian change of sides meant the Soviet Union controlled the country which it was now 'liberating' rather than conquering. Nevertheless Romanian forces fought hard alongside their new Soviet allies to free Transylvania and then Czechoslovakia from the Germans and Hungarians.

After the war Romania was allowed to keep northern Transylvania but Bessarabia, northern Bukovina and southern Dobruja were lost. In February 1945 a set of ten surtaxed stamps celebrated the liberation of northern Transylvania from Hungary. The 75l+75L featured King Michael and his revered grandfather King Carol I (reigned 1881-1914) by a map (75l+75l). (19.1) However several stamps pictured leading figures

19.1 15l Michael the Brave, 25l Andrei Saguna, 35l Avram Iancu, 55l Horea, Closca and Crisan: from set February 1945.

in the 1848 revolution - such as the lawyer and writer Avram Iancu (1824-72) (35l), philosopher Simion Barnutui (1808-64) (41l), poet Andrei Muresanu (1816-73) (50l), and Romanian Orthodox Bishop Andrei Saguna (1809-73) (25b). They had sought autonomy for Transylvania within the Austrian Empire rather than union with Hungary - a policy that angered Hungarian independence campaigners such as Louis Kossuth. Other stamps featured earlier figures campaigning for the greater civic recognition of Romanians in Transylvania, including the cultural historian Samuil Micu (1745-1806) (4l50), nationalist teacher and writer Gheorghe Sincai (1754-1816) (11l), campaigner for Romanian language schools Gheorghe Lazar (1779-1823) (31l), and philosopher Petru Maior (1756-1821) (61l). Two stamps harked back to more distant heroes. The 55l featured Horea, Closca and Crisan (officially Vasile Ursu Nicola, Ion Oarga and Marcu Giurgiu) who led the Transylvanian peasants revolt of 1784-85 against serfdom. Targeting the nobles and Imperial officials, the uprising was crushed by Austrian forces and the three leaders executed. The 15l portrayed the national hero Prince Michael the Brave (1558-1601). He succeeded in uniting (very briefly in 1600-01) Wallachia, Moldavia and Transylvania under one ruler against the might of the Hapsburg Empire, Ottoman Empire and Polish-Lithuanian Commonwealth.

After dismissing Antonescu King Michael had made the loyal General Constantin Sanatescu prime minister but the growing influence of the Communists soon led the Socialist Petru Groza (1884-1958) of the Ploughman's Front Party to be appointed the head of a coalition government with Communists heading several ministries. Groza instigated female suffrage and land reforms, and felt strong enough to ignore the king's objections and refusal to sign legislation. Riots erupted in November 1945 between monarchist and populist crowds which Soviet troops had to repress. In elections held in November 1946 the allied Communist and Socialist parties were credited with over 80% of the votes, although fraud and intimidation were widespread. The Western Allies made protests, the Romanian government maintained the pretence of a monarchy working closely with a coalition government, but events were moving fast.

With the Soviet army still present and the Communists growing in strength (not least because many sensed the trend and switched allegiance from other parties and associated organisations), the government moved swiftly to condemn and execute pro-Nazi Romanians, including Antonescu, and to discredit and imprison leaders of centrist and monarchist parties. Interest in Romania by the Western Allies faded sharply once the 1947 Peace Treaty was signed; there was little they could

19.2 55l King Michael: from definitive set March 1945+.

do about Soviet interference, and of course in 1944 Churchill had agreed with Stalin that Romania was primarily a Russian sphere of influence - although perhaps he did not anticipate to what extent.

Trials and terror went hand in hand, until on 30 December 1947 Petru Groza and his hard-line Communist colleague Gheorghe Gheorghiu-Dej (1901-65) walked into the royal palace and demanded the king's abdication. With the palace surrounded and all communications cut, Michael had no choice but to sign. On the same day Parliament abolished the monarchy, and declared the country a People's Republic. Groza remained prime minister, but Gheorghiu-Dej was the far more influential First Secretary of the Communist Party. On 13 April 1948 a new constitution took effect. Based upon that of the Soviet Union it seemed to guarantee all manner of freedoms while in practice confirming the state's freedom to repress all dissent. The Romanian Orthodox Church remained in being but strictly subservient, and the Romanian economy was subordinated to the needs of the Soviet Union.

Stamp issues had always proliferated in Romania, but from 1945 new ones appeared every few weeks to promote some aspect of Communist policy. The only exception was the definitive series portraying King Michael until his departure in 1947 (19.2), and several stamps which suggested (largely falsely) his support for Groza's radical change.

An early example of convoluted Communist propaganda was the War Victims' Relief Fund set and miniature sheet issued on 30 April 1945 inscribed *APARAREA PATRIOTICA (PATRIOTIC DEFENCE) and VICTIMELE TEROAREI HITLERISTE (VICTIMS OF HITLERITE TERROR)*.(19.3) Three stamps featured major inter-war politicians, all Liberal but far from being Communists. Ion Gheorghe Duca (1879-1933) (12l+188l) was a Liberal politician who was murdered by Iron Guards soon after becoming prime minister and seeking to suppress them. Virgil Madgearu (1887-1940) (16l+184l) was a fiercely anti-Fascist government minister from the left wing Peasants' Party killed by by Iron Guards. Nicolae Iorga (1871-1940) (20l+170l) was a writer, National Party politician, and briefly prime minister (1931-32) who was killed for challenging the

19.3 16l+184l Virgil Madgearu and 36l+164l Filimon Sarbu: from set 30 April 1945 (see also 19.51).

19.4 75l+225l Drawn curtain revealing Moscow light and 80l+420l Nevski and Vladimirescu: from set 20 May 1945.

rise of the Iron Guards. Alongside the portraits are scenes of thuggish Iron Guards. Three other stamps featured young Communists killed in the war. Ilie Pintilie (1903-40) (32l+168l) was a railway worker and frequently arrested Communist activist who died in prison during the wartime Vrancea earthquake. Bernath Andrei (1908-44) (35l+165l) was a Communist resistance fighter shot by the Germans. Filimon Sarbu (1916-41) (36l+164l) was a Communist saboteur based in Constanta arrested and shot by the Romanian secret police. Alongside the portraits are scenes of the victims' heroic actions and martyrdom. All six are portrayed as preparing the ground for Romania's radical new era.

On 20 May 1945 a set and miniature sheet supported the first Romanian-Soviet Union Congress ostensibly organised by the Romanian Society for Friendship with the Soviet Union (its acronym was *ARLUS*). It was the successor to a similar Romanian society suppressed in the 1930s.(19.4) Accumulatively the four very different stamps made the permanence of the international connection explicit. The 20l+80l featured identical Romanian and Soviet Marxist text books or manifestos, and the 35l+165l displayed the two countries flags flying together. The 75l+225l featured a curtain being drawn back to allow in the Communist sun shining from the Kremlin. The 80l+420l portrayed the Russian hero Alexander Nevski (1221-63) who held together the medieval Russian lands in desperate times against German and Swedish invaders, and the Romanian Tudor Vladimirescu (c1780-1821) whom the Communists elevated to heroic status for seeking Russian approval and support for his Wallachian uprising in 1812 against the Ottoman Empire.

The set was quickly followed on 30 June 1945 by one marking the *CONFEDERATIA GENERALA A MUNCII (TRADES UNION CONGRESS)* in Bucharest.(19.5) A second inscription proclaimed *TRAIASCA UNITATEA SINDICALA (LONG LIVE THE UNITY OF THE UNIONS)* and as the three stamps portrayed the Communist ideologues Karl Marx and Friedrich Engels and their major interpreter and implementer Vladimir Lenin, not surprisingly a third inscription repeated the Communist cry *PROLETARI DIN TOATE TARILE UNITI-VAI (WORKERS FROM ALL COUNTRIES UNITE)*. The inculcation of enthusiasm for a more equitable society through the abolition of privilege was a key to Communist success - and obedient enthusiasm was required of the unions.

On 23 August 1945 the first anniversary of Romania's wartime change of sides saw three new issues. The first included two stamps inscribed *23 AUGUST 1944 - 23 AUGUST 1945*.(19.6) One showed a farm worker shaking hands with a factory worker by a sheaf of corn and farm implements, and the other, with heavy symbolism, featured the two workers supporting a heavy plinth inscribed *Romania* with King Michael beneath. The king was there to mask, and conversely seemingly accept, the steady enhancement of Communist authority.

The second issue was a single charity stamp inscribed *ASISTENTA COPIII (CHILD WELFARE)* and *APARAREA PATRIOTICA (PATRIOTIC DEFENCE)* featuring destitute war orphans protected by a cloaked figure with sword and shield.(19.7) Perhaps deliberately

19.5 155l+445l Lenin: from set 30 June 1945.

it is not clear whether it represents the state or charity - or perhaps both. The third issue ran to twelve heavily surtaxed Patriotic Defence Fund stamps.(19.8) There were six illustrations and values, each printed twice in different colours. Three highlighted postwar 'Amnesties' or 'Freedoms' with the 20l+580l portraying the release of a political prisoner, the 40l+560l showing a released soldier, and the 55l+545l featuring a peasant breaking his chains as peace returns. In practice amnesties tended to apply solely to those in sympathy with the increasingly left-wing regime. The 100l+500l portrayed King Michael amidst wartime ruins as workers began rebuilding the shattered economy. The 60l+540l portrayed the newly exalted hero Tudor Vladimirescu, and the 80l+520l Vasili Ursu Nicola (known as Horea) (1731-85), the Transylvanian craftsman who co-led the ill-fated peasants revolt against the harsh serfdom imposed by their feudal lords.

In most sets the economy and the contribution of the dedicated proletariat to its development were to the fore. Interestingly in these troubled years for King Michael, on 26 September 1945 he appeared with King Carol I on a stamp whose lengthy inscription translates as the '50th Anniversary of the Bridge over the Danube at Fetesti'. (19.9) Opened in September 1895 this massive box truss bridge with its ornate towers crossed the marshy river basin to connect the newly won province of northern Dobruja (after the 1877-78 Russo-Turkish War) with the rest of Romania at Fetesti. A town called Cernavoda was created on the Dobruja side. Known as the King Carol I Bridge during the monarchy the stamp deliberately omitted his name - the era of blackening Carol's name as a pawn of the Kaiser and enemy of the people was about to start. However King Michael remained popular after the war, and Romanian Communists had had little support prior to 1944. Indeed many Romanians had approved of the war against the Russians and feared rather than welcomed their arrival. The Communists recognised the value of the monarchy and a coalition government as a short-term cover, both nationally and internationally, for their covert accumulation of political control.

19.6 100l+400l Industrial and agricultural workers and 200l+800l King Michael and workers: set 23 August 1945.

19.7 40l Protecting destitute children: 23 August 1945.

19.9 80l The Cernavoda-Fetesti bridge: 26 September 1945.

19.8 20L+580l 'Political Amnesty', 40l+560l 'Military Amnesty', and 100l+500l King Michael and 'Reconstruction': from set 23 August 1945.

19.10 80l Allegory of Learning (Journal 'Gazeta Matematica'): from set 5 September 1945.

Technology soared in status. On 5 September 1945 the 50th anniversary of the founding of the Romanian Journal of Mathematics was marked by two stamps: the 80l featured a dignified allegory of learning against a background of an aeroplane flying over the Cernavoda-Fetesti bridge, and the 2l portrayed four distinguished members and editors - Vasile Cristescu (1859-1929), Ion Ionescu (1870-1946), Gheorghe Titeica (1873-1939 and A.G. Idachimescu (1895-1943).19.10

During October 1945 a surtaxed set and miniature sheet, issued both perforated and imperforate, supported the 16th Congress of the General Association of Romanian Engineers.(19.11) Established in 1881 to promote the exchange of technical skills and to advance the country, the organisation was supported by successive governments, and perfectly suited Communist purposes. The 10l+490l featured an electric train and the 55l+445l the Ploesti oil wells: the former was more a statement of intent as overhead electrification was fifteen years away, while the latter was a greatly valued investment soon to be nationalised. The 20l+490l was an allegory of scholarship alongside the Coats of Arms of various trades and professions, the 25l+475l depicted a truck on an arterial road, and the 100l+400l an allegory of Agriculture. One triangular Airmail stamp featured a distant aeroplane flying over an industrial plant and a Classically draped figure holding a scribing compass (80l+420l) and another a Lockheed 14 Super Electra flying over mountains where stood the brave but arrogant Icarus whose wax and feather wings melted when he flew too near the Sun. (200l+800l). In 1945 the inter-war Romanian State-Operated Airlines *(LARES)* was replaced by the jointly owned Romanian-Soviet *TARS (TRANSPORTURI AERIENE ROMANO-SOVIETICE)*. TARS began operations in 1946 and was stocked with Russian Lisunov and Ilyushin aircraft, but the American Lockheed shown on this 1945 stamp was probably one of the four supplied to LARES in the later 1930s.

On 5 December 1945 a surtaxed set supported the important World Trade Union Congress in Paris which in October had formally established the World Federation of Trades Unions (WFTU) after a preliminary conference in London that February. (19.12) American, British and Russian unionists had led the initiative which used the new United Nations charter to guide its aims of promoting peace and social and economic progress. The WFTU was envisaged as the workers' international pressure group, but in 1948-49, as the Cold War developed and the WFTU was perceived as Soviet political instrument, many western trades unions departed to found the International Confederation of Free Trades Unions. The four stamps had centre pictures featuring a globe behind clasped hands (80l+920l), a dove of peace (160l+1840l), a hand wielding a hammer (320l+1680l) and scaffolding (440l+2560l).

From 6 March 1946 a set publicised the government's agrarian reforms - even though they had met with significant resistance.(19.13 The Communists hoped to gain favour with Stalin by redistributing land previously owned by Germans, or by Romanians deemed 'war criminals', or who fled abroad, neglected their farms, or owned more than 50 hectares. It was hoped this would

19.11 10l+490l Electric train, 55l+445l Ploesti oil wells, and 200l+800l Lockheed 14 Super Electra and Icarus: from set 1 October 1945+.

19.12 80l+920l World Trade Union Congress, Paris: from set 5 December 1945.

19.13 50l+450l Distributing title deeds, 80l Blacksmith and ploughman, and 200l+800l Laden ox-drawn wagon: from set 6 March 1946+.

In common with the Soviet Union's policy elsewhere, thousands of people holding German citizenship, and others held to be enemies of the state, were interned in Romanian camps from 1944 onwards. Other camps housed former prisoners-of-war awaiting repatriation, and forced labourers and displaced civilian workers awaiting processing and, hopefully, identity papers and travelling documents. The Red Cross made valiant efforts to ameliorate their conditions and assist with their documentation wherever possible, and stamps were supplied to the Red Cross for permitted internees mail. In May 1946 a wartime King Michael Postal Tax set was made available to the Red Cross with the border overprinted *SERVICIUL PRIZONIERILOR DE RAZBOI (PRISONERS OF WAR SERVICE)* and the value overprinted with a Red Cross and *SCUTIT DE TAXA POSTALA (EXEMPTED FROM POSTAL TAX)*.(19.14) Controversy exists over whether many were used.

In November 1946 three similarly inscribed stamps featuring King Michael's mother, Queen Helen (1896-1982), probably originally printed in the war, were issued for the Red Cross.(19.15) Helen had been a high profile supporter of wartime humanitarian initiatives, including the Red Cross. In 1947 King Michael's Fund (a royal charity succeeding the King Carol I Foundation) also issued a special postage-exempt set, including an Airmail stamp, for use on its charitable business.(19.16). From time to time other issues levied a compulsory postal tax to support war invalids *(invalizi)*, orphans *(orfani)* and widows *(vaduve)*.(19.17)

On 26 April 1946 a set marked the 25th anniversary of the Bucharest Philharmonic Orchestra.(19.18) The stamps featured the orchestra's magnificent Athenaeum, a musical score and a portrait of George Enescu (1881-

be a preliminary step towards collectivisation. In the event some 143,000 owners lost land, and around 910,000 peasant families had received an extra hectare or so by the end of 1948. The disruption caused widespread anxiety and a dangerous decline in production, but despite this in 1949 a collectivisation programme began which made the social and economic situation worse - but at least Stalin was ameliorated. The stamps were meant to be optimistic, although several showed antiquated methods. The 50l+450l (and Airmail miniature sheet) showed a particularly statuesque official - possibly Prime Minister Petru Groza himself - distributing new title deeds. The 80l depicted a blacksmith and oxen pulling a plough, the 100l+900l the sun shining behind a hand sower, the 200l+800l oxen drawing a loaded waggon, and the 400l+1600l a plough and its hoped for replacement, a tractor.

19.14 4l Postal Tax (issued 1943) overprinted *SERVICIUL PRIZONIERILOR DE RAZBOI* and *SCUTIT DE TAXA POSTALA*: from set May 1946.

19.15 Queen Helen: Romanian Red Cross Postal Tax Exempt: from set November 1946.

119.16 King Michael's Fund Postal Tax Exempt: from set September 1947+.

19.17 1l Allegory of Hope: from I.O.V.R. Postal Tax set 1948.

19.18 80l George Enescu: from set 26 April 1946.

19.19 200l Students and 10,000l May Day miniature sheet: from set 1 May 1946.

1955) who is regarded as one of Romania's greatest composers and conductors. His symphonies, *Romanian Rhapsodies*, and chamber music, much of it influenced by Romanian folk music, brought him international fame between the wars. After 1945 he lived in personally imposed exile in Paris, but regularly conducted works by modern Romanian composers, and remained in favour during the Communist era. Soon after his death the orchestra was named after him. The Orchestra maintained its high profile but its long-term conductor George Georgescu (1887-1964) was branded as a Nazi collaborator for organising concerts throughout occupied countries during the war and lost his post - although his international status led him to recover it in 1953.

On 1 May 1946 a set inscribed ZIUA MUNCHII (LABOUR DAY) began the annual celebration of this key Communist anniversary.(19.19) Embracing gender, education and the rural and urban economy one 10l portrayed a building worker, another a female mechanic, the two 20l stamps pictured male and female peasants, and the 200l students. An additional Labour Day Airmail miniature sheet selling for 10,000l showed an aeroplane writing *1 Mai* in the sky.

Labour Day in 1947 was belatedly celebrated philatelically on 15 June with stamps inscribed 1 Mai featuring smiling and confident workers.(19.20) They included a miner and a railway (1000l+1000l), a farm worker and a tractor (1500l+1500l) a countrywoman and a hay waggon (2000l+2000l), a scientist with a microscope by a research institute (the sun of new knowledge shines over the scene) (2500l+2500) and a worker plus hammer by a vast factory (3000l+3000l). One 3000l Airmail stamp featured the date 1 *MAI* dropping from parachutes, another the huge column topped by a flying man forming the Monument to the Heroes of the Air unveiled in 1935, and third a four engine passenger aeroplane (supposedly the American Douglas DC-4) flying over land and sea.(19.21) It might have been a visiting airliner, and certainly DC-4s were used to bring in supplies during the terrible Romanian famine of 1946-47 (see 19.28 and 19.39) There is no evidence, though, that DC-4s were used by Romania's state airlines - the pre-war *LARES* and post-war *TARS* - and there was no Soviet variant. *LARES* did, though, have several two engined DC-3s.

The Communist obsession with healthy exercise, worker fitness, the mental and physical discipline of training, and national glory stemming from sporting

19.20 2,000l+2,000l Female farm workers and 2,500l+2,500l Researcher and institute: from set 15 June 1947.

19.22 16l+184l Diving and 20l+180l Skiing: from set 5 August 1945.

19.21 3,000l Monument to the Heroes of the Air and 3,000l aeroplane: from set 15 June 1947.

competitions, led to an early surtaxed set on 5 August 1945 featuring discus throwing, diving, skiing, volleyball and, significantly, a stamp symbolising the fit sportsman as the strong healthy worker. (19.22) Significantly, the foremost skier wore a military cap and carried a rifle. To ram home the message the inscription read *TOATE SPORTURILE PENTRU POPOR (ALL SPORTS ARE FOR THE PEOPLE).*

Every post-war Romanian Sports stamp also possessed the letters *OSP* within a shield. They stood for *ORGANIZATIA SPORTULUI POPULAR (THE PEOPLE'S SPORT ORGANISATION)* which had been set up by the state soon after the war to develop mass participation but also subordinate the programme and its participants to Communist ideologies. In common with the associated Youth programmes most Sports sets had high surtaxes to help pay for the initiatives.

A surtaxed Youth issue on 28 July 1946 promoted the activities expected of young people in a Communist state.(19.23) Meritocracy was the key, and everyone had to be aspirational in the service of the state. Young people were encouraged to work alongside rural and urban labourers, and indeed indoctrinate them, and the 10l+100l featured a sower and the 80l+300l a young man and a factory. The 10l+200l featured hurdlers, the 80l+200l a student, and the 200l+400l young people with banners on the march. The accompanying Airmail stamps featured a young pilot and aeroplanes parked and flying.

Healthy exercise featured soon afterwards with a set plus costly miniature sheet on 1 September 1946 featuring football (10l), diving (20l), running (50l),

19.23 10l+100l, Sower, 80l+200l Student, 200l+400l On the march, and 500l Pilot: from set 28 July 1946.

19.24 10l Football and 80l Mountaineering: from set 1 September 1946.

19.25 10l+10l Parade of athletes: from OSP set 31 December 1948.

19.26 100l Cultural ties, 300l Economic ties, and 6,000l Dove of Peace: from set 20 October 1946.

mountaineering (80l) and ski-jumping (160l+1340l), with two Airmail stamps picturing an aeroplane taking off (300l).(19.24) In December 1948 an OSP set included runners (5l+5l), an Airmail stamp showing a boy with a model aeroplane (20l+20l), and perhaps most significant of all the 10l+10l pictured the mass ranks of proud male and female athletes waving patriotic banners.(19.25)

On 20 October 1946, just before the fraudulent elections that November, a set marked the Friendship Pact between Romania and the Soviet Union.(19.26) The two countries had already signed a long term economic agreement that created numerous *Sovroms* - joint-stock companies that ensured Russia secured goods cheaply and tax free and controlled all Romania's main sources of income, notably oil and uranium. The stamps featured a bewigged eighteenth century figure signifying historical links (80l), a book, paint brush, mask and a Russian or Gypsy guitar representing cultural ties (100l), trees, corn, oil well and factory highlighting economic ties (300l), and a dove bearing a sprig of olive (300l+1,200l). The 6,000l miniature sheet is inscribed *DE ZIUA PRIETENIEI ROMANO-SOVIETICE (ON THE DAY OF ROMANIAN-SOVIET FRIENDSHIP)*

On 20 November 1946 a surtaxed set and miniature sheet inscribed *FEDERATIA DEMOCRATA A FEMEILOR DIN ROMANIA* supported the Romanian Women's Democratic Federation.(19.27) It was affiliated to the Women's International Democratic Federation founded in Paris in 1945 but soon banned in France as an instrument of Communist propaganda. It relocated to East Berlin and despite all suspicions it retained a powerful voice on women's behalf. Communism preached the equality of women and their need for good education, healthcare, and careers. They became equal before the law but rarely economically independent even though many young women received a sound education after the war and found employment. Nevertheless as in many Balkan satellite countries stereotyped sex roles persisted as men took the higher paid jobs in modernised plants while most women took menial posts and were still expected to run the home. Ironically the set featured women's traditional roles. The 80l showed a girl at a handloom, the 80l+320l a Banat girl working a distaff, the 140l+360l a Wallachian girl carrying a sheaf of wheat, the 300l+450l a Transylvanian girl on a horse, the 600l+900l a Moldavian girl carrying water, and the 500l+9,000l Airmail miniature sheet featured dancing girls in regional costumes.

King Michael proved useful in 1947 when the Peace Treaty was signed defining the new borders and including optimistic clauses promising freedom of the press, worship, political opinions and public meetings.

19.28 600l King Michael and relief and 1,500l+3,500l Winged figure and relief: from set 15 January 1947.

19.27 80l+320l Banat girl, 300l+450l Transylvanian girl, 600l+900l Moldavian girl: from set 20 November 1946.

19.29 300l King Michael and Victory chariot and 3,000l Allied flags: from set 25 February 1947.

On 15 January 1947 he appeared on a stamp (600l) showing lorries and carts transporting vital food supplies during the recent famine.(19.28) The other three stamps, without the king, pictured hands bringing food to the starving (300l and 3,700l+5,300l) and a winged figure - more likely a general allegory of relief than an angel - bringing food and clothing (1,500l+3,500l). The inscription on each was *AJUTOR INFOMETATILOR SI ASISTENTEI SOCIALE (HELP & SOCIAL ASSISTANCE FOR THE HUNGRY)*. Coming after the devastation of war, the drought of 1946-47 accentuated food shortages across Romania and famine blighted much of the country, especially Moldavia, Transylvania and northern Dobruja. Other causes were the Soviet Union's appropriation of farm produce and imposition of heavy war reparation on Romania, the chaos of land reform and the Romanian government's own brutal attempts to stop starving people moving from towns and villages to seek food. Thousands perished. The USA, Red Cross and foreign religious and secular charities did much to supply food, but the basically Communist Romanian government only belatedly took humanitarian action, probably to save its diplomatic face. The portrait of the king - as notional head of government - was possibly included to direct any blame for negligence onto him rather than give him recognition for the relief programme.

The Peace Treaty was celebrated with four stamps on 25 February 1947.(19.29) The 300l featured a four-horse Roman triumphal chariot carrying Peace and a medallion portrait of King Michael - who had been awarded Russia's prestigious Order of Victory as well as the USA's Legion of Merit for his contribution to victory. The 600l portrayed a winged statue of Peace, the 3,000l the flags of the USA, the USSR, the UK and France, and the 7,200l a dove carrying a sprig of olive. Unfortunately for King Michael the treaty gave the Communists the security and confidence to reveal their hand and declare the republic.

In March 1947 the *CONFEDERATIA GENERALA A MUNCII DIN ROMANIA (ROMANIAN GENERAL CONFEDERATION OF LABOUR)* - analogous to a Trades Union Congress but by 1947 a strictly circumscribed state supporting enterprise - was marked by three stamps featuring a map of Romania, as confirmed by the recent Peace Treaty, above clasped hands and a Marxist book (or national manifesto). (19.30) They were encircled by the ubiquitous Communist ears of corn and cogwheel, and inscribed *CGM*. One Airmail stamp had an added passenger aeroplane, no doubt the Lisunov Li-2, and a second, issued in sheets of four, featured a smiling worker holding a flaming torch symbolising the optimistic future brought about by, and for, the nation's proletariat.

19.30 600l CGM symbols, 1,100l CGM symbols and aeroplane, and 3,000l+7,000l Worker and torch miniature sheet: from set March 1947.

19.31 2l+10l Workers and 11l Aeroplane over CGM rally: from set 10 November 1947.

Another CGM set in November that year glorified the enthusiastic Communist worker.(19.31) The 2l+10l portrayed a scientist, countryman and factory worker, the 7l+10l featured an allegory of 'Work' - a winged worker holding a hammer and sickle, and the Airmail 11l showed a Lisunov Li-2 flying over a CMG demonstration. The values were in the new Leu (each worth 100 old Lei) introduced in August 1947.

A few months earlier, on 5 March 1947, a surtaxed set inscribed *CASA SCOALELOR SI A CULTURII POPORULUI 1896/1946 (THE PLACES OF THE PEOPLE'S EDUCATION & CULTURE 1896/1946)* shrewdly placed the new Communist educational initiatives within an historical context.(19.32) Four stamps pictured boys' reading lessons (200l+200l), girls' practical schooling (300l+300l), an engineering class (600l+600l), and a major school building (1,200l+1,200l) from times (and indeed recent times) when only a minority of the population had access to education. The final stamp (1,500l+1,500l) and miniature sheet, though, featured an allegory of 'Learning' in the form of youngsters looking eagerly upwards at a figure holding books in the rays of the sun heralding a new era of universal, free and compulsory education. In the following year, 1948, all private and church schools were transferred to the state without compensation, and religious education was abolished. Teachers and pupils followed the state directed curriculum with its own interpretations of history, culture, patriotism, family life and careers.

Soon afterwards, in June 1947, the newly created Institute of Romanian-Soviet Studies marked its partisan activities with a set of nine surtaxed stamps each valued 1,500l+1,500l.(19.33) Although several scholarly Romanian societies already existed this one's aims were to link scientific and cultural achievements to political needs. It represented the sycophantic Romanian Communist Party's complete subservience to Moscow. Five figures on the stamps were Russian; just three Romanian. An accompanying Airmail miniature sheet featuring the Russian Lisunov Li-2 had the celebratory inscription *CULTURA TECHNICA PROGRES 1947*.

The Russians were:

Petru Movila (1596-1647), the Eastern Orthodox Metropolitan of Kiev, founded numerous schools across the vast Polish-Lithuanian Commonwealth (covering much of Ukraine, Belarus, Poland and the Baltic States), all with a wide curriculum, and using the universal language of Latin.

19.32 200l+200l Boys' lesson, 300l+300l Girls' lesson, and 1,500l+1,500l Allegory of learning: from set 5 March 1947.

Mikhail Lomonosov (1711-65), the co-founder of Moscow University with Count Ivan Shuvalov, and a scientist who suggested, and some say proved, the wave theory of light, the law of mass conservation in chemical reaction, the atmosphere existing on Venus and how icebergs must be formed on land.

Ilya Repin (1844-1930) an internationally renowned artist, famous for his vast paintings of historic Russian life and events, and admired by Imperial and Bolshevik Russia alike.

Alexander Puskin (1799-1837) the celebrated poet, playwright and novelist whose *Ode to Liberty* led to exile under Tsar Alexander I. The Soviet Union praised his works while forgetting his aristocratic lineage.

Pytor Tchaikovsky (1840-93) the famous composer, was honoured by Tsar Alexander III in his lifetime, and later by the Soviet Union, for reflecting the complex Russian character and raising the reputation of Russian music internationally.

The Romanians were:

Mihai Eminescu (1850-89), a renowned Romantic poet whose works celebrated the nation's folklore and history, especially during its liberation in the 1877-78 Russo-Turkish War.

Nicolae Grigorescu (1838-1907), an artist whose outdoor works were widely exhibited, notably in Paris. Several major works stemmed from his time as a frontline artist in the 1877-78 war.

Victor Babes (1854-1926), a Romanian research scientist, a founder of modern microbiology and promoter of public health services.

Ironically as King Michael's reign neared its end his portrait appeared on several new issues. Nine new definitives appeared in March 1947, and on 6 September one of them appeared overprinted 2+3 *LEI* (the new currency) and *C.B.A.1947* to promote the *CAMPIONATUL DE BALCANIC ATLETISM (BALKAN ATHLETICS CHAMPIONSHIP)* held in Bucharest. (19.34) This was the second unofficial post-war Games as the official ones did not restart until 1953. Stalin had little interest in the various satellite countries coming together for anything - and certainly not in any federation - and this may well explain the modest philatelic commemoration. Much later, on 20 February 1948, a surtaxed set of five stamps featuring male and female athletes and an aeroplane flying over a stadium recalled the 1947 Games, perhaps to raise funds to offset

19.33 1,500l+1,500l Ilya Repin, Pytor Tchaikovsky, Mihai Eminescu and Victor Babes: from set June 1947.

19.34 5,500l and 36,000l King Michael: from set March 1947, with the latter overprinted 2+3 LEI and C.B.A. 1947: 8 September 1947.

19.35 1l+1l Discus thrower and 7l+7l Aeroplane over running track: from set 20 February 1948.

19.36 50b Harvesting and 5l Curtea de Arges Cathedral: from set 15 August 1947, the latter overprinted ARLUS 1-7.XI.1947: 30 October 1947.

the event's debts and mark Romania's nine (unofficial) gold medals (three by the celebrated runner Ion Moina).

King Michael's portrait adorned a lengthy set issued from August 1947 in the new currency.(19.36) They featured a range of national scenes and recently nationalised industries. The 50b featured harvesting - a vital event in this year of famine, the 1l rafts of timber floating down a river, the 2l a steamer on the Danube, the 3l the vast steel works at Reshitza in the Banat, the 20l the oil wells in Prahova, much of whose production went cheaply to the USSR, and the 12l and 36l the Fetesti-Cernavoda Bridge.

The 5l pictured the Byzantine style Romanian Orthodox cathedral in Curtea de Arges, the burial place of royalty. Perhaps the reason for its inclusion lay more in the well-known legend of its Master Builder Manole who was threatened with execution by Prince Rudu the Black, its founder, when the walls kept crumbling and progress halted. In a dream Manole was told only the sacrifice of a beloved person built into the walls would resolve the awful dilemma. The masons agreed that the first wife they saw the following day would be selected, and sadly it was Manole's pregnant wife who alone braved a terrifying storm to be with her husband. The story perfectly suited the Communist regime with its theme of great personal sacrifice for the common good. Interestingly, on 30 October 1947 this stamp was selected for overprinting with *+5l ARLUS 1-7. XI. 1947* to mark that year's Romanian-Soviet Amity Congress.

The 10l featured the Royal Palace in Bucharest and King Carol I's statue. Built in 1936-37 after a fire destroyed the old building, the Palace was badly damaged by German bombing on 24 August 1944 in retaliation for King Michael's arrest of the pro-Nazi leader, Ion Antonescu, the previous day. Afterwards King Michael lived in the villa owned by his aunt, Elisabeta, the former Queen Consort, and it was here that he was forced to abdicate. In 1948 the palace became the National Museum of Art and the throne room, devoid of all royal insignia, was used as the Hall of the State's Council.(19.37) The 15l and 32l showed the small Romanian liner MS *Transilvania* at the Black Sea port of Constantza (see also 19.55). Built in Denmark in 1938, she was the sister of MS *Basarabia* which had been ceded to the Soviet Union as a war reparation and renamed MS *Ukraina*. Both ships spent most of their lives in the Black Sea and Mediterranean.

Modernising the economy dominated the images on the 1 October 1947 set supporting the 17th Congress of the General Association of Romanian Engineers. *AGIR (ASOCIATIA GENERALA A INGINERILOR DIN ROMANIA)* was its acronym.(19.38) The 1l+1l pictured a tractor and processing mill, the 2l+2l a saw mill and cable transporter, the 3l+3l an oil refinery, the 4l+4l a steel works, and the 5l+5l Airmail gliders soaring over the forests and mountains.

19.37 10l Royal Palace, Bucharest and 15l MS 'Transilvania' at Constantza: from set 15 August 1947 (see also 19.55).

19.38 1l+1l Tractor and mill and 4l+4l Steel works: from set 1 October 1947.

19.40 12l Savings Day: 31 October 1947.

19.41 12l 1948 Census: 25 January 1948.

19.42 6l 75th anniversary of the State Stamp Printing Works: from set 12 February 1948+.

On 7 November 1947 a surtaxed Patriotic Defence set eulogised the state's relief and welfare initiatives over the past three years of war and tenuous peace.(19.39) No doubt its lacklustre performance during the famine was uppermost in mind. The 1l+1l inscribed *AJUTORAREA ARDEALULUI SI MOLDOVEI (HELPING TRANSYLVANIA AND MOLDAVIA)* was dated November 1944 - July 1945 and featured a motorised food convoy heading to regions devastated by war. The 2l+2l inscribed *TOTUL PENTRU FRONT - TOTUL PENTRU VICTORIE (EVERYTHING FOR THE FRONT - EVERYTHING FOR VICTORY)* was dated December 1944 - 9 May 1945 and showed parcels reaching front line troops when Romania had switched allegiance to the Allies. The 3l+3l inscribed *SA LECUIM RANILE RAZBOIULUI (LET'S HEAL THE WOUNDS OF WAR)* was dated June 1945 and pictured a family being welcomed at a modern hospital. The 4l+4l inscribed *AJUTORAREA REGIUNILOR SECETOASE (HELPING DROUGHT REGIONS)* was dated September 1946 and pictured hungry children enjoying a meal. Finally the 5l+5l ensured there was no doubt about the government's success by picturing a hand breaking free from chains and waving the national flag. It was inscribed *APARAREA PATRIOTICA 3 ANI DE ACTIUNE (PATRIOT DEFENCE 3 YEARS OF ACTION)*.

19.39 1l+1l Food convoy, 4l+4l Famine relief, and 5l+5l '3 Years of Action': from set 7 November 1947.

On 31 October 1947 a stamp picturing the beehive symbol, had marked Savings Day, always a major Communist theme.(19.40) Banks operated under increasingly strict state control, and the prudent management of finance by citizens was a key Communist message and indeed a test of loyalty.

On 30 December 1947 King Michael abdicated and the People's Republic was declared. The first stamp inscribed *REPUBLICA POPULARA ROMANA* on 25 January 1948 publicised a new census (19.41), and on 12 February 1948 (and 20 May) similarly titled new stamps celebrated the 75th anniversary of the State Stamp Printing Works.(19.42)

Making a brutal point, however, in March 1948 all eleven stamp issued in 1947 featuring King Michael and national scenes were reissued with the king's portrait and crown heavily overprinted with a bar and *R.P.R.* for *REPUBLICA POPULARA ROMANA*.(19.43)

19.43 1l Timber raft, 2l River Danube, and 3l Reshitza steel works overprinted R.P.R.: from set March 1948.

19.44 12l Workers and new constitution: from set 8 April 1948.

19.45 2l Republic's new emblem: from set 8 July 1948+.

19.46 10l Newspaper titles, 10l+10l Pen, torch and flag, and 15l+15l Alexandru Sahia: from set 12 September 1948.

Henceforth, with Stalin's approval and backed by the Soviet military presence, the Communists reigned openly supreme, and duly consolidated power. On 13 April 1948 a Soviet-style Constitution was adopted which promised freedom of speech and religion (as long as their expression was not deemed 'fascist and antidemocratic'), subordinated the judiciary to the government, promised free elections (but opposition parties were banned), and promoted the superiority of nationalisation to individual or corporate ownership. On 8 April (three days before ratification) three stamps pictured workers looking up at a statuesque female figure holding aloft the constitution from which shone rays of light.(19.44)

Between July and October 1948 six stamps appeared with the new republic's emblem which, not surprisingly, was modelled on that of the Soviet Union.(19.45) It featured an oval of sheaves of corn bound together by a ribbon of blue, gold and red inscribed R P R enclosing a picture of the sun shining behind mountains, forests and an oil well. This replaced the first emblem lasting from January to March 1948 whose main features were a red tractor in a circle of stylised corn. In 1952 a red star was added at the apex.

On 12 September 1948 a set marked Press Week (SAPTAMANA PRESAI).(19.46) The constitution declared a free press, but the stamps featured the main Communist controlled newspapers including *Scanteia* (The Spark) and *Romania Munciteare* (The Working Romanian) and the Romanian emblem on a flag. The 15l+15l was equally explicit in picturing Alexandru Sahia (1908-37) whose short life - he died of TB - was spent searching for a cause to serve until he visited the Soviet Union in the 1930s, found Communism, and wrote the celebratory USSR Today. A decade after his death he was exalted as a Romanian working class hero. A stamp on 22 March 1949 honoured Ion Frimu (1871-1919) on the 30th anniversary of his death. A fervent

19.47 20l Ion Frimu: 22 March 1949.

19.48 32l Romanian-Bulgarian Friendship: 28 March 1948.

Socialist and co-founder of *Romania Muncitoare* in the days when it was a subversive newspaper, he died in prison after being found guilty of instigating a general strike of typesetters.(19.47)

The new Soviet republic was internationally isolated and economically chaotic, and its leaders responded warmly to Bulgaria's overtures about economic co-operation and even federation. In January 1948 a Treaty of Friendship, Cooperation and Mutual Assistance was signed, but Stalin's opposition to any close ties between 'his' satellites meant no further progress was made. On 28 March 1948 a stamp showing a dancing Bulgarian and Romanian in national costumes marked the friendship - and the end of further hopes.(19.48)

Far more pointed and significant was the set on 29 October 1948 marking Romanian-Russian Amity. (19.49) The 10l pictured the flag waving Russian soldier topping the Soviet Soldiers' Monument in Bucharest near the graves of colleagues killed fighting for the city. A label attached to it repeated Stalin's words claiming *The Soviet army is an army that respects other peoples - it is the army of peace-keeping between different countries.* The 10l+10l featured the *ARLUS* emblem with a label exclaiming *Long live Romanian-Soviet friendship*, the 15l+15l pictured the guiding light of Communism shining from the summit of the Spasskaya Tower in Moscow, and the 20l+20l featured an Lisunov Li-2 aeroplane between two attached labels - one showing Bucharest, the other Moscow.

Further issues flattered the Soviet Union. On 20 May Romania ensured Russia's revered poet Alexander Pushkin was honoured on the 150th anniversary of his birth (actually on 20 June 1799).(19.50) On 23 August 1949 Romania duly celebrated the fifth anniversary of Russian troops entering Bucharest with an image of cheering crowds greeting a tank.(19.51) An even more sycophantic 'double' stamp marked Romanian-Soviet Friendship Week in November 1949.(19.52) On one side radiant young people waved flowers at a medallion picturing Lenin and Stalin, and on the other side demonstrators marched with banners adorned with the hammer and sickle. One inscription read *Long live the Romanian Soviet friendship*, and the other noted the special national committee that had organised the week of celebrations (1-7 November).

Special sets proliferated throughout 1948 and 1949 celebrating and promoting Communist ideology, especially with the young, and reiterating the need for military strength, economic development and friendship with the Soviet Union. All opposition, suspected or real, was eliminated, and young people

19.49 10l Soviet Soldiers' Monument, Bucharest, 15l+15l Spasskaya Tower, Moscow, and 20l+20l Li-2 aeroplane linking Bucharest and Moscow: from set 29 October 1948.

19.50 30l Alexander Pushkin: from set 20 May 1949.

19.51 50l Fifth anniversary of Russian army's entry to Bucharest: 23 August 1949.

19.52 20l Romanian-Soviet Friendship Week: 1 November 1949.

19.53 3l+3l Female harvester and 8l+8l Youth parade honouring Filimon Sarbu: from set 15 March 1948.

Labour Day (1 May) in 1948 was celebrated with stamps showing smiling young country folk admiring farmland (10l+10l), a stern factory worker holding a cogwheel (12l+12l), and a four engined aeroplane flying beneath an Icarus-like figure (20l+20l).(19.54) Stanley Gibbons says it is a Heinkel He 116A, the high-speed long-range German mail plane developed in the late 1930s. However only eight were built, but it is possible one was sold to, or seized by, the USSR or Romania. The distinctive 8l+8l features the Marxist cry *Workers from*

were not immune to arrest. Starting in 1948 youth organisations as well as schools were restructured along Soviet lines and anyone dismissed from them as 'dangerous elements' had little chance of a career, even if prison was avoided. Most existing youth groups were abolished or merged into the new state Union of Working Youth, and on 15 March 1948 this development was marked with a set picturing a determined factory worker and hammer (2l+2l), a joyful farm girl celebrating harvest (3l+3l), a serious looking student (5l+5l), a triangular stamp showing youths waving a banner honouring the wartime partisan Filimon Sarbu (8l+8l), and an Airmail stamp showing barn swallows and a four-engined passenger plane.(19.53)

19.54 8l+8l Marxist slogan, 10l+10l Rural couple and 20l+20l Icarus and aeroplane: from set 1 May 1948.

19.55 3l+3l Fighter, 7l50+7l50 Tank, and 8l+8l Destroyer: from set 9 May 1948.

19.57 5l+5l Barque 'Mircea' and 10l+10l Liner 'Transilvania': from set 26 July 1948.

19.56 2l+2l Goppingen Go3 Minimoa glider and 5l+5l Aurel Vlaicu's 'Crazy Fly': from set 26 July 1948.

all countries unite set against the background of wheatsheaves, globe, an open book, anvil and hammer, and smoking factory chimneys.

After 1945 the Soviet Union's military establishment took control of Romania's armed forces, purged them of undesirable elements, remodelled them on Russian lines, sold them Soviet equipment, and ensured they had plenty of Soviet advisors and senior officers. On 9 May 1948 a set marking Army Day was inscribed TRAIASCA FRATIA DE ARME ROMANO-SOVIETICA (LONG LIVE THE ROMANIAN-SOVIET BROTHERHOOD OF ARMS) with the all-important dates 23 August 1944 - 9 May 1945 when the Soviet Union stopped being the overwhelming enemy and became the overwhelming ally.(19.55) The 1.50l+1.50l pictured a Romanian and Russian soldier, the 2l+2l cutting a barbed wire entanglement, the 3l+3l an Ilyushin Il-2M3 Stormovik fighter plane scoring a victory, the 4l+4l artillery firing, the 5l+5l a Petlyakov Pe-2 dive bomber in action, the 7.50l+7.50l infantry advancing alongside a Russian made tank, probably a T44, and the 8l+8l a Russian destroyer, which looked like one of the large *Ognevoy* class armed with twin 5.1" guns completed during and after the war.

In contrast, on 26 July 1948 Air Force and Navy Day was marked, surprisingly, with a set of peaceful craft. Flying was represented by four stamps. The 2l+2l featured the pre-war German Goppingen Go3 Minimoa single seat glider that established an altitude record of almost 22,000' in 1938. and the 5l+5l pictured the Romanian pioneering aircraft designer Aurel Vlaicu attempting to fly across the Carpathian Mountains in his *Crazy Fly* (which led to his death) in 1913.(19.56) The others featured a Russian made Lisunov Li-2 aircraft flying over farmland (8l+8l) and mountains (10l+10l). Ships were represented by yachting (2l+2l), the cadet training barque *Mircea* built in 1938, seized by the Soviet Union in 1945, and returned in 1946 (5l+5l), a River Danube paddle steamer (8l+8l), and the small liner *Transilvania* (10l+10l).(19.57)

Between these two sets the Wallachian and Transylvanian Revolts of 1848 had been remembered with five stamps. Wallachia and Moldavia stretched north from the River Danube to the River Prut. In 1848 they remained nominally within the fading Ottoman Empire, were ruled by a reactionary oligarchy of an elected prince and semi-independent boyars, and subject to repressive Russian political and economic interests. The provinces were an important Russian bridgehead into the Balkans. When much of Europe was wracked by revolutions in 1848, like-minded conspirators calling themselves 'The Brotherhood' led by Nicolae Balcescu ejected the ruling oligarchy and set up a revolutionary government promising wide-ranging social and economic reforms. Although the Turks were not unsympathetic, seeing the revolt primarily as an anti-Russian move, the Russian Tsar pressurised the Sultan to eject the new government. The revolt was suppressed.

Nevertheless the core of intellectuals and soldiers leading the revolt were fortunate that when Russia relinquished its interests in the region after defeat in the Crimean War of 1854-56, and the Ottoman Empire was in no position to exert full control, Wallachia and Moldavia agreed to unify as Romania. In 1859 Alexandru Cuza, a Moldavian army officer active in the 1848 revolution, was elected Prince and ruled only nominally subject to Turkish suzerainty. In 1866 the increasingly autocratic Cuza was ousted and replaced by the German Prince Carol who became King Carol I soon after Romania achieved full independence in 1878. Although the revolutionaries were far from Communists, and indeed split into warring liberal and conservative factions over land reforms and universal suffrage after 1848, a century later the Romanian Communists celebrated them as nationalists and liberators and used them to publicise the post-war Communist regime as the final victory of these historic but forward looking revolutionaries.

Alexandru Cuza is pictured at the top of the 36l+18l while the key figure of the soldier, writer and historian Nicolae Balcescu (1819-52) appears alone on the 2l+2l and also alongside others on the 5l+5l, 10l+10l and 36l+18l.(19.58) Among the diverse other figures were Ion Heliade Radulescu (1802-72) (5l+5l) whose historical writings helped stimulate the cultural revival, Ana Ipatescu (1805-75) (5l+5l) whose oratory inspired pro-revolutionary crowds, Avram Iancu (1824-72) (10l+10l) who led the ill-fated Transylvanian revolt, fighting both Hungarians and Austrians, Simion Barnutiu (1808-64) (10l+10l) a Liberal Transylvanian politician who sought regional self-government, Vasile Alecsandri (1821-90) (36l+18l), a renowned poet, and cultural nationalist dedicated to the creation of Romania, and Mihail Kogalniceanu (1817-91) (36l+18l) who was the ideologue of the 1848 Moldavian revolt, and rose to be Prime Minister under Cuza and Foreign Minister under King Carol I. The 11l featured people on 9 June 1848 at the Proclamation at Islaz in Wallachia of the revolutionary programme of civil rights and self-government written by Ion Radulescu. The stamp was inscribed PATRIA TUTUROR CELOR CE MUNCESC CU BRATELE SI CU MINTEA DELA SATE SI DELA ORASE which translates as THE HOMELAND OF ALL THOSE WHO WORK WITH THEIR HANDS AND MINDS IN VILLAGES AND CITIES.

19.58 2l+2l Nicolae Balcesu, 36l+18l Balescu, Alexandru Cuza, Vasile Alecsandri and Mihail Kogalniceanu, and 11l Proclamation: from set 1 June 1948.

On 20 December 1948 another stamp portrayed Nicolae Balcescu.(19.59) By that date a century earlier the Wallachian uprising was over and Balcescu had been hiding in Serbia. However he now emerged for talks with Louis Kossuth, the Hungarian revolutionary, and Avram Iancu, the Transylvanian patriot. Their different partisan aims left little room for concerted action against Austria or Russia but at least they avoided further military action against each other and agreed that a self-governing Romania within the Ottoman Empire and a self-governing Hungary under the Hapsburgs were their ultimate ambitions. Both came to pass, the former in 1859, the latter in 1867. On 24 January 1949 a stamp featuring regional folk dancers celebrated the 90th anniversary of the union of Wallachia and Moldavia. (19.60) However under the 1867 Austro-Hungarian agreement establishing the 'Dual Monarchy' Transylvania fell under Hungarian rule.

Other sets at this time reinforced the importance of communications and transport to the economy. Two Airmail stamps on 22 November 1948 pictured what appears to be Lisunov Li-2s flying over oil fields (30l), over tractors busy providing food for distant factories (50l), and over trains, lorries and liners (100l).(19.61) A little later, on 10 December 1948, a set and miniature sheet featured dockers loading a freighter (1l+1l), lorries and telephone engineers at work (3l+3l), a Lisunov Li-2 being prepared for flight (11l+11l) and a steam train at speed (15l+15l).(19.62)

On 10 December 1949 two stamps featuring coaches, trains and aeroplanes set against the globe marked the Congress of the International Transport Workers

19.59 20l Nicolae Balcescu: 20 December 1948.

19.60 10l 90th anniversary of the union of Wallachia and Moldavia: 24 January 1949.

19.61 30l Aeroplane over oil field and 50l Aeroplane over farm and factory: from set 22 November 1948.

19.62 3l+3l Lorry and telephone engineers: from set 10 December 1948.

19.63 11l International Transport Workers Federation Congress: from set 10 December 1949.

19.64 5l First anniversary of the People's Republic: 30 December 1948.

19.65 20l 25th anniversary of the death of Lenin: 21 January 1949.

Federation made up of transport unions across the world.(19.63) Founded in 1896, its headquarters moved to England from Amsterdam in 1939. It campaigned (and still does) for better safety measures and employment conditions and creating international solidarity among its members.

On 30 December 1948 a stamp showing hands breaking a chain over the date 30 December 1947 - the day King Michael abdicated - celebrated the first anniversary of the People's Republic.(19.64) On 21 January 1949 a stamp marked the 25th anniversary of the death of Lenin (19.65), and on 21 December 1949 a stamp celebrated Stalin's 75th birthday.(19.65) Romania's status as a strict Communist state taking its political, social and economic direction from Moscow could not have been made clearer.

CHAPTER 20

BULGARIA

The early twentieth century saw Bulgaria lurch dramatically from hopes of dominating the Balkans to confronting utter humiliation. Tsar Ferdinand (reigned 1887-1918) decided a Bulgarian alliance with Germany and Austria-Hungary in the First World War would gain his country swathes of new territory, at the expense of his neighbours, only to see Bulgarians become disenchanted with the slaughter of fellow Slavs and mounting economic hardship, and increasingly susceptible to Bolshevik propaganda. In 1918 Ferdinand abdicated amidst his country's chaos, and his son Boris III spent the inter-war decades striving to cope with the violent political battles, and sometimes outright violence, between the right and left wing parties. In 1935 Boris managed to garner enough political support to establish his own authoritarian regime - but it was a tense time in European affairs and the neutrality he sought was increasingly hard to sustain.

Faced with overwhelming pressure from Germany and Italy, in 1941 Boris had little option but to join the Axis powers and allow German troops through Bulgaria on their way to attack Greece. He never declared war on the Soviet Union, although his warships did engage with those of Russia when Bulgarian shipping was attacked in the Black Sea. Across the Balkans Bulgarian forces helped garrison and administer German occupied parts of Macedonia, Thrace and Yugoslavia, and were drawn into regular combat against resistance groups, many of them Communist. Many Jews were dispatched to concentration camps. In December 1941 Bulgaria formally declared war on Great Britain and the USA which laid Sofia, the capital, open to Allied bombing raids. And as early as the summer of 1942 the underground Bulgarian Communist Party set up the anti-Nazi Fatherland Front which attracted many members, both Communist and non-Communist.

In August 1943 Boris died suddenly - possibly poisoned after a stormy meeting with Hitler over the king's refusal to send troops to the Eastern Front and be more active in the deportation of Jews. His son Simeon, aged six, succeeded him. A regency council was established which sought to avoid Soviet occupation by opening tentative talks with the western Allies. By the summer of 1944 Soviet forces neared Bulgaria. On 23 August Romania changed sides, thus easing Soviet access to Bulgaria which declared itself neutral on the 27th. Hearing this, the increasingly Communist-inspired Fatherland Front launched an armed rebellion against the government on the same day but failed to take over. Nevertheless Soviet pressure on Bulgaria mounted. German forces undertook a strategic withdrawal without fighting the Bulgarians, but soon afterwards Stalin declared war on Bulgaria to 'liberate' it from pro-Nazi politicians. On 8 September 1944 Soviet forces crossed the border, but the Bulgarian government ordered its troops not to resist, and declared war on Germany.

On the following day, 9 September 1944, the Fatherland Front, supported by the army, successfully seized power and began releasing Communists from prison and repatriating Allied prisoners of war. In addition in the volte-face Bulgarian armies started to fight alongside Soviet ones against the Germans in Yugoslavia, Macedonia and Hungary. Early in 1945 several dozen senior members of the wartime regency council, government and armed forces were tried and executed, and hundreds more 'counter-revolutionaries' imprisoned. Once it became clear that the western Allies were content, or felt obliged, to let Bulgaria become a Soviet 'sphere of interest' the destruction of Bulgaria's professional and capitalist elite was assured. On 15 September 1946 a referendum was held and as a

20.1 3l King Simeon II: 21 March 1944.

20.2 50l and 100l Parcel Post overprinted ALL FOR THE FRONT: from set 25 January 1945.

20.3 1l King Boris III overprinted COLLECT ALL RAGS, 2l COLLECT OLD IRON, and 4l COLLECT WASTE PAPER: from set March 1945.

20.5 50st, 2l and 5l Bulgarian Lion definitives: from set 26 April 1945+, and 50st with star above lion: from set 20 August 1948+.

result the monarchy was abolished, Simeon went into exile, and a people's republic declared. Georgi Dimitrov, a Bulgarian ally of Stalin, became prime minister after the Constitutional Assembly elections in October 1946 gave the Communists a majority. In December 1947 the constituent assembly ratified a new constitution based on that of the Soviet Union. Other political parties, and notably the hitherto influential Agrarian National Union, had to align themselves closely with the Communists or be dissolved. From 1948 Muslim, Protestant and Roman Catholic organisations were strictly controlled or suppressed, and the hitherto popular Bulgarian Orthodox Church neutralised when state nominees occupied many of its important posts.

Just one stamp depicted the young King Simeon, a 3l on 12 June 1944.(20.1) Otherwise issues by the dominant Fatherland Front at this time concentrated on the fight against Fascism and the assertion of the Front's right to rule. On 25 January 1945 Parcel Post stamps featuring the historic Bulgarian Lion Coat of Arms were issued overprinted *ALL FOR THE FRONT* in Cyrillic (20.2), and in March stocks of King Boris definitives were thought good enough to be overprinted *COLLECT ALL RAGS, COLLECT OLD IRON* or *COLLECT WASTE PAPER*.(20.3)

In March and April a set featuring a symbolic tree and its sturdy branches reaching maturity marked the All Slav Congress organised in Sofia by Mrs Tsola Dragoicheva (1898-1993), General Secretary of the Fatherland Front and ardent pro-Moscow Communist

20.4 50l All Slav Congress: from set 8 March 1945+.

minister.(20.4) Georgi Dimitrov remained warmly receptive to Tito's ideas on a South Slav Federation, but Stalin's earlier enthusiasm for uniting Slavs against the Germans was soon to fade in favour of entirely separate, relatively weak and more easily controllable satellite states.

From April 1945 new definitives and official stamps featured the Bulgarian Lion emblem in various formats, and on some values the crown was joined by proletarian tufts and sheaves of corn. In 1948 the Communist star appeared above the historic lion.(20.5) Nationalist and Communist sentiment were effectively entwined, the former giving some legitimacy to the latter.

Three other sets in 1945 highlighted the Fatherland Front. On 4 June a long set and two miniature sheets, all with particularly high values, helped promote and finance the state's Liberty Loan for post-war recovery projects.(20.6) The stamps, inscribed Liberty Loan, featured a worker breaking chains (50l), a hand offering a coin, (100l), a symbolic stream powering a mill, (150l) and rays from a coin turning the machinery of rural and urban production (200l).

Significantly, two sets highlighted the number 9. Belatedly, on 1 September 1945 two small stamps marked Victory in Europe Day.(20.7) They were inscribed 9, not 8, May 1945 as the German surrender in Berlin late on the 8 May meant its announcement in Moscow was early on the 9th. The date suited the Fatherland Front as on 7 September 1945 a set with a 9 at its centre celebrated the Communist-led coalition's first anniversary (on 9 September) of assuming power and allying with the Soviet Union.(20.8)

A series of sets revealed Communist propaganda at work. They harked back to the wartime partisans,

20.6 50l Chain breaker, 150l Water mill, and 200l Powering the economy: from set 4 June 1945.

20.7 10l Victory in Europe: from set 1 September 1945.

20.8 4l and 10l First anniversary of the Fatherland Front Coalition: from set 7 September 1945.

20.9 2l Refugee children, 35l Red Cross train, and 50l Nurse and wounded soldier: from set 4 April 1946.

commemorated carefully chosen figures in Bulgaria's remote and recent past, promoted welfare projects and celebrated the close links with the USSR and, occasionally, other emerging Slav satellites. A revisionist cultural history was tied as tightly as possible to Communist ideology and national improvement.

On 4 April 1946 a set promoted the continuing work of the Red Cross, with haunting images of refugee children (2l and 10l), a soldier on a stretcher (4l and 20l), a nurse and emaciated soldier (30l and 50l), and a Red Cross train (35l and 50l).(20.9) The set was reissued on 31 January 1947 in different colours. In-between the two, on 30 December 1946, another haunting set on behalf of the Winter Relief Fund featured children gathering around a nurse (1l, 10l and 50l), a child bearing gifts (4l and 9l), a hungry child (20l and 40l) and a destitute mother and child (30l).(20.10)

Memories of wartime were kept constantly to the fore to entwine heroic images of Bulgarian courage with personal sacrifices for the state and gather them together under the Communist banner. On 9 August 1946 a set of eleven action packed stamps featured wartime scenes of grenade throwers and machine gunners (2l, 4l and 20l), horse drawn artillery and cavalry charges (5l, 10l and 30l), tanks entering rivers and soldiers building pontoons (9l and 60l), and horses and carts and lorries bringing up supplies (40l and 50l). (20.11) The date *25 X 1944* on the 4l and *3 XI 1944* on the 60l made it clear the soldiers were fighting alongside the Russians. Interestingly the set highlights how much horses contributed to the war alongside mechanisation. Nevertheless Bulgaria had had plentiful supplies of German arms, including the dive-bombing 'Stukas' (Junkers Ju 87B) that eventually were turned against the Germans, as pictured in the 6l. After the war the Bulgarian army remained strong and was rearmed by the Soviet Union.

On 26 August 1946 it seemed as though the Fatherland Front set was honouring an early Bulgarian saint. One stamp portrayed St Ivan Rilski (876-c946), a hermit renowned for performing miracles, and the other four

20.10 1l Nurse and children, 4l Child with gifts, and 20l Hungry child: from set 30 December 1946.

20.13 5l and 10l Partisans: from set 2 December 1946.

20.11 6l 'Stuka' dive bombers, 40l Supply column, and 60l Tank and infantry attack: from set 9 August 1946.

20.12 1l St Ivan Rilski and 10l Rila Monastery: from set 26 August 1946.

featured views of Rila Monastery founded in his memory.(20.12) However Rila was celebrated not only as a Bulgarian cultural centre but also as the hiding place of leading nineteenth century revolutionaries against Ottoman rule, notably a key leader, Vasili Levski (1837-73). Churches were not specifically targeted for repression until 1948.

On 2 December 1946 another set featured partisans in actions.(20.13) The 1l and 20l featured an attack led by male and female partisans and a soldier. The 5l and 50l portrayed an armed partisan, the 4l and 10l pictured partisans behind a tree preparing an ambush, and the 30l pictured a partisan attack. The Fatherland Front had grown out of the anti-German resistance movement after Hitler had broken his pact with Stalin and invaded the USSR in June 1941. In 1943 resistance groups had been organised into the People's Liberation Rebel Army operating from various key zones. All this created an armed power base across the country to assist the Communist-led takeover.

Several sets marked the Fatherland Front's steady progress towards complete dominance by the Communists under Georgi Dimitrov. In 1945 the government had nationalised banks and taken control of their investments, but it left the popular Post Office Savings Bank with a modicum of independence to encourage small savers. Its 50th anniversary was marked by four stamps on 12 April 1946 featuring its beehive emblem (4l), saving certificates (10l), a child and her money box (20l), and the reassuringly solid bank building (50l).(20.14) In common with many countries, occasional sets of surtaxed stamps supported Bulgaria's Postal Employees' Relief Fund. Highlighting both traditional and more modern roles, on 5 November 1947 a set featured a postman (4l+2l), an engineer up a telegraph pole (10l+5l), telephonists (20l+10l) and wireless masts (40l+20l).(20.15) Control of communications, and notably broadcasting, was a key Communist aim, and so was securing control of trades unions. On 29 February 1948 two stamps (one Airmail)

20.14 4l Savings Bank emblem and 20l Child and money box: from set 12 April 1946.

20.16 4l Worker and banner (Second General Workers' Union Congress): from set 29 February 1948.

20.15 20l+10l Telephonists and 40l+20l Wireless masts: from set 5 November 1947.

20.17 100l (Unofficial) Balkan Games: 6 July 1946.

20.18 4l Bulgarian-Soviet Union Congress: 23 May 1946+.

featuring workers and factories marked the Second Congress of the Bulgarian General Workers' Union. (20.16) Here, as at most annual meetings, delegates could discuss issues as long as they did not imply criticisms of the Party, especially its leadership, and ideally promoted greater efficiency. Coincidentally 1948 was the year the left wing Social Democratic Workers Party ended its days as an independent coalition member of the Fatherland Front and was forced to merge with the Communist Party.

On 6 July 1946 a stamp picturing the emblems of Albania, Bulgaria, Romania and Yugoslavia publicised the unofficial restoration of the Balkan Games - with its strong symbolism of Slav cooperation and possible federation that Stalin came to dislike.(20.17) In May and July 1946 stamps featuring national emblems and symbolic acorns on an oak branch marked a Bulgarian-Soviet Union Congress which helped tighten the association between the minor satellite and its major partner.(20.18) A few months later, on 15 September 1946 three stamps featuring a sword wielding female figure marked the Bulgarian referendum leading to the republic.(20.19) It was claimed that over 95% of votes favoured this result. Young King Simeon went into exile, and henceforth the Communists made little effort to pretend a left-wing coalition ran the country.

In a significant state decision, amidst these last three issues a stamp appeared on 13 June 1946 marking the 23rd anniversary of the violent death of Aleksandur Stamboliski (1879-1923), leader of the left-wing Agrarian Party and Bulgaria's elected prime minister from 1919 until 1923.(20.20) Clearly it was important not to wait for the more usual 25th anniversary. Stamboliski had introduced major land reforms and encouraged collectivisation but within a progressive market economy. His downfall, though, was signing the 1923 Treaty of Nis confirming Yugoslav ownership of north-west Macedonia, as laid down by the Treaty of Paris in 1919. This infuriated the Internal Macedonian Revolutionary Organisation (IMRO) which ran its terror campaign against Greek and Yugoslav interests in Macedonia largely from Bulgaria. Stamboliski agreed to suppress IMRO, but he was overthrown in a right-wing coup supported by the army and IMRO, and murdered soon afterwards. The Bulgarian Communist Party had

20.19 50l Allegory of the new republic: from set 15 September 1946.

20.20 100l Aleksandur Stamboliski: 13 June 1946.

20.21 10l Male and female revolutionaries (1923) and 70l Soldier addressing crowd (1944): from set 21 January 1947.

20.22 4l Dimitur Blageov, 9l Gabril Genov, and 60l Youth parade: from set 6 September 1948.

seen Stamboliski as a Socialist rival and failed to oppose the coup. However Stalin was furious, and the humiliated Bulgarian Communists felt obliged to stage a hastily organised uprising which the new regime speedily crushed. In 1946, though, it was convenient for Bulgarian Communists to hail Stamboliski as a proletarian leader martyred at the hands of selfish conservative interests.

The Bulgarian Communists made further attempts to turn the humiliating political events of 1923 into some sort of armed triumph. A set on 21 January 1947 specifically highlighted the Bulgarian Communist Party's opposition to the 1923 coup, as well as its continuing opposition to Axis forces from 1941 when Bulgaria was Hitler's ally to 1944 when Bulgaria was Stalin's ally.(20.21) The 10l and 20l featured advancing partisans, and the 70l a soldier addressing a crowd. On 6 September 1948 another set commemorated the 25th anniversary of the belated 1923 uprising. (20.22) The 4l portrayed Dimitur Blageov, the founder of the Bulgarian Communist Party who advocated a Soviet Socialist Republic but, in the event, opposed the uprising as too little too late, the 9l Gabril Genov who led the ultimately unsuccessful rebel advance on Vratsa, the 20l a train carrying revolutionaries, and the 60l modern Communist Youth on parade.

On 28 February 1947 stamps picturing an olive branch and dove of peace - and the emblems of the USSR, USA, UK and Bulgaria (but not France) - marked the Treaty of Paris.(20.23) Bulgaria ceded north west Macedonia to Yugoslavia and east Macedonia to Greece, but perhaps surprisingly as a defeated Axis country, it ended up keeping Southern Dobruja.

There was a flurry of stamps highlighting the wider world. On 16 June 1947 a surtaxed stamp supported the 30th Esperanto Conference held in Sofia.(20.24) Earlier Airmail stamps in June 1946 had blandly featured wings, birds and aeroplanes, but on 31 May 1947 a surcharged Airmail stamp boldly promoted the Bulgarian stand at New York's Philatelic Exhibition.(see 1.8)

On 23 May 1948 an Airmail stamp for Stamp Day featured a Russian twin engined Petlyakov Pe-2 bomber flying over Balduin's Tower in the Tsarevets Fortress guarding the historic city of Tarnovo.(20.25) It seemed innocuous enough, but undoubtedly symbolised Russia's role as 'liberator' of Bulgaria. In 1877 the Russian General Joseph Gourko had ridden through Tarnovo with Grand Prince Ferdinand (later Tsar Ferdinand of

20.23 4l Treaty of Paris: from set 28 February 1947.

20.24 20l+10l Esperanto Conference, Sofia: 16 June 1947.

20.25 50l Petlyakov Pe-2 over Tarnovo: 23 May 1948.

intensified in the 1950s.(20.27) The 20l featured the state's emblem of industry - a hammer and anvil within a cogwheel.

A further stamp portraying coal miners appeared on 7 October 1948 at the time production was scheduled to soar once the government's Five Year Industrial and Agricultural Plan got underway.(20.28) On 5 August 1949 a set marked the Plan with images of a hydro-electric plant (4l), cement works (9l), heavy tractor making a road (20l), farm tractor (15l) and symbolic cogs and sheaves of corn being powered by electricity. (20.29) Heavy industry was planned to grow by 220%, light industry by 75% and agriculture by 59%, but the all-important mechanisation of farming failed to materialise sufficiently to free workers who could be sent into industry. In addition the Soviet Union took too many products at rock bottom prices to allow sufficient profit for reinvestment.

Another reinvigorated aspect of the economy after the wartime losses was shipping, celebrated by a stamp on 19 December 1947 featuring the *Rodina* which was the first post-war cargo ship to be purchased - in June 1946. (20.30) Her construction started in German occupied Copenhagen in 1944 but she was sunk by saboteurs,

20.26 1l President's Palace and 9l National Theatre, Sofia: from set 1 July 1947+.

Bulgaria) after the largely Russian victories had ended almost five centuries of Ottoman rule. After 1945 the Russians supplied the Bulgarian Air Force with Pe-2 bombers and, after the 1947 Peace Treaty, they supplied the new Bulgarian airlines (which the Soviet Union co-owned) with Lisunov Li-2 aeroplanes which were basically copies of the American Douglas DC-3.

The next sets turned sharply inwards and reflected the government's control of reconstruction and output, its promotion of literature, drama and music promoting Communist ideals, and its encouragement of sporting activities that kept workers disciplined and healthy. During 1947 and 1948 a set proudly featured key state buildings in Sofia - the General Post Office's headquarters, the National Theatre, Parliament Building, and President's Palace.(20.26) On 6 August 1947 four stamps highlighted the state's investment in dams and hydro-electric plants (4l) (although none were completed until the mid 1950s), and its encouragement of coal and copper mining (9l), and the mechanisation of agriculture (40l), although passive resistance to collectivisation remained a significant hurdle until state coercion

20.27 4l Dam and power station and 40l Mechanised ploughing: from set 6 August 1947.

20.28 4l Coal miner: 7 October 1948.

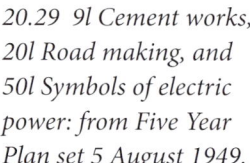

20.29 9l Cement works, 20l Road making, and 50l Symbols of electric power: from Five Year Plan set 5 August 1949.

then raised and completed in Autumn 1945. In due course Bulgaria expanded its own shipyards at Rousse, Burgas and Varna.

On 31 August 1947 four striking stamps promoted the revival of Plovdiv's International Trade Fair.(20.31) Thousands of visitors from across the world, but mainly from Communist states, were offered goods from across the world, including the USA, but the Fair primarily sought to promote the forced economies of Communist states, especially Bulgaria itself. The 4l pictured the Exhibition Hall, the 20l roses and grapes against a cogwheel, and the 40l an aeroplane over Plovdiv. The 9l featured the striking house in Plovdiv where the celebrated French poet and republican politician Alphonse de Lamartine (1790-1869) stayed for a few days in 1833 on his way home from the Middle East. His inclusion probably rested most on his celebrated role in overthrowing the French monarchy and establishing the Second Republic in 1848.

Sport, education, and the purposeful use of leisure were regularly highlighted, and were closely linked in Communist policies. On 29 September 1947 a set picturing Balkan flags (60l), cycling (2l), basketball (4l), football (20l) and the Communist favourite, chess (9l), marked the second unofficial Balkan Games. (20.32) It was held in Bucharest and was extended to the central European countries of Hungry, Czechoslovakia and Poland. It was a successful but relatively low key affair, not least as by then Stalin was less than enthusiastic about closer links between satellite countries.

Schools were essential in imparting both utilitarian skills and Communist ideologies and versions of history. In October 1947 and February 1948 two different stamps portrayed Vasil Aprilov (1789-1847), a major figure in the Bulgarian Renaissance when the region was still part of the Ottoman Empire. He founded the first secular schools to ensure children remained culturally 'Bulgarian'.(20.33)

20.30 50l Cargo ship 'Rodina': 19 December 1947.

20.31 9l Lamartine's house and 40l Aeroplane over Plovdiv: from set 31 August 1947.

20.32 9l (Unofficial) Balkan & Central European Games: 29 September 1947.

20.33 *40l Vasil Aprilov: from set 19 October 1947+.*

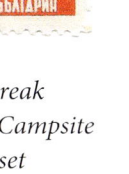

20.34 *4l Work break reading and 20l Campsite accordion: from set 31 March 1948.*

20.35 *5l Tunnelling, 20l Tractor driving, and 40l Lorry with workers waving banners: from set 6 April 1949.*

20.36 *4l Throwing javelin and grenade and 9l Leaping hurdles and barbed wire: from set 5 September 1949.*

On 31 May 1948 four stamps pictured people reading a book and listening to music against a background of their workplace (4l and 40l) while others were playing an accordion and exercising with a ball at a campsite (20l and 60l).(20.34). Government approved books and music were encouraged in work breaks, and carefully choreographed camping breaks for young people were key components of the Communist education system.

A further set on 6 April 1949 celebrated Bulgaria's version of the USSR's Komsomol, the National Youth Movement for those aged 14 to 28. It mixed sport and cultural activities with political education and voluntary labour, and expected the youngsters to be an inspiration to children and older people, especially rural peasants with whom they sometimes worked alongside.(20.35). The stamps featured road building (4l), tunnel building (5l), a railway (9l), and eager workers on the back of a lorry waving a banner (40l). Two close up images pictured young women in a textile factory (10l) and driving a farm tractor (20l). Founded in 1944, members took an oath to Georgi Dimitrov to 'fight selflessly' towards the victory of Communism.

The link between between sport and military service was made explicit in a set on 5 September 1949 promoting physical culture. The 4l featured a javelin thrower and grenade thrower, the 9l a hurdler and soldier leaping barbed wire, the 20l a motor cyclist and heavy vehicle driver, and the 50l a male and female athlete marching military style.(20.36)

Bulgaria's numerous mineral springs and warm baths had long been popular for their health giving properties and remained so under Communism. The same was true of the challenges of skiing and mountaineering, notably in the Rila Mountains in the south-west. A set issued at various times in 1948 and 1949 promoted both activities.(20.37)

On 8 December 1947 a set of eleven stamps, five of which were surtaxed, celebrated the 50th anniversary of Sofia's National Theatre and supported the Actors Benevolent Fund.(20.38) It marked, too, the state's interest in controlling public performances even though the sequence of actors and directors portrayed on the stamps conveyed an apparently seamless continuity within the venerable institution. The set featured medallion portraits and performance images of Geno Kirov (1866-1944) (50st), Zlatina Nedeva (1878-1941)

20.37 5l Malyovitsa peak, Rila Mountains and 10l Mineral Bath, Gorna Banya, Sofia: from set 20 August 1948+.

(1l), Ivan Popov (1865-1966) (2l), husband and wife Atanas Kirchev (1879-1912) (3l) and Elena Snezhina (1881-1944) (4l), Stoyan Buchvarov (1878-1949) (5l), husband and wife Khristo Ganchev (1877-1912) (9l+5l) and Adriana Budevska (1878-1955) (10l+6l), Vasil Kirkov (1870-1931) (15l+7l), Sava Ognyanov (1876-1933) (20l+15l), and Krustyu Sarafov (1876-1952) (30l+20l).

All the actors were nationally famous, and key figures in the creation of a national theatre in the late nineteenth and early twentieth centuries. They were the nation's first generation of stars performing in classical plays from across the world and showcasing Bulgarian works. Some died young, some appeared on radio and in films, such as Ivan Popov and Stoyan Buchvarov, and a few were still working after the war. The National Theatre itself was finished in fashionable Art Nouveau style in 1906. After the Second World War the management was purged, and wider European works disappeared from the repertoire to be replaced by politically acceptable Soviet and Bulgarian ones with Socialist Realism the primary consideration. When this set was issued many Bulgarians might have recalled seeing Geno Kirov and Zlatina Nedeva performing in the National Theatre. They might have known, too, that Adriana Budevska had chosen to return to the country after a long absence in South America to perform under Communist rule, and that Krustyu Sarafov was a member of the Communist Party and recently created People's Artist of the Republic. In 1952 the National Theatre was renamed after him.

Linked to this set was another on 18 May 1948 honouring selected Bulgarian poets.(20.39) They included Nikola Vaptsarov (1909-42) (4l), a sailor and worker poet who became a Communist partisan and was executed by the Germans, Peyu Yavorov (1878-1914) (9l), a Romantic poet within the Macedonian Revolutionary Movement, Khristo Smirmenski (1898-1923) (15l), a Communist whose lyrical poems dreamt of future happiness during the troubled years after 1918, and Ivan Vazov (1850-1921) (20l), a poet and dramatist whose life and works stretched from the 1877-78 war to

20.38 50st Geno Kirov, 1l Zlatina Nedeva, 10l+6l Adriana Budevska, and 30l+20l Krustyu Sarafov: from set 8 December 1947.

20.39 4l Nikola Vaptsarov: from set 18 May 1948.

promoting the National Theatre. Finally there was Petko Slaveikov (1827-95) (45l) a Bulgarian Renaissance poet and politician actively engaged in the events of 1877-78 and later imprisoned for opposing the suspension of the democratic constitution by Prince Alexander (who reigned as the first prince of an autonomous Bulgaria from 1879 until 1886 when he was ousted in a coup). Khristo Smirmenski whose poems particularly appealed to the idealistic young, featured on two more stamps on the 50th anniversary of his birth on 2 October 1948. (20.40)

1948 and 1949 saw sets harking back to the revolutionaries of 1848-49 and 1877-78. On 5 July 1948 a particularly pointed set promoted the idea of a monument to the Soviet Army for its part in the country's liberation.(20.41) The 4l pictured a Russian soldier, the 10l peasants welcoming Russian soldiers with bread and flowers, and the 60l the Spasskaya Tower

20.40 16l Khristo Smirmenski: from set 2 October 1948.

20.42 20l Khristo Botev and 9l Riverboat 'Radetzky': from set 21 December 1948+.

and, for the first time on a Bulgarian stamp, a portrait of Stalin. The 20l featured Russian soldiers of 1878 and 1944, and in the background is the massive memorial at Shipka Pass in Bulgaria where the Russians aided by Bulgarian forces defeated the Ottoman Turks in 1877. The bright light of a Communist star shines over the historic scene. The huge post-1945 Soviet Army Monument in Sofia was not completed until 1954. It was topped with a triumphant Russian soldier standing protectively by a Bulgarian family.

On 21 December 1948 a set marked the centenary of the birth of the celebrated poet and revolutionary Khristo Botev (1848-76).(20.42) Heavily influenced by Russian liberal and socialist writers, his early poems, articles and speeches against repression by the Ottoman Turks and their wealthy Bulgarian collaborators forced him into hiding along with the revolutionary leader Vasil Levski. After Levski's capture and execution in February 1873, Botev planned an insurrection thinking thousands would join him. In 1876 he and an armed party around 200 strong boarded and seized the Danube riverboat Radetzky, landed on Bulgarian territory to find few supporters but numerous Ottoman patrols searching for them. They held off repeated attacks while vainly seeking reinforcements until finally trapped on Mount Okoltchitza where Botev was killed and most of his company captured and executed. His Russian links, revolutionary fervour, contempt for the conservative bourgeoisie, and poetry that empathised with the oppressed, made him both a national and international hero. The dramatist and revolutionary Ivan Vazov (1850-1921), who knew Botev well, was a major contributor to his legendary status. The set features his birthplace in Kalofer (1l), Kalofer itself (15l), his mother and part of a poem (40l), two portraits,(4l and 20l), the *Radetzky* (named after the Austrian general who had crushed several of the 1848-49 Italian revolts) (9l) and a crossed quill, pistol and wreath (50l).

1948 and 1949 included several sets which showed how firmly Bulgaria was in Stalin's grasp. On 1 November 1948 three optimistic stamps (two of them Airmail) publicised Bulgaria's Treaty of Friendship, Cooperation & Mutual Assistance with Romania signed by Georgi Dimitrov in Bucharest earlier in the year. (20.43) The 100l featured the jointly proposed Danube Bridge linking the two countries, the 40l the Parliamentary Buildings in Sofia and Bucharest, and the dramatic 20l honoured the Romanians who won the hard fought Battle of Grivitsa alongside the Russians against the Turks in 1877. On Dimitrov's return he made public his commitment to creating a Balkan Confederation but soon afterwards humiliatingly withdrew it in the face of Stalin's fury. The Soviet Union had no intention of allowing its small satellites to become a power bloc, and no interest in harmonious relations between them. However the truss bridge across the Danube at Ruse was opened in 1954, the year after Stalin's death. It was the first one between the two countries.

On 24 January 1949 two stamps featuring Lenin marked 25 years since his death with the 20l reproducing the famous 'scarlet' painting by Alexander Gerassimov of him as a revolutionary orator. (20.44) On 10 July 1949 two stamps marked the sudden death of Georgi Dimitrov

20.41 10l Peasants greeting Russian soldiers, 20l Soldiers of 1878 and 1944, and 60l Stalin and Spasskaya Tower: from Soviet Army Monument set 5 July 1948.

20.43 20l Battle of Grivitsa, 40l Sofia and Bucharest, and 100l Proposed Danube bridge: set 1 November 1948.

20.44 20l Lenin: from set 24 January 1949.

20.45 20l Death of Georgi Dimitrov: from set 10 July 1949.

20.46 40l Stalin: from set 21 December 1949.

20.47 9l 'Unanimity' and 20l Couple with spade sand wheel barrow: from Fatherland Front set 13 December 1949.

20.48 4l Frontier guard and village elder, 20l Guard on coast, and 60l Guard in mountains: set 31 October 1949.

a week or so earlier in Moscow. The ruthless purge of senior Eastern Bloc Communists instigated that year by Stalin (notably over Yugoslavia) did nothing to quell the rumours that Dimitrov was also one of his victims. (20.45) Nevertheless in due obeisance, on 21 December 1949 four Bulgarian stamps portrayed Stalin for his 70th birthday.(20.46)

On 13 December 1949 four stamps featured aspects of life under the Fatherland Front. The 4l pictured Dimitrov, the 9l an allegory called 'Unanimity', the 20l a couple with a spade and wheelbarrow, and the 50l young people marching.(20.47) Significantly, a little earlier, on 31 October 1949 three stamps had pictured armed frontier guards overlooking a village with a village elder (4l), patrolling the coast (20l), and with a dog in the mountains.(20.48) They seem to be protecting the country from possible external aggressors, and to some extent that was true as Bulgaria's long southern border was with Greece and Turkey but the guards were numbered in thousands and very much concerned with stopping Bulgarians fleeing Communist rule.

CHAPTER 21

GREECE

In September 1939 Greece strove to remain neutral but became the target of an Italian invasion in October 1940 from neighbouring Italian-occupied Albania. Humiliatingly the Greeks drove the Italians back to Albania only for Hitler to come to Mussolini's rescue in April 1941 and invade Greece via Bulgaria and Yugoslavia. King George II fled and a much despised puppet government took office.

Germany kept control of the key regions of Athens, an area around Thessalonika and several major islands, Bulgaria got much of Macedonia and Thrace, and until Italy surrendered in 1943 it administered the rest of the country, most of it rural and mountainous. In the German regions, the Greeks suffered relentless exploitation, with food and raw materials, and even complete factories, sent to Germany. Tens of thousands died, and but for International Red Cross supplies many more would have perished. Italian rule was a little lighter, but not without atrocities, but when the Germans swiftly took over in 1943 they brought harsher measures with them, especially against the Jews. Bulgaria imposed a brutal programme of subjugation and ethnic cleansing. The rise in resistance activities often made things worse for communities as reprisals usually included the burning of villages, destruction of crops and mass executions. And when the mutually hostile royalist/nationalist and Communist/republican partisans were not fighting the Germans, Italians and Bulgarians, they were fighting each other. Cooperation between them was rare, tentative and brief, and usually broke down amidst accusations of treachery.

As time went by each major faction became increasingly concerned with securing control of the country once the war was over. Nevertheless in February 1944 the various organisations signed the Plaka Bridge agreement whereby all efforts would be directed against the Germans, not each other. In May a further agreement placed all factions within a 'Government of National Unity' with the Communists holding a quarter of the cabinet seats. In September all the resistance 'armies' came together under the British military authority of Lieutenant General Sir Ronald Scobie in order to sweep out the Germans and establish a provisional government representing a broad swathe of opinion. This was achieved in October 1944, but the opposition to partisan disarmament, the resignation of left-wing ministers and violent left-wing street demonstrations in Athens revealed the country's inherent instability - especially under a fractious and internally warring administration so obviously losing overall control of events. British and nationalist Greek troops eventually gained the upper hand but although some Communist groups were disarmed many others disappeared into hiding.

Amidst all the battles and chaos sets of specially overprinted stamps sought funds to relieve at least a little of the wartime distress. (21.1, 21.2)

A nationalist coalition won the March 1946 general election, and civil war erupted, or rather re-erupted, when the Greek Communist Party formed a break-away provisional government, and with the support of Yugoslavia, Albania and Bulgaria mobilised its ex-partisan forces as its battle-hardened military wing. Later that year a referendum brought King George back to Greece, and this reinforced the anti-Communist campaign. Most crucial, though, was Stalin's attitude, and he had decided to abide by the wartime Allied

21.1 75d Edessa (from set 1 September 1942+) overprinted 5,000d for Postal Staff Anti-TB Fund: 1 July 1944.

21.2 10d East Wind (from set 15 September 1943) overprinted 50,000+450,000d for Children's Convalescent Camp Fund: from set 20 July 1944.

21.3 50l Diagoras of Rhodes (from set 24 January 1937+) overprinted New Drachmas: from set 11 November 1944+.

21.4 1d Glory of Psara: from reissued set 1 March 1945+.

agreement that Greece was to be largely a British sphere of influence. Although he refused to support the Greek Communist Party its violent campaign continued unabated. Much of the countryside was ravaged as both sides ransacked villages for supplies, and families were subjected to ideological pressure and, on the slightest suspicion of disloyalty, to atrocities.

In 1947 the USA joined the British in supporting the Greek army, and the Communists made the tactical mistake of making full scale attacks on towns which proved costly failures. Although Communist forces numbered tens of thousands, American and British support ensured many Greek counterattacks were successful. In 1948 Stalin and Tito severed relations, largely over Yugoslavia's support for the Greek Communists who, to their dismay, had to choose between the two leaders. After bitter internal controversy, they chose Stalin. Tito closed his borders to Greek Communist forces, and they suffered a massive defeat by the Greek army. Gradually they were hounded across the countryside and dispersed into small isolated units. Most left Greece for camps in the Soviet Union or satellite Balkan countries, and late in 1949 hostilities ground to a halt. Up to 100,000 Communists and their sympathisers were executed, exiled or imprisoned, the economy was in ruins and political extremism remained unabated.

The Greek army retained considerable political sway, Communist ranks were considerably depleted, American support remained strong, and state visits by King Paul (reigned 1947-64) positively aided new trade and diplomatic links. And notwithstanding the constant undercurrents of disruptive republicanism, Greece moved towards membership of NATO in 1952, and became a symbol of a nation's fierce resistance to right wing Fascism and left wing Communism.

Greece's stamps tell the story, although increasingly from the right wing nationalist perspective. When Greece was liberated in October 1944 its economy was virtually paralysed, with domestic production very low and bank credit almost non-existent due to hyperinflation. In November a 'new drachma' was introduced equal to fifty billion old drachma and 600 new drachmas were linked to £1. It failed to work and the currency was not stabilised until the Bank of Greece and Greek government poured money into the rural and urban economy in the later 1940s, and aid arrived from the USA and UNRRA (United Nations Relief & Rehabilitation Administration). The first issue after liberation on 11 November 1944 comprised four 'low value' stamps from a 1937-38 set overprinted 'New drachmas' in Greek.(21.3) They highlighted Classical Greek culture and victories. The 50l featured the Olympic boxer Diagoras of Rhodes being carried into the stadium by his two sons after they, too, had become Olympic champions in 448BC. The 2d featured the naval Battle of Salamis where the allied Greek states destroyed the Persian fleet of King Xerxes in 480BC. The 5d pictured a chariot used in the Panathenaic Games, and the 6d Alexander the Great at the Battle of Issus, now in Turkey, where he defeated King Darius and the Persians.

On 1 March 1945 five stamps appeared picturing the 'Glory of Psara', the allegorical figure of Doxa dressed in a white chiton recording the names of the Greek revolutionary heroes of Psara.(21.4) It was painted by the Greek artist Nikolaos Gyzis in 1898 who was inspired by a poem by Dionysios Solomis written in 1825 soon after the avenging Turks retook the small Aegean island. Rather than surrender, the Greek defenders blew up the fortified town centre killing themselves but also many Turks as they broke through. Doxa is a difficult word to translate as it embraces elements of the True Way, Honour and Glory. On 10 August 1945 higher values up to 200d were added revealing the continuing instability of the currency. The design had been used in a 1937-38 set, but it possessed particular poignancy in 1945 recalling the sacrifices made in the earlier Greek wars of independence.

Throughout 1946 and 1947 the wartime inflation set of 1942-4 featuring monasteries, islands and towns was reissued overprinted with 'new drachma' values.(21.5)

21.5 2,000d Corfu (from set 1 September 1942+) overprinted 10 new drachmas: from set 10 February 1946.

21.8 20d OXI (NO); from set 28 October 1945.

21.6 40l Delphic Amphictyonic League coin (from set 24 January 1937+) overprinted 20 new drachmas for Postal Staff Anti-TB Fund: 11 March 1946.

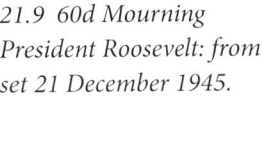

21.9 60d Mourning President Roosevelt: from set 21 December 1945.

21.7 50l Queens Olga and Sophia (from set 1 February 1939) overprinted 50 new drachmas for Red Cross Fund: 20 June 1946.

In 1946 increasingly higher new drachma overprints had to be printed. And in the immediate post-war years a mix of pre-war stamps continued to be re-issued overprinted in support of the Red Cross and the postal workers anti-TB fund.(21.6, 21.7) The relentless wartime and post-war fighting had led to economic chaos, and epidemics and starvation across the country.

On 28 October 1945 two completely new stamps celebrated Greek's resistance to the Italian call to surrender on that day in 1940. The Greek flag flies across a Classical column above the single word OXI (NO).(21.8) On 21 December 1945 three black-edged mourning stamps marked the death of President Roosevelt (on 12 April 1945) who had openly praised Greek resistance against the Germans, although it was only under his successor, Harry S Truman (1945-53), that the USA actively supported the Greek government's anti-Communist campaign.(21.9)

On 25 March 1946 two high value stamps portrayed the controversial republican politician, Eleftherios Venezelos (1864-1936), a month after the tenth anniversary of his death.(21.10) Prime minister for most of the time between 1910 and 1920, and also from 1928 to 1933, he contributed much to Greece's territorial expansion in the 1912-13 Balkan Wars and as an Allied supporter in the First World War. King Constantine (reigned 1913-17 and 1920-22) had preferred neutrality or a German alliance and the ensuing disagreement created to a bitter republican-royalist schism that led, for several damaging years, to a Venezelos controlled republic of Greece across the north of the country while the royalists ruled in Athens and the south. His later ministry signed several treaties of friendship with other countries, including the old enemy Turkey, but his attempts to restrict civil liberties and suppress Communism during the general unrest of the Great Depression led to his electoral defeat - although this did not stop him backing two violent but unsuccessful

21.10 130d Eleftherios Venezelos: from set 15 November 1946.

coups in the mid 1930s and fleeing to avoid a death sentence. Despite everything, his achievements ensured many revered him as the founder of modern Greece.

As the republican Liberals held office from November 1945 until the end of March 1946, probably it was no coincidence that the stamps honouring Venezelos, their founder, appeared just as the unresolved question of the return of King George II was moving up the political agenda. Such was Greece's tumultuous history he had succeeded as king in 1922, been deposed after a referendum in 1924, restored after another referendum in 1935, and exiled in 1941 after the German invasion. Many Greeks feared, although many others hoped, the king would seek to reimpose an autocratic right wing government. On 31 March 1946 the pro-monarchy People's Party won the election which, in a significant error of judgement, the Communists boycotted, and on 1 September a referendum marked by significant fraud claimed 68% of voters wanted the monarchy restored. George returned from wartime exile on 26 September 1946 to a wrecked palace and a nation in turmoil. Four stamps from the 1937-38 set portraying him were re-issued on 28 September hurriedly overprinted *1-9-1946*

 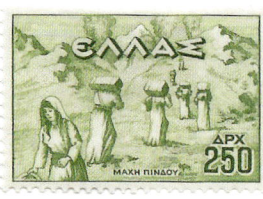

21.14 100d Torpedoing of 'Helle' and 250d Women carrying munitions: from set 28 October 1946+.

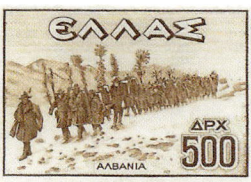 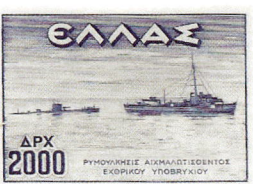

21.15 500d Column of infantry and 2,000d HMS Hyacinth towing the submarine Perla: from set 28 October 1946+.

21.11 1d King George II (from set 24 January 1947) overprinted 50d and 1-9-1946: from set 28 September 1946.

21.12 As 21.10 but with black mourning border: from set 6 April 1947.

21.13 600d Panagiotis Tsaldaris: from set 15 November 1946.

and new values.(21.11) The king died the following April and three values reappeared equally hurriedly edged in black.(21.12)

Interestingly on 15 November 1946 two stamps marked the tenth anniversary of the death of a prominent Conservative prime minister, Panagiotis Tsaldaris (1868-1936).(21.13) A royalist at heart, he led the People's Party throughout the politically tortuous years of 1922 to 1936. He was prime minister between 1932 to 1935, during which time he suppressed a pro-Venezelos coup, and although finally toppled from power by an armed forces coup impatient for a restored monarchy he had, in fact, been working diplomatically and peacefully towards a general consensus, and hopefully a referendum, for the king's return from exile.

There had just been time during the king's brief return for the first stamp (250d) in the first Victory set to be issued on 28 October 1946. The rest appeared on the 1 May 1947. No stamp in the set of eight commemorated the mutually hostile partisans; three marked the initial defeat of the Italians and five celebrated the achievements of the forces loyal to the royal government-in-exile in Great Britain.(21.14, 21.15) The 100d featured the Italian torpedoing of the Greek cruiser *Helle* at anchor off the island of Tinos on 15 August 1940, two months before the outbreak of war. The 250d recalled the crucial role of local women in

21.16 1,000d The battle for Crete: 15 September 1948.

21.17 1,000d Allied flags and map of Crete: 28 April 1950.

carrying munitions to Greek soldiers in the Pindos Mountains during their successful counterattack against the Italians in 1940, and the 500d showed a column of Greek infantry pursuing the Italians back into Albania. Later, in exile, Greeks served on Allied convoys (50d), fought in North Africa (5,000d) and Italy (600d), and flew Spitfires (1,000d). The 2,000d shows the captured Italian submarine *Perla* being towed into port by the British corvette HMS Hyacinth in July 1942. Soon afterwards the *Perla* was transferred the Hellenic Navy as the Matrosos, and in 1943 HMS *Hyacinth* became the Greek *Apostolis*.

The second Victory issue was a single stamp on 15 September 1948 dramatically portraying the battle for Crete.(21.16) Seeing the strategic value of Crete, British, Australian and New Zealand forces had reinforced Greek troops there in late October 1940. Although anticipating a German amphibious attack, the Allies were caught by a surprise paratrooper landing the following May. A combination of lacklustre leadership, poor communications, inadequate weapons and failure to hold the airfields led to an Allied defeat by a skilled and determined enemy. However the Greek units fought heroically, and were instrumental in buying time for many Allied troops to be evacuated. The battle was remembered in a second stamp on 28 April 1950 that included a map, flags of the Allied forces and a portrait of King George II.(21.17)

A lengthy series beginning in November 1947 celebrated the Treaty of Paris formally returning the Dodecanese Islands from Italian to Greek ownership. The attractive stamps ranged across a variety of island artefacts, scenes and people.(21.18, 21.19) Some featured a Dodecanese vase, a woman in a local costume, the god Apollo's head, and the revolutionary Emmanuil Xanthos (1772-1852). He was a leader of a secret society dedicated to achieving Greek independence - which came about in 1821, but did not include the Dodecanese. The 'Apollo' stamps contained a reprint of the unofficial 1912 stamp proclaiming Union with Greece which was immediately suppressed by the incoming Italian military authorities. Other Treaty of Paris stamps ranged across the islands. They pictured the fortress guarding the island of Castelrosso, St John's Convent on Patmos, the Colossus of Rhodes (the sun god Helios), the statue of Hippocrates the physician on Kos, and a wooden warship off the island of Casos. In a turbulent history the islands had been held by Greeks, briefly the Persians, for centuries the Roman and then the Byzantines, briefly the Knights Hospitaller, and then for centuries the Ottoman Turks who sold them in 1912 to Italy much to Greek fury. In 1945 the British allowed the islands to unite informally with Greece pending a treaty.

Two other sets recalled recent events. On 25 January 1948 a single stamp featured St Demetrius who was believed to have been a Christian Roman pro-consul in his home region of Thessalonika martyred during the Emperor Galerian's early third century persecution. It was issued to promote the restoration of churches, notably those damaged or destroyed in the war. It may well have been significant that Thessalonika is in

21.18 20d Fortress at Castelrosso and 30d Dodecanese vase: from set 20 November 1947+.

21.19 250d Emmanuil Xanthos and 450d Apollo stamp from 1912 Union with Greece Committee: from set 20 November 1947.

21.20 50d St Demetrius: 25 January 1948.

21.21 Abduction of Greek children: set 1 February 1949

Macedonia where the Communists were particularly strong and retained a stranglehold on many village communities.

On 1 February 1949, a set dramatically highlighted a highly controversial Civil War practice. The 450d featured a column of women and children, the 1000d a map of Greece and captive children, and the 1800d a hand menacing a woman and child. By this date many Communists, staring defeat, imprisonment and possible execution in the face, were fleeing Greece into sympathetic Communist countries and taking tens of thousands of children with them to be brought up as the next generation of Communists. Contemporary reports vary widely in saying how far this diaspora was willingly agreed by families who faced hunger and disease at home, and violence at the hands of the warring forces. They agree, though, that many families, especially in northern Greece and Macedonia, were torn apart as the guerrillas sought safety in what was already being termed the Eastern Bloc: many men, women and children perished on the journey and many surviving children never saw their parents again. Not surprisingly the Greek government played heavily on the heartlessness of Communist attitudes towards family life, and the severing of the mother and child bond. It alleged that many children were brutally seized from non-Communist parents.

The Civil War ground to a halt in 1949, but as late as August 1952 a set celebrated the Communist defeat with stamps portraying a priest blessing troops and an allegory of Victory standing over soldiers in battle.

BIBLIOGRAPHY

Applebaum, A., *Iron Curtain: the Crushing of Eastern Europe 1944-56*, Penguin, 2013

Armour, I., *A History of Eastern Europe 1918 to the Present: Modernisation, Ideology and Nationality*, Bloomsbury Academic. 2016

Beaton, R., *Greece: Biography of a Modern Nation*, Penguin, 2020

D'haen T., Damrosch, D., & Kadir D. (Eds.), *Routledge Companion to World Literature*, Routledge, 2013

Fenby, J., *The History of Modern France: From the Revolution to the War with Terror*, Simon & Schuster, 2015

Fulbrook, M., *History of Germany 1918-2014: The Divided Nation*, Wiley Blackwell, 2014

Ginsborg, P., *A History of Contemporary Italy 1943-1980*, Penguin, 1990

Glenny, M., *The Balkans 1804-2012: Nationalism, War & The Great Powers*, Granta, 2012

Hastings, M., *All Hell Let Loose: The World at War 1939-1945*, Collins, 2012

Hennessy, P., *Never Again: Britain 1945-51*, Vintage, 1993

Jelavich, C.& B., *The Establishment of the Balkan National States 1804-1920*, Washington, USA, 1986

Judt, T., *Postwar: A History of Europe since 1945*, Vintage, 2010

Kershaw, I., *The End: Germany 1944-45*, Penguin, 2012

Lowe, K., S*avage Continent: Europe in the Aftermath of World War II*, Penguin, 2013

Mason, D., *A Concise History of Modern Europe: Liberty, Equality, Solidarity*, Orient Black Swan, 2018

Service, R., *The Penguin History of Modern Russia: From Tsarism to the Twenty-First Century*, Penguin, 2015

Webb, A. (Ed.), *Routledge Companion to Central & Eastern Europe since 1919*, Routledge, 2008

Zamoyski, A., *Poland: A History*, Hippocrene, 2012

Stamp Catalogues: Michel, Scott and Stanley Gibbons.

Britannica.com and en.wikipedia.org for numerous biographies, events and places

INDEX

The entries in this Index refer to the themes of single stamps and sets of stamps from each country

Air Mail/Aircraft
    Belgium, 12
    Germany, 27, 28, 30
    Soviet Union, 48, 60-62
    France, 72-73
    Belgium, 83-84
    Luxembourg, 93
    Poland, 123, 124
    Czechoslovakia, 138
    Austria, 150
    Italy, 163, 169, 171-172
    Yugoslavia, 178, 181, 183
    Hungary, 200-201
    Romania, 209, 210, 211-212, 214-215, 221, 222, 223-224
    Bulgaria, 230-231, 232
    Greece, 241

Animals,
    Germany, 28-29
    Soviet Union, 50
    Austria, 150
    Italy, 170

Anniversaries, national (see also Revolutionaries)
    Poland, 122
    Czechoslovakia, 139, 141-142
    Austria, 148, 155
    Italy, 159, 164-165
    Albania, 186-188
    Romania, 224
    Greece, 238

Anti-Fascist commemorations
    Germany, 33-34, 38-39
    France, 69, 74
    Belgium, 81, 83, 85
    Poland, 124, 130
    Czechoslovakia, 135
    Austria, 149, 152-153
    Yugoslavia, 180
    Albania, 188-189

    Hungary, 197-198, 199
    Romania, 206-207
    Greece, 239

Anti-TB Campaign,
    France, 69, 76-77
    Belgium, 81-82
    Finland, 112,113
    Poland, 129
    Austria, 154
    Yugoslavia, 178
    Greece, 239

Architecture/notable buildings (see also Reconstruction)
    Germany, 19, 20, 22, 23, 24, 25, 29-30, 35-36, 41
    Soviet Union, 54-56, 63
    Netherlands, 98
    Norway, 104
    Finland, 109, 113-114
    Poland, 125-126
    Czechoslovakia, 136
    Austria, 152
    Italy, 158-159, 163-164, 170
    Yugoslavia, 182
    Hungary, 198, 200
    Romania, 208, 217
    Bulgaria, 231

Armed Forces (Historic Battles/Leaders)
    Germany, 27
    Soviet Union, 45, 60-61
    France, 71
    Belgium, 84-85
    Netherlands, 98
    Norway, 105-106
    Poland, 118, 120, 128, 132

Armed Forces (Second World War/Modern)
    Soviet Union, 47-49, 60-61, 64

    France, 71-72, 74, 75
    Luxembourg, 90-91
    Netherlands, 95
    Norway, 103-105
    Poland, 116-118
    Romania, 222
    Bulgaria, 227-228, 236

Artists
    Soviet Union, 60-62
    France, 75, 78-79
    Belgium, 85-86
    Poland, 126-127
    Austria, 150, 154-155
    Italy, 167-168
    Romania, 216

Cathedrals/Churches/Abbeys
    Germany, 19, 22, 23, 24, 28, 35-36
    Soviet Union, 55, 56
    France, 69-71
    Luxembourg, 90-91, 92-93
    Austria, 149, 150, 153, 155
    Italy, 159, 169
    Italy, 172-173 (Campione)
    Yugoslavia, 177
    Hungary, 200
    Romania, 217

Charities (see also Red Cross and Anti-TB Campaign)
    Germany, 26, 28, 34, 41
    France, 69, 76-77, 78-79
    Belgium, 81, 83-85
    Luxembourg, 91, 92-93
    Netherlands, 96-99
    Denmark, 101
    Finland, 109
    Poland, 126-127
    Czechoslovakia, 140
    Austria, 152-153, 155, 156
    Yugoslavia, 180

INDEX

Hungary, 195, 197-198, 202
Romania, 207-208, 213-214
Bulgaria, 227-229
Greece, 237

Coats of Arms
Germany, 21
Soviet Union, 51-52, 64
France, 68
Belgium, 81-82
Austria, 147, 153
Italy, 161
Yugoslavia, 176-177
Hungary, 11, 196, 197, 203-204
Bulgaria, 225, 226

Composers
Germany, 23, 26-27
Luxembourg, 92
Finland, 111
Poland, 127
Czechoslovakia, 142-143
Austria, 151, 156
Italy, 166, 167
Romania, 210-211, 216

Congresses/Conferences (Professional Bodies/Trades Unions)
Germany, 25-26, 42
France, 76
Poland, 124, 125, 131
Czechoslovakia, 143-144
Yugoslavia, 180
Albania, 188
Hungary, 198, 202-203
Romania, 207, 214-215, 217-218, 223-224
Bulgaria, 229

Congresses/Conferences (Political Parties)
Germany, 39
Poland, 125
Czechoslovakia, 143-144
Yugoslavia, 182 (Slavic Conference), 184-185
Albania, 186-188
Romania, 207, 209, 217
Bulgaria 226 (All Slav Congress), 229

Constitutions/Manifestos
Poland, 125
Italy, 165-166
Yugoslavia, 179-180
Albania, 187-188
Hungary, 198-199, 203-204
Romania, 218-219
Bulgaria, 229-230

Costumes, national and regional
Germany, 22
Austria, 153-154

Education,
Germany, 28
Finland, 111
Poland, 128
Czechoslovakia, 141
Romania, 209, 215-216
Bulgaria, 232-233

Esperanto
Austria, 156
Bulgaria, 230-231

European Recovery Programme
Germany, 31
Italy, 161

Explorers
Soviet Union, 50
France, 75-76,
Belgium, 86-87
Norway, 105, 106, 107

Fairs
East and West Germany, 17-18, 20, 35, 40, 41
Czechoslovakia, 144
Italy, 167, 171-172
Yugoslavia, 180
Bulgaria, 232

Farming/Farm workers
Germany, 17-18, 23, 27, 33, 34, 35
Soviet Union, 48-49, 57, 58, 59
France, 77, 78
Finland, 108, 110
Poland, 130

Czechoslovakia, 143
Austria, 150
Italy, 170
Yugoslavia, 179-180
Albania, 190
Hungary, 199
Romania, 207-208, 211-212, 217-218, 221, 224
Bulgaria, 231, 233

Five Year Plans
Soviet Union, 56-59, 63-64
Bulgaria, 231-232

Government-in-exile
Norway, 103-104
Poland, 116, 117

Health/Spas
Soviet Union, 52-53
Finland, 112
Italy, 168
Bulgaria, 233

Labour Day
Italy, 171-172 (Yugoslav issue for Trieste)
Albania, 191
Romania, 211, 221

Land reforms
Germany, 34
Finland, 110
Albania, 190
Hungary, 199
Romania, 209-210

Liberated territory/regional issues
Poland, 118-119
Czechoslovakia, 133-135
Italy, 157, 160-161
Yugoslavia, 176-177
Romania, 205-206
Greece, 241

Liberation
France, 68
Netherlands, 95-96
Denmark, 101-102
Poland, 118-119, 121, 122, 131-132

245

EUROPEAN STAMP ISSUES AND THE AFTERMATH OF THE SECOND WORLD WAR: 1944–1949

Czechoslovakia, 136-137
Austria, 147
Yugoslavia, 179
Hungary, 194
Romania, 220-221
Bulgaria, 226-227

Literary figures/Philosophers
Germany, 20, 21, 23, 30-31, 37, 38, 39-40
Soviet Union, 50-51, 56, 61-62
France, 71, 78-79
Luxembourg, 92
Norway, 103-104, 106-107
Finland, 111
Poland, 126, 127, 128
Czechoslovakia, 137, 142-143
Austria, 150
Italy, 161, 166, 167
Yugoslavia, 181-182, 183
Hungary, 199-201
Romania, 205-206, 216, 220-221, 223
Bulgaria, 233-235

Medals
Soviet Union, 45-47, 48, 49, 53-54

Memorials/Memorial issues
France, 69, 74
Belgium, 81, 83-84, 87-88
Luxembourg, 90, 91
Netherlands, 98-99
Norway, 104
Poland, 122, 123, 124, 130
Czechoslovakia, 134-135
Bulgaria, 234-235

Occupation of Albania
Overprinted Italian stamps, 186-187

Occupation of Austria
Russian Zone, 146-147
British, French & American Zones, 14

Occupation of Germany
Allied Military Post, 17
British, American & Soviet Zones, 17-18
British & American Zones, 19-20
Federal Republic & Democratic Republic, 40-42
French Zone, 21-26
Overprinted Third Reich stamps, 16-17, 31-32
Russian Zone (local and zonal issues), 31-40
Saar, 26-29
West Berlin, 29-31

Occupation of Italy
Overprinted Italian stamps by Allies, 157,
Overprinted Italian stamps by Italian Social Republic, 158
Yugoslav-Italian occupation of Trieste & Venetia-Giulia, 169-172

Olympic Games
United Kingdom, 14
Austria, 155-156

Parades, political/military
Soviet Union, 53, 59-60
Yugoslavia, 184
Romania, 220-221

Partisans (in Second World War)
Italy, 171-172 (Yugoslav issue for Trieste)
Yugoslavia, 177-179, 185
Albania, 188-189
Bulgaria, 228

Peace/Peace Treaties
United Kingdom, 13, 14
Soviet Union, 48
France, 73-74
Belgium, 80-81
Finland, 108
Poland, 124,
Hungary, 192-193
Romania, 213-214, 220
Bulgaria, 226-227, 230-231, 235
Greece, 240-241

Political leaders and premiers (see also Royalty)
Soviet Union, 51
France, 66
Finland, 108-109, 111
Poland, 131
Czechoslovakia 135-136, 139, 141-142
Austria, 148-149
Italy, 172
Yugoslavia, 177, 178-179
Albania, 188, 191
Hungary, 202, 204
Romania, 207-208, 224
Bulgaria, 229-230, 235-236
Greece, 239-240

Postal Services (see also UPU)
Germany, 25, 42
Norway, 105-106
Finland, 109
Hungary (inflation overprints), 195-196
Bulgaria, 231

Railways
Germany, 29, 35
Soviet Union, 55, 57, 59
Belgium, 88
Denmark, 101-102
Poland, 130-131
Austria, 154
Yugoslavia, 180-181
Albania, 190
Hungary, 197
Romania, 209
Bulgaria, 227, 233

Reconstruction (see also Land Reform)
Germany, 17-18, 19, 25, 27, 29-30, 32, 34-35, 36, 38,
France, 69-70, 77
Belgium, 81, 88-89
Netherlands, 99
Poland, 123, 124, ,129-130
Czechoslovakia (Two Year Plan), 139
Austria, 150, 154
Italy, 162, 168

INDEX

Hungary, 198
Romania, 207-208, 218
Bulgaria, 231, 236

Red Cross
   Germany, 24-24
   Netherlands, 99
   Denmark, 100
   Norway, 104-105
   Finland, 109, 110, 111, 112
   Poland, 124
   Czechoslovakia, 144
   Yugoslavia, 178
   Albania, 187-188
   Romania, 210
   Bulgaria, 227
   Greece, 239

Revolutions/Revolutionaries
   1794, 1830, 1863, 1919-21
      Poland, 119, 120, 121, 128
   1844
      Italy, 159
   1848-49
      Germany, 25-26
      France, 77-78
      Czechoslovakia, 140-141
      Italy, 165-166, 171
      Hungary, 201-202
      Romania, 205-206, 222-223, 224
   1876
      Bulgaria, 235
   1918-1919
      Germany, 38-39
      Hungary, 203
   1923
      Bulgaria, 229-230
   Bolshevik
      Soviet Union, 59
   Various dates
      Hungary, 199-200
      Romania, 205-206, 208

Royalty (historic and present)
   United Kingdom, 13
   Germany, 22, 23
   France, 11, 66, 75
   Belgium, 81-83, 84-85, 87-88
   Luxembourg, 90, 91-92, 94
   Netherlands, 95-97

Denmark, 100, 101
Norway, 104-105, 106
Austria, 149
Italy, 157, 158, 159, 165-166
Yugoslavia, 174-175
Hungary, 193-194
Romania, 206, 210-211, 216-217
Bulgaria, 225-226
Greece, 240

Saints
   Germany, 26, 41
   Belgium, 87
   Luxembourg, 91-92
   Czechoslovakia, 137
   Austria, 153
   Italy, 164-165
   Hungary, 193
   Bulgaria, 227-228
   Greece, 241-242

Savings Banks
   Finland, 113
   Hungary, 202-203
   Romania, 218
   Bulgaria, 228-229

Scientists/Inventors
   Germany, 23
   Soviet Union, 49, 50
   France, 71-72
   Denmark, 101, 102
   Poland, 127
   Italy, 167, 168
   Hungary, 200-201
   Romania, 216

Ships
   Germany, 34
   Soviet Union, 50, 57, 58, 60
   France, 71-72
   Belgium, 83, 86-87, 89
   Netherlands, 95
   Poland, 122-123, 130
   Yugoslavia, 181
   Romania, 217, 222
   Bulgaria, 231-232, 235
   Greece, 240

Sport (see also Olympic Games)
   Germany, 20, 28
   Soviet Union, 53-54
   Finland, 112
   Poland, 129
   Czechoslovakia, 139-140
   Austria, 155-156
   Yugoslavia, 184, 185
   Albania, 188
   Romania, 211-213, 216
   Bulgaria, 229, 232, 233

Stamp Days and Exhibitions
   Austria, 10
   Bulgaria, 10
   Finland, 10
   France, 11
   Hungary, 10
   Poland, 10
   Luxembourg, 93
   Italy, 171

Stamp Anniversaries
   United Kingdom (centenary), 13
   Germany (centenary), 41-42
   Soviet Union (25th), 12, 52
   Belgium (centenary), 12
   Czechoslovakia (30th), 12
   Yugoslavia, (invention of
      adhesive stamps),183
   Hungary (75th), 11, 198-199,
      203

United Nations Organisation (inc
UNICEF, UNESCO, WHO)
   France 73-74
   Austria, 148, 156
   Italy, 168

Universal Postal Union (75th
Anniversary, 1949)
   United Kingdom, 14
   Germany, 17-18, 25, 30, 41-42
   France, 79,
   Belgium, 88
   Luxembourg, 10
   Netherlands, 9
   Denmark, 10
   Norway, 107
   Finland, 10

Czechoslovakia, 9
Austria, 155
Italy, 9
Yugoslavia, 183-184
Romania, 9
Greece, 10

Victory (see Peace)

Views/landscapes
Germany, 22, 23, 24, 28, 29
France, 73
Luxembourg, 93, 94
Austria, 148, 150, 153

Women/Women's Day
Germany, 22, 23, 38-39, 41
Soviet Union, 53, 64
Poland, 126-127
Albania, 188
Hungary, 194, 203
Romania, 213

Youth/Youth Clubs, Festivals
Soviet Union, 53
France, 76-77
Poland, 129
Czechoslovakia, 137-138
Yugoslavia, 180